Sufficient Provision for Seekers of the Path of Truth

[Al-Ghunya li-Ṭālibī Ṭarīq al-Ḥaqq]

VOLUME FOUR

Sufficient Provision for Seekers of The Path of Truth

[Al Ghunya li-Ṭālibī Ṭarīq al-Ḥaqq]

A COMPLETE RESOURCE ON THE INNER AND OUTER ASPECTS OF ISLAM

VOLUME FOUR

SHAIKH ʿABD AL-QĀDIR AL-JĪLĀNĪ
TRANSLATED FROM THE ARABIC BY MUHTAR HOLLAND

AL-BAZ PUBLISHING, INC.
HOLLYWOOD, FLORIDA

"He [Allāh] is the Truth." Qur'ān (22:6)

Cover Design: Rohana Filippi

Using watercolor and wax to combine the beauty of Arabic script with the Qur'ānic message on paper, Italian artist Rohana Filippi has developed her own artistic style through personal research and inner inspiration. Her art is entirely devoted to "expressing Allāh's presence everywhere."
Ms. Filippi, who currently resides in Colombia, has lived and worked in Italy, England, Mexico, and the United States.

Cover Design: Dryden Design, Houston, Texas
Cover Preparation: Susan Lee Graphic Design, Ft. Lauderdale, Florida

Body text set in Jilani and Ghazali fonts by Al-Baz Publishing, Inc.

Printed on acid-free paper.

Second Edition: January 2008

Library of Congress
Catalog Card Number: 95–75589

ISBN: 1–882216–10–5
Sufficient Provision for Seekers of the path of Truth, Vol. 4
ISBN: 1–882216–12–1
Sufficient Provision for Seekers of the path of Truth, set of 5 volumes

Published by Al-Baz Publishing, Inc.

8807 148th Ave. NE, Building E, Redmond 98052
Phone: (425) 869-3923 E-mail: albaz@bellsouth.net

Contents

Sufficient Provision for Seekers of the Path of Truth

[Al-Ghunya li-Ṭālibī Ṭarīq al-Ḥaqq]

VOLUME FOUR

بِسْمِ ٱللَّهِ ٱلرَّحْمَٰنِ ٱلرَّحِيمِ

So remember Me,
and I will remember you...
(Qur'ān 2:152)

CHAPTER SEVEN

Concerning the practice of fasting all year long *[ṣiyām ad-dahr]*, and the spiritual reward and recompense due to someone who observes it.

Shaikh Abū Naṣr Muḥammad ibn al-Bannā' has informed us, citing traditional authority for his report,[1] that Allāh's Messenger (Allāh bless him and give him peace) once said:

> The most meritorious form of fasting *[ṣiyām]* is the fasting of David *[Dāwūd]*,[2] and if someone fasts throughout the entire year *[ṣāma 'd-dahr kulla-hu]*, he has already given himself to Allāh (Exalted is He).

According to Abū Mūsā al-Ash'ari (may Allāh be well pleased with him), the Prophet (Allāh bless him and give him peace) once said:

> If a person fasts all year long *[ṣāma 'd-dahr]*, Hell will become too narrow for him, [as it keeps shrinking] like this...

—and he clenched his fists repeatedly, as if making a finger-count up to ninety *['aqada tis'īn]*.

According to a report from Shu'aib, it was Sa'd ibn Ibrāhīm who said: "'Ā'isha (may Allāh be well pleased with her) used to fast all year long *[kānat taṣūmu 'd-dahr]*."

Ya'qūb is reported as having said: "My father once told us that Sa'd (may Allāh be well pleased with him) made a constant practice of fasting throughout the last forty years of his life."

[1] ***Author's note***: Shaikh Abū Naṣr Muḥammad ibn al-Bannā' cites the following chain of transmission *[isnād]* for this report: **His own father, Shaikh Abū 'Alī ibn Aḥmad ibn 'Abdi'llāh ibn al-Bannā'—Abu'l-Ḥasan 'Alī ibn Aḥmad al-Muqrī—Ibrāhīm ibn Aḥmad al-Qarmainī—al-Ḥasan ibn Suhail—Yaḥyā—Ibrāhīm ibn Abī Najā—Ṣafwān ibn Salīm—'Alqama ibn Abī 'Alqama—'Umar ibn al-Khaṭṭāb** (may Allāh be well pleased with him)**—the Prophet** (Allāh bless him and give him peace).

[2] As reported on the authority of 'Abdu'llāh ibn 'Umar (may Allāh be well pleased with him and with his father), Allāh's Messenger (Allāh bless him and give him peace) once said:

> The best kind of fasting *[ṣiyām]* is the fasting of David *[Dāwūd]* (peace be upon him), for he made it his practice to fast on alternate days throughout the entire year *[niṣf ad-dahr]*.

Abū Idrīs ʿĀʾidhu'llāh is reported as having said: "Abū Mūsā al-Ashʿarī (may Allāh be well pleased with him) kept fasting until he become as slim as a toothpick, so I said to him: 'O Abū Mūsā, how about giving your poor self a break?' But he replied: 'Give it a break? What I want is to see it overtaking all the lean horses in the race!'"

Abū Isḥāq ibn Ibrāhīm is reported as having said: "ʿAmmār, the Christian monk *[rāhib]*, once told me about a remarkable dream-experience of his, which he described in these words: 'I saw [the holy spiritual being called] Sakīna aẓ-Ẓafāriyya in my dream. She was present with us at the religious gathering *[majlis]* convened by ʿĪsā ibn Zādhān at al-Abla, having come down from al-Baṣra for the specific purpose of paying him a visit. So I said to her: "O Sakīna, what has ʿĪsā done [to deserve your attention]?" She laughed, then she replied: "He has donned the raiment of splendid beauty *[bahāʾ]*!" The servants circled around him with pitchers [of water for his ablution], then he put on his clothes, and someone was heard to exclaim: "O reader of Scripture *[yā qāriʾ]*, you must recite an incantation *[ruqya]*, for—by my life—your fasting has left you utterly emaciated!" ʿĪsā had fasted indeed, to the point where his body was bent in a stoop, and he had lost his voice.'"

Anas [ibn Mālik] (may Allāh be well pleased with him) is reported as having said: "Abū Ṭalḥa (may Allāh be well pleased with him) did no fasting at all, during the lifetime of Allāh's Messenger (Allāh bless him and give him peace), on account of [his constant involvement in] military campaigns *[ghazw]*. But after Allāh's Messenger (Allāh bless him and give him peace) had died, I never once saw him break his daily fast, except on the Day of Breaking Fast *[Yawm al-Fiṭr]* [at the end of the month of Ramaḍān], and on the Day of Sacrifice *[Yawm an-Naḥr]* [at the end of the Pilgrimage]."

As we learn from a traditional report, it was Abū Bakr ibn ʿAbd ar-Raḥmān ibn al-Ḥarth ibn Hishām who said: "Someone told me that, on a summer's day, he had seen Allāh's Messenger (Allāh bless him and give him peace) pouring water over his head, on account of the extreme intensity of the heat and thirst, even though he was fasting at the time."

ʿAlī [ibn Abī Ṭālib] (may Allāh be well pleased with him) is reported[3] as having said: "Allāh's Messenger (Allāh bless him and give him

[3] ***Author's note***: The chain of transmission *[isnād]* for this report goes back to: **Sufyān [ath-Thawrī]—Abū Isḥāq—al-Ḥarth—ʿAlī [ibn Abī Ṭālib]** (may Allāh be well pleased with him).

peace) used to fast for a day, then go for a day without fasting."

In the traditional account *[ḥadīth]* that has come down to us on the authority of Jābir (may Allāh be well pleased with him), we find that he said:[4]

"ʿUmar [ibn al-Khaṭṭāb] (may Allāh be well pleased with him) once asked the Prophet (Allāh bless him and give him peace): 'O Prophet of Allāh *[yā Nabiyya'llāh]*, inform us about [the condition of] a man who fasts throughout the entire year *[yaṣūmu 'd-dahr kulla-hu]*?' To this he replied (Allāh bless him and give him peace):

> 'May that person neither fast nor break fast *[lā ṣāma dhālika wa lā afṭara]*!'"[5]

When properly construed, this remark must apply to a man who has fasted literally throughout the year, without breaking fast on the days of the Two Festivals *[al-ʿĪdain]* and during the Days of *Tashrīq*[6] [when fasting is actually forbidden]. Such was the construction placed upon it by Imām Aḥmad ibn Ḥanbal[7] (may Allāh bestow His mercy upon him). As for someone who breaks fast on these particular days, and devotes the rest of the year to fasting, no prohibition is applicable in his case. On the contrary, indeed, he is entitled to all the excellent merits we have mentioned above.

[4] For a more detailed version of this traditional report, see Vol. 3, p. 46 .

[5] In one version of this traditional report, the Prophet (Allāh bless him and give him peace) is said to have exclaimed: "He who fasts all the time, may he neither fast nor return to what is good in normal everyday life *[man ṣāma 'd-dahra fa-lā ṣāma wa lā āla]*! In either case, according to traditional authorities, this is an imprecation uttered by the Prophet (Allāh bless him and give him peace), "lest a man should come to believe that this kind of fasting has been ordained by Allāh (Exalted is He); or, through physical incapacity, should become insincere; or because, by fasting all the days of the year, he would do so even on the days when fasting is strictly forbidden." (See: E. W. Lane, *Arabic-English Lexicon*, art. ʾ-W-L.)

[6] See note 344 on p. 248 below; also Vol. 3, pp. 262–66 and 270–71.

[7] Imām Aḥmad ibn Ḥanbal (may Allāh bestow His mercy upon him) was the founder of one of the four schools *[madhāhib]* of Islamic jurisprudence. He died in the year A.H. 241/855 C.E. The legal doctrines of the Ḥanbalī school were those studied most intensively by the author, Shaikh ʿAbd al-Qādir al-Jīlānī (may Allāh be well pleased with him) as a young man.

Concerning the merit of fasting *[ṣiyām]* in general.

On this subject, as we are reliably informed by Shaikh Abū Naṣr,[8] Allāh's Messenger (Allāh bless him and give him peace) once said:

> If someone devotes a single day to fasting, for the purpose of gaining the countenance of Allāh (Exalted is He), Allāh will keep him at a distance from Hell—at the distance covered by a raven *[ghurāb]* that takes flight when it is merely a chick, and then stays airborne till it dies of old age.

It is said that the raven *[ghurāb]* has a normal lifespan of fifty years!

According to a report from Abu'd-Dardā' (may Allāh be well pleased with him), Allāh's Messenger (Allāh bless him and give him peace) also said:

> If someone devotes a single day to fasting, for the sake of Allāh's cause *[fī sabīli 'llāh]*, Allāh will install a trench *[khandaq]* between him and the Fire of Hell, and the width thereof will be as great as the distance between the heaven and the earth.

According to a another traditional report, this one from Abū Sa'īd al-Khudrī (may Allāh be well pleased with him), Allāh's Messenger (Allāh bless him and give him peace) once said:

> If someone devotes a single day to fasting, for the sake of Allāh's cause *[fī sabīli 'llāh]*, Allāh will reward him for it by keeping his face at a distance from the Fire of Hell, for seventy autumn seasons.

'Ā'isha (may Allāh be well pleased with her) is reported as having said: "I once heard Allāh's Messenger (Allāh bless him and give him peace) say:

> "'Whenever a servant [of the Lord] embarks upon the morning in a state of fasting, the gates of heaven are opened up for him, the members of his body glorify the Lord, and the inhabitants of the heaven of this lower world *[ahl samā' ad-dunyā]* seek forgiveness on his behalf, until the world disappears behind the veil [of night]. If that servant also performs one or two cycles of ritual prayer

[8] ***Author's note***: Shaikh Abū Naṣr Muḥammad ibn al-Bannā' narrates this report on the authority of his father, citing a chain of transmission *[isnād]* from **'Amr ibn Rabī'a—Salām ibn Qais** (may Allāh be well pleased with him)—**the Prophet** (Allāh bless him and give him peace).

> *[ṣallā rak'a aw rak'atain]*, as a voluntary act of devotion *[taṭawwu'an]*, the heaven will radiate a light for his benefit, and his wives among the lovely-eyed brides of Paradise *[al-ḥūr al-'īn]*[9] will say: "O Allāh, fetch him here to us, for we are eagerly yearning to set our eyes upon him!" If he also declares the Uniqueness of Allāh *[hallala]*,[10] or proclaims His Glory *[sabbaḥa]*,[11] his utterances will be received by seventy thousand angels, who will go on recording them until the world disappears behind the veil [of night].'"

As reported by Abū Ṣāliḥ, on the authority of Abū Huraira (may Allāh be well pleased with him), the Prophet (Allāh bless him and give him peace) also said:

> Every good deed performed by the human being *[ibn Ādam]* is [known to be counted] as from ten good deeds to a hundred good deeds, or up to seven hundred good deeds, with the exception of fasting *[ṣawm]*, for Allāh (Exalted is He) has said in one of His Books: "Fasting is Mine, and I determine its reward."[12] As for the odor of the mouth of someone who is fasting, it is more fragrant to Allāh than the scent of musk.

'Alī [ibn Abī Ṭālib] (may Allāh be well pleased with him) is reported as having said: "I once heard Allāh's Messenger (Allāh bless him and give him peace) say:

> Though a person is prevented, by keeping the fast, from taking the food and drink for which he has an appetite, Allāh will feed him from the fruits of the Garden of Paradise, and He will quench his thirst from the pure drink thereof.

According to a report from Abū Huraira (may Allāh be well pleased with him), Allāh's Messenger (Allāh bless him and give him peace) once said:

> For all those people who perform good work, there is a particular gate, among the gateways of the Garden of Paradise, through which they will be invited to enter, as a reward for that good work. As for the people who practice fasting, there is a special gate through which they will be invited to enter, and it is called *ar-Rayyān* ["plump and juicy"].

[9] The 'houries' *[ḥūr* or *ḥawrā']* of Paradise are mentioned in several verses *[āyāt]* of the Qur'ān. Literally, according to the Arabic lexicographers, the term means 'women whose eyes are characterized by intense whiteness of the part that is white, and intense blackness of the part that is black,' or, more poetically, 'women with eyes resembling those of the gazelle.' (See: E.W. Lane, *Arabic-English Lexicon*, art. *Ḥ–W–R*.)

[10] The Arabic verb *hallala*, of which *tahlīl* is the corresponding verbal noun, means "to declare the Uniqueness of Allāh, by saying: 'There is no god but Allāh *[lā ilāha illa'llāh]*.'"

[11] The Arabic verb *sabbaḥa*, of which *tasbīḥ* is the corresponding verbal noun, means "to proclaim the Glory of Allāh, by saying: 'Glory be to Allāh *[subḥāna 'llāh]*.'"

[12] Variants of this Divine Saying *[Ḥadīth Qudsī]* have been recorded by several of the most highly respected traditional authorities. For a scholarly study of six of these variants (none of them quite identical with either of those quoted in the above subsection), see: William A. Graham. *Divine Word and Prophetic Word in Early Islam*. The Hague and Paris: Mouton, 1977; pp. 186–190.

When Abū Bakr (may Allāh be well pleased with him) heard this, he said: "O Messenger of Allāh, will some folk be invited to enter through all of these gates?" "Yes," replied the Prophet (Allāh bless him and give him peace), "and I do hope that you will be one of them, O Abū Bakr!" He also said (Allāh bless him and give him peace):

> Everything has its own gate or doorway, and the doorway to worshipful service *[ʿibāda]* is fasting.

According to a another traditional report, this one transmitted on the authority of Anas ibn Mālik (may Allāh be well pleased with him), Allāh's Messenger (Allāh bless him and give him peace) once said:

> You must be sure to practice fasting, for your hearts will be then be purified.

As reported on the authority of Abū Huraira (may Allāh be well pleased with him), Allāh's Messenger (Allāh bless him and give him peace) once said:

> Fasting is one half of patience *[aṣ-ṣawmu niṣfu 'ṣ-ṣabr]*. Everything has to pay some form of alms-due *[zakāt]*, and the alms-due of the physical body is fasting.

As reported on the authority of Abū Awfā (may Allāh be well pleased with him), the Prophet (Allāh bless him and give him peace) once said:

> The sleep of one who fasts is an act of worshipful service *[ʿibāda]*, his silence is a glorification of the Lord *[tasbīḥ]*,[13] and his good work is sure to be accepted.

According to a another traditional report, this one transmitted on the authority of Ibn ʿAbbās (may Allāh be well pleased with him and with his father), Allāh's Messenger (Allāh bless him and give him peace) once said:

> A table made of gold will be spread, on the Day of Resurrection *[Yawm al-Qiyāma]*, before those who now observe the practice of fasting. It will be laden with fish, so they will eat thereof, while the rest of the people look on.

This next report has come to us from Aḥmad ibn Abi'l-Ḥawārī, who said that he heard it from Abū Sulaimān, when the latter told him: "Abū ʿAlī al-Aṣamm ['the Deaf'] has brought me the finest traditional saying *[ḥadīth]* I ever heard in this world. This is how it goes:

"A table will be laid before those who now practice fasting, and they will eat from it while the rest of the people are being subjected to the Reckoning. 'O Lord,' the latter will say, 'how is it that we are being called to account, while those folk are busy eating?' So He will explain: 'For such a long time, they would be engaged in fasting, while you would

[13] See note 11 on p. 9 above.

be breaking fast, and they would be keeping night vigil, while you would be sleeping.'"

As reported by Ibn 'Abbās (may Allāh be well pleased with him and with his father), Allāh's Messenger (Allāh bless him and give him peace) once said:

> When they emerge from their graves [at the Resurrection], the fragrant aroma of musk will issue from the mouths of those who now practice fasting. A table will be brought to them from the Garden of Paradise, and from it they will eat, while sitting in the shade of the Heavenly Throne *['Arsh]*.

It was Sufyān ibn 'Uyaina who said: "According to my information, someone who keeps the fast will not be called to account [at the Resurrection] for what he takes when he breaks his fast."

As reported by Abū Ṣāliḥ, on the authority of Abū Huraira (may Allāh be well pleased with him), Allāh's Messenger (Allāh bless him and give him peace) once said:

> Allāh (Almighty and Glorious is He) says: "Fasting is Mine, and I determine its reward. He abstains from his carnal appetite, his food, and his drink for My sake. Fasting is a protective shield *[junna]*." For someone who keeps the fast, there are two delights in store: one delight at the moment of breaking his fast, and one delight at the moment of meeting his Lord. As for the odor of the mouth of someone who is fasting, it is more fragrant to Allāh than the scent of musk.

According to a another traditional report, this one transmitted on the authority of Jābir ibn 'Abdi'llāh (may Allāh be well pleased with him and with his father), Allāh's Messenger (Allāh bless him and give him peace) once said:

> Fasting is a protective shield *[junna]*, by means of which the servant [of the Lord] is shielded from the Fire of Hell.

According to Sa'īd ibn Jubair, who heard the report from Ibn 'Umar (may Allāh be well pleased with him and with his father), 'Umar ibn al-Khaṭṭāb (may Allāh be well pleased with him) once said:

"I feel no keen sense of regret over anything belonging to this world, which I shall have to leave behind me, apart from fasting in the midday heat *[hājira]* and walking to the ritual prayer *[ṣalāt]*."

As reported by Mujāhid, on the authority of Abū Huraira (may Allāh be well pleased with him), Allāh's Messenger (Allāh bless him and give him peace) once said:

> If a man were to fast voluntarily *[taṭawwu'an]*, for the sake of Allāh, even if he were to be given enough gold to fill the earth, he would not have received his reward in full, this side of the final Reckoning.

Traditional reports concerning the recitation of various litanies *[awrād]* during the observance of night vigil *[qiyām al-lail]*, which is a practice to be encouraged.

As for the recitation of nighttime litanies *[awrād al-lail]*, and the incentive to keep vigil *[qiyām]*, there are many traditional reports in favor of the practice. Some of these reports, the authenticity of which is unanimously accepted, are recorded in the two *Ṣaḥīḥ*'s,[14] while some are mentioned in other books [of tradition]. Let us therefore quote a number of examples from these sources:

As reported on the authority of Shafīq, it was ʿAbdu'llāh (may Allāh be well pleased with him) who said: "A certain man was mentioned in the presence of the Prophet (Allāh bless him and give him peace), to whom someone said: 'O Messenger of Allāh, so-and-so spent the whole night asleep, right through to the break of day. He never got up to perform any [voluntary] ritual prayers.' On hearing this, the Prophet (Allāh bless him and give him peace) exclaimed:

> 'The devil *[shaiṭān]* must have pissed in that man's ear!'"

According to one traditional report *[khabar]* [the Prophet (Allāh bless him and give him peace) once said]:

> While a man is sleeping, the devil *[shaiṭān]* ties knots on his head, three knots in all. If the sleeper sits up and remembers Allāh (Exalted is He), one knot will be undone. If he performs the minor ritual ablution *[wuḍūʾ]*, a second knot will be untied, and if he performs two cycles of ritual prayer *[ṣallā rakʿatain]*, all the knots will be loosened. In that case, when morning comes, he will be fresh and in a cheerful mood; otherwise, however, the morning will find him sluggish and bad-tempered.

According to another traditional report *[khabar]* [the Prophet (Allāh bless him and give him peace) also said]:

> The devil *[shaiṭān]* has a kind of snuff *[saʿūṭ]*, a kind of syrup *[laʿūq]* and a kind of powder *[dharūr]*. When he gets the servant [of the Lord] to take this snuff,

[14] These are the two most famous collections of Prophetic traditions, separately entitled *Ṣaḥīḥ al-Bukhārī* and *Ṣaḥīḥ Muslim*. (The term *ṣaḥīḥ* means "correct; authentic.")

the man becomes badly behaved. When he administers the syrup, the man acquires a sharp and evil tongue. Then, when he applies the powder, the man sleeps right through the night till the break of day.

It is customary[15] to prolong the upright posture *[ṭūl al-qiyām]* in the course of the [voluntary] nighttime ritual prayer *[ṣalāt al-lail]*, which is performed in two sets of two cycles *[mathnā mathnā]*. (In the [voluntary] daytime ritual prayer *[ṣalāt an-nahār]*, on the other hand, it is customary to emphasize the frequency of bowing *[rukūʿ]* and prostration *[sujūd]*.) Nevertheless, if the worshipper wishes to perform it as a four-cycle prayer, with one concluding salutation *[taslīma]*, it is permissible for him to do so.

In the case of the Prophet himself (Allāh bless him and give him peace), the nighttime ritual prayer *[ṣalāt al-lail]* was [more than] a supererogatory devotion *[nāfila]*; it was also an obligatory duty *[farīḍa]*, an act of drawing near [to Allāh] *[qurba]*, and a charismatic event *[karāma]*. In the case of his Community *[Umma]*, it is a complement and supplement to the obligatory observances *[farāʾiḍ]*.

As reported on the authority of Sālim, it was Ibn ʿUmar (may Allāh be well pleased with him and with his father) who said:

"Whenever a man experienced an unusual dream, during the lifetime of Allāh's Messenger (Allāh bless him and give him peace), he would be sure to recount it to Allāh's Messenger (Allāh bless him and give him peace). I dearly wished that I might also experience such a dream, so that I could then recount it to Allāh's Messenger (Allāh bless him and give him peace). At the time I am recalling, during the lifetime of Allāh's Messenger (Allāh bless him and give him peace), when I was quite a young fellow and still a bachelor, I would often sleep in the mosque *[masjid]*. It was there that I eventually saw a vision in my sleep: It seemed as if two angels had seized me and carried me toward the Fire of Hell, which appeared to be sunk in a hole, like the hole of a well. It also appeared to have two horns, like the horns [or posts] of a well. I noticed the presence of people I knew, so I set about saying: 'I take refuge with Allāh from the Fire of Hell. I take refuge with Allāh from the Fire of Hell.' At this point, another angel approached us and said: 'It will come as no surprise to me, if you really do end up here!'"

[15] By "customary" we mean following the exemplary custom [*sunna* in Arabic] of the Prophet (Allāh bless him and give him peace).

Ibn ʿUmar (may Allāh be well pleased with him and with his father) went on to say: "I recounted this experience to [my sister] Ḥafṣa, and Ḥafṣa (may Allāh be well pleased with her) recounted it in turn to [her husband] the Messenger of Allāh (Allāh bless him and give him peace). When he had heard the story, Allāh's Messenger (Allāh bless him and give him peace) said: 'Yes, the man is the servant of Allāh. If only he would perform the ritual prayer *[yuṣallī]* during part of the night!'"

Sālim concluded this report with the observation: "From that moment on, Ibn ʿUmar (may Allāh be well pleased with him and with his father) spent very little of the night asleep."

As reported on the authority of Abū Salama, it was ʿAbdu'llāh ibn ʿAmr al-ʿĀṣ (may Allāh be well pleased with him and with his father) who said: "Allāh's Messenger (Allāh bless him and give him peace) once said to me:

> "'You must not be like so-and-so, who used to stay awake at night *[kāna yaqūmu 'l-lail]*, but neglected to observe the practice of night vigil *[qiyām al-lail]*.'"

According to one traditional report,[16] al-Ḥusain ibn ʿAlī (may Allāh be well pleased with him and with his father) was told by his father, ʿAlī ibn Abī Ṭālib (may Allāh be well pleased with him), that Allāh's Messenger (Allāh bless him and give him peace) once paid a nighttime visit to him and his [wife, the Prophet's] daughter, Fāṭima (may Allāh be well pleased with her and with her husband), only to find them both sound asleep.

[The report continues in ʿAlī's own words (may Allāh be well pleased with him)]: "He said: 'Are you not performing your prayers?' So I replied: 'O Messenger of Allāh, our souls are surely in the hand of Allāh (Exalted is He), so if He wishes to arouse us, He will surely arouse us!'" Allāh's Messenger (Allāh bless him and give him peace) moved away, when I said that to him, and he did not offer any direct response, but I could hear him slapping his thigh, as he recited (Allāh bless him and give him peace):

But man is more than anything prone to disputation. (18:54)'"	*wa kāna 'l-insānu akthara shaiʾin jadalā.*

[16] ***Author's note***: For this report, the chain of transmission *[isnād]* goes back through the following links: **Abū Ṣāliḥ—Ibn Shihāb—ʿAlī ibn al-Ḥusain—his father, al-Ḥusain ibn ʿAlī** (may Allāh be well pleased with him and with his father)—**his father, ʿAlī ibn Abī Ṭālib** (may Allāh be well pleased with him).

Shaikh Abū Naṣr Muḥammad ibn al-Bannā' has informed us, citing traditional authority for his report,[17] that the Prophet (Allāh bless him and give him peace) once said:

> Two cycles of ritual prayer *[rak'atān]*, performed in the middle of the night, are better than this world and all that it contains. But for the hardship it would have caused my Community *[Ummatī]*, I would have made their performance compulsory for them.

As we are reliably informed by Shaikh Abū Naṣr,[18] Abū Muslim once asked Abū Dharr (may Allāh be well pleased with him): "Which nighttime prayer *[ṣalāt al-lail]* is the most meritorious?" Abū Dharr (may Allāh be well pleased with him) responded by saying: "I once asked Allāh's Messenger (Allāh bless him and give him peace) that very same question, and he told me:

> "'[The most meritorious is the prayer in] the middle of the night *[jawf al-lail]*—(or he may have said: 'the halfway point of the night *[niṣf al-lail]*')—though few indeed are they who perform it.'"

According to certain traditional reports *[akhbār]*, the Prophet David *[Dāwūd an-Nabī]* (peace be upon him) once asked a similar question of his Lord (Almighty and Glorious is He), for he said: "My God *[Ilāhī]*, I dearly wish to offer You my worshipful service, so which time is most appropriate?" Allāh (Exalted is He) thereupon conveyed to him *[awḥā ilai-hi]* by way of inspiration: "O David, do not keep vigil in either the first part of the night or the last part thereof, because if someone keeps vigil in the first part, he will sleep through the last part, and if someone keeps vigil in the last part, he will not keep vigil in the first part. You should rather keep vigil in the middle of the night, for then you will be alone with Me, and I will be Alone with you. You should also offer up your needs to Me [at that time of night]."

As reported on the authority of Yaḥyā ibn al-Mukhtār, it was al-Ḥasan [al-Baṣrī] (may Allāh bestow His mercy upon him) who said: "The servant [of the Lord] can perform no deed that is more soothing to the

17 ***Author's note***: Shaikh Abū Naṣr Muḥammad ibn al-Bannā' cites the following chain of transmission *[isnād]* for this report: **His own father, Shaikh Abū 'Alī ibn Aḥmad ibn 'Abdi'llāh ibn al-Bannā'—Sufyān ath-Thawrī—Abu'z-Zubair—Jābir ibn 'Abdi'llāh** (may Allāh be well pleased with him and with his father)—**the Prophet** (Allāh bless him and give him peace).

18 ***Author's note***: Shaikh Abū Naṣr Muḥammad ibn al-Bannā' narrates this report on the authority of his father, citing a chain of transmission *[isnād]* from **Abu'l-'Āliya—Abū Muslim—Abū Dharr** (may Allāh be well pleased with him)—**the Prophet** (Allāh bless him and give him peace).

eye, or lighter on the back, or more cheering to the spirit, than vigil kept from the middle of the night to the very end—unless it be the spending of wealth on a worthy cause."

Abu'd-Dardā' (may Allāh be well pleased with him) used to say: "O you people, for you I am a faithful counsellor *[nāṣiḥ]*, for you I am a caring sympathizer *[shafīq]*, [so hear me when I say]: 'Perform the ritual prayer in the darkness of the night, in preparation for the lonely desolation of the graves. Keep the fast here in this world, in preparation for the blistering heat of the Day of Resurrection *[Yawm an-Nushūr]*. Be active in charitable giving, for fear of a day of great hardship *[yawm ʿasīr]*.[19] O you people, for you I am a faithful counsellor *[nāṣiḥ]*, for you I am a caring sympathizer *[shafīq]*!"

Shaikh Abū Naṣr Muḥammad ibn al-Bannā' has also informed us, citing traditional authority for his report,[20] that the Prophet (Allāh bless him and give him peace) once said:

> When a third of the night is still remaining, Allāh (Exalted is He) descends to the lowest heaven *[as-samā' ad-dunyā]*, and He keeps saying, until the dawn breaks: "Is there anyone ready to appeal to Me, so that I may answer his plea? Is there anyone ready to seek My forgiveness, so that I may forgive him? Is there anyone ready to ask Me for sustenance, so that I may sustain him? Is there anyone seeking the removal of harm, so that I may remove it from him?"

Shaikh Abū Naṣr Muḥammad ibn al-Bannā' has further informed us, citing traditional authority for his report,[21] that the Prophet (Allāh bless him and give him peace) once said:

> Our Lord (Almighty and Glorious is He) descends every night to the lowest heaven *[as-samā' ad-dunyā]*, during the last third of the night, and He says: "Is there anyone seeking forgiveness, so that I may forgive him? Is there anyone offering a supplication, so that I may respond to him? Is there anyone making a petition, so I may grant his petition?

This is surely enough to explain why they [our righteous predecessors] would always recommend the performance of ritual prayer *[ṣalāt]* during the last part of the night!

[19] This is an allusion to Q. 74:8–10

[20] ***Author's note***: Shaikh Abū Naṣr Muḥammad ibn al-Bannā' cites the following chain of transmission *[isnād]* for this report: **His own father, Shaikh Abū ʿAlī ibn Aḥmad ibn ʿAbdi'llāh ibn al-Bannā'—Yaḥyā ibn Abī Kathīr—Abū Jaʿfar—Abū Huraira** (may Allāh be well pleased with him)—**the Prophet** (Allāh bless him and give him peace).

[21] ***Author's note***: Shaikh Abū Naṣr Muḥammad ibn al-Bannā' narrates this report on the authority of his father, citing a chain of transmission *[isnād]* from **Abū Huraira** (may Allāh be well pleased with him)—**the Prophet** (Allāh bless him and give him peace).

Abū Umāma (may Allāh be well pleased with him) is reported as having said: "When someone asked Allāh's Messenger (Allāh bless him and give him peace): 'Which part of the night is best for the hearing [of supplications]?' he replied:

> "'The middle of the last part of the night, and the ends of the prescribed ritual prayers *[adbār aṣ-ṣalawāt al-maktūba]*.'"

As reported on the authority of ʿAbdu'llāh ibn ʿUmar (may Allāh be well pleased with him and with his father), Allāh's Messenger (Allāh bless him and give him peace) once said:

> The best kind of fasting *[ṣiyām]* is the fasting of David *[Dāwūd]* (peace be upon him), for he made it his practice to fast on alternate days throughout the entire year *[niṣf ad-dahr]*. The best kind of ritual prayer *[ṣalāt]* is likewise the ritual prayer of David *[Dāwūd]* (peace be upon him), for he used to sleep for half of the night, then devote the last part of the night to ritual prayer, until one sixth of the night still remained.

In differently worded version *[lafẓ]* of this report from ʿAbdu'llāh ibn ʿUmar (may Allāh be well pleased with him and with his father), the saying attributed to Allāh's Messenger (Allāh bless him and give him peace) reads as follows:

> The ritual prayer *[ṣalāt]* that is dearest to Allāh is the ritual prayer of David *[Dāwūd]* (peace be upon him). He used to sleep for half of the night, then wake up and keep vigil. Then he would sleep in the last part of the night. He would thus keep vigil for the third of the night after its halfway point.

Abū Huraira (may Allāh be well pleased with him) once said: "I divide the night into thirds. During one third I sleep, during one third I perform the ritual prayer *[uṣallī]*, and during one third I memorize the tradition *[ḥadīth]* of Allāh's Messenger (Allāh bless him and give him peace)."

It was Ibn Masʿūd (may Allāh be well pleased with him) who said: "The superior merit of the [voluntary] nighttime ritual prayer *[ṣalāt al-lail]*, as opposed to the [voluntary] daytime ritual prayer *[ṣalāt an-nahār]*, is comparable to the superior merit of charitable donation *[ṣadaqa]* made in secret, as opposed to charitable donation made in public."

ʿAmr ibn al-ʿĀṣ (may Allāh be well pleased with him) once said: "A single cycle of ritual prayer *[rakʿa]*, performed in the nighttime, is better than ten performed in the daytime."

It is reported that Allāh's Messenger (Allāh bless him and give him peace) once asked Gabriel *[Jibrīl]* (peace be upon him): "Which part of the night is best for the hearing [of supplications]?" He received the reply: "The Heavenly Throne *[ʿArsh]* is positively tingling during the pre-dawn interlude *[saḥar]*."

The Prophet (Allāh bless him and give him peace) once said:

> You must be sure to maintain the keeping of night vigil *[qiyām al-lail]*, for it has been the regular practice of the righteous *[ṣāliḥīn]* before you. The keeping of night vigil is a means of drawing near to Allāh (Exalted is He), of atoning for evil deeds, of preventing the commission of sins, and of driving sickness away from the physical body.

Shaikh Abū Naṣr Muḥammad ibn al-Bannā' has also informed us, citing traditional authority for his report,[22] that Allāh's Messenger (Allāh bless him and give him peace) once said:

> In the course of the night, there is an hour so special that, if a servant [of the Lord] asks something of Allāh (Exalted is He) at a moment coinciding with that hour, He will certainly grant his request.

There is one such hour in the course of every night. They [the religious scholars] have stated that this is a general occurrence, corresponding [in its mysterious character] to the special hour on Friday, the Day of Congregation *[Yawm al-Jumʿa]*, and to the Night of Power *[Lailat al-Qadr]* in the last ten days of the month of Ramaḍān.[23]

It is also said that, in the course of the night, there is a particular time when everyone is bound to go to sleep, when every conscious individual is bound to experience the loss of consciousnees, with the sole exception of the Ever-Living, the Eternally Self-Sustaining *[al-Ḥayy al-Qayyūm]*, the One who never dies. For all we know, it may be this very same hour.

In the tradition *[ḥadīth]* reported by ʿAmr ibn ʿUtba, we are told that the Prophet (Allāh bless him and give him peace) once said:

> You must be sure to perform the ritual prayer *[ṣalāt]* of the last part of the night, for it is witnessed and attended *[mashhūda maḥḍūra]*. It is attended by the angels of the night, and also by the angels of the day *[malā'ikat al-lail wa malā'ikat an-nahār]*.

[22] ***Author's note***: Shaikh Abū Naṣr Muḥammad ibn al-Bannā' cites the following chain of transmission *[isnād]* for this report: **His own father, Shaikh Abū ʿAlī ibn Aḥmad ibn ʿAbdi'llāh ibn al-Bannā'—al-Aʿmash—Abū Sufyān—Jābir** (may Allāh be well pleased with him)—**the Prophet** (Allāh bless him and give him peace).

[23] In the Seventh Discourse of the present work, Shaikh ʿAbd al-Qādir al-Jīlānī (may Allāh be well pleased with him) has quoted a long traditional report, containing a vivid description of the wonders of the nights of the month of Ramaḍān. (See Vol. 3, p. 89.)

Concerning the ritual prayer *[ṣalāt]* performed by Allāh's Messenger (Allāh bless him and give him peace) at certain times during the night.

On the subject of the ritual prayer *[ṣalāt]* performed by Allāh's Messenger (Allāh bless him and give him peace) at certain times during the night, many traditional reports are recorded in the collections that are unanimously accepted as authentic. Let us therefore quote some examples from these reliable sources:

Abū Isḥāq is reported as having said: "I once paid a visit to al-Aswad ibn Yazīd. He was a spiritual brother of mine, and a good friend, so I said to him: 'O Abū ʿAmr, tell me what ʿĀʾisha (may Allāh be well pleased with her) related to you about the ritual prayer *[ṣalāt]* of Allāh's Messenger (Allāh bless him and give him peace).' In response to my request, he told me that she had said (may Allāh be well pleased with her):

""'The Prophet (Allāh bless him and give him peace) used to sleep during the first part of the night, and devote the latter part of it to keeping vigil. Then, if he needed to attend to his family, he would take care of the need in question. Without touching water, he would then go straight to sleep. As soon as he heard the first call [to prayer], he would jump up *[wathaba]*," ('No, by Allāh, she did not say: "he would stand up *[qāma]*,"') "and pour water on himself." ('No again, by Allāh, she did not say: "and perform the major ablution *[ightasala]*." I know what you have in mind!') "If he was not in a state of major ritual impurity *[junub]*, he would perform his minor ablution *[wuḍūʾ]* in preparation for the ritual prayer *[ṣalāt]*. Then he would perform the prayer *[ṣallā]*."'""

As reported on the authority of Kuraib, the freedman *[mawlā]* of Ibn ʿAbbās: "Ibn ʿAbbās (may Allāh be well pleased with him and with his father) once spent a night in the home of Maimūna, the Mother of the Believers *[Umm al-Mu'minīn]* (may Allāh be well pleased with her). He [Ibn 'Abbās] said:

"'So I laid myself down to rest in a crosswise position on the cushion *[wisāda]*, while Allāh's Messenger (Allāh bless him and give him peace) and his wife reclined on it lengthwise. Allāh's Messenger (Allāh bless him and give him peace) slept until the night was halfway through, or slightly before that point, or slightly after it. Then Allāh's Messenger (Allāh bless him and give him peace) awoke, sat up, and rubbed the sleep from his face with his hand. Then he recited the ten Qur'ānic verses *[āyāt]* that form the concluding section *[al-āyāt al-khawātim]* of the Sūra of the Family of 'Imrān *[Sūrat Āl 'Imrān]*, beginning with the words of Allāh (Almighty and Glorious is He):

[There are signs for] those	*alladhīna yadhkurūna*
who remember Allāh,	*'llāha qiyāman*
standing and sitting	*wa qu'ūdan*
and on their sides, and who	*wa 'alā junūbi-him*
reflect upon the creation	*wa yatafakkarūna*
of the heavens	*fī khalqi 's-samāwāti*
and the earth:	*wa 'l-arḍ:*
"Our Lord, You have not	*Rabba-nā mā khalaqta*
created this in vain.	*hādhā bāṭilā:*
Glory be to You! So guard	*subḥāna-ka fa-qi-nā*
us against the torment of the Fire."	*'adhāba 'n-nār.*
(3:191)	

—and ending with His words (Exalted is He):

O you who believe,	*yā ayyuha 'lladhīna*
endure with patience,	*āmanu 'ṣbirū*
outdo all others	*wa ṣābirū*
in patient endurance, be ready,	*wa rābiṭū:*
and observe your duty to Allāh,	*wa 'ttaqu 'llāha*
in order that you may succeed.	*la'alla-kum tufliḥūn.*
(3:200)	

"'Then he stood up, reached for a dangling waterskin, and drew water from it for his minor ablution *[wuḍū']*, which he performed in a most thorough fashion. He then stood at the ready, and proceeded to perform the ritual prayer *[qāma fa-ṣallā]*.'"

"Ibn 'Abbās (may Allāh be well pleased with him and with his father) went on to say: 'So I got up too, and did the same things that Allāh's

Messenger (Allāh bless him and give him peace) had done. Then I went and stood by his side, at which point Allāh's Messenger (Allāh bless him and give him peace) placed his right hand on my head, took hold of my right ear, and gave it a twist. Then he proceeded to perform two cycles of ritual prayer *[rak'atain]*, then two more cycles, then two more cycles, then two more cycles, and then two more cycles. Then he concluded the odd-numbered prayer *[awtara]* with a single cycle *[rak'a]*. Then he lay down to rest, until the muezzin *[mu'adhdhin]* came by. Then he got up again, and performed two simple, unprotracted cycles of ritual prayer *[ṣallā rak'atain khafīfatain]*. Then he went out [to the mosque] and performed the [prescribed] prayer of daybreak *[ṣalla 'ṣ-ṣubḥ]*.'"

As reported on the authority of Abū Salama, 'Ā'isha (may Allāh be well pleased with her) once said: "I would never find the Prophet (Allāh bless him and give him peace) in any position, during the late pre-dawn interlude *[saḥar]*, except that of lying asleep beside me." (This was her way of saying: "after the *witr* prayer.")

Masrūq is reported as having said: "'Ā'isha (may Allāh be well pleased with her) once told me: 'The Prophet (Allāh bless him and give him peace) was always pleased by work performed with consistent regularity.' So I asked her: 'Which part of the night did he often say [that he liked best]?' and she replied: 'When he heard the crowing of the rooster *[ṣārikh]*.'"

As reported on the authority of al-Ḥasan [al-Baṣrī] (may Allāh bestow His mercy upon him), Allāh's Messenger (Allāh bless him and give him peace) once said:

> Perform the ritual prayer *[ṣallū]* in the course of the night, if only four [cycles]. Perform the ritual prayer, if only two cycles *[rak'atain]*. Whenever the members of a given household are recognized [in heaven], as people known to practice ritual prayer *[ṣalāt]* in the nighttime, an angelic crier will cry out to them: "O members of that household there, wake up to perform your ritual prayer *[qūmū li-ṣalāti-kum]*!"

According to a report from Abū Salama, on the authority of Abū Huraira (may Allāh be well pleased with him), Allāh's Messenger (Allāh bless him and give him peace) once said:

> Allāh has never listened to anything as much as He has listened to a Prophet *[Nabī]* with a beautiful voice, chanting the Qur'ān.

According to yet another traditional report, this one transmitted on the authority of ʿUrwa, ʿĀʾisha (may Allāh be well pleased with her) once said: "The Prophet (Allāh bless him and give him peace) once heard a man reciting a Sūra [of the Qurʾān] during the night, so he said (Allāh bless him and give him peace):

> 'May Allāh bestow His mercy upon him! He has reminded me of such-and-such a verse *[āya]*, which I had omitted from the Sūra of such-and such.'"

As for the amount of ritual prayer *[ṣalāt]* the Prophet (Allāh bless him and give him peace) used to perform during the nighttime, we may cite the following traditional report, conveyed to us by Shaikh Abū Naṣr Muḥammad ibn al-Bannāʾ:[24]

ʿUrwa (may Allāh bestow His mercy upon him) said that ʿĀʾisha (may Allāh be well pleased with her) once told him: "In the course of the night, Allāh's Messenger (Allāh bless him and give him peace) used to perform thirteen cycles [of voluntary prayer] and the two cycles of the dawn prayer *[rakʿatayi 'l-fajr]*."

It is also reported that, in the course of the night, the Prophet (Allāh bless him and give him peace) would perform twelve cycles of ritual prayer, then he would conclude the odd-numbered prayer *[awtara]* with a single cycle *[rakʿa]*. According to some accounts, however, [he would perform not twelve but only] ten cycles, then he would conclude the odd-numbered prayer *[awtara]* with a single cycle *[rakʿa]*.

[24] ***Author's note***: Shaikh Abū Naṣr Muḥammad ibn al-Bannāʾ cites the following chain of transmission *[isnād]* for this report: **His own father, Shaikh Abū ʿAlī ibn Aḥmad ibn ʿAbdi'llāh ibn al-Bannāʾ—Muḥammad ibn Aḥmad ibn Abi'l-Fawāris—Aḥmad ibn Yūsuf—Aḥmad ibn Ibrāhīm ibn Malḥān—Abū Bakr—al-Laith—Ibn Abī Ḥabīb—ʿArrāk—ʿUrwa** (may Allāh bestow His mercy upon him)—**ʿĀʾisha** (may Allāh be well pleased with her).

Qur'ānic verses *[āyāt]* concerning those who perform the ritual prayer *[ṣalāt]* during the night.

Allāh (Exalted is He) has mentioned those who keep vigil by night *[al-qā'imīn bi'l-lail]* in His Glorious Book [the Qur'ān], for He has told us (Almighty and Glorious is He):

They used to sleep only a little	*kānū qalīlan*
during the night, and with	*mina 'l-laili mā yahja'ūn:*
the dawning of each day,	*wa bi'l-asḥāri*
they would seek forgiveness.	*hum yastaghfirūn.*
(51:17,18)	

He has also said (Glorious and Exalted is He):

Their sides shun their couches,	*tatajāfā junūbu-hum 'ani 'l-maḍāji'i*
as they call on their Lord	*yad'ūna Rabba-hum*
in fear and hope. (32:16)	*khawfan wa ṭama'ā.*

He has also said (Exalted is He):

Or is he who is obedient	*am-man huwa qānitun*
in the watches of the night,	*ānā'a 'l-laili*
bowing and standing erect,	*sājidan wa qā'iman*
being wary of the hereafter	*yaḥdharu 'l-ākhirata*
and hoping for the mercy	*wa yarjū raḥmata*
of his Lord...?	*Rabbi-h: qul*
Say: "Are they equal,	*hal yastawi 'lladhīna*
those who know and those	*ya'lamūna*
who do not know?"	*wa 'lladhīna lā ya'lamūn:*
Only those with powers	*inna-mā yatadhdhakaru*
of understanding will remember	*ulu 'l-albāb.*
and take heed. (39:9)	

He has also said (Blessed and Exalted is He):

and who spend the night	*wa 'lladhīna yabītūna*
before their Lord,	*li-Rabbi-him*
prostrate and standing; (25:65)	*sujjadan wa qiyāmā:*

He has also said (Glorious and Exalted is He):

And as for the night, keep vigil during a part of it, as a supererogatory work of devotion for you; it may be that your Lord will raise you up to a praiseworthy station. (17:79)	*wa mina 'l-laili fa-tahajjad bi-hi nāfilatan la-k: ʿasā an yabʿatha-ka Rabbu-ka maqāman maḥmūdā.*

The Prophet (Allāh bless him and give him peace) once said:

> When, on the Day of Resurrection *[Yawm al-Qiyāma]*, Allāh assembles those of ancient times and those who came later, an angelic herald will cry out: "Let them now arise, all those whose sides used to shun their couches, as they called upon their Lord in fear and hope!" They will thereupon arise, but they will be very few.
>
> Then the herald will return, and this time he will cry: "Let them now arise, all those whom neither commerce nor trafficking diverted from the remembrance of Allāh!" They will thereupon arise, but they will be very few.
>
> The herald will then return again, and this time he will cry: "Let them now arise, all those who used to praise Allāh (Almighty and Glorious is He) in good times and in bad." They will thereupon arise, but they will be very few. The rest of the people will then be called to account in turn.

The Prophet (Allāh bless him and give him peace) also said:

> You must take advantage of the pre-dawn meal *[ṭaʿām as-saḥar]*, to help you prepare for the daytime fasting, and of the daytime siesta *[qailūla]*, to help you prepare for the nighttime vigil *[qiyām al-lail]*. The addict of sleep will come away bankrupt *[muflis]*, and no one spends the whole length of the night asleep, unless the devil *[shaiṭān]* has pissed in his ear.

Allāh's Messenger (Allāh bless him and give him peace) would often repeat a Qurʾānic verse *[āya]* until the break of dawn, and ʿĀʾisha (may Allāh be well pleased with her) once said:

"Allāh's Messenger (Allāh bless him and give him peace) lay sleeping [close beside me] one night, until his skin became stuck to my skin, then he said: 'O ʿĀʾisha, would you permit me to devote the night to worshipping my Lord?' So I told him: 'By Allāh, I love your nearness, but I prefer to respect your dearest wish.' He then stood erect (Allāh bless him and give him peace) and proceeded to recite the Qurʾān. He wept as he did so, until the upper parts of his chest were drenched with tears. Then he sat down and continued to recite, still weeping, until his sides and loins were drenched with tears. Then he lay down on the floor, still weeping and reciting, until the area next to the ground was also drenched with tears.[25]

[25] For an essentially similar, yet interestingly different version of this lengthy report from ʿĀʾisha (may Allāh be well pleased with her), see Vol. 5, pp. 132–33.

"Bilāl (may Allāh be well pleased with him) eventually came to him and said: 'By my father and my mother, surely Allāh has forgiven you!' To this he replied (Allāh bless him and give him peace):

"'O Bilāl, should I not be a very thankful servant [*ʿabd shakūr*]? Sent down to me this night were the words of divine revelation:

Surely in the creation of the heavens and the earth, and the alternation of night and day, there are signs for men with understanding minds.	*inna fī khalqi 's-samāwāti wa 'l-arḍi wa 'khtilāfi 'l-laili wa 'n-nahāri la āyātin li-uli 'l-albāb.*
[There are signs for] those who remember Allāh, standing and sitting and on their sides, and who reflect upon the creation of the heavens and the earth: "Our Lord, You have not created this in vain. Glory be to You! So guard us against the torment of the Fire." (3:190,191)	*alladhīna yadhkurūna 'llāha qiyāman wa quʿūdan wa ʿalā junūbi-him wa yatafakkarūna fī khalqi 's-samāwāti wa 'l-arḍ: Rabba-nā mā khalaqta hādhā bāṭilā: subḥāna-ka fa-qi-nā ʿadhāba 'n-nār.*

ʿĀʾisha (may Allāh be well pleased with her) also said: "At no time did I ever see Allāh's Messenger (Allāh bless him and give him peace) performing the whole of his nighttime ritual prayer [*ṣalāt al-lail*] in a sitting posture—not until he entered the period of old age, when he did start to perform his prayers while sitting down. When he still had thirty or forty verses of a Sūra left to recite, he would stand up and complete their recitation, then he would adopt the bowing posture (Allāh bless him and give him peace).

It was Yaʿmar ibn Bishr who said: "I once came to the door of ʿAbdu'llāh ibn Mubārak, after the time of the [prescribed] late evening prayer [*al-ʿishāʾ al-ākhira*], and I found him performing [voluntary] prayers. I heard him reciting:

When the heaven is split asunder, and when the stars are scattered, and when the seas are made to overflow, and when the tombs are overthrown, then a soul will know what it has sent on ahead, and what it has left behind. (82:1–5)	*idha 's-smāʾu 'nfaṭarat: wa idha 'l-kawākibu 'ntatharat: wa idha 'l-biḥāru fujjirat: wa idha 'l-qubūru buʿthirat: ʿalimat nafsun mā qaddamat wa akhkharat.*

—until he reached:

What has deceived you concerning your Lord, the All-Generous? (82:6)	*mā gharra-ka bi-Rabbi-ka 'l-Karīm:*

"He paused at this point, but then he kept repeating this same recitation, over and over again, until a good part of the night had elapsed. So I went back home, and returned to his place when the light of dawn had appeared, only to find him still repeating it. When he noticed the light of dawn, he finally stopped. Then he said: 'Your tolerance and my ignorance! Your tolerance and my ignorance *[ḥilmu-ka wa jahlī]*!' So I went away and left him.'"

The Prophet (Allāh bless him and give him peace) once said:

> The winter is the springtime of the true believer *[mu'min]*. His day gets shorter, so he devotes it to fasting, and his night grows longer, so he devotes it to vigil.

It was Ibn Mas'ūd (may Allāh be well pleased with him) who said: "It should always be possible to recognize the reader of the Qur'ān: by his [vigil in the] nighttime, when other people are sleeping; by his [fasting in the] daytime, when other people are breaking fast; by his weeping, when other people are laughing; by his pious caution and restraint *[wara']*, when other people are freely mixing [the lawful with the dubious, or even with the unlawful]; by his humble and modest bearing, when other people are strutting about and parading their self-importance; by his sadness, when other people are behaving merrily; and by his remaining silent, when other people are plunging without hesitation into argument and gossip.

Concerning the special merit of the [voluntary] ritual prayer *[ṣalāt]* performed between the two [prescribed] evening prayers *[al-ʿishāʾain]*.[26]

Shaikh Abū Naṣr Muḥammad ibn al-Bannāʾ has informed us, citing traditional authority for his report,[27] that Allāh's Messenger (Allāh bless him and give him peace) once said:

> If someone performs six cycles of [voluntary] ritual prayer *[ṣallā sitta rakaʿāt]* after the [prescribed prayer of] sunset *[baʿda'l-maghrib]*, without talking in the space between them, they will be counted as equal in merit to the worshipful service *[ʿibāda]* of twelve whole years.

In the traditional report *[ḥadīth]* of Zaid ibn al-Ḥabbāb, the wording is:

> —without talking about anything bad in the space between them....

In the first two cycles *[rakʿatain]*, it has also been said, the worshipper is recommended to recite [the Sūras that begin with] "Say: 'O you unbelievers *[qul yā ayyuha 'l-kāfirūn]*,'"[28] and "Say: 'He is Allāh, One! *[qul Huwa 'llāhu Aḥad]*.'"[29] He should perform these first two cycles

[26] That is to say, between the prescribed prayer of sunset *[ṣalāt al-maghrib]* and the prescribed prayer of the late evening *[ṣalāt al-ʿishāʾ al-ākhira]*.

[27] ***Author's note***: Shaikh Abū Naṣr Muḥammad ibn al-Bannāʾ cites the following chain of transmission *[isnād]* for this report: **His own father, Shaikh Abū ʿAlī ibn Aḥmad ibn ʿAbdi'llāh ibn al-Bannāʾ—Abu'l-Fatḥ Muḥammad ibn Aḥmad ibn Abi'l-Fawāris al-Ḥāfiẓ—Bishr—Muḥammad ibn Sulaimān al-Maṣīṣī—Zaid ibn al-Ḥabbāb—ʿUmar ibn ʿAbdi'llāh ibn Khathʿam—Yaḥyā ibn Abī Bakr—Abū Salama—Abū Huraira** (may Allāh be well pleased with him)—**the Prophet** (Allāh bless him and give him peace).

[28] This is the Sūra entitled "The Unbelievers *[al-Kāfirūn]*," which reads:

Say: "O unbelievers, I do not worship	*qul yā ayyuha 'l-kāfirūn:*
that which you worship.	*lā aʿbudu mā taʿbudūn:*
And you do not worship that which I worship.	*wa lā antum ʿābidūna mā aʿbud:*
And I shall not worship that which you worship.	*wa lā ana ʿābidun mā ʿabadtum*
Nor will you worship that which I worship.	*wa lā antum ʿābidūna mā aʿbud:*
To you your religion,	*la-kum dīnu-kum*
and to me my religion!" (109:1–6)	*wa liya dīn.*

[29] This is the Sūra of Sincere Devotion *[Sūrat al-Ikhlāṣ]*, which reads:

Say: "He is Allāh, One!	*qul Huwa 'llāhu Aḥad:*
Allāh, the Everlasting Refuge!	*Allāhu 'ṣ-Ṣamad:*
He does not beget, nor was He begotten;	*lam yalid wa lam yūlad:*
and there is none	*wa lam yakun la-hu*
comparable unto Him." (112:1–4)	*kufuwan aḥad.*

quickly, because then, it is said, they will be raised up [to heaven] together with the sunset prayer *[ṣalāt al-maghrib]*. Then, as he goes on to perform the rest of them, he may prolong any of their ingredients to whatever extent he wishes.

According to the traditional report *[ḥadīth]* of Ibn ʿAbbās (may Allāh be well pleased with him and with his father) the Prophet (Allāh bless him and give him peace) once said:

> If someone performs six cycles of [voluntary] ritual prayer *[ṣallā sitta rakaʿāt]*, after the [prescribed prayer of] sunset *[baʿda'l-maghrib]* and before he has talked to anybody, they will be raised up for him to the Highest Heaven *[ʿIlliyūn]*. He will be just like someone who is present on the Night of Power *[Lailat al-Qadr]* in the Farthest Mosque *[al-Masjid al-Aqṣā]*, and that is better than devoting half a night to vigil.

As we are reliably informed by Shaikh Abū Naṣr,[30] Abū Bakr aṣ-Ṣiddīq [the Champion of Truth] (may Allāh be well pleased with him) once said: "I heard the Prophet (Allāh bless him and give him peace) say:

> "'If someone performs the [prescribed] prayer of sunset *[maghrib]*, and then performs four [voluntary cycles] after it, he will be just like someone who performs one Pilgrimage after another *[man ḥajja baʿda Ḥijja]*.'

"So I asked him: 'What if he performs six [cycles] after it?' To this he replied:

> "'He will be forgiven the sins of fifty years.'"

Allāh's Messenger (Allāh bless him and give him peace) is reported[31] as having said:

> If someone secludes himself between the [prescribed prayers of] sunset and late evening *[baina 'l-maghrib wa 'l-ʿishā']*, in a congregational mosque *[masjid jamāʿa]*, and if he utters no speech at all, apart from [what is required] in performing a ritual prayer *[ṣalāt]* or a Qur'ānic recitation, it will be incumbent upon Allāh to have two palatial mansions built for him in the Garden of Paradise. A tour of either of these mansions would take a hundred years to complete. In the area between them, He will cultivate a plantation vast enough to accommodate all the people of this world, if they happened to pay him a visit.

Shaikh Abū Naṣr Muḥammad ibn al-Bannā' has informed us, citing

[30] ***Author's note***: Shaikh Abū Naṣr Muḥammad ibn al-Bannā' narrates this report on the authority of his father, citing a chain of transmission *[isnād]* from **Ṭāriq ibn Shihāb—Abū Bakr aṣ-Ṣiddīq** [the Champion of Truth] (may Allāh be well pleased with him).

[31] ***Author's note***: For this report, the chain of transmission *[isnād]* goes back through the following links: **Saʿīd ibn Jubair—Thawbān** (may Allāh be well pleased with him)**—the Prophet** (Allāh bless him and give him peace).

traditional authority for his report,[32] that Allāh's Messenger (Allāh bless him and give him peace) once said:

> No ritual prayer *[ṣalāt]* is dearer to Allāh (Exalted is He) than the [prescribed] prayer of sunset *[ṣalāt al-maghrib]*. With it the servant [of the Lord] begins his time of night, and with it he concludes his time of day. In no case may it be abbreviated, neither by the traveler *[musāfir]* nor by the resident *[muqīm]*.
>
> If a worshipper duly performs it, and then performs four [voluntary cycles] after it, without engaging in conversation while seated [in the interval], Allāh will have two palatial mansions built for him. Each of these will be crowned with pearls and sapphires, and in the area between them there will be Gardens of Paradise, the description whereof is known only to Allāh (Exalted is He).
>
> If a worshipper duly performs it, and then performs six [voluntary cycles] after it, without engaging in conversation while seated [in the interval], He will grant him forgiveness for [the sins of] forty years.

Abū Huraira (may Allāh be well pleased with him) used to perform twelve cycles of [voluntary] ritual prayer between the two [prescribed] evening prayers *[baina 'l-ʿishā'ain]*.

According to a report transmitted from ʿĀ'isha (may Allāh be well pleased with her),[33] Allāh's Messenger (Allāh bless him and give him peace) once said:

> If a worshipper performs twenty [voluntary] cycles of ritual prayer, between the [prescribed prayers of] sunset and late evening *[baina 'l-maghrib wa 'l-ʿishā']*, Allāh will have a house built for him in the Garden of Paradise.

It is traditionally related that Anas ibn Mālik (may Allāh be well pleased with him) used to perform [voluntary] ritual prayers between the [prescribed prayers of] sunset and late evening *[baina 'l-maghrib wa 'l-ʿishā']*, and that he used to say: "It is the time when the night sets in *[nāshi'at al-lail]*."[34]

[32] ***Author's note***: Shaikh Abū Naṣr Muḥammad ibn al-Bannā' cites the following chain of transmission *[isnād]* for this report: **His own father, Shaikh Abū ʿAlī ibn Aḥmad ibn ʿAbdi'llāh ibn al-Bannā'—Hishām ibn ʿUrwa—ʿĀ'isha** (may Allāh be well pleased with her)—**the Prophet** (Allāh bless him and give him peace).

[33] ***Author's note***: For this report, the chain of transmission *[isnād]* goes back through the following links: **Hishām ibn ʿUrwa—his father—ʿĀ'isha** (may Allāh be well pleased with her)—**the Prophet** (Allāh bless him and give him peace).

[34] Anas ibn Mālik (may Allāh be well pleased with him) was alluding to a verse *[āya]* in the Sūra of the Enshrouded One *[Sūrat al-Muzzammil]*, the 73rd Sūra of the Qur'ān:

The time when the night sets in is indeed the time when impressions are strongest and speech most direct. (73:6)	*inna nāshi'ata 'l-laili hiya ashaddu waṭ'an wa aqwamu qīlā.*

As related by ʿAbd ar-Raḥmān ibn al-Aswad, his paternal uncle once said: "Not once did I pay a visit to ʿAbdu'llāh ibn Masʿūd (may Allāh be well pleased with him), without finding him performing the [voluntary] ritual prayer between the [prescribed prayers of] sunset and late evening *[baina 'l-maghrib wa 'l-ʿishāʾ]*. He used to say: 'It is [all too often] an hour of heedless neglect.'"

It was during it [the interval between the sunset and late evening prayers], some say, that down came [the words of divine revelation]:

Their sides shun their couches,	*tatajāfā junūbu-hum ʿani 'l-maḍājiʿi*
as they call on their Lord	*yadʿūna Rabba-hum*
in fear and hope. (32:16)	*khawfan wa ṭamaʿā.*

According to another traditional report, transmitted on the authority of ʿAbdu'llāh ibn Abī Awfā (may Allāh be well pleased with him and with his father), the Prophet (Allāh bless him and give him peace) once said:

> If a worshipper recites, after the [prescribed prayer of] sunset *[maghrib]*, [the Sūras beginning with]:
>
> | | |
> |---|---|
> | Alif, Lām, Mīm. | *Alif–Lām–Mīm.* |
> | The revelation of the Book, | *tanzīlu 'l-Kitābi* |
> | of which there is no doubt, | *lā raiba fī-hi* |
> | is from the Lord of All the Worlds. | *min Rabbi 'l-ʿālamīn.* |
>
> —that is to say, the Sūra of Prostration *[Sūrat as-Sajda]*,[35] and:
>
> | | |
> |---|---|
> | Blessed is He in whose Hand | *tabāraka 'lladhī* |
> | is the Sovereignty.[36] | *bi-yadi-hi 'l-mulk.* |
>
> —when he comes forth on the Day of Resurrection *[Yawm al-Qiyāma]*, his face will be like the moon on the night when it is at the full *[lailat al-badr]*, and he will certainly do justice to that night."

Regarding these [voluntary] cycles of ritual prayer *[rakaʿāt]*, to which we find so many references in the traditional reports *[akhbār]*, it is possible that they are meant to be kept separate from the two cycles of the regular customary prayer *[ar-rakʿatain as-sunna]*,[37] though it is also possible that they are meant to be performed in combination with the latter.

[35] The Sūra of Prostration *[Sūrat as-Sajda]* is the 32nd Sūra of the Qurʾān.

[36] This is the first verse *[āya]* of the Sūra of Sovereignty *[Sūrat al-Mulk]*, the 67th Sūra of the Qurʾān.

[37] See pp. 141–46 below.

Concerning the two [voluntary] cycles *[rakʿatān]* sometimes performed before the [prescribed] sunset prayer *[ṣalāt al-maghrib]*.

Aḥmad ibn Ḥanbal (may Allāh bestow His mercy upon him) was once asked about the two [voluntary] cycles *[rakʿatān]* performed before the [prescribed] sunset prayer *[ṣalāt al-maghrib]*. He responded by telling the questioner:

"As far as I am concerned, I do not perform them, but if any man does perform them, there is no harm in his doing so."

Ibn ʿUmar (may Allāh be well pleased with him and with his father) was also asked about the performance of those same two cycles of ritual prayer *[ṣalāt]*. He said in reply:

"I never saw anyone perform them during the lifetime of Allāh's Messenger (Allāh bless him and give him peace)." It should be noted, however, that Ibn ʿUmar (may Allāh be well pleased with him and with his father) did not forbid their performance.

Anas ibn Mālik (may Allāh be well pleased with him) is reported as having said: "During the liftetime of Allāh's Messenger (Allāh bless him and give him peace), we used to perform two [voluntary] cycles of ritual prayer *[rakʿatain]* after the setting of the sun *[ghurūb ash-shams]* and before the [prescribed] ritual prayer of sunset *[ṣalāt al-maghrib]*." [The reporter said:] "So I asked him: 'Did Allāh's Messenger (Allāh bless him and give him peace) also perform them?' To this he replied: 'Allāh's Messenger (Allāh bless him and give him peace) often saw us performing them, but he never directly instructed us to do so, nor did he ever tell us that the practice was forbidden."

It was Ibrāhīm an-Nakhaʿī (may Allāh bestow His mercy upon him) who said: "Some of the very best of the Companions *[Aṣḥāb]* of Allāh's Messenger (Allāh bless him and give him peace) were at one time based in Kūfa, including ʿAlī ibn Abī Ṭālib, Ibn Masʿūd, Ḥudhaifa ibn al-Yamān, ʿAmmār ibn Yāsir, Abū Masʿūd al-Anṣārī and others (may Allāh be well pleased with them all)—and I never saw a single one of them performing a ritual prayer before the [prescribed prayer of] sunset *[qabla 'l-maghrib]*. Nor were these two particular cycles *[rakʿatain]* ever performed by Abū Bakr, ʿUmar, or ʿUthmān (may Allāh be well pleased with them all)."

More traditional reports concerning the [voluntary] ritual prayer *[ṣalāt]* performed between the two [prescribed] evening prayers *[al-ʿishāʾain]*, with special reference to the vision of the Prophet (Allāh bless him and give him peace).

Abū Ṭība Karaz ibn Wabra al-Ḥārithī (may Allāh bestow His mercy upon him) was one of the *Abdāl* [Spiritual Deputies].[38] He is reported[39] as having said:

"I once received a visit from a spiritual brother of mine, an inhabitant of the region of Damascus, who presented me with a gift. 'O Karaz,' he said to me, 'accept from me this gift, for it is truly an excellent present!' So I asked him: 'O my brother, and who gave you this gift?' To this he replied: 'It was given to me by Ibrāhīm at-Taimī (may Allāh the Exalted bestow His mercy upon him),' so I said: 'Well, did you ask Ibrāhīm who gave this gift to him?' 'Yes, of course,' said he, then he told me the following story:

"'I was sitting in the area in front of the Kaʿba [in Mecca], and I was engrossed in affirming the Uniqueness of Allāh *[tahlīl]*,[40] in proclaiming His Glory *[tasbīḥ]*,[41] and in offering praise to Him *[taḥmīd]*.[42] Then a man came up to me, greeted me with the salutation of peace *[sallama*

[38] In the Sixth Discourse of *Revelations of the Unseen [Futūḥ al-Ghaib]*, Shaikh ʿAbd al-Qādir (may Allāh be well pleased with him) gives the following explanation of the term *Abdāl*:

Annihilation *[fanāʾ]* is the aim and object, the final destination of the journey of the saints. This was the direction sought by all previous saints and *Abdāl*: to become extinct to their own will, and let the will of the Almighty and Glorious Truth take its place, as a permanent transformation, lasting until death. That is why they came to be called *Abdāl* [lit: 'substitutes'] (may Allāh be well pleased with them all).

[39] ***Author's note***: For this report, the chain of transmission goes back through the following links: **ʿAbd ar-Raḥmān ibn Ḥabīb al-Ḥārithī al-Baṣrī—Saʿīd ibn Saʿd—Abū Ṭība Karaz ibn Wabra al-Ḥārithī** (may Allāh bestow His mercy upon him).

[40] See note 10 on p. 9 above.

[41] See note 11 on p. 9 above.

[42] The Arabic verb *ḥammada*, of which *taḥmīd* is the corresponding verbal noun, means "to extol Allāh, by saying: 'Praise be to Allāh *[al-ḥamdu 'llāh]*.'"

ʿalayya], and seated himself to my right. Well, never in all my days had I seen anyone more handsome in facial features, more handsome in style of attire, more fragrantly perfumed, or with a fairer complexion. So I said: 'O servant of Allāh, who are you? Where do you come from, and what are you?' He replied: 'I am al-Khiḍr.[43] I have come to say, "Peace be upon you," and because I have a feeling of love toward you, for the sake of Allāh. I also come bearing a gift, which I intend to present to you.'

"'Well then,' said I, 'please tell me about this gift of yours. What is it?' To this al-Khiḍr (peace be upon him) replied: 'You must recite the following, before the sun rises and spreads its light over the earth, and also before it sets:

- The Sūra of Praise *[Sūrat al-Ḥamd]*[44]—seven times.
- The Sūra that begins with:

Say: "I take refuge with the Lord of mankind." (114:1)	*qul aʿūdhu bi-Rabbi 'n-nās.*

—seven times.

- The Sūra that begins with:

Say: "I take refuge with the Lord of the Daybreak." (113:1)	*qul aʿūdhu bi-Rabbi 'l-falaq.*

—seven times.

- The Sūra that begins with:

Say: "He is Allāh, One!" (112:1)	*qul Huwa 'llāhu Aḥad.*

—seven times.

- The Sūra that begins with:

Say: "O unbelievers...." (109:1)	*qul yā ayyuha 'l-kāfirūn....*

—seven times.

- The Verse of the Throne *[Āyat al-Kursī]*[45]—seven times.

You must also say:

• Glory be to Allāh!	*subḥāna 'llāh.*
• Praise be to Allāh!	*al-ḥamdu li'llāh.*

[43] See Vol. 2, note 87 on p. 63.

[44] The Sūra of Praise *[Sūrat al-Ḥamd]* is another name for the Opening Sūra of the Book *[Fātiḥat al-Kitāb]*, which begins with the verse *[āya]*:

Praise be to Allāh, Lord of All the Worlds.	*al-ḥamdu li'llāhi Rabbi 'l-ʿālamīn.*

[45] Q. 2:255.

• There is no god but Allāh!	*lā ilāha illa 'llāh.*
• Allāh is Supremely Great!	*Allāhu Akbar.*

—seven times.

You must invoke blessings upon the Prophet (Allāh bless him and give him peace)—seven times.

You must seek forgiveness for yourself, for your parents, and for all the believing men *[mu'minīn]* and all the believing women *[mu'mināt]*—seven times.

Immediately after the appeal for forgiveness *[istighfār]*, you must say:

O Allāh, my Lord, do with us	*Allāhumma Rabbi 'f'al bī*
and with them,	*wa bi-him*
both in the short term	*'ājilan*
and in the long term,	*wa ājilan*
in matters of religion,	*fi 'd-dīni*
this world and the hereafter,	*wa 'd-dunyā wa 'l-ākhirati*
that of which You are Capable.	*mā Anta la-hu Ahl:*
Do not do with us, O our Master,	*wa lā taf'al bi-nā yā Mawlā-nā*
that of which we are capable!	*mā naḥnu la-hu ahl:*
You are Forgiving, Forbearing,	*inna-ka Ghafūrun Ḥalīmun*
Generous, Noble, Kind,	*Jawādun Karīmun Barrun*
Gentle, Compassionate	*Ra'ūfun Raḥīm.*

—seven times.

"'See to it that you carry out this practice without fail, both in the morning and in the evening, for he who gave it to me told me: "You must say it at least once in your lifetime." When I said to him: 'I would like you to tell me who gave you this gift,' he said: 'It was Muḥammad (Allāh bless him and give him peace) who gave it to me.'

"I then said to al-Khiḍr (peace be upon him): 'Tell me something. Suppose I see the Prophet (Allāh bless him and give him peace) in one of my dreams, should I ask him if he gave you this gift?' So he said to me: 'Are you doubting my veracity?' I said: 'No, by Allāh, but I would love to hear that directly from Allāh's Messenger (Allāh bless him and give him peace).'

"He then told me: 'If you wish to see the Prophet (Allāh bless him and give him peace) in one of your dreams, this is what you need to know: As soon as you have performed the [prescribed] prayer of sunset *[ṣallaita 'l-maghrib]*, you must proceed to perform [voluntary] ritual prayers until the time of the [prescribed prayer] of late evening *[al-'ishā' al-ākhira]*, without talking to any human being. You must concentrate on the ritual prayer *[ṣalāt]* in which you are engaged. You must pronounce the salutation *[taslīma]* after each set of two cycles *[rakʿatain]*. In the course of each cycle *[rakʿa]*, you must complete the following Qurʾānic recitations:

- the Sūra of Praise *[Sūrat al-Ḥamd]*[46]—one time only, and
- the Sūra that begins with:

Say: "He is Allāh, One!" (112:1)	*qul Huwa 'llāhu Aḥad.*

—seven times.

You must then perform the [prescribed] ritual prayer of late evening *[ṣalāt al-ʿatama]*,[47] as a member of the congregation *[jamāʿa]*. On no account must you talk to anyone [after that], until you reach your own place of residence, and there perform the odd-numbered prayer *[ṣalāt al-witr]*. You must also perform two cycles of prayer *[rakʿatain]* at the point where you are about to take your sleep, reciting in each cycle *[rakʿa]*:

- the Sūra of Praise *[Sūrat al-Ḥamd]*, and
- the Sūra that begins with:

Say: "He is Allāh, One!" (112:1)	*qul Huwa 'llāhu Aḥad.*

—seven times.

Then you must perform an act of prostration, after the ritual prayer *[ṣalāt]*. While in your posture of prostration *[sujūd]*, you must seek forgiveness of Allāh (Exalted is He)—seven times. You must also say:

• Glory be to Allāh!	*subḥāna 'llāh.*
• Praise be to Allāh!	*al-ḥamdu li'llāh.*
• There is no god but Allāh!	*lā ilāha illa 'llāh.*
• Allāh is Supremely Great!	*Allāhu Akbar.*
• There is no might	*lā ḥawla*
nor any power except	*wa lā quwwata illā*
with Allāh, the All-High,	*bi'llāhi 'l-ʿAliyyi 'l-*
the Almighty.	*ʿAẓīm.*

—seven times.

Then you must raise your head from the posture of prostration *[sujūd]*, hold yourself steady in a sitting position, lift up your hands, and say:

O Ever-Living One,	*yā Ḥayyu*
O Self-Sustaining One!	*yā Qayyūm.*

[46] See note 44 on p. 34 above.

[47] The term *ṣalāt al-ʿatama* is synonymous with *ṣalāt al-ʿishāʾ al-ākhira*. See p. 139 below.

O Possessor of Majesty and Honor!	*yā Dha 'l-Jalāli wa 'l-Ikrām*
O God of the first and the last [of mankind]!	*yā Ilāha 'l-awwalīna wa 'l-ākhirīn.*
O All-Merciful of this world	*yā Raḥmāna 'd-dunyā*
and the hereafter,	*wa 'l-ākhira*
and All-Compassionate of both worlds!	*wa Raḥīma-humā*
O Lord, O Lord, O Lord!	*yā Rabb yā Rabb yā Rabb.*
O Allāh, O Allāh, O Allāh!	*yā Allāh yā Allāh yā Allāh.*

"'Then you must stand erect, and repeat the same invocations in your upright posture *[qiyām]*. Then you must prostrate yourself again, and repeat the same invocations in your posture of prostration *[sujūd]*. Then you must raise your head. At this point, you may lie down to sleep wherever you wish, facing the *Qibla* [direction of the Kaʿba] and invoking blessings on the Prophet (Allāh bless him and give him peace). You must keep this up until sleep overwhelms you.'

"I said to him [to al-Khiḍr (peace be upon him)]: 'I would like you to tell me from whom you heard this prayer of supplication *[duʿāʾ]*.' So he said to me: 'Are you doubting my veracity?' I said: 'By the One who sent Muḥammad (Allāh bless him and give him peace) as a Prophet bearing the Truth *[bi'l-Ḥaqqi Nabiyyan]*, I am not doubting your veracity.' He then went on (peace be upon him) to tell me: 'I was in the presence of Muḥammad (Allāh bless him and give him peace) when he was taught this prayer of supplication *[duʿāʾ]*, and I was beside him when it was entrusted to him, so I learned it from the One who taught it to him.'"

"Ibrāhīm continued: 'So I said to him: "Tell me about the spiritual reward of this prayer of supplication *[duʿāʾ]*," and al-Khiḍr (peace be upon him) told me: "When you meet Muḥammad (Allāh bless him and give him peace), you should ask him about its spiritual reward."'"

"Ibrāhīm went on to say: 'So I did what al-Khiḍr (peace be upon him) had told me to do. I kept invoking blessings upon the Prophet (Allāh bless him and give him peace) while I lay in my bed, and sleep departed from me, due to my intense delight with all that al-Khiḍr (peace be upon him) had taught me, and the hope of meeting the Prophet (Allāh bless him and give him peace). I was still in that state when morning came, so I performed the [prescribed] ritual prayer of dawn *[ṣallaitu 'l-fajr]*, then sat in my prayer niche *[miḥrāb]* until the full light of day had appeared. Then I performed the [voluntary] forenoon prayer *[ṣallaitu 'ḍ-ḍuḥā]*, saying to myself: "If I am still alive tonight, I shall do this all over again, just as I did it last night!"

"'It was then that sleep overwhelmed me, and the angels came and carried me away. They took me inside the Garden of Paradise, where I saw palatial mansions built of red rubies, and palatial mansions built of green emeralds, and palatial mansions built of white pearls. I also saw rivers of honey and milk and wine. In one of those palatial mansions, I saw a maiden looking down at me, and I noticed that the radiance of her face was brighter than the light of the unclouded sun. She had locks of hair that fell to the ground, all the way down from the top of the palatial mansion. So I asked the angels who had brought me inside: "To whom does this palace belong, and to whom does this maiden belong?" They replied: "To someone who performs the kind of good work you perform."

"'Needless to say, they did eventually remove me from those Gardens of Paradise, but not until they had given me some of its fruits to eat, and quenched my thirst with some of that refreshing drink. Only then did they take me away, and return me to the spot where I had been before.

"'It was then that Allāh's Messenger (Allāh bless him and give him peace) came to me, accompanied by seventy Prophets and seventy rows of angels, each row extending all the way from the East to the West. He greeted me with the salutation of peace *[sallama ʿalayya]*, and took me by my hand, so I said: "O Messenger of Allāh (may Allāh bless you and give you peace!), al-Khiḍr has told me that he heard this saying *[ḥadīth]* from you." The Prophet (Allāh bless him and give him peace) responded to this by saying: "Yes, al-Khiḍr has told you the truth, but then every story he tells is always true. He is the savant *[ʿālim]* of the people of the earth. He is the chieftain of the Spiritual Deputies *[raʾīs al-Abdāl]*, and he is one of Allāh's soldiers *[junūd]* upon the earth."

"'I then said: "O Messenger of Allāh, if someone does exactly as I have done, yet does not see what I have seen in my dream, will he nevertheless be given something of that which I have been given?" To this he replied (Allāh bless him and give him peace): "By the One who sent me as a Prophet bearing the Truth *[bi'l-Ḥaqqi Nabiyyan]*, that person will surely receive forgiveness for all the major sins *[kabāʾir]* he has ever committed, and Allāh will relieve him of His anger and His displeasure.

By the One who sent me as a Prophet bearing the Truth *[bi'l-Ḥaqqi Nabiyyan]*, if anyone matches this performance [of yours], even if he does not see the Garden of Paradise in one of his dreams, he will surely be given something comparable to that which you have been given.

""""An angelic herald will proclaim in the heaven above: "Allāh has already granted forgiveness, not only to the one who has worked so hard for his [the Prophet's] sake, but to his entire Community *[Umma]* (Allāh bless him and give him peace), consisting of all the believing men *[mu'minīn]* and believing women *[mu'mināt]* in the East and in the West. [The recording angel called] the Companion of the Left *[Ṣāḥib ash-Shimāl]* will be instructed not to record anything against any one of them, in the way of misdeeds, until the year that lies ahead.""""

"Ibrāhīm continued further: 'So then I said to him: "Let my father and my mother be your ransom, O Messenger of Allāh! By the One who has allowed me to behold your beauty, and has shown me the Garden of Paradise, am I to understand that this will be that person's spiritual reward?" He said: "Yes, he will be given all of that!" So I said: "O Messenger of Allāh, it is surely most important for all the believing men *[mu'minīn]* and believing women *[mu'mināt]* to learn this practice, and to teach it to others, since it is endowed with spiritual reward and merit of such magnitude!"

"'The Prophet (Allāh bless him and give him peace) replied: "By the One who sent me as a Prophet bearing the Truth *[bi'l-Ḥaqqi Nabiyyan]*, no one can do this, unless Allāh has created him as a fortunate individual, and no one can neglect to do it, unless Allāh has created him as an unlucky wretch." So I said: "O Messenger of Allāh, will anything else be given to someone who performs this work?"

"The Prophet (Allāh bless him and give him peace) replied: "By the One who sent me as a Prophet bearing the Truth *[bi'l-Ḥaqqi Nabiyyan]*, if someone performs this work for just one night, good deeds will be record in his favor, to the count of every drop of rain that has fallen from the sky, from the moment when Allāh created this world till the Day [of Resurrection] when the blast shall be blown on the Trumpet. By the same token, bad deeds will be erased from his record, to the number of every seed that has ever grown in the earth. These benefits will accrue to him, as well as to all the believing men *[mu'minīn]* and believing women *[mu'mināt]* who have put this advice into practice, whether in ancient or in later times.'"'"

As reported by al-A'raj, on the authority of Abū Huraira (may Allāh be well pleased with him), Allāh's Messenger (Allāh bless him and give him peace) once said:

> If a worshipper performs two [voluntary] cycles of ritual prayer *[ṣallā rak'atain]* on the night of Friday, the Day of Congregation *[lailat al-Jum'a]*, reciting in each cycle *[rak'a]*:
>
> • the Opening Sūra of the Book *[Fātiḥat al-Kitāb]* and the Verse of the Throne *[Āyat al-Kursī]*
>
> —one time only, and:
>
> • the Sūra that begins with:
>
> Say: "He is Allāh, One!" (112:1) *qul Huwa 'llāhu Aḥad.*
>
> —fifteen times, and if he says, at the end of his ritual prayer *[ṣalāt]*:
>
> O Allāh, bless Muḥammad, the unlettered Prophet! *Allāhumma ṣalli 'alā Muḥammadini 'n-Nabiyyi 'l-ummī.*
>
> —one thousand times, he will see me in one of his dreams. What is more, he will see me before the next Friday *[Jum'a]* is over. If someone sees me [in one of his dreams], it means that he is assured of the Garden of Paradise, and that he will be forgiven his former and his later sins.

Traditional references to the [voluntary] ritual prayer *[ṣalāt]* performed after the [prescribed] late evening prayer *[al-ʿishāʾ al-ākhira]*.

On this subject, as we are reliably informed by Shaikh Abū Naṣr Muḥammad ibn al-Bannāʾ,[48] it was Ibn ʿAbbās (may Allāh be well pleased with him and with his father) who said:

"If a worshipper performs four [voluntary cycles], after the [prescribed] ritual prayer of late evening *[al-ʿishāʾ al-ākhira]*, he will be just like one who arrives in time to experience the Night of Power *[Lailat al-Qadr]* in the Sacred Mosque *[Masjid al-Ḥarām]*."

A similar saying has been transmitted from Kaʿb al-Aḥbār, namely:

"If a worshipper performs four [voluntary cycles], after the [prescribed] ritual prayer of late evening *[al-ʿishāʾ al-ākhira]*, and with a fine Qurʾānic recitation, he will be entitled to a spiritual reward like that of the Night of Power *[Lailat al-Qadr]*."

In other words, it will be as if he had actually performed his ritual prayer on the Night of Power *[Lailat al-Qadr]*.

Shaikh Abū Naṣr Muḥammad ibn al-Bannāʾ has also informed us, citing traditional authority for his report,[49] that the Prophet himself (Allāh bless him and give him peace) once said:

> If a worshipper performs two [voluntary] cycles *[rakʿatain]*, after the [prescribed] ritual prayer of late evening *[al-ʿishāʾ al-ākhira]*, reciting:
>
> - the Opening Sūra of the Book *[Fātiḥat al-Kitāb]* —one time only, and
> - the Sūra that begins with:
>
> Say: "He is Allāh, One!" (112:1) *qul Huwa 'llāhu Aḥad.*
>
> —twenty times, Allāh will have two palatial mansions built for him in the Garden of Paradise, so impressive that the people of Paradise will point them out as landmarks!

[48] ***Author's note***: Shaikh Abū Naṣr Muḥammad ibn al-Bannāʾ narrates this report on the authority of his father, citing a chain of transmission *[isnād]* from **Ibn ʿAbbās** (may Allāh be well pleased with him and with his father).

[49] ***Author's note***: Shaikh Abū Naṣr Muḥammad ibn al-Bannāʾ cites the following chain of transmission *[isnād]* for this report: **His own father, Shaikh Abū ʿAlī ibn Aḥmad ibn ʿAbdi'llāh ibn al-Bannāʾ—Thābit al-Bannānī—Anas ibn Mālik** (may Allāh be well pleased with him)—**the Prophet** (Allāh bless him and give him peace).

Concerning the nighttime prayer called *witr*,[50] and the time of night most suitable for its performance.

As for the nighttime prayer called *witr* ["odd-numbered"], the time most suitable for its performance must be the last part of the night, in view of all that has been explained above, concerning the special merit of keeping vigil *[qiyām]* during the last part of the night. For further confirmation of this, we may adduce the following evidence:

As we learn from one traditional report, transmitted by Nāfi' on the authority of Ibn 'Umar (may Allāh be well pleased with him and with his father), a man once asked the Prophet (Allāh bless him and give him peace) about [the ritual prayer performed during] the night vigil *[qiyām al-lail]*, so he said:

> [The nighttime ritual prayer should be performed] in sets of two cycles *[mathnā mathnā]*, so, if you are afraid [of not finishing before] the dawn, one [separate cycle] will make what has preceded it count as your *witr*.

'Umar al-Fārūq (may Allāh be well pleased with him) used to perform the *witr* prayer during the last part of the night, whereas Abū Bakr aṣ-Siddīq [the Champion of Truth] (may Allāh be well pleased with him) performed his *witr* during the first part of the night. This came to the notice of the Prophet (Allāh bless him and give him peace), so he asked the two of them about it.

"When do you perform the *witr* prayer?" he said first to Abū Bakr (may Allāh be well pleased with him), and the latter replied: "In the first part

[50] The term *witr* [lit., odd number] is used to denote the ritual prayer, consisting of an odd number of cycles, that is performed after the late evening prayer *[ṣalāt al-'ishā']* and before the dawn of day *[ṣubḥ]*. The number of cycles is usually three, five, or seven, but may be as many as thirteen. Performance of the *witr* prayer is considered customary *[sunna]* by most traditional authorities, with the exception of Imām Abū Ḥanīfa (may Allāh bestow His mercy upon him), who took a stricter view. According to the Ḥanafī school *[madhhab]* of Islāmic jurisprudence *[fiqh]*, the observance of the *witr* prayer is classed as necessary *[wājib]*. (See: A.J. Wensinck, art. WITR in *Shorter Encyclopaedia of Islam*; and: Thomas Patrick Hughes, *Dictionary of Islam*, art. WITR.)

of the night, before I go to sleep." Then he asked ʿUmar (may Allāh be well pleased with him): "When do you perform the *witr* prayer?" and he received the answer: "During the last part of the night." The Prophet (Allāh bless him and give him peace) then said, with reference to Abū Bakr (may Allāh be well pleased with him): "This one is cautious," and with reference to ʿUmar (may Allāh be well pleased with him): "This one is strong."

ʿUmar (may Allāh be well pleased with him) is also reported as having said: "The shrewd ones *[akyās]* perform the *witr* prayer during the first part of the night, while the stong *[aqwiyāʾ]* perform it during the last part of the night, and the latter practice is more meritorious." There are some who maintain, however, that the first part of the night is actually more meritorious, in view of the practice of Abū Bakr (may Allāh be well pleased with him).

ʿUthmān [ibn ʿAffān] (may Allāh be well pleased with him) is reported as having said: "As for myself, I perform the *witr* prayer during the first part of the night. If I wake up [later], I perform one cycle of ritual prayer *[rakʿa]*, thereby converting my [odd-numbered] *witr* into part of an even-numbered set. I can only compare it to a stray she-camel, whom I am reuniting with her sisters. Then I perform an odd cycle at the very end of my ritual prayer *[ṣalāt]*." It is widely known, in fact, that he made it his practice (may Allāh be well pleased with him) to keep vigil throughout the whole of the night, while performing one single cycle of prayer *[rakʿa]*, in which he would recite the entire Qurʾān. That was his *witr* prayer.

Abū Huraira is reported as having said: "My bosom friend *[khalīlī]*, Abu'l-Qāsim[51] (Allāh bless him and give him peace) alerted me to the value of three practices: (1) the *witr* prayer before going to sleep, (2) devoting three days out of every month to fasting, and (3) the two cycles of the forenoon prayer *[rakʿatayi 'ḍ-ḍuḥā]*. [The early performance of the *witr* is recommended] especially in the case of someone who is afraid of not waking up until after the rising of the dawn, since the best course for him is to sleep on the *witr*."

ʿAlī [ibn Abī Ṭālib] (may Allāh be well pleased with him) once said: "The *witr* can be approached from any of these three angles: (1) If you wish, you may perform an odd number of prayer-cycles in the first part

[51] Abu'l-Qāsim [the Father of al-Qāsim] is one of the names of the Prophet Muḥammad (Allāh bless him and give him peace), assumed in memory of his son, who died in infancy.

of the night, then [perform any later nighttime prayers in] sets of two cycles *[rak'atain rak'atain]*. (2) If you wish, you may perform one single cycle *[rak'a]* as a *witr* prayer [before going to sleep]. Then, if you wake up [later in the night], you may add another to it [to make an even pair]. You may then perform an odd number of cycles during the last part of the night. (3) If you wish, you may postpone the *witr* until the very end of your [nighttime performance of the] ritual prayer *[ṣalāt]*."

As reported on the authority of Jābir ibn 'Abdi'llāh (may Allāh be well pleased with him and with his father), the Prophet (Allāh bless him and give him peace) once said:

> If someone is afraid that he may not wake up during the last part of the night, let him perform the *witr* prayer in the first part of the night, then let him go to sleep. On the other hand, if someone has a strong urge to get up during the last part of the night, let him postpone it [till then]. Vigil in the last part of the night is a practice restricted [to a few], and therefore more meritorious.

'Ā'isha (may Allāh be well pleased with her) is reported as having said: "As soon as Allāh's Messenger (Allāh bless him and give him peace) had performed his *witr* prayer, in the last part of the night, he would approach his wives, if he needed to do so; otherwise, he would lie down and take a nap in his place of prayer *[muṣallā]*, until Bilāl (may Allāh be well pleased with him) arrived to summon him with the call to prayer."

'Ā'isha (may Allāh be well pleased with her) also said: "Of the night as a whole, Allāh's Messenger (Allāh bless him and give him peace) sometimes performed the *witr* prayer in the first part, and sometimes in the middle section, and the very latest time for his *witr* was toward the pre-dawn interlude *[saḥar]*."

According to one traditional report *[khabar]*, Allāh's Messenger (Allāh bless him and give him peace) would perform the *witr* at the time of the [pre-dawn] call to prayer *[adhān]*, then he would perform the two [customary] cycles *[rak'atain]* at the time of the final announcement *[iqāma]* [immediately before the prescribed prayer of daybreak].

The Companions *[Aṣḥāb]* of Allāh's Messenger (Allāh bless him and give him peace) would perform the [prescribed] prayer of late evening *[al-'ishā']*, then they would perform two [voluntary] cycles *[rak'atain]*, then four [more of the same]. After that, if anyone saw fit to do so, he would perform the *witr* prayer, and if anyone was ready for sleep, he would go to sleep.

Two opinions concerning the annulment of the *witr* prayer, when someone performs it in the first part of the night, then proceeds to perform the prayers called *tahajjud*.[52]

If someone performs the *witr* prayer during the first part of the night, then gets up [after some sleep] to perform the prayers called *tahajjud*, must he annul his *witr*, or may he perform whatever additional prayers he wishes, without annulling the *witr?* On this question, there are two conflicting versions of the doctrine attributed to Imām Aḥmad ibn Ḥanbal (may Allāh bestow His mercy upon him).

According to one account, he is not required to invalidate the *witr*. In the version related by al-Faḍl ibn Ziyād, he [Imām Aḥmad] said: "While performance of the *witr* during the last part of the night is more meritorious, it may happen that a man is afraid of sleeping [through that period], in which case he ought to perform the *witr* during the first part of the night. Then, if he does get up during the last part of the night, he should perform the ritual prayer in sets of two cycles *[rak'atain rak'atain]*, but he should not perform the *witr* again." According to the other account, however, he must actually render it invalid.

"I once asked Aḥmad [ibn Ḥanbal]," said al-Faḍl ibn Ziyād: 'Do you see him as having to invalidate the *witr?*' 'No,' he replied, 'and even if he must render it invalid, that is hardly a serious problem. 'Umar, 'Alī, Usāma, Ibn 'Umar, Ibn 'Abbās and Abū Huraira (may Allāh be well pleased with them)—all of them did that!'"

Here is a step-by-step description of what is involved in the invalidation

[52] The term *tahajjud* is sometimes synonymous with *ṣalāt al-lail* [the prayer of night vigil]. In some contexts, however, it refers to the voluntary prayers performed after the compulsory prayer of late evening *[ṣalāt al-'ishā']*. The corresponding verb, in the imperative form *tahajjad*, occurs in Q. 17:78 and 17:79.

[naqḍ] and annulment *[faskh]* of the *witr* prayer [as a separate, odd-numbered entity]:

• The person concerned performs the *witr* in the first part of the night, as a ritual prayer consisting of one single cycle.

• He goes to sleep.

• He gets up in the course of the night, in order to perform more ritual prayers.

• He performs one single cycle of ritual prayer *[rakʿa wāḥida]*, with the specific intention that it should invalidate [the separate, odd-numbered status of] his previous *witr*, and convert it into the first of two elements forming a pair.

• He pronounces the concluding salutation [to mark the completion of this latest cycle of prayer], so now all his prayers up to this point have become even-numbered.

• He may then go on to perform further prayers, as many as he wishes, so long as they are in sets of two cycles *[mathnā mathnā]*.

• Finally, he may perform the *witr* before the rising of the dawn *[ṭulūʿ al-fajr]*, by completing one single, unpaired cycle of ritual prayer *[rakʿa wāḥida]*.

That is all quite clear, in light of the practice of ʿUthmān ibn ʿAffān (may Allāh be well pleased with him), which we have described above [in the preceding subsection.]

It is not permissible to leave the first *witr* in its original condition, and then perform the *witr* a second time, because the Prophet (Allāh bless him and give him peace) once said:

> There must not be two performances of the *witr* in a single night.

As for the case where someone does not render his *witr* invalid, but simply goes on to perform whatever [even-numbered] prayers he wishes, we have already explained the permissibility thereof.

Concerning the supplication *[duʿāʾ]* to be offered at a certain point in the *witr* prayer.

In the final cycle *[rakʿa]* of the *witr* prayer, at the point where he raises his head from the bowing posture *[rukūʿ]*, the worshipper should offer the following supplication *[duʿāʾ]*:

O Allāh, we appeal to You for help,	*Allāhumma innā nastaʿīnu-ka*
and guidance, and forgiveness.	*wa nastahdī-ka wa nastaghfiru-ka*
We believe in You,	*wa nuʾminu bi-ka*
and in You we place all our trust.	*wa natawakkalu ʿalai-ka*
We extol You	*wa nuthnī*
for all that is good.	*ʿalai-ka 'l-khaira kulla-hu*
We give thanks to You,	*nashkuru-ka*
and we are not ungrateful to You.	*wa lā nakfiru-ka*
We dismiss and abandon those	*wa nakhlaʿu wa natruku*
who sinfully disobey You.	*man yafjuru-ka*
O Allāh, You Alone do we worship.	*Allāhumma iyyā-ka naʿbudu*
To You we pray	*wa la-ka nuṣallī*
and make prostration,	*wa nasjudu*
and we are quick to serve	*wa ilai-ka nasʿā*
and obey You.	*wa naḥfidu*
We hope for Your mercy	*narjū raḥmata-ka*
and we dread Your chastisement.	*wa nakhshā ʿadhāba-ka*
Surely Your extreme chastisement	*inna ʿadhāba-ka 'l-jidda*
will be applied to the unbelievers.	*bi'l-kuffāri mulḥaq.*
O Allāh, guide me among those	*Allāhumma 'hdi-nī*
whom You have guided aright.	*fī-man hadaita*
Pardon me among those	*wa ʿāfi-nī*
to whom You have granted pardon.	*fī-man ʿafaita*
Take care of me among those	*wa tawalla-nī*
of whom You have taken care.	*fī-man tawallaita*
Bless me among those	*wa bārik lī*
to whom You have	*fī-man*
granted Your blessing,	*aʿṭaita*
and guard me against the evil	*wa qi-nī sharra*
of that which You have decreed.	*mā qaḍaita*
Surely You make judgment,	*inna-ka taqḍī*

and judgment is not	*wa lā yuqḍā*
made against You.	*ʿalai-k.*
Those whom You treat as friends	*inna-hu lā yadhillu*
are surely not to be despised,	*man wālaita*
and those whom You	*wa lā*
treat as enemies	*yaʿizzu*
are not worthy of respect.	*man ʿādaita*
Blessed are You, Our Lord,	*tabārakata Rabba-nā*
and Exalted are You!	*wa taʿālait.*
O Allāh, I take refuge	*Allāhumma innī aʿūdhu*
with Your good pleasure	*bi-riḍā-ka*
from Your disapproval,	*min sukhṭi-ka*
and with Your pardon	*wa bi-ʿafwi-ka*
from Your punishment,	*min ʿuqūbati-ka*
and I take refuge with You	*wa aʿūdhu bi-ka*
from You!	*min-ka*
I can never extol You enough, for	*lā aḥṣī thanāʾan ʿalai-ka*
You are as You have	*Anta ka-mā athnaita*
extolled Yourself.	*ʿalā Nafsi-k.*

If the supplicant chooses to add more to this, it is permissible for him to do so. He should then pass his hand over his face, according to one of two accounts [of the Ḥanbalī doctrine]. According to the other, he should pass it over his breast.

If he is acting as prayer leader *[imām]* in the month of Ramaḍān, he must use the first-person plural in every appropriate instance, saying: "Guide *us* and grant *us* well-being *[ihdi-***nā** *wa ʿāfi-***nā***]*," and so on through to the end of the supplication.

Concerning the best course to be followed by someone who is overcome by drowsiness *[nu'ās]*, while devoting the night to ritual prayer *[yuṣalli 'l-lail]*.

If a worshipper is one of those who devote the night to ritual prayer *[yuṣalli 'l-lail]*, but he is overcome by drowsiness *[nu'ās]*, the best course for him is to get some sleep. This advice is based on the traditional report, recorded in the two *Ṣaḥīḥ*'s,[53] according to which 'Ā'isha (may Allāh be well pleased with her) said that Allāh's Messenger (Allāh bless him and give him peace) once said:

> If one of you is overcome by drowsiness, while performing the ritual prayer *[ṣalāt]*, let him lie down to rest until sleep departs from him, for, if he prays while he is feeling drowsy, perhaps he will go away to seek forgiveness, since he may attribute the blame to himself.

As reported on the authority of 'Abd al-'Azīz ibn Ṣuhaib, it was Anas ibn Mālik (may Allāh be well pleased with him) who said:

"Allāh's Messenger (Allāh bless him and give him peace) once entered the mosque *[masjid]*, where he noticed that a rope had been strung between the two columns. 'What is this?' he exclaimed, so they told him: 'It was put there for Zainab to use, while she is performing the ritual prayer. Whenever she feels sluggish or listless, she grasps it with her hand.' He said: 'Unfasten it!' Then he went on to say (Allāh bless him and give him peace):

> "'Let each one of you perform the prayer while he has the energy *[nashāṭ]* for it, then, if he feels too sluggish or listless, let him sit down and take a rest.'"

According to a report from 'Urwa, 'Ā'isha (may Allāh be well pleased with her) once had with her a woman from the tribe of Banī Asad. When the Prophet (Allāh bless him and give him peace) came in, he asked: "Who is this?" She said: "This is so-and-so, who never

[53] See n. 14 on p. 12 above.

sleeps in the night." It was then that the Prophet (Allāh bless him and give him peace) said:

> All of you must do as much work as you are capable of doing, for, by Allāh, Allāh (Almighty and Glorious is He) has never had enough until you have had enough!

ʿĀʾisha (may Allāh be well pleased with her) once said: "The work that is dearest to Allāh (Exalted is He) is that which is pursued with diligence and perseverance by its practitioner, even if it does not amount to very much. Whenever Allāh's Messenger (Allāh bless him and give him peace) instructed them to do as much work and they were capable of doing, they [his Companions] used to say: 'O Messenger of Allāh, we are not in the same situation as you. Allāh (Almighty and Glorious is He) has forgiven you your earlier and your later sins.' This would make him feel so angry that it showed on his face."

It can thus be stated that, in the case of a worshipper who is overwhelmed by sleep, to the point where it distracts him from the ritual prayer *[ṣalāt]* and the remembrance of Allāh *[dhikr]*, the Sunna[54] requires him to sleep until he is relieved of the burden of slumber, so that he feels completely ready for worshipful service *[ʿibāda]*, and can fully understand what he is saying.

Ibn ʿAbbās (may Allāh be well pleased with him and with his father) is said to have disapproved of sleep in a sitting position.

In the words of one traditional report *[khabar]*, we are told: "Do not challenge the night [by trying to go through it without any sleep at all]."

Among the righteous *[ṣāliḥīn]* there were some who deliberately trained themselves to sleep [at an early time], in order to be fortified thereby in the middle of the night. There were others who disapproved of any deliberate attempt to sleep, and who did not sleep at all until slumber overwhelmed them with irresistible force.

It is said that Wahb ibn Munabbih al-Yamānī (may Allāh bestow His mercy upon him) did not once lay his side on the ground, in all of thirty years. He kept a cushion *[miswara]* made of leather, on which he would place his breast, when sleep overwhelmed him. Then, after dozing off for a few minutes *[khafaqa khafaqāt]*, he would wake up with a start and resume his vigil. He would often say: "I would much prefer to see a devil *[shaiṭān]* in my house, rather than to see a pillow *[wisāda]* in it." (By this he meant: "because the pillow would represent an invitation to sleep.")

[54] The Sunna is the customary practice established by the Prophet (Allāh bless him and give him peace). See also n. 57 on p. 52 below.

When one of the righteous was asked to give a description of the *Abdāl* [Spiritual Deputies],[55] he said: "Their eating is of sheer necessity, their sleep is induced by overwhelming force, their speech is in response to urgent need, their silence is a mark of wisdom *[ḥikma]*, and their knowledge is a form of power *[qudra]*."

When another of the righteous was asked to give a description of those who fear the Lord *[al-khā'ifīn]*, he said: "Their diet is the diet of the sick, and their sleep is the sleep of the drowned."

One's attention should not be primarily focused, however, on the spiritual states and actions of the righteous *[ṣāliḥīn]*, but rather on that which has been reported concerning Allāh's Messenger (Allāh bless him and give him peace). That is where reliance should be placed, until the servant [of the Lord] moves into a spiritual condition by which he is distinctly singled out from others.

According to Umm Salama (may Allāh be well pleased with her), 'Ā'isha (may Allāh be well pleased with her) once said: "Allāh's Messenger (Allāh bless him and give him peace) was asked: 'Which kind of work is the most meritorious?' He replied:

> "'[The most meritorious kind of work is] that which is most diligently and persistently performed, even if it does not amount to very much.'"

As reported on the authority of 'Alqama, 'Ā'isha (may Allāh be well pleased with her) once said: "For Allāh's Messenger (Allāh bless him and give him peace), the ritual prayer *[ṣalāt]* was a constant practice. That is why Allāh's Messenger (Allāh bless him and give him peace) used to keep vigil during various segments of the night. On one night, it would be for half of the night; on one night, for a third of it; on one night, for half of the night, plus half of one sixth of it. He would sometimes keep vigil for one quarter of the night, and no more than that. He would sometimes keep vigil for one sixth of the night, and that would be enough. All of this is mentioned in the Sūra of the Enshrouded One *[Sūrat al-Muzzammil]*."[56]

The Prophet (Allāh bless him and give him peace) is reported as having said:

> Devote some part of the night to ritual prayer, even if only as long as it takes to milk a sheep *[ṣalli mina 'l-laili wa law qadra ḥalbi shāt]*.

[55] See n. 18 on p. 33 above.

[56] The Sūra of the Enshrouded One *[Sūrat al-Muzzammil]* is the 73rd Sūra of the Qur'ān.

That could be the time it takes to perform four cycles of prayer *[rakaʿāt]*, or it may only be enough for two cycles *[rakʿatain]*.

He also said (Allāh bless him and give him peace):

> Two cycles of ritual prayer *[rakʿatān]*, performed by the servant [of the Lord] in the middle of the night, are better than this world and all that it contains. But for the hardship it would have caused my Community *[Ummatī]*, I would have made them obligatory.

All of this was intended to make it easy for his Community *[Umma]* to keep night vigil *[qiyām al-lail]* and to practice worshipful service *[ʿibāda]*. He did not wish it to be burdensome for them, and for worshipful service to be unpleasant for them, so that they would become weary and bored. Far from it! He simply steered them (Allāh bless him and give him peace) toward the keeping of night vigil *[qiyām al-lail]*, by mentioning its excellent merit and its spiritual reward, so that they would not confine themselves exclusively to the obligatory religious duties *[farāʾiḍ]* and established customary practices *[sunan]*.[57]

For the keeping of vigil, one third is the fraction of the night that is most strongly recommended, while the least recommended is one sixth. This is because the Prophet (Allāh bless him and give him peace) never once kept vigil throughout the whole of a night until morning. He would always take some sleep in the course of it. Nor did he ever sleep throughout the whole of a night until morning. He would always keep vigil during some part of it, as we have explained.

It has been said that the ritual prayer *[ṣalāt]* of the first part of the night is for those who observe *tahajjud*;[58] the vigil *[qiyām]* kept in the middle part of it is for the humbly devout *[qānitīn]*; the vigil kept in the last part of it is for worshippers devoted to the ritual prayer *[muṣallīn]*; and the vigil kept at the break of dawn *[qiyām al-fajr]* is for the heedless.

Yūsuf ibn Mihrān (may Allāh bestow His mercy upon him) is reported as having said: "Beneath the Heavenly Throne *[ʿArsh]*, as I have been informed, there is an angel in the shape of a rooster *[dīk]*. Its talons are of pearl and its spurs of green topaz. When the first third of

[57] The term *sunna* (of which *sunan* is the plural form) may be applied to a particular practice recommended by Allāh's Messenger (Allāh bless him and give him peace), as well as to his exemplary conduct in general. Although there are no capital letters in the Arabic script, it is convenient to mark the distinction, in transliteration, between the specific *sunna/sunan* and the general *Sunna*.

[58] See n. 52 on p. 45 above.

the night has elapsed, its flaps its wings, crows and says: 'Let those who pray *[muṣallūn]* arise!' When half of the night has gone by, it again flaps its wings, crows and says: 'Let those who observe *tahajjud* arise!' Then, when two thirds of the night have passed, it once more flaps its wings, crows and says: 'Let the humbly devout *[qānitūn]* arise!' Finally, when the dawn breaks, it flaps its wings, crows and says: 'Let the heedless now arise, bearing the weight of their sins!'"

It was one of the truly wise *[ʿārifīn]* who said: "During the watches of the night *[asḥār]*, Allāh (Exalted is He) looks into the hearts of those who are vigilantly wakeful, and He fills their hearts with radiant lights. The benefits accrue to their hearts, so they become enlightened. Then the beneficial effects spread from their hearts to the hearts of the negligent and heedless."

It has been related that Allāh (Exalted is He) conveyed *[awḥā]* these words to one of the champions of the truth *[ṣiddīqīn]*, by way of inspiration: "Among My servants, I have some servants who love Me, and whom I love. They yearn for Me, and I yearn for them. They remember Me, and I remember them. They look toward Me, and I look toward them. So, if you follow their example, I shall love you too, but if you turn away from them, I shall despise you."

"O my Lord," he said, "what is their distinctive feature?" His Lord replied: "They tend the shadows by day, just as the caring shepherd tends his flocks. They yearn for the setting of the sun, just as the birds yearn for their nests around the time of sunset. Then, when the night lowers its veil upon them, and the darkness becomes pervasive, and the mattresses are spread, and the couches are prepared, and every friend forsakes his friend, they direct their footsteps toward Me, and stretch their faces toward Me. They whisper to Me in My way of speaking, and they coax Me with My kind of grace.

"Between one who is crying and one who is weeping, between one who is moaning and one who is complaining, between one who is standing and one who is sitting, between one who is bowing *[rākiʿ]* and one who is making prostration *[sājid]*, within My sight is whatever they are suffering for My sake, and within My hearing is whatever they are complaining about because of My love.

"First of all, I shall give them beams of My light, projected into their hearts, so they will get to know about Me, as I know all about them. As for My second gift, even if the seven heavens and all that they contain were [weighted against them] in their balances, I would reduce the weight thereof to the point of insignificance. As for My third gift, I shall turn My noble countenance toward them. Then, as you will see, when I turn My noble countenance toward someone, that person will recognize one of the gifts I intend to give him."

Concerning the observance of vigil *[qiyām]* throughout the whole of the night.

As for the keeping of vigil *[qiyām]* throughout the whole of the night, that is the practice of the strong, of those who have already been assured of providential care *[ʿināya]* from Him, those for whom custodial protection *[riʿāya]* has been permanently established, those whose hearts have been enveloped by enabling guidance *[tawfīq]*, by the light of Divine Majesty *[Jalāl]* and, then again, of Divine Beauty *[Jamāl]*.

According to traditional reports, ʿUthmān ibn ʿAffān (may Allāh be well pleased with him) used to enliven the night by performing a single cycle *[rakʿa]* of ritual prayer, in which he would recite the whole of the Qurʾān, from beginning to end. (We have mentioned this in a previous subsection.[59])

Tradition also tells of forty men, from among the Successors *[Tābiʿūn]*, who used to keep vigil throughout the entire night, performing the dawn prayer *[ṣalāt al-ghadāh]* with the ritual ablution of the last evening prayer *[wuḍūʾ al-ʿishāʾ al-ākhira]*. They made this their practice for forty years. The traditional reports concerning them are of verified authenticity, and have been widely disseminated. Here are the names of some of them:

Saʿīd ibn Jubair, Ṣafwān ibn Salīm, Abū Ḥāzim and Muḥammad ibn al-Munkadir (of the people of Medina); Fuḍail ibn ʿIyāḍ and Wahb ibn al-Ward (of the people of Mecca); Ṭāwūs and Wahb ibn Munabbih (of the people of Yemen); ar-Rabīʿ ibn Khaitham and al-Ḥakam (of the people of Kūfa); Abū Sulaimān ad-Dārānī and ʿAlī ibn Bakkār (of the people of Damascus); Abū ʿAbdu'llāh al-Khawwāṣ and Abū ʿĀṣim (of the people of ʿAbadān); Ḥabīb Abū Aḥmad and Abū Jāʾiz al-Salmānī (of the people of Persia); Mālik ibn Dīnār, Sulaimān at-Taimī, Zaid ar-Ruqāshī, Ḥabīb ibn Abī Thābit, and Yaḥyā al-Bakkāʾ (of the people of Baṣra).

It would take too long to list all the others. May Allāh bestow His mercy and His good pleasure upon them all.

[59] See p. 43 above.

On how a person should extricate himself from a state of utter negligence, in which mistakes and sins prevent him from keeping night vigil *[qiyām al-lail]*.

Let us now consider the predicament of someone whose heedless neglect has reached the utmost extreme, whose serious mistakes have hemmed him in from all sides, and whose errors and sins have bound him in chains, thereby preventing him from keeping night vigil *[qiyām al-lail]*. We are speaking of someone who, despite this condition, would dearly love to keep his vigil, and to enter the company of the humbly obedient *[qānitīn]*, of those who seek forgiveness in the watches of the night *[asḥār]*.[60] In order to extricate himself from his terrible predicament, this is what he must do:

He must beg forgiveness of Allāh (Exalted is He), three times, whenever he is ready for sleep, and whenever he lies down to rest. Then he must recite:

In the Name of Allāh, the All-Merciful, the All-Compassionate.	*Bismi'llāhi 'r- Raḥmāni 'r- Raḥīm.*

Then he must recite ten verses *[āyāt]* from the beginning of the Sūra of the Cave *[Sūrat al-Kahf]*, and ten from the last part of the same. He must also recite [the last part of the Sūra of the Cow *(Sūrat al-Baqara)*, beginning with the words]:

The Messenger believes in that which has been sent down to him from his Lord, and so do the believers. (2:285)	*āmana 'r-Rasūlu bi-mā unzila ilai-hi min Rabbi-hi wa 'l-mu'minūn.*

—and [the Sūra that begins with]:

Say: "O unbelievers.... (109:1)	*qul yā ayyuha 'l-kāfirūn....*

[60] This is a clear allusion to several verses *[āyāt]* of the Qur'ān, notably 3:17.

—for then Allāh (Exalted is He) will awaken him and prepare him for the night vigil *[qiyām al-lail]*, through His all-encompassing grace, His all-embracing forgiveness, and His all-inclusive care for the true believers *[mu'minīn]* among His servants.

He must also say:

O Allāh, awaken me in the hours	*Allāhumma aiqiẓ-nī*
that are dearest to You,	*fī aḥabbi 's-sā'āti ilai-ka*
and employ me in the deeds	*wa 'sta'mil-nī*
that are dearest to You,	*bi-aḥabbi 'l-a'māli ladai-k:*
that will draw me	*allatī tuqarribu-nī*
most closely to You,	*ilai-ka zulfā*
and keep me far removed	*wa yub'idu-nī*
from Your displeasure.	*min sukhṭi-ka bu'dā.*
I am begging You,	*as'alu-ka*
so You will grant what I ask.	*fa-tu'ṭiya-nī*
I am seeking Your forgiveness,	*astaghfiru-ka*
so You will forgive me.	*fa-taghfira lī*
I am beseeching You,	*ad'ū-ka*
so You will answer my plea.	*fatastajība lī.*
O Allāh, let me not feel safe	*Allāhumma lā*
from Your cunning,	*tu'min-nī makra-ka*
and do not entrust me	*wa lā tuwalli-nī*
to anyone but You.	*ghaira-ka*
Do not deprive me	*wa lā tarfa'*
of Your protection,	*'an-nī sitra-ka*
let me not forget	*wa lā tunsi-nī*
Your remembrance,	*dhikra-ka*
and do not include me	*wa lā taj'al-nī*
among the heedless.	*mina 'l-ghāfilīn.*

—for it is said that, if someone pronounces these words, when he is about to go to sleep, Allāh (Almighty and Glorious is He) will send down to him three angels, who will arouse him for the ritual prayer *[ṣalāt]*. Then, if he performs the prayer and offers a supplication *[ṣallā wa da'ā]*, they will say "*Āmīn*" to his supplication *[du'ā']*. Even if he does not get up to pray, the angels will worship in the air, and the spiritual reward of their act of worship *['ibāda]* will be recorded in his favor.

He should also repeat the words mentioned in the following quotation, since the Prophet (Allāh bless him and give him peace) is reported as having said:

> If someone positively enjoys waking up in the course of the night, let him say, at the moment when he lies down to rest:

O Allāh,	*Allāhumma 'b'ath-nī*
arouse me from my couch,	*min maḍja'i-nī*
to remember You,	*li-dhikri-ka wa shukri-ka*
to thank You,	*wa ṣalāti-ka*
to perform Your prayer,	*wa 'stighfāri-ka*
to seek Your forgiveness,	*wa tilāwati Kitābi-ka*
to recite Your Book,	*wa ḥusni*
and to serve You well.	*'ibādati-k.*

Then let him proclaim the Glory of Allāh *[li-yusabbiḥ]*,[61] thirty-three times. Let him give praise to Allāh *[li-yuḥammid]*,[62] thirty-three times. Let him also proclaim the Supreme Greatness of Allāh *[li-yukabbir]*,[63] thirty-three times.

If he prefers, he may say, twenty-five times:

Glory be to Allāh,	*subḥāna 'llāhi*
and praise be to Allāh,	*wa 'l-ḥamdu li'llāhi*
and there is no god but Allāh,	*wa lā ilāha illa 'llahu*
and Allāh is Supremely Great!	*wa 'llāhu Akbar.*

—since that will be simpler for him, and it will add up to a total of one hundred component parts, counting from the beginning.

'Ā'isha (may Allāh be well pleased with her) is reported as having said: "Whenever Allāh's Messenger (Allāh bless him and give him peace) was on the point of going to sleep, resting his cheek on his right hand, and recognizing that he might die in the course of that very night, these are the last words he would say:

O Allāh,	*Allāhumma*
Lord of the seven heavens	*Rabba 's-samāwāti 's-sab'i*
and Lord of the Mighty Throne,	*wa Rabba 'l-'Arshi 'l-'Aẓīm:*
Our Lord	*Rabba-nā*
and the Lord of every thing,	*wa Rabba kulli shai':*
Revealer of the Torah, the Gospel	*Munazzila 't-Tawrāti*
and the Criterion,	*wa 'l-Injīli wa 'l-Furqān:*
Splitter of the grain	*Fāliqa 'l-ḥabbi*
and the date-stone,[64]	*wa 'n-nawā*
I take refuge with You from the evil	*a'ūdhu bi-ka min sharri*
of everything capable of evil,	*kulli dhī sharr:*
and from the evil	*wa min sharri*
of every crawling creature	*kulli dābbatin*
that You are grasping	*Anta ākhidhun*
by its forelock.[65]	*bi-nāṣiyati-hā.*

[61] See n. 11 on p. 9 above.

[62] See n. 42 on p. 33 above.

[63] The Arabic verb *kabbara*, of which *takbīr* is the corresponding verbal noun, means "to proclaim the Supreme Greatness of Allāh, by saying: 'Allāh is Supremely Great *[Allāhu Akbar]*.'"

[64] This is an allusion to Q. 6:96.

[65] This is an allusion to Q. 11:56.

O Allāh, You are the First,
for there is nothing before You,
and You are the Last,
for there is nothing after You,
and You are the Outer,
for there is nothing above You,
and You are the Inner,
for there is nothing below You.
Settle the debt for me,
and relieve me of poverty.

Allāhumma Anta 'l-Awwalu
fa-laisa qabla-ka shaiʾ:
wa Anta 'l-Ākhiru
fa-laisa baʿda-ka shaiʾ:
wa Anta 'ẓ-Ẓāhiru
fa-laisa fawqa-ka shaiʾ:
wa Anta 'l-Bāṭinu
fa-laisa dūna-ka shaiʾ:
iqḍi ʿan-ni 'd-daina
wa aghnī ʿan-ni 'l-faqr.

Concerning the need to make a constant practice of *tahajjud,*[66] after one has received a blessing through the observance of night vigil *[qiyām al-lail]* and the performance of certain supererogatory devotions *[nawāfil]*.

When someone has received a blessing through the observance of night vigil *[qiyām al-lail]*, and the performance of certain supererogatory devotions *[nawāfil]*, it is incumbent upon him to make a constant practice of *tahajjud*, provided that he is capable of doing so, and that he has no valid excuse for not doing so.

This assertion is based on the fact that, according to a report from ʿĀʾisha (may Allāh be well pleased with her), Allāh's Messenger (Allāh bless him and give him peace) once said:

> If someone embarks on an act of worshipful service *[ʿibāda]* for the sake of Allāh (Glory be to Him), but then abandons it on account of boredom, Allāh (Exalted is He) will despise him.

Āʾisha (may Allāh be well pleased with her) also said: "If sleep overwhelmed him, or if he was sick, Allāh's Messenger (Allāh bless him and give him peace) would not keep vigil that night. He would perform twelve [voluntary] cycles of ritual prayer during the daytime [instead]."

As stated in the traditional report *[khabar]*: "Of all good works, that which is dearest to Allāh (Exalted is He) is that which is most diligently and persistently performed, even if it does not amount to very much."

[66] See n. 52 on p. 45 above.

Concerning the recommended utterances to be made by someone who devotes part of the night to the practice of *tahajjud*.[67]

When someone intends to devote part of the night to keeping vigil, in order to perform the prayers called *tahajjud*, it is considered commendable for him to say:

Praise be to Allāh, who restored me to life after causing me to die; and unto Him is the Resurrection.	*al-ḥamdu li'llāhi 'lladhī* *aḥyā-nī* *ba'da an amāta-nī* *wa ilai-hi 'n-nushūr.*

He should also recite the ten Qur'ānic verses *[āyāt]* from the last part of the Sūra entitled *Āl 'Imrān* [The Family of 'Imrān]:

[There are signs for] those who remember Allāh, standing and sitting and on their sides, and who reflect upon the creation of the heavens and the earth: "Our Lord, You have not created this in vain. Glory be to You! So guard us against the torment of the Fire."	*alladhīna* *yadhkurūna 'llāha qiyāman* *wa qu'ūdan* *wa 'alā junūbi-him* *wa yatafakkarūna* *fī khalqi 's-samāwāti wa 'l-arḍ:* *Rabba-nā mā khalaqta* *hādhā bāṭilā: subḥāna-ka* *fa-qi-nā* *'adhāba 'n-nār.*
Our Lord, whomever You cause to enter the Fire, him You will have abased, and for the evildoers there will be no helpers.	*Rabba-nā inna-ka* *man tudkhili 'n-nāra* *fa-qad akhzaita-h:* *wa mā li'z-zālimīna* *min anṣār.*
Our Lord, we have heard a crier calling us to faith, saying: "Believe in your Lord!" So we have believed. Our Lord, forgive us our sins and acquit us	*Rabba-nā* *inna-nā sami'nā munādiyan* *yunādī li'l-īmāni an* *āminū bi-Rabbi-kum* *fa-āmannā Rabba-nā* *fa-'ghfir la-nā* *dhunūba-nā wa kaffir*

[67] See n. 52 on p. 45 above.

of our evil deeds, and	*ʿan-nā sayyiʾāti-nā*
let us die in the company	*wa tawaffa-nā*
of the righteous.	*maʿa 'l-abrār.*
Our Lord, give us that	*Rabba-nā wa āti-nā*
which You have promised us	*mā waʿadta-nā*
through Your Messengers,	*ʿalā Rusuli-ka*
and do not put us to shame	*wa lā tukhzi-nā*
on the Day of Resurrection.	*yawma 'l-qiyāma:*
Surely You will not fail	*inna-ka lā*
to keep the tryst!	*tukhlifu 'l-mīʿād.*
And their Lord has answered them:	*fa-'stajāba la-hum Rabbu-hum*
"I do not waste	*annī lā uḍīʿu*
the labor of any laborer among you,	*ʿamala ʿāmilin*
whether make or female;	*min-kum min dhakarin aw unthā:*
the one of you is from the other.	*baʿḍu-kum min baʿḍ:*
So those who emigrated,	*fa-'lladhīna hājarū*
and were driven	*wa ukhrijū*
from their homes,	*min diyāri-him*
and suffered for My cause,	*wa ūdhū fī sabīlī*
and fought and were slain,	*wa qātalū wa qutilū*
I shall surely acquit	*la-ukaffiranna*
them of their evil deeds,	*ʿan-hum sayyiʾāti-him*
and I shall admit	*wa la-udkhilanna-hum*
them to Gardens	*jannātin*
underneath which rivers flow—	*tajrī min*
a reward from Allāh,	*taḥti-ha 'l-anhār: thawāban*
and with Allāh	*min ʿindi 'llāh: wa 'llāhu*
is the fairest reward."	*ʿinda-hu ḥusnu 'th-thawāb.*
Let it not delude you,	*lā yaghurranna-ka*
that those who disbelieve	*taqallubu 'lladhīna*
enjoy freedom of action in the land.	*kafarū fi 'l-bilād.*
A little enjoyment,	*matāʿun qalīl:*
but then their habitation	*thumma maʾwā-hum*
will be Hell, an evil cradle!	*jahannam: wa biʾsa 'l-mihād.*
But those who keep	*lākini 'lladhīna 'ttaqaw*
their duty to their Lord,	*Rabba-hum la-hum*
for them there will be Gardens	*jannātun*
underneath which rivers flow,	*tajrī min taḥti-ha 'l-anhāru*
dwelling therein forever,	*khālidīna fī-hā nuzulan*
a welcome from their Lord.	*min ʿindi 'llāh:*
That which Allāh has in store	*wa mā ʿinda 'llāhi*
is better for the righteous.	*khairun li'l-abrār.*
And of the People of the Book	*wa inna min Ahli 'l-Kitābi*
there are some who believe	*la-man yuʾminu*

in Allāh and what has been sent	*bi'llāhi wa mā unzila*
down to you,	*ilai-kum*
and what has been sent down	*wa mā unzila*
to them, humble toward Allāh,	*ilai-him khāshiʿīna li'llāhi*
not selling Allāh's signs	*lā yashtarūna bi-āyāti 'llāhi*
for a small price.	*thamanan qalīlā: ulāʾika*
Their reward is with their Lord.	*la-hum ajru-hum ʿinda Rabbi-him*
Allāh is Swift at reckoning.	*inna 'llāha Sarīʿu 'l-ḥisāb.*

O you who believe, be patient,	*yā ayyuha 'lladhīna āmanu 'ṣbirū*
and vie in patience; be steadfast,	*wa ṣābirū wa rābiṭū:*
and observe your duty to Allāh,	*wa 'ttaqu 'llāha*
in order that you may succeed.	*laʿalla-kum tufliḥūn.*
(3:191–200)	

Next, he should proceed to clean his teeth with a toothbrush *[siwāk]*, and perform the minor ritual ablution *[wuḍūʾ]*. Then he should say:

Glory be to You,	*subḥāna-ka*
and with Your praise!	*wa bi-ḥamdi-ka*
There is no god but You.	*lā ilāha illā Anta*
I seek Your forgiveness	*astaghfiru-ka*
and I beg You to accept	*wa asʾalu-ka 't-*
my repentance,	*tawba:*
so forgive me and relent toward me,	*fa-'ghfir lī wa tub ʿalayya*
for You are the Ever-Relenting,	*inna-ka Anta 't-Tawwābu'r-*
the All-Compassionate.	*Raḥīm.*

O Allāh, let me be	*Allāhumma 'jʿal-nī*
one of those who repent.	*mina 't-tawwābīn:*
Let me be one of those	*wa 'jʿal-nī*
who purify themselves.	*mina 'l-mutaṭahhirīn:*
Let me be very patient	*wa 'jʿal-nī ṣabūran*
and very thankful,	*shakūrā:*
Let me be one of those	*wa 'jʿal-nī mim-man*
who remember You	*yadhkur-ka dhikran*
very, very often,	*kathīrā:*
and who glorify You	*wa yusabbiḥ-ka*
both early and late.	*bukratan wa aṣīlā.*

Then he should raise his head heavenward and say:

I bear witness	*ashhadu an*
that there is no god but Allāh,	*lā ilāha illa 'llāhu Waḥda-h:*
Alone, without partner.	*lā sharīka la-h:*
I also bear witness that	*wa ashhadu*
Muḥammad is His servant	*anna Muḥammadan ʿabdu-hu*
and His Messenger.	*wa Rasūlu-h.*
I take refuge with Your pardon	*aʿūdhu bi-ʿafwi-ka*
from Your torment.	*min ʿadhābi-ka*

I take refuge with Your good pleasure	*wa aʿūdhu bi-riḍā-ka*
from Your disapproval,	*min sukhṭi-ka*
and I take refuge with You	*wa aʿūdhu bi-ka*
from You!	*min-ka*
I can never extol You enough, for	*lā aḥṣī thanāʾan ʿalai-ka*
You are as You have extolled Yourself	*Anta ka-mā athnaita ʿalā Nafsi-k.*
I am Your servant,	*ana ʿabdu-ka*
and the son of Your servant.	*wa 'bnu ʿabdi-ka*
My forelock is in Your hand.[68]	*nāṣiyatī bi-yadi-k.*
Let Your judgment be in my favor!	*jāri fiyya ḥukma-k:*
Let Your verdict be fair to me!	*ʿaddil fiyya qaḍā'a-k.*
These are my hands,	*hādhihi yadāya*
with what they have earned,	*bi-mā kasabat*
and this is my soul,	*wa hādhihi nafsī*
with what it has produced.	*bi-mā akhrajat.*
There is no god but You.	*lā ilāha illā Anta*
Glory be to You.	*subḥāna-k:*
I have been one of the wrongdoers.	*innī kuntu mina 'ẓ-ẓālimīn:*
I have acted badly	*ʿamiltu sūʾan*
and wronged myself,	*wa ẓalamtu nafsī*
so forgive me my enormous sin.	*fa-'ghfir lī dhanbi 'l-ʿaẓīm:*
You are indeed my Lord.	*inna-ka Anta Rabbī*
Surely no one	*inna-hu lā*
forgives sins but You.	*yaghfiru 'dh-dhunūba illā Ant.*

Then, when he stands ready to perform the ritual prayer *[ṣalāt]*, facing toward the *Qibla*, he should say:

Allāh is Supremely Great,	*Allāhu Akbar*
immensely so!	*kabīrā:*
And praise be to Allāh,	*wa 'l-ḥamdu li'llāhi*
abundantly!	*kathīrā:*
And glory be to Allāh,	*wa subḥāna 'llāhi*
both early and late.	*bukratan wa aṣīlā:*

He should also say:

Glory be to Allāh!	*subḥāna 'llāh.*

—ten times;

Praise be to Allāh!	*al-ḥamdu li'llāh.*

—ten times;

There is no god but Allāh!	*lā ilāha illa 'llah.*

—ten times, and:

Allāh is Supremely Great!	*Allāhu Akbar.*

—ten times.

[68] See n. 65 on p. 58 above.

He should also say:

Allāh is Supremely Great! [He is]	*Allāhu Akbaru*
the Owner of the Kingdom	*Dhu 'l-Malakūti*
and the Dominion,	*wa 'l-Jabarūti*
of the Grandeur and the Might,	*wa 'l-Kibriyā'i wa 'l-'Aẓamati*
of the Majesty and the Power.	*wa 'l-Jalāli wa Qudra.*

If he wishes to utter the following words, he may do so in the knowledge that they have been transmitted *[ma'thūra]* from Allāh's Messenger (Allāh bless him and give him peace), who used to utter them in his observance of the *tahajjud*[69] prayers:

O Allāh, to You belongs the praise!	*Allāhumma la-ka 'l-ḥamd:*
You are the Light of the heavens	*Anta nūru 's-samāwāti*
and the earth,	*wa 'l-arḍi*
and to You belongs the praise!	*wa la-ka 'l-ḥamd:*
You are the Splendor of the heavens	*Anta Bahā'u 's-samāwāti*
and the earth,	*wa 'l-arḍi*
and to You belongs the praise!	*wa la-ka 'l-ḥamd:*
You are the Beauty of the heavens	*Anta Zainu 's-samāwāti*
and the earth,	*wa 'l-arḍi*
and to You belongs the praise!	*wa la-ka 'l-ḥamd:*
You are the Eternal Sustainer	*Anta Qayyūmu 's-samāwāti*
of the heavens and the earth,	*wa 'l-arḍi*
and of those therein	*wa man fī-hinna*
and those thereon.	*wa man 'alai-hinn.*
You are the Truth,	*Anta 'l-Ḥaqqu*
and from You comes	*wa min-ka 'l-*
what is real and true.	*ḥaqq:*
The Garden is real and true	*wa 'l-jannatu ḥaqqun*
and the Fire is real and true.	*wa 'n-nāru ḥaqqun*
The Prophets are real and true,	*wa 'n-Nabiyyūna ḥaqqun*
and Muḥammad (Allāh bless him	*wa Muḥammadun*
and give him peace) is real and true.	*(ṣalla 'llāhu 'alai-hi wa sallam) ḥaqq.*
O Allāh, to You I have surrendered,	*Allāhumma la-ka aslamtu*
in You I have believed,	*wa bi-ka āmantu*
and in You I have placed my trust.	*wa 'alai-ka tawakkaltu*
With Your aid I have argued	*wa bi-ka*
my case	*khāṣamtu*
[against my unbelieving foes],	
and to You I have	*wa ilai-ka*
submitted the judgment.	*ḥākamt:*
So grant me forgiveness	*fa-'ghfir*
for whatever [sins]	*lī mā qaddamtu*
I have committed,	*wa mā akhkhartu*

69 See n. 52 on p. 45 above.

in earlier and later times,	*wa mā asrartu*
in secret and in public.	*wa mā aʿlant.*
You are the Accelerator,	*Anta 'l-Muqaddimu*
and You are the Postponer.	*wa Anta 'l-Muʾakhkhir:*
There is no god but You.	*lā ilāha illā Anta.*
O Allāh,	*Allāhumma*
grant my soul its true devotion,	*āti nafsī taqwā-hā*
and cause it to grow in purity.	*wa zakki-hā*
You are the One best qualified	*Anta Khairu*
to purify it.	*man zakkā-hā*
You are its Custodian	*Anta Waliyyu-hā*
and its Master.	*wa Mawlā-hā.*
O Allāh, guide me	*Allāhumma 'hdi-nī*
toward the best of deeds,	*li-aḥsani 'l-aʿmāli*
for none guides to the best	*fa-inna-hu lā yahdī*
of them but You,	*li-aḥsani-hā illā Anta*
and avert from me	*wa 'ṣrif*
the worst of them,	*ʿan-nī sayyiʾa-hā*
for none averts the worst	*fa-inna-hu lā yaṣrifu*
of them but You.	*sayyiʾa-hā illā Ant.*
My request to You	*asʾalu-ka masʾalata 'l-*
is that of a wretched beggar,	*bāʾisi 'l-miskīni*
and my plea to You	*wa adʿū-ka duʿāʾa 'l-*
is that of a miserable pauper,	*muftaqiri 'dh-dhalīl:*
so do not treat me as a rogue,	*fa-lā tajʿal-nī*
my Lord, for supplicating You.	*bi-duʿāʾi-ka Rabbi shaqiyyan*
Be Kind to me, and Compassionate,	*wa kun bī Raʾūfan Raḥīman*
O Best of those who are asked,	*yā Khaira 'l-masʾūlīna*
and Most Generous of those who give!	*wa Akrama 'l-muʿṭīn.*

As we learn from a traditional report, conveyed to us by Shaikh Abū Naṣr Muḥammad ibn al-Bannāʾ,[70] it was Abū Salama ibn ʿAbd ar-Raḥmān who said:

"I once asked ʿĀʾisha (may Allāh be well pleased with her): 'What expressions did the Prophet (Allāh bless him and give him peace) usually utter, when proclaiming the Supreme Greatness of Allāh and commencing his ritual prayer *[ṣalāt]*, while he was keeping vigil through part of the night?' She answered by telling me: 'He used to proclaim the Supreme Greatness of Allāh and commence [his ritual prayer] by saying:

"O Allāh, Lord of Gabriel	*Allāhumma Rabba Jibrīla*
and Michael and Isrāfīl,	*wa Mīkāʾīla wa Isrāfīl:*
Creator of the heavens	*Fāṭira 's-samāwāti*
and the earth,	*wa 'l-arḍ:*

[70] ***Author's note***: Shaikh Abū Naṣr Muḥammad ibn al-Bannāʾ narrates this report on the authority of his father, citing a chain of transmission *[isnād]* from **Yaḥyā ibn Abī Kathīr—Abū Salama ibn ʿAbd ar-Raḥmān—ʿĀʾisha** (may Allāh be well pleased with her).

Knower of the unseen	*ʿĀlima 'l-ghaibi*
and the visible,	*wa 'sh-shahāda:*
You will judge	*Anta taḥkumu*
between Your servants	*baina ʿibādi-ka*
concerning that over which	*fī-mā*
they used to be at odds.[71]	*kānū yakhtalifūn:*
Guide me to that	*ihdi-nī*
over which they were at odds—	*li-ma 'khtalafū fī-hi*
to the Truth, by Your leave.	*mina 'l-ḥaqqi bi-idhni-k:*
You surely guide whomever You will	*inna-ka tahdī man tashāʾu*
to a path that is straight."""	*ilā ṣirāṭin mustaqīm.*

[71] This is an obvious allusion to Q. 22:69.

Concerning the recommended approach to the observance of nighttime prayer *[ṣalāt al-lail]*.

When the worshipper gets up to perform the nighttime prayer *[ṣalāt al-lail]*, he should follow these recommendations:

He should open his ritual prayer *[ṣalāt]* with two simple, unprotracted cycles *[rak'atain khafīfatain]*.

He should not take anything in the way of food and drink, until he has concluded whatever Allāh graciously bestows upon him in the way of performing the ritual prayer *[fi'l aṣ-ṣalāt]* and the proclamation of His glory *[tasbīḥ]*. This is because, when he wakes up from his sleep, he is undisturbed in his feelings and free from distracting concerns. As soon as he eats or drinks, however, the clear state of his heart will alter and turn murky. His best course, therefore, is to postpone the consumption of food and drink until later, unless he is very hungry indeed, to the point where hunger would make him inattentive, or if he is afraid of excessive daytime hunger in the month of Ramaḍān, and therefore dreads the break of dawn. In cases like these, the recommended course is to take one's meal at an earlier stage.

Concerning the recommended number of Qur'ānic verses *[āyāt]* to be recited before the nighttime worshipper goes to sleep.

In order to be admitted into the company of the worshipful servants *[zumrat al-'ābidīn]*, and not to be registered as one of those who are negligent and heedless *[ghāfilīn]*, the keeper of vigil must conform to the recommended practice, which means that he must not go off to sleep until he has recited three hundred Qur'ānic verses *[āyāt]*. He is therefore well advised to recite the Sūra of the Criterion *[Sūrat al-Furqān]*[72] and the Sūra of the Poets *[Sūrat ash-Shu'arā']*,[73] since the two of them together contain a total of three hundred verses *[āyāt]*.

If he does not know these two Sūras well enough, he may recite from the the Sūra of the Morning Star *[Sūrat aṭ-Ṭāriq]*[74] right through to the very end of the Qur'ān, since that whole section also includes three hundred verses *[āyāt]*.

It will be even better for him, and more complete in respect of merit, if he recites one thousand verses *[alf āya]*, that is to say, from the Sūra[75] that begins with the words of Allāh (Almighty and Glorious is He):

Blessed is He in whose Hand is the Sovereignty.	*tabāraka 'lladhī bi-yadi-hi 'l-mulk.*

—through to the very end of the Qur'ān.

If he does not know the Qur'ān well enough [to be able to adopt any of these suggestions], he may recite [the short Sūra that begins with His words (Exalted is He)]:[76]

Say: "He is Allāh, One!"	*Qul Huwa 'llāh Aḥad.*

[72] The Sūra of the Criterion *[Sūrat al-Furqān]* is the 25th Sūra of the Qur'ān.

[73] The Sūra of the Poets *[Sūrat ash-Shu'arā']* is the 26th Sūra of the Qur'ān.

[74] The Sūra of the Morning Star *[Sūrat aṭ-Ṭāriq]* is the 86th Sūra of the Qur'ān.

[75] Often referred to as the Sūra of Sovereignty *[Sūrat al-Mulk]*, this is the 67th Sūra of the Qur'ān.

[76] See note 28 on p. 27 above.

—two hundred and fifty times, for that will add up to a grand total of one thousand verses *[alf āya]*.

It is important for him not to omit the recitation, throughout the entire course of the night, of four particular Sūras, namely: (1) the Sūra that begins with the words of Allāh (Almighty and Glorious is He):

Alif, Lām, Mīm.	*Alif–Lām–Mīm.*
The revelation of the Book,	*tanzīlu 'l-Kitābi*
of which there is no doubt,	*lā raiba fī-hi*
is from the Lord of All the Worlds.	*min Rabbi 'l-'ālamīn.*

—that is to say, the Sūra of Prostration *[Sūrat as-Sajda]*,[77] (2) the Sūra entitled *Yā-Sīn*,[78] (3) the Sūra that begins with the words of Allāh (Blessed and Exalted is He):

Ḥā-Mīm.	*Ḥā-Mīm:*
By the Book that makes plain;	*wa 'l-Kitābi 'l-mubīni*
We sent it down	*innā anzalnā-hu*
on a blessed night.... (44:1-3)	*fī lailatin mubārakatin.*

—that is to say, the Sūra of Smoke *[Sūrat ad-Dukhān]*,[79] and (4) the Sūra that begins with His words (Exalted is He):

Blessed is He in whose Hand	*tabāraka 'lladhī*
is the Sovereignty.	*bi-yadi-hi 'l-mulk.*

—that is to say, the Sūra of Sovereignty *[Sūrat al-Mulk]*.[80]

He will do better still if he also recites, together with these four, the Sūra of the Enshrouded One *[Sūrat al-Muzzammil]*[81] and the Sūra of the Event *[Sūrat al-Wāqi'a]*.[82]

It is said that the Prophet (Allāh bless him and give him peace) would never go off to sleep until he had recited the Sūra of Prostration *[Sūrat as-Sajda]*[83] and the Sūra that begins with the words of Allāh (Almighty and Glorious is He):

Blessed is He in whose Hand	*tabāraka 'lladhī*
is the Sovereignty.	*bi-yadi-hi 'l-mulk.*

[77] The Sūra of Prostration *[Sūrat as-Sajda]* is the 32nd Sūra of the Qur'ān.

[78] The Sūra entitled *Yā–Sīn* is the 36th Sūra of the Qur'ān.

[79] The Sūra of Smoke *[Sūrat ad-Dukhān]* is the 44th Sūra of the Qur'ān.

[80] See n. 75 on p. 69 above.

[81] The Sūra of the Enshrouded One *[Sūrat al-Muzzammil]* is the 73rd Sūra of the Qur'ān.

[82] The Sūra of the Event *[Sūrat al-Wāqi'a]* is the 56th Sūra of the Qur'ān.

[83] See n. 77 above.

—that is to say, the Sūra of Sovereignty *[Sūrat al-Mulk]*.[84]

According to another traditional report *[khabar]*, the Prophet (Allāh bless him and give him peace) would never go off to sleep until he had recited the Sūra of the Children of Israel *[Sūra Banī Isrāʾīl]*[85] and the Sūra of the Troops *[Sūrat az-Zumar]*.[86]

According to yet another traditional report *[khabar]*, the Prophet (Allāh bless him and give him peace) would never go off to sleep until he had recited the Sūras of Glorification *[al-Musabbiḥāt]*.[87] These are said to include one particular verse *[āya]* that is more excellent than a hundred thousand verses.

It is because they share one very significant feature, that the Sūras of Glorification *[al-Musabbiḥāt]* have been given this collective title. Each of them begins with a verse *[āya]* in which the first Arabic word is *subḥāna* [glory], or *sabbaḥa* [has glorified], or *yusabbiḥu* [glorifies], or *sabbiḥ* [glorify]. As for the separate titles of the Sūras concerned, and their opening verses *[āyāt]*, they are as follows:

• The Sūra of the Children of Israel *[Sūra Banī Isrāʾīl]*, also known as the Sūra of the Night Journey *[Sūrat al-Isrāʾ]*, which begins with the words of Allāh (Almighty and Glorious is He):

Glory be to the One who carried	*subḥāna 'lladhī asrā*
His servant by night	*bi-ʿabdi-hi lailan*
from the Sacred Place of Worship	*mina 'l-Masjidi 'l-Ḥarāmi*
to the Far Distant	*ila 'l-Masjidi 'l-*
Place of Worship,	*Aqṣa 'lladhī*
the precincts	*bāraknā*
of which We have blessed,	*ḥawla-hu*
that We might show him	*li-nuriya-hu*
some of Our signs!	*min āyāti-nā:*
Surely He, only He	*inna-hu*
is the All-Hearing,	*Huwa 's-Samīʿu 'l-*
the All-Seeing. (17:1)	*Baṣīr.*

• The Sūra of Iron *[Sūrat al-Ḥadīd]*, which begins with the words of Allāh (Blessed and Exalted is He):

All that is in the heavens	*sabbaḥa li'llāhi*
and the earth has glorified Allāh,	*mā fi 's-samāwāti wa 'l-arḍ:*

[84] See n. 75 on p. 69 above.

[85] The Sūra of the Children of Israel *[Sūra Banī Isrāʾīl]* is the 17th Sūra of the Qurʾān. It is also known as the Sūra of the Night Journey *[Sūrat al-Isrāʾ]*.

[86] The Sūra of the Troops *[Sūrat az-Zumar]* is the 39th Sūra of the Qurʾān.

[87] The Sūras of Glorification *[al-Musabbiḥāt]* are the 17th, 57th, 59th, 61st, 62nd, 64th and 87th Sūras of the Qurʾān.

and He is the Omnipotent,	*wa Huwa 'l-'Azīzu 'l-*
the All-Wise. (57:1)	*Ḥakīm.*

• The Sūra of Exile *[Sūrat al-Ḥashr]*, which begins with the words of Allāh (Glorious and Exalted is He):

All that is in the heavens	*sabbaḥa li'llāhi*
has glorified Allāh,	*mā fi 's-samāwāti*
and all that is in the earth,	*wa mā fi 'l-arḍ:*
and He is the Omnipotent,	*wa Huwa 'l-'Azīzu 'l-*
the All-Wise. (59:1)	*Ḥakīm.*

• The Sūra of the Ranks *[Sūrat aṣ-Ṣaff]*, which begins with the words of Allāh (Exalted is He):

All that is in the heavens	*sabbaḥa li'llāhi*
has glorified Allāh,	*mā fi 's-samāwāti*
and all that is in the earth,	*wa mā fi 'l-arḍ:*
and He is the Omnipotent,	*wa Huwa 'l-'Azīzu 'l-*
the All-Wise. (61:1)	*Ḥakīm.*

• The Sūra of the Congregation *[Sūrat al-Jumu'a]*, which begins with His words (Almighty and Glorious is He):

All that is in the heavens	*yusabbiḥu li'llāhi*
glorifies Allāh,	*mā fi 's-samāwāti*
and all that is in the earth,	*wa mā fi 'l-arḍi 'l-*
[for He is] the King,	*Maliki 'l-*
the All-Holy, the Omnipotent,	*Quddūsi 'l-'Azīzi 'l-*
the All-Wise. (62:1)	*Ḥakīm:*

• The Sūra of Mutual Disillusion *[Sūrat at-Taghābun]*, which begins with the words of Allāh (Exalted is He):

All that is in the heavens	*sabbaḥa li'llāhi*
has glorified Allāh,	*mā fi 's-samāwāti*
and all that is in the earth.	*wa mā fi 'l-arḍ:*
To Him belongs the sovereignty	*la-hu 'l-mulku*
and to Him belongs the praise,	*wa la-hu 'l-ḥamd:*
and He is Capable of all things. (64:1)	*wa Huwa 'alā kulli shai'in Qadīr.*

• The Sūra of the Most High *[Sūrat al-A'lā]*, which begins with the words of Allāh (Glory be to Him and Exalted is He):

Glorify the Name	*sabbiḥi 'sma*
of your Lord the Most High,	*Rabbi-ka 'l-A'lā:*
who created, and then shaped,	*alladhī khalaqa fa-sawwā:*
and who determined, then guided. (87:1–3)	*wa 'lladhī qaddara fa-hadā.*

As for the verse *[āya]* that is said to be "more excellent than a hundred thousand verses," most of the scholars maintain that its specific identity is concealed from our knowledge, like the exact date of the Night of Power *[Lailat al-Qadr]*,[88] or the precise time of the Special Hour on Friday, the Day of Congregation *[Sā'at al-Jum'a]*.[89] According to 'Abd al-Ḥaqq, however, it is most probably either the final verse *[āya]* of the Sūra of Exile *[Sūrat al-Ḥashr]*, in which Allāh (Almighty and Glorious is He) has said:

He is Allāh, the Crearor,	*Huwa 'llāhu 'l-Khāliqu 'l-*
the Maker, the Shaper.	*Bāri'u 'l-Muṣawwiru*
His are the Most Beautiful Names.	*la-hu 'l-asmā'u 'l-ḥusnā.*
All that is in the heavens	*yusabbiḥu la-hu*
glorifies Him	*mā fi 's-samāwāti*
and all that is in the earth,	*wa mā fi 'l-arḍ:*
and He is the Omnipotent,	*wa Huwa 'l-'Azīzu 'l-*
the All-Wise. (59:24)	*Ḥakīm.*

—or the first verse *[āya]* of the Sūra of Iron *[Sūrat al-Ḥadīd]*, in which Allāh (Exalted is He) has said:

All that is in the heavens	*sabbaḥa li'llāhi*
and the earth has glorified Allāh,	*mā fi 's-samāwāti wa 'l-arḍ:*
and He is the Omnipotent,	*wa Huwa 'l-'Azīzu 'l-*
the All-Wise. (57:1)	*Ḥakīm.*

[88] As Shaikh 'Abd al-Qādir al-Jīlānī (may Allāh be well pleased with him) has explained, in the Sixth Discourse of the present work:

Concerning the wisdom in the decision of Allāh (Exalted is He) to make known [the date of] the Night of Absolution, while concealing [that of] the Night of Power, it has been said to lie in the fact that the Night of Power is the night of mercy and forgiveness and emancipation from the fires of Hell, which Allāh (Almighty and Glorious is He) has kept hidden so that there can be no discussion about it. He has made known the Night of Absolution, however, because it is the night of regulation and decree, the night of displeasure and approval, the night of acceptance and rejection, of attainment and obstruction, the night of bliss and woe, of grace and cleansing. (See Vol. 3, p. 67.)

[89] See p. 18 above, and especially Vol. 3, pp. 295–325.

Concerning various things from which help should be sought, in preparation for the observance of night vigil *[qiyām al-lail]*.

In order to prepare himself for the observance of night vigil *[qiyām al-lail]*, the worshipper should turn to several things for assistance, including the following:

• Keeping to a lawful diet *[akl al-ḥalāl]*.

• Charting a straight course toward repentance *[tawba]*, by using fear of the threatened penalty *[waʿīd]* as the negative pole of the compass, and hope of the promised reward *[mawʿūd]* as the positive pole thereof.

• Taking care to avoid the consumption of things that are of dubious legality *[shubuhāt]*, and steering clear of persistence in the commission of sins.

• Ridding the heart of the dominant influence of worldly concern and attachment, by remembering death, and by reflecting on the Resurrection *[Maʿād]* and what one will encounter after death.

A man once said to al-Ḥasan [al-Baṣrī] (may Allāh bestow His mercy upon him): "O Abū Saʿīd, I have rejected my own excuses. I love the idea of keeping night vigil, and I prepare my state of ritual purity [in order to be ready for it], so what can be wrong with me? Why do I not get up to observe the vigil in practice?" To this al-Ḥasan replied: "Your sins have tied you down."

It was ath-Thawrī (may Allāh bestow His mercy upon him) who said: "I was banned from keeping night vigil *[qiyām al-lail]* for five long months, and all because of a sin I had committed." When someone asked him what that sin had been, he explained: "I saw a man shedding tears, so I said to myself: 'This fellow is nothing but an ostentatious hyprocrite *[murāʾin]*!'"

Al-Ḥasan [al-Baṣrī] (may Allāh bestow His mercy upon him) used to say: "It may happen that the servant [of the Lord] commits a sin, and then finds himself banned, because of it, from both nighttime vigil *[qiyām al-lail]* and daytime fasting *[ṣiyām an-nahār]*."

As someone has wisely expressed it: "Many a meal has prevented the keeping of night vigil *[qiyām al-lail]*, just as many a glance has banned the recitation of a Qur'ānic Sūra. The servant [of the Lord] may gobble the meal, or commit some act [of impropriety], only to find himself banned, because of it, from observing the customary[90] practice *[qiyām as-sunna]*. Through the art of careful scrutiny *[tafaqqud]*, he will come to recognize the difference between excess and deficiency, and by committing fewer sins he will master the art of careful scrutiny."

Abū Sulaimān (may Allāh the Exalted bestow His mercy upon him) once said: "No one ever misses a congregational prayer *[ṣalāt jamā'a]*, except on account of a sin." He also used to say: "The nocturnal emission of sperm *[iḥtilām]* is a punishment, and the [resulting] state of major ritual impurity *[janāba]* is a state of remoteness [from the Lord]."

Other practices that are helpful, in preparation for the observance of night vigil, include reducing one's intake of food and drink to the bare minimum, and keeping the stomach as empty as possible. This advice is supported by the following traditional report, related by 'Awn ibn 'Abdi'llāh (may Allāh bestow His mercy upon him):

"Among the Children of Israel *[Banī Isrā'īl]* there were people who devoted themselves to worshipful service, so, when their time of breaking fast *[fiṭr]* was at hand, a superintendent would address them, saying: 'Do not eat too much, for, if you eat a lot, you will also sleep a lot. Then, if you sleep a lot, you will do very little praying."

The tendency to sleep a lot, it has been said, can also result from the frequent drinking of water. As a matter of fact, this is said to represent the unanimous view of seventy champions of the truth *[sab'īn ṣiddīqan]*, all of whom maintain that much sleeping results from much drinking of water.

In his preparation for keeping night vigil, the worshipper will also find it helpful to accustom his heart to anxiety, to grief and to sorrow, as well as to constant alertness, for he will thereby enliven his heart. He should also maintain a constant contemplation of the Heavenly Kingdom *[al-Malakūt]*. He should take a nap or siesta during the daytime, and avoid overtiring his physical limbs and organs in dealing with the affairs of this world.

[90] By "customary" we mean following the exemplary custom [*sunna* in Arabic] of the Prophet (Allāh bless him and give him peace).

If he so chooses, he may spend the first part of the night awake, until sleep overwhelms him. Then he may sleep, and then renew his vigil when he wakes up. Then he may sleep again, when sleep overwhelms him, and then arise to spend the last part of the night in vigil. In the course of the night, he will thus experience two awakenings *[qawmatān]* and two bouts of sleeping *[nawmatān]*. He will thereby brave the stresses and strains of the night, which is the hardest of deeds to accomplish.

Such is the spiritual state of the people of present awareness *[ḥuḍūr]*, conscious alertness *[yaqẓa]*, reflection *[fikr]* and contemplation *[tadhakkur]*. Such, it has also been said, are some of the charateristics of Allāh's Messenger (Allāh bless him and give him peace). The ordinary nighttime worshipper is likely to experience very irregular bouts of waking and sleeping. As for the ability to strike a perfectly even balance between vigil and slumber, that is peculiar to the Prophet (Allāh bless him and give him peace), because his heart is in a permanent state of alertness. The inspiration *[waḥy]* received from Allāh (Glory be to Him), telling precisely what to do and what not to do, and exactly when to wake up and when to sleep, and indicating the need for change and movement—that is peculiar to him, and quite beyond the scope of ordinary creatures.

Concerning two reasons why the keeper of night vigil is recommended to catch some sleep during the last part of the night.

The keeper of night vigil *[man qāma 'l-lail]* is recommended to catch some sleep during the last part of the night, for these two reasons:

1. Drowsiness *[nuʿās]* will thereby leave him unaffected in the early morning *[ghadāh]*. It is considered reprehensible to sleep in the early morning, which explains why they used to instruct a drowsy person *[nāʿis]* to sleep after the [prescribed] prayer of dawn *[ṣalāt aṣ-ṣubḥ]*, and to refrain from sleeping before the same. As we learn from traditional sources, Allāh's Messenger (Allāh bless him and give him peace) would usually take a nap after the [prescribed] prayer of daybreak *[ṣalāt al-fajr]*.

2. Sleep during the last part of the night is effective in ridding the face of a pallid complexion *[ṣufra]*. If a person forces himself to go without the sleep he needs, and does not even take a nap, his complexion will retain its state of pallor. That is something against which he ought to be on guard, because it is a doorway that leads into a blind alley *[bāb ghāmiḍ]*. It is conducive to hidden ambition *[shahwa khafiyya]* and concealed polytheism *[shirk khafī]*, because people will point him out as someone special. He will acquire an imaginary reputation as a model of righteousness *[ṣalāḥ]*, as one who is devoted to vigilant wakefulness and fasting, and who is motivated by the fear of Allāh (Almighty and Glorious is He)—and all on account of that pallid complexion he wears on his face. We take refuge with Allāh from attributing partners to Him *[shirk]*, and from hypocritical display *[riyāʾ]*, as well as from every signpost that points in the direction thereof!

It is also important for the keeper of vigil to drink only a minimal amount of water in the course of the night. This is because the drinking of water tends to bring on sleep, as we have explained above,[91] and

[91] See p. 75 above.

because it contributes to the pallid complexion of the face, especially in the last part of the night, but also at the time of waking up from sleep.

As we are told in the words of the traditional report *[khabar]*: "When the Prophet (Allāh bless him and give him peace) had performed the *witr* prayer at the end of the night, he used to lie down and take a nap, reclining on his right side, until Bilāl (may Allāh be well pleased with him) came to give him the call, at which point he would go out with him to perform the ritual prayer *[ṣalāt]*."

Our righteous predecessors *[as-salaf]* were very much in favor of this practice of reclining and taking a nap, after the *witr* and before the dawn prayer *[ṣalāt aṣ-ṣubḥ]*. Some of them even went so far as to make it an established customary practice *[sunna]*, notably Abū Huraira (may Allāh be well pleased with him) and those who followed his example in this respect.

When they recommended this practice so highly, they did so for very good reasons. It is of the utmost value to the people of direct vision *[mushāhada]* and present awareness *[ḥuḍūr]*, because they receive insights into the Heavenly Kingdom *[al-Malakūt]*, they are enlightened by all kinds of knowledge from the Heavenly Dominion *[al-Jabarūt]*, they grasp the mysterious subtleties of the law and the sciences *[gharā'ib al-ḥukm wa 'l-'ulūm]*, and they come to recognize what had been concealed from them, in the way of destiny's allotted shares and portions, meaning what has been prepared for them by the Lord of the realm of creation *[Rabb al-khalīqa]*, the Knower of the invisible realms *['Allām al-Ghuyūb]*. It is also of value to the dutiful workers *['ummāl]* and those engaged in the sacred struggle *[ahl al-mujāhada]*, since in their case it represents a much-needed opportunity for rest and relaxation.

This explains why Allāh's Messenger (Allāh bless him and give him peace) forbade the performance of ritual prayer *[ṣalāt]* in the interval between the rising of the dawn *[ṭulū' al-fajr]* and the rising of the sun *[ṭulū' ash-shams]*, and in the interval between the afternoon *['aṣr]* and the setting of the sun *[ghurūb ash-shams]*, thereby allowing periods of rest for those who observe the nocturnal and diurnal litanies *[ahl awrād al-lail wa 'n-nahār]*.

It is likewise recommended, for the keeper of vigil, that he should punctuate the phases of the nighttime prayer *[ṣalāt al-lail]* with a period of sitting still, in which he recites one hundred glorifications *[yusabbiḥ mi'a tasbīḥa]*. This will be helpful to him in the performance of the prayer itself, for it will allow his physical limbs and organs to take a rest. The lower self *[nafs]* may cease to regard the vigil with an attitude of weary boredom, and may even acquire a positive liking for nighttime worship *[tahajjud]* and the ritual prayer *[ṣalāt]*. Be that as it may, this recommendation is clearly in accordance with the words of Allāh (Almighty and Glorious is He):

And in the night	*wa mina 'l-laili*
proclaim His praise,	*fa-sabbiḥ-hu*
and at the setting of the stars.	*wa idbāra 'n-nujūm.*
(52:49)	

—and with His words (Exalted is He):

And in the night	*wa mina 'l-laili*
proclaim His praise,	*fa-sabbiḥ-hu*
and at the ends of the prostrations.	*wa adbāra 's-sujūd.*
(50:40)	

Concerning how to make up for having missed the night vigil [qiyām al-lail] on account of sleep or preoccupation [with worldly matters].

I f someone misses the night vigil [qiyām al-lail] on account of sleep or preoccupation [with worldly matters], and if he then makes up for it [with devotions performed] between the rising of the sun and the sun's decline from the meridian, he is just like a worshipper who has performed the prayer at its proper time in the night.

This assertion is based on a traditional report, conveyed to us by Shaikh Abū Naṣr Muḥammad ibn al-Bannā',[92] to the effect that ʿUmar ibn al-Khaṭṭāb (may Allāh be well pleased with him) once heard Allāh's Messenger (Allāh bless him and give him peace) say:

> Four cycles of ritual prayer [rakaʿāt], performed before the point of noon [qabl aẓ-ẓuhr]—which is just after the sun's decline from the meridian [baʿd az-zawāl] —will be reckoned as equal to their counterparts in the period before daybreak [as-saḥar].

Likewise reported on the authority of ʿUmar ibn al-Khaṭṭāb (may Allāh be well pleased with him) is a statement of similar import, though differently worded, in which the Prophet (Allāh bless him and give him peace) said:

> If someone fails to recite his section of the Qurʾān [ḥizb] in the course of the night, due to oversleeping or simply forgetting about it, and if he then recites it in the period between the dawn prayer [ṣalāt al-fajr] and the noon prayer [ṣalāt aẓ-ẓuhr], it will be just as if he had recited it during the night.

One of our righteous forebears [as-salaf] is reported as having said: "On this point, the members of the family of Muḥammad (Allāh bless him and give him peace) are unanimously agreed. They all maintain that, if someone performs his litany [wird]—after missing it during the

---

[92] **Author's note**: Shaikh Abū Naṣr Muḥammad ibn al-Bannā' cites the following chain of transmission [isnād] for this report: **His own father, Shaikh Abū ʿAlī ibn Aḥmad ibn ʿAbdi'llāh ibn al-Bannā'**—ʿAbdu'llāh ibn Ghanam—ʿUmar ibn al-Khaṭṭāb (may Allāh be well pleased with him)—**the Prophet** (Allāh bless him and give him peace).

night—before the sun's decline from the meridian, he is just like someone who actually performed it during the night."

If he is unable to do this, he should make up for it between the noon *[ẓuhr]* and the afternoon *[ʿaṣr]*.

Allāh (Exalted is He) has said:

And He it is who has made	*wa Huwa 'lladhī jaʿala 'l-*
the night and day a succession,	*laila wa 'n-nahāra khilfatan*
for him who desires to remember,	*li-man arāda an yadhdhakkara*
or desires thankfulness. (25:62)	*aw arāda shukūrā.*

—in other words, He has caused them to be a pair of alternating successors *[khalafain]*, which follow one after the other in priority, replacing each other by turns.

Concerning the five litanies of the nighttime *[awrād al-lail]*, and their respective times.

From all that has been mentioned and discussed above, we may reach the conclusion that the litanies of the nighttime *[awrād al-lail]* are five in number, namely:

1. The litany *[wird]* that is recited between sunset and nightfall *[baina 'l-ʿishā'ain]*.[93]
2. That which is recited after the late evening prayer *[al-ʿishā' al-ākhira]*, and before the time when the worshipper goes off to sleep.
3. That which is recited in the middle of the night *[jawf al-lail]*.
4. That which is recited in the final third of the night.
5. That which is recited in the last interval *[saḥar]* before the appearance of the second dawn *[al-fajr ath-thānī]*.[94] This is the period of time during which it is forbidden to perform the ritual prayer *[ṣalāt]*,[95] and this is why the Prophet (Allāh bless him and give him peace) once said:

> The [voluntary] nighttime ritual prayer *[ṣalāt al-lail]* is properly performed in sets of two cycles *[mathnā mathnā]*, but if you are afraid [that you may not finish before the appearance] of the dawn *[fajr]*, you must perform one separate cycle of prayer *[awtir bi-rakʿa]*, and what has preceded it will then be counted as part of your *witr* prayer.

O Allāh, [let him not resort to this] unless he happens to have missed his *witr* prayer and his litany *[wird]* through oversleeping, for he ought to perform his ritual prayer at this [the appropriate] hour, in accordance with the explanation given above, in the subsection concerning the performance of the *witr*.[96]

[93] Literally, "between the two evening times."

[94] The second dawn *[al-fajr ath-thānī]* is also known as the true dawn *[al-fajr aṣ-ṣādiq]*.

[95] See p. 109 below.

[96] See pp. 42–44 above.

Subsections *[fuṣūl]* concerning the litanies of the daytime *[awrād an-nahār]*.

Concerning the five litanies of the daytime *[awrād an-nahār]*, and their respective times.

As for the litanies of the daytime *[awrād an-nahār]*, these are also five in number, namely:

1. The litany *[wird]* recited in the period between the appearance of the second dawn *[al-fajr ath-thānī]*[97] and the rising of the sun.
2. That which is recited between the forenoon ritual prayer *[ṣalāt aḍ-ḍuḥā]* (or the corresponding time, if that prayer is not performed)[98] and the moment of the sun's decline from the meridian *[zawāl]*.
3. That which is recited in conjunction with four cycles *[rakaʿāt]* [of voluntary ritual prayer], after the sun's decline from the meridian *[zawāl]*, with a beautiful Qurʾānic recitation and a single salutation *[salām]*. It has been said that the gates of heaven are opened up to receive it.
4. That which is recited between the time of the noon prayer and the time of the afternoon prayer *[baina 'z-zuhr wa 'l-ʿaṣr]*.
5. That which is recited after the time of the afternoon prayer, and before the sunset *[baʿda 'l-ʿaṣr wa qabla 'l-ghurūb]*.

[97] The second dawn *[al-fajr ath-thānī]* is also known as the true dawn *[al-fajr aṣ-ṣādiq]*. (See p. 118 below.)

[98] The forenoon prayer *[ṣalāt aḍ-ḍuḥā]* is not one of the five obligatory daily prayers. The Prophet (Allāh bless him and give him peace) once described it as "the prayer of those who frequently repent *[ṣalāt al-awwābīn]*." According to one authority cited by E.W. Lane in his *Arabic-English Lexicon*, art. ʾ–W–B, the time for its [optional] performance is "when the young camels feel the heat of the sun from the parched ground." According to Thomas Patrick Hughes (*Dictionary of Islam*, art. ṢALĀT), the forenoon prayer *[ṣalāt aḍ-ḍuḥā]* consists of eight cycles *[rakaʿāt]*, and the time for its optional performance is around 11 a.m.

Concerning the first litany *[wird]* of the daytime.

As for the first litany *[wird]* of the daytime, the recommended procedure is as follows: The worshipper should remain in a sitting posture, from just after the dawn prayer *[ṣalāt al-fajr]* until the rising of the sun. He should devote that period to the remembrance of Allāh (Exalted is He), either by reciting the Qur'ān, or through some other suitable practice, such as glorification *[tasbīḥ]*,[99] or reflection *[tafakkur]*, or contemplation *[tadhakkur]*, or providing religious instruction *[ta'līm]*, or sitting as a student in the company of a religious scholar *['ālim]*. The same applies to the period between the end of the afternoon prayer *[ṣalāt al-'aṣr]* and the setting of the sun, because both are periods of time in which it is forbidden to perform supererogatory ritual prayers *[tanafful bi'ṣ-ṣalāt]*.

This is based on a traditional report, conveyed to us by Shaikh Abū Naṣr Muḥammad ibn al-Bannā',[100] to the effect that the Prophet (Allāh bless him and give him peace) once said:

> To sit with a group of people, from just after the dawn prayer *[ṣalāt al-fajr]* until the rising of the sun, remembering Allāh (Exalted is He), proclaiming His Supreme Greatness *[ukabbiru]*[101] and affirming His Uniqueness *[uhallilu]*[102] — that is even dearer to me than securing the emancipation of a pair of slaves. As for remembering Allāh (Almighty and Glorious is He) from just after the afternoon prayer *[ṣalāt al-'aṣr]* until the sun sets, that is even dearer to me than securing the emancipation of four slaves, from among the offspring of Ishmael *[Ismā'īl]*.

[99] See n. 11 on p. 9 above.

[100] ***Author's note***: Shaikh Abū Naṣr Muḥammad ibn al-Bannā' cites the following chain of transmission *[isnād]* for this report: **His own father, Shaikh Abū 'Alī ibn Aḥmad ibn 'Abdi'llāh ibn al-Bannā'—Abū 'Alī Ismā'īl ibn Muḥammad ibn Ismā'īl al-Khaṭṭī —Muḥammad ibn Ya'qūb—Hudaiba ibn Khālid al-Qaisī—Aḥmad ibn Salama—'Alī ibn Zaid—ash-Sha'bī—Abū Umāma** (may Allāh be well pleased with him)—**the Prophet** (Allāh bless him and give him peace).

[101] See n. 63 on p. 58 above.

[102] See n. 10 on p. 9 above.

According to another traditional report, transmitted on the authority of Anas ibn Mālik (may Allāh be well pleased with him), Allāh's Messenger (Allāh bless him and give him peace) once said:

> You must not sleep at the expense of seeking your provisions *[arzāq]*!

"O Anas," someone asked, "what did Allāh's Messenger (Allāh bless him and give him peace) mean, when he said: 'You must not sleep at the expense of seeking your provisions *[arzāq]*'?" So Anas explained: "As soon as you have performed the dawn prayer *[ṣallaitum al-fajr]*, [instead of going off to sleep] you should say, thirty-three times:

- Praise be to Allāh! — *al-ḥamdu li'llāh.*
- Glory be to Allāh! — *subḥāna 'llāh.*
- There is no god but Allāh! — *lā ilāha illa 'llāh.*
- Allāh is Supremely Great! " — *Allāhu Akbar.*

According to another traditional report *[ḥadīth]*, the worshipper should say:

- Glory be to Allāh! — *subḥāna 'llāh.*

—thirty-three times,

- Praise be to Allāh! — *al-ḥamdu li'llāh.*

—thirty-three times, and:

- Allāh is Supremely Great! — *Allāhu Akbar.*

—thirty-four times.

Then, to set the seal on his devotions, he should conclude by saying:

There is no god but Allāh,	*lā ilāha illa 'llāhu*
Alone, without partner.	*Waḥda-hu lā sharīka la-h:*
To Him belongs the sovereignty	*la-hu 'l-mulku*
and to Him belongs the praise.	*wa la-hu 'l-ḥamd:*
He brings to life and causes death,	*yuḥyī wa yumītu*
while He is Ever-Living and never dies.	*wa Huwa Ḥayyun lā yamūt:*
All goodness is in His Hand,	*bi-yadIhi 'l-khairu*
and He is Capable of all things.	*wa Huwa 'alā kulli shai'in Qadīr.*

The same procedure should be followed in the wake of the afternoon prayer *[ba'da 'l-'aṣr]*, and again when the time for sleep is at hand.

Shaikh Abū Naṣr has also informed us[103] that az-Zubair (may Allāh be

[103] ***Author's note:*** Shaikh Abū Naṣr Muḥammad ibn al-Bannā' narrates this report on the authority of his own father, citing a chain of transmission *[isnād]* from **'Urwa ibn az-Zubair—his father** (may Allāh be well pleased with him)—**the Prophet** (Allāh bless him and give him peace).

well pleased with him) once heard Allāh's Messenger (Allāh bless him and give him peace) say:

> An errand in the early morning or the evening *[ghadwa aw rawḥa]*, in fighting for Allāh's cause *[fī sabīli 'llāh]*, is better than this world and all that it contains.

A man then said: "O Messenger of Allāh, so what about someone who is unable to take part in a military campaign *[ghazw]*?" To this he replied:

> If a worshipper remains in a sitting posture, from the time when he performs the prayer of sunset *[yuṣalli 'l-maghrib]*, remembering Allāh (Exalted is He) until he performs the prayer of late evening *[yuṣalli 'l-ʿishā']*, that session *[majlis]* of his will count as an evening errand in the cause of Allāh *[rawḥa fī sabīli 'llāh]*. As for one who remains in a sitting posture, from the time when he performs the prayer of daybreak *[yuṣalli 'l-ghadāh]*, remembering Allāh (Exalted is He) until the sun rises, that session *[majlis]* of his will be just like an early morning errand in the cause of Allāh *[ghadwa fī sabīli 'llāh]*.

As we are reliably informed by Shaikh Abū Naṣr Muḥammad ibn al-Bannā',[104] Allāh's Messenger (Allāh bless him and give him peace) once said:

> If any servant [of the Lord] recites, in the wake of the [prescribed] ritual prayer of daybreak *[ṣalāt al-ghadāh]*:

There is no god but Allāh,	*lā ilāha illa 'llāhu*
Alone, without partner.	*Waḥda-hu lā sharīka la-h:*
To Him belongs the sovereignty	*la-hu 'l-mulku*
and to Him belongs the praise.	*wa la-hu 'l-ḥamd:*
He brings to life and causes death,	*yuḥyī wa yumītu*
while He is Ever-Living	*wa Huwa Ḥayyun*
and never dies.	*lā yamūt:*
All goodness is in His Hand,	*bi-yadIhi 'l-khairu*
and He is Capable of all things.	*wa Huwa ʿalā kulli shai'in Qadīr.*

> —ten times, Allāh will certainly reward him for those ten recitations. He will do so by recording ten good deeds in his credit column, and by erasing ten bad deeds from his debit column. He will also promote him by ten spiritual degrees. Those ten recitations will be equivalent to [the emancipation of] ten slaves, and he will not be harmed by any sin he may commit that day, unless it be some form of *shirk* [associating partners with Allāh].

> If any servant [of the Lord] performs the ritual ablution *[wuḍū']* really well, so that he washes his face as Allāh (Exalted is He) has commanded, Allāh will certainly relieve him of the burden of every sin at which his eyes have ever looked, or of which his tongue has ever spoken. If any servant [of the Lord] is careful to wash his hands, as Allāh (Almighty and Glorious is He) has commanded, Allāh will certainly relieve him of the burden of every sin that his hands have ever touched.

[104] ***Author's note:*** Shaikh Abū Naṣr Muḥammad ibn al-Bannā' narrates this report on the authority of his own father, citing a chain of transmission *[isnād]* from **Abū Umāma** (may Allāh be well pleased with him)—**the Prophet** (Allāh bless him and give him peace).

> Then, if he wipes his head and his ears, as Allāh (Exalted is He) has commanded, Allāh will certainly relieve him of the burden of every sin to which his ears have ever listened.
>
> Then, if he washes his feet as Allāh (Exalted is He) has commanded, Allāh will certainly relieve him of the burden of every sin to which his feet have walked, until he stands ready to perform the ritual prayer *[ṣalāt]*. That ritual prayer will therefore be an excellent one.
>
> If any servant [of the Lord] falls asleep in a state of ritual purity, while practicing remembrance *[dhikr]*, then offers a prayer of supplication *[daʿwa]* as soon as he recovers consciousness, his supplication is sure to receive a positive response. If any servant [of the Lord] throws a spear, in fighting for the cause of Allāh *[fī sabīli 'llāh]* (Almighty and Glorious is He), regardless of whether he hits his target or misses his mark, he will surely be rewarded for his effort, as he would for the freeing of a slave.
>
> If any servant [of the Lord] grows one gray hair, while fighting for Allāh's cause *[fī sabīli 'llāh]*, he will surely be granted compensation for it, in the form of a light on the Day of Resurrection *[Yawm al-Qiyāma]*.
>
> If any servant [of the Lord] emancipates a slave, that freed slave will surely be his ransom from the Fire of Hell *[Nār Jahannam]*, one limb for every limb.

As we are reliably informed by Shaikh Abū Naṣr Muḥammad ibn al-Bannā',[105] al-Ḥasan ibn ʿAlī (may Allāh be well pleased with him and with his father) once heard Allāh's Messenger (Allāh bless him and give him peace) say:

> If someone performs the [prescribed] ritual prayer of daybreak *[ṣalāt al-ghadāh]* in his place of worship *[masjid]*, then remains in a sitting posture, remembering Allāh (Exalted is He) until the suns rises—and if, once it has risen, he praises Allāh (Exalted is He) and stands up to perform two [voluntary] cycles of ritual prayer *[rakʿatain]* —Allāh will grant him, for each cycle, a million *[alf alf]* palatial mansions in the Garden of Paradise. Inside each palatial mansion, there will be a million heavenly brides *[ḥawrā']*,[106] and each heavenly bride will be accompanied by a million menservants. Moreover, in the sight of Allāh, that worshipper will be one of those who truly repent *[al-awwābīn]*.[107]

As reported on the authority of Nāfiʿ, it was Ibn ʿUmar (may Allāh be well pleased with him and with his father) who said: "When Allāh's Messenger (Allāh bless him and give him peace) performed the ritual

[105] ***Author's note***: Shaikh Abū Naṣr Muḥammad ibn al-Bannā' cites the following chain of transmission *[isnād]* for this report: **His own father, Shaikh Abū ʿAlī ibn Aḥmad ibn ʿAbdi'llāh ibn al-Bannā'—al-Ḥasan ibn ʿAlī** (may Allāh be well pleased with him and with his father)—**the Prophet** (Allāh bless him and give him peace).

[106] See note 9 on p. 9 above.

[107] This is an allusion to the verse *[āya]* of the Qur'ān:

Your Lord is best aware of what is in your souls. If you are righteous, He is ever Forgiving to those who truly repent. (17:25)	*Rabbu-kum aʿlamu bi-mā fī nufūsi-kum: in kuntum ṣāliḥīna fa-inna-hu kāna li-'l-awwābina Ghafūrā.*

prayer of dawn *[ṣalla 'l-fajr]*, he would not get up from his sitting position *[majlis]*, until the prayer itself enabled him to do so."

The Prophet (Allāh bless him and give him peace) once said:

> If a worshipper performs the [prescribed] ritual prayer of daybreak *[ṣalāt aṣ-ṣubḥ]*, then stays in his sitting position *[majlis]* until the prayer itself enables him [to get up], that prayer will be at the same degree as a Pilgrimage *[Ḥajj]* and a Visitation *['Umra]*, both of which have been accepted.

When Ibn 'Umar (may Allāh be well pleased with him and with his father) performed the [prescribed] ritual prayer of daybreak *[ṣalāt al-ghadāh]*, he used to remain in a sitting posture until the rising of the sun. Someone asked him: "Why do you do this?" So he explained: "I regard it as the established customary practice *[sunna]*."[108]

As we are reliably informed by Shaikh Abū Naṣr Muḥammad ibn al-Bannā',[109] Allāh's Messenger (Allāh bless him and give him peace) once said:

> If a worshipper performs the [prescribed] ritual prayer of the dawn *[ṣalāt aṣ-fajr]*, in a congregation *[jamā'a]*, then withdraws in seclusion *['akafa]* until the rising of the sun, then performs four consecutive cycles of [voluntary] ritual prayer *[raka'āt mutawāliyāt]*, reciting in the first cycle *[rak'a]*:
>
> - the Opening Sūra of the Book *[Fātiḥat al-Kitāb]*,
> - the Verse of the Throne *[Āyat al-Kursī]*[110]—three times, and
> - the Sūra that begins with:
>
> Say: "He is Allāh, One!" (112:1) *qul Huwa 'llāhu Aḥad.*
>
> —seven times; then, in the second cycle *[rak'a]*:
>
> - the Opening Sūra of the Book *[Fātiḥat al-Kitāb]*—one time only, and:
> - the Sūra that begins with:
>
> By the sun and its brightness. (91:1) *wa 'sh-shamsi wa ḍuḥā-hā*
>
> —then, in the third cycle *[rak'a]*:
>
> - the Opening Sūra of the Book *[Fātiḥat al-Kitāb]*, and:
> - the Sūra that begins with:
>
> By the heaven and the morning star. (86:1) *wa 's-samā'i wa 'ṭ-ṭāriq.*

[108] See n. 57 on p. 52 above.

[109] ***Author's note***: Shaikh Abū Naṣr Muḥammad ibn al-Bannā' cites the following chain of transmission *[isnād]* for this report: **His own father, Shaikh Abū 'Alī ibn Aḥmad ibn 'Abdi'llāh ibn al-Bannā'—'Ikrima—Ibn 'Abbās** (may Allāh be well pleased with him and with his father)—**the Prophet** (Allāh bless him and give him peace).

[110] Q. 2:225

and then, in the fourth cycle *[rak'a]*:

- the Opening Sūra of the Book *[Fātiḥat al-Kitāb]*, and
- the Verse of the Throne *[Āyat al-Kursī]*—one time only, and
- the Sūra that begins with:

Say: "He is Allāh, One!" (112:1) *qul Huwa 'llāhu Aḥad.*

—three times, Allāh (Exalted is He) will send seventy angels to him, ten angels from each of the seven heavens. They will come bearing trays peculiar to the Garden of Paradise, as well as handkerchiefs *[manādīl]* peculiar to the Garden of Paradise, and they will load that prayer *[ṣalāt]* onto those trays, then they will carry it aloft. Whenever they pass by a company of the angels, they will seek forgiveness on behalf of the owner of the prayer, and when it is placed between the hands of the All-Compelling One *[al-Jabbār]*, Allāh (Exalted is He) will say: "My servant, you have performed the ritual prayer for My sake *[lī ṣallaita]*, and Me you have worshipped *[iyyā-ya 'abadta]*, so start work anew, for I have forgiven you!"

This ritual prayer *[ṣalāt]* provides us with an explanatory interpretation *[tafsīr]* of the following saying, reported by Prophet (Allāh bless him and give him peace) from his Lord (Almighty and Glorious is He):

> O son of Adam, you must perform, for My sake, four cycles of ritual prayer *[ṣalli araba'a raka'āt]* in the first part of the day, so that I may grant you sufficient recompense for so doing.

Some of the commentators have interpreted this as referring to the ritual prayer of the dawn *[ṣalāt]*, [counting the two cycles of] its obligatory performance *[farḍ]* and [the two cycles of] its customarily recommended counterpart *[masnūn]*. The correct interpretation, however, is the one we have mentioned above.

Concerning the second litany *[wird]* of the daytime.

As for the second litany *[wird]* of the daytime, it coincides with the ritual prayer of the forenoon *[ṣalāt aḍ-ḍuḥā]*,[111] which is also known as the ritual prayer of those who truly repent *[ṣalāt al-awwābīn]*.[112]

Is the regular performance of this prayer a recommended practice, or not? There are two conflicting answers to this question, according to the doctrine of our [Ḥanbalī] colleagues. The basic guidance on this subject is contained in the following traditional reports:

As we are reliably informed by Shaikh Abū Naṣr Muḥammad ibn al-Bannā',[113] Allāh's Messenger (Allāh bless him and give him peace) once said:

> The ritual prayer of the forenoon *[ṣalāt aḍ-ḍuḥā]* is the ritual prayer of those who truly repent *[ṣalāt al-awwābīn]*.

According to another report, transmitted by the same chain of authorities *[isnād]*, he also said (Allāh bless him and give him peace):

> The ritual prayer of the forenoon *[ṣalāt aḍ-ḍuḥā]* is the greater part of the ritual prayer of David *[ṣalāt Dāwūd]* (peace be upon him).

Shaikh Abū Naṣr has informed us[114] that the Prophet (Allāh bless him and give him peace) once said:

> One of the gates of the Garden of Paradise is called "The Forenoon *[aḍ-Ḍuḥā]*." When the Day of Resurrection *[Yawm al-Qiyāma]* is at hand, an angelic herald will cry out: "Where are those who used to perform the ritual prayer of the forenoon *[ṣalāt aḍ-ḍuḥā]*, making it their regular practice? Cause them to enter the Garden of Paradise, through the mercy of Allāh!"

[111] See n. 98 on p. 83 above.

[112] See n. 107 on p. 87 above.

[113] ***Author's note***: Shaikh Abū Naṣr Muḥammad ibn al-Bannā' cites the following chain of transmission *[isnād]* for this report: **His own father, Shaikh Abū 'Alī ibn Aḥmad ibn 'Abdi'llāh ibn al-Bannā'—Yaḥyā ibn Abī Kathīr—Abū Salama—Abū Huraira** (may Allāh be well pleased with him)—**the Prophet** (Allāh bless him and give him peace).

[114] ***Author's note***: Shaikh Abū Naṣr Muḥammad ibn al-Bannā' narrates this report on the authority of his father, citing a chain of transmission *[isnād]* from **Abū Huraira** (may Allāh be well pleased with him).

In the time of the Commander of the Faithful *[Amīr al-Muʾminīn]*, ʿUmar ibn al-Khaṭṭāb, and that of ʿAlī (may Allāh be well pleased with them both), the worshippers used to perform the [prescribed] ritual prayer of daybreak *[ṣalāt aṣ-ṣubḥ]*, then they would wait for the moment assigned to the ritual prayer of the forenoon *[ṣalāt aḍ-ḍuḥā]*, and perform it in the mosque *[masjid]*.

As reported on the authority of aḍ-Ḍaḥḥāk ibn Qais, Ibn ʿAbbās (may Allāh be well pleased with him and with his father) once said: "At a certain stage in time, we realized that we did not understand the significance of this Qurʾānic verse *[āya]*:

They proclaim the glory [of the Lord]	*yusabbiḥūna*
in the evening and at sunrise. (38:18)	*bi'l-ʿashiyi wa'l-ishrāqi.*

—until we noticed people performing the ritual prayer of the forenoon *[ṣalāt aḍ-ḍuḥā]*.

It was Ibn Abī Makīla (may Allāh bestow His mercy upon him) who said: "Someone asked Ibn ʿAbbās (may Allāh be well pleased with him and with his father) about the ritual prayer of the forenoon *[ṣalāt aḍ-ḍuḥā]*, so he replied: 'It is definitely mentioned in the Book of Allāh (Exalted is He)." Then he recited this Qurʾānic verse *[āya]*:

In houses [of worship]	*fī buyūtin*
Allāh has allowed to be raised up,	*adhina 'llāhu an turfaʿa*
and in which [He has allowed]	*wa yudhkara*
His Name to be commemorated;	*fī-ha 'smu-hu*
glorifying Him therein,	*yusabbiḥu la-hu*
in the mornings and the evenings (24:36)'	*fī-hā bi'l-ghuduwwi wa 'l-āṣāl.*

"Ibn ʿAbbās (may Allāh be well pleased with him and with his father) would often perform the two cycles of the forenoon prayer *[rakʿatayi 'ḍ-ḍuḥā]*, but he did not become completely addicted to it."

This explains why, when ʿIkrima was asked about how Ibn ʿAbbās (may Allāh be well pleased with him and with his father) performed the ritual prayer of the forenoon *[ṣalāt aḍ-ḍuḥā]*, he replied: "He used to perform it one day, then leave it out for ten."

It was an-Nakhaʿī (may Allāh bestow His mercy upon him) who said: "They [the Companions] used to disapprove of making the ritual prayer of the forenoon *[ṣalāt aḍ-ḍuḥā]* a regular practice, so they would sometimes perform it, and sometimes leave it out, to keep it from acquiring the same status as those prayers that are strictly prescribed *[maktūba]*."

Concerning the number of cycles *[rakaʿāt]* to be performed in the forenoon prayer *[ṣalāt aḍ-ḍuḥā]*.[115]

As for the number of cycles *[rakaʿat]* required in the ritual prayer of the forenoon *[ṣalāt aḍ-ḍuḥā]*, the minimum is two cycles, the best medium is eight cycles, and the maximum is twelve cycles. With respect to the two cycles *[rakʿatān]*, as we are reliably informed by Shaikh Abū Naṣr Muḥammad ibn al-Bannāʾ,[116] Allāh's Messenger (Allāh bless him and give him peace) once said:

> Within the human body there are three hundred and sixty joints. It is therefore incumbent upon the human being to make a charitable donation on behalf of every single joint—one charitable donation *[ṣadaqa]* each day [of the year].

His listeners asked: "And who is capable of that, O Messenger of Allāh?" So he replied (Allāh bless him and give him peace):

> [It will count as a charitable donation] if someone notices a clot of phlegm or mucus in the mosque *[masjid]*, and takes the trouble to bury it, or if he clears some nuisance from the path. If he cannot [do anything like that], the two cycles of the ritual prayer of the forenoon *[ṣalāt aḍ-ḍuḥā]* will adequately compensate for it.

We may also cite the traditional report *[ḥadīth]* of Abū Huraira (may Allāh be well pleased with him), who said: "My bosom friend *[khalīlī]* Abu'l-Qāsim[117] (Allāh bless him and give him peace) alerted me to the value of three practices: (1) the *witr* prayer before going to sleep, (2) devoting three days out of every month to fasting, and (3) the two cycles of the forenoon prayer *[rakʿatayi 'ḍ-ḍuḥā]*."

[115] See note 98 on p. 83 above.

[116] ***Author's note***: Shaikh Abū Naṣr Muḥammad ibn al-Bannāʾ narrates this report on the authority of his own father, citing a chain of transmission *[isnād]* from **ʿAbdu'llāh ibn Buraida—his father** (may Allāh be well pleased with him)—**the Prophet** (Allāh bless him and give him peace).

[117] See n. 51 on p. 43 above.

According to one traditional report, however, four cycles are required. This has been mentioned in a previous subsection, where we cited the relevant saying *[ḥadīth]* of the Prophet (Allāh bless him and give him peace), transmitted by ʿIkrima on the authority of Ibn ʿAbbās (may Allāh be well pleased with him and with his father).

As reported by Muʿādha, ʿĀʾisha (may Allāh be well pleased with her) once said: "The Prophet (Allāh bless him and give him peace) performed the ritual prayer of the forenoon *[ṣalāt aḍ-ḍuḥā]*, sometimes as a prayer of four, but then sometimes as one of six cycles *[rakaʿāt]*."

As reported on the authority of Ḥamīd aṭ-Ṭawīl, it was Anas ibn Mālik (may Allāh be well pleased with him) who said: "The Prophet (Allāh bless him and give him peace) used to perform the the ritual prayer of the forenoon *[ṣalāt aḍ-ḍuḥā]*, sometimes as a prayer of six cycles, but then sometimes as one of eight cycles *[rakaʿāt]*."

According to another report, this one transmitted on the authority of ʿIkrima ibn Khālid, it was Umm Hāniʾ bint Abū Ṭālib (may Allāh be well pleased with her) who said: "When Allāh's Messenger (Allāh bless him and give him peace) approached [the city], at the time of the conquest—the conquest of Mecca *[fatḥ Makka]*—he made a halt on the upper side of Mecca, while he performed a ritual prayer of eight cycles *[rakaʿāt]*. So I asked: "O Messenger of Allāh, what is this ritual prayer *[ṣalāt]*?" He said (Allāh bless him and give him peace): "The ritual prayer of the forenoon *[ṣalāt aḍ-ḍuḥā]*."

Aḥmad ibn Ḥanbal (may Allāh the Exalted bestow His mercy upon him) declared: "It is reliably established," and the preferred choice, in the opinion of the experts in religious knowledge (may Allāh bestow His mercy upon them all), is definitely eight cycles *[rakaʿāt]*.[118] Should further confirmation be needed, we could cite yet another traditional report, transmitted by Abū Saʿīd (may Allāh be well pleased with him) from the Prophet himself (Allāh bless him and give him peace).

As far as ʿĀʾisha is concerned (may Allāh be well pleased with her), she is also reported as having performed the ritual prayer of the forenoon *[ṣalāt aḍ-ḍuḥā]* as a prayer of eight cycles *[rakaʿāt]*. In the words of al-Qāsim ibn Muḥammad (may Allāh bestow His mercy upon him): "ʿĀʾisha (may Allāh be well pleased with her) would often perform the ritual prayer of the forenoon *[ṣalāt aḍ-ḍuḥā]* as a prayer of eight cycles

[118] See note 98 on p. 83 above.

[raka'āt], and she would spend a long time in the process. While she was performing it, she would keep her door locked. Then again, if she preferred, she would perform ten cycles, or even twelve cycles *[raka'āt]*, the latter being her favorite option."

This should come as no surprise, for, as we are reliably informed by Shaikh Abū Naṣr,[119] Anas ibn Mālik (may Allāh be well pleased with him) once heard Allāh's Messenger (Allāh bless him and give him peace) say:

> If a worshipper performs the ritual prayer of the forenoon *[ṣalāt aḍ-ḍuḥā]*, as a prayer of twelve cycles *[raka'āt]*, Allāh (Exalted is He) will have a golden palace built for him in the Garden of Paradise.

Shaikh Abū Naṣr has also informed us, citing traditional authority for his report,[120] that Allāh's Messenger (Allāh bless him and give him peace) once said:

> If a worshipper performs twelve cycles of ritual prayer *[raka'āt]*, in the daytime, Allāh (Exalted is He) will have a house built for him in the Garden of Paradise.

As we are reliably informed by Shaikh Abū Naṣr,[121] Allāh's Messenger (Allāh bless him and give him peace) once turned to Abū Dharr (may Allāh be well pleased with him) and said:

> O Abū Dharr, the daytime consists of twelve hours, so you must be ready to provide one act of bowing *[rak'a]*[122] and two acts of prostration *[sajdatain]* for each of those hours, for that will ward off from you whatever sin it may harbor.
>
> O Abū Dharr, if a worshipper performs two cycles of prayer *[rak'atain]*, he will not be included among the heedless. If someone performs four, he will be

[119] ***Author's note***: Shaikh Abū Naṣr Muḥammad ibn al-Bannā' cites the following chain of transmission *[isnād]* for this report: **His own father, Shaikh Abū 'Alī ibn Aḥmad ibn 'Abdi'llāh ibn al-Bannā'—Ḥamza ibn Mūsā ibn Anas ibn Mālik al-Anṣārī—his uncle, Thumāma ibn Anas—his grandfather, Anas ibn Mālik** (may Allāh be well pleased with him)—**the Prophet** (Allāh bless him and give him peace).

[120] ***Author's note***: Shaikh Abū Naṣr Muḥammad ibn al-Bannā' narrates this report on the authority of his father, citing a chain of transmission *[isnād]* from **Umm Ḥabība** (may Allāh be well pleased with her).

[121] ***Author's note***: Shaikh Abū Naṣr Muḥammad ibn al-Bannā' cites the following chain of transmission *[isnād]* for this report: **His own father, Shaikh Abū 'Alī ibn Aḥmad ibn 'Abdi'llāh ibn al-Bannā'—Ibrāhīm at-Taimī—his father—Abū Dharr** (may Allāh be well pleased with him)—**the Prophet** (Allāh bless him and give him peace).

[122] The term *rak'a* [an act of bowing] has acquired an extended meaning, since it is generally used to denote the whole series of movements and postures—including the bowing posture *[rukū']*—that constitute one cycle of the ritual prayer *[ṣalāt]*. (The dual and plural forms, corresponding to the singular form *rak'a*, are *rak'atān/-ain* and *raka'āt*, respectively.)

recorded as one of those who practice remembrance. If someone performs six, no sin will stick to him that day, unless it be that of associating partners *[shirk]* with Allāh (Exalted is He). If someone performs twelve cycles of prayer, a house will be constructed for him in the Garden of Paradise.

When Abū Dharr heard this, he said: "O Messenger of Allāh, [should they be performed] in combination, or separately?" He replied (Allāh bless him and give him peace): "You need not concern yourself with that *[lā ʿalaik]*."

Concerning the proper time [*waqt*] for the performance of the ritual prayer of the forenoon [*ṣalāt aḍ-ḍuḥā*].

As for the proper time [*waqt*] for its performance, there are actually two such times. The first, which is simply permissible [*jā'iz*], is the period after the rising of the sun, until the [prescribed] prayer of noon [*ṣalāt aẓ-ẓuhr*]. The other, which is positively recommended [*mustaḥabb*], is the time when the young camels, newly weaned from their mothers, are seriously affected by the scorching heat [*turmaḍu 'l-fiṣāl*],[123] at the point when the sun is about to decline from the meridian ['*inda qurb az-zawāl*]. In support of the recommended status assigned to its performance at this latter time, we may cite the following as evidence:

According to a traditional report, Zaid ibn Arqam (may Allāh be well pleased with him) once noticed a group of people performing the ritual prayer of the forenoon [*yuṣallūna 'd-ḍuḥā*] in the mosque [*masjid*] of Qubā'. So he said: "As you must surely be aware, it is more meritorious to perform the prayer [*ṣalāt*] at a different hour from this! Allāh's Messenger (Allāh bless him and give him peace) has said:

> "'The ritual prayer of those who truly repent [*ṣalāt al-awwābīn*][124] [should be performed] at the time when the young camels, newly weaned from their mothers [*fiṣāl*], are seriously affected by the scorching heat [*turmaḍu 'l-fiṣāl*].'"

It must also be permissible to perform it after the sun's decline from the meridian, in view of the report from 'Awf ibn Mālik (may Allāh be well pleased with him), who stated that Allāh's Messenger (Allāh bless him and give him peace) once said:

> The hour of the supererogatory prayer [*sā'at aṣ-ṣubḥa*] is moment when the sun declines from the center of the sky.

---

[123] Some say that this expression accounts for the name of the month of Ramaḍān. (See Vol. 3, p. 79.)

[124] See p. 90 above.

It is also known as the ritual prayer of those who humble themselves *[ṣalāt al-mukhbitīn]*. The best time for its performance is when the heat of the day is extremely intense. If a worshipper has not performed it by the time he performs the [prescribed] ritual prayer of noon *[ṣalāt aẓ-ẓuhr]*, he should make up for it later, in accordance with the [abovementioned] recommendation *[istiḥbāb]*.

Concerning the Qur'ānic recitation appropriate to the ritual prayer of the forenoon *[ṣalāt aḍ-ḍuḥā]*.

As for the Qur'ānic recitation appropriate to the the ritual prayer of the forenoon *[ṣalāt aḍ-ḍuḥā]*, Prophet (Allāh bless him and give him peace) is reported as having said:

> The ritual prayer of the forenoon *[ṣalāt aḍ-ḍuḥā]* should include the recitation of the Sūra [that begins with]:
>
> By the sun and its brightness. (91:1)   *wa 'sh-shamsi wa ḍuḥā-hā*
>
> —and [the Sūra of] the Bright Forenoon *[Surat aḍ-Ḍuḥā]*.[125]

According to one traditional report,[126] Allāh's Messenger (Allāh bless him and give him peace) once said:

> When a worshipper performs the twelve cycles of the ritual prayer of the forenoon *[ṣalāt aḍ-ḍuḥā]*, he should recite in each cycle *[rak'a]*:
>
> - the Opening Sūra of the Book *[Fātiḥat al-Kitāb]*—one time only,
> - the Verse of the Throne *[Āyat al-Kursī]*[127]—one time only, and
> - [the Sūra that begins with]:
>
> Say: "He is Allāh, One!" (112:1)   *qul Huwa 'llāhu Aḥad*—three times.
>
> Seventy thousand angels will thereupon descend from every heaven, bearing white sheets of paper and pens made of light, and they will go on recording good deeds in his favor, until the blast is blown on the Trumpet. Then, when the Day of Resurrection *[Yawm al-Qiyāma]* has arrived, the angels will come to him, and each of the angels will bring a fine suit of clothes and a gift. They will stand by his grave, and they will say: "O occupant of the grave, arise, by the permission of Allāh (Almighty and Glorious is He), for you are one of those who are safe and secure *[āminīn]*."

[125] The Sūra of the Bright Forenoon *[Surat aḍ-Ḍuḥā]* is the 93rd Sūra of the Qur'ān. (In some translations, it is entitled "The Sūra of the Morning Hours.")

[126] ***Author's note:*** The chain of transmission *[isnād]* for this report goes back to: **'Urwa ibn Shu'aib—his father—his grandfather** (may Allāh be well pleased with him)—**the Prophet** (Allāh bless him and give him peace).

[127] Q. 2:255.

Traditional reports unfavorable to the practice of the forenoon prayer *[ṣalāt aḍ-ḍuḥā]*.

It has been reported that some of the Companions *[Ṣaḥāba]* (may Allāh be well pleased with them all) denied the validity of the ritual prayer of the forenoon *[ṣalāt aḍ-ḍuḥā]*. According to one such report,[128] Ibn ʿUmar (may Allāh be well pleased with him and with his father) once said:

"I have never performed the ritual prayer of the forenoon *[ṣalāt aḍ-ḍuḥā]* since I first accepted Islām *[aslamtu]*, except when I am circumambulating the House *[uṭawwif bi'l-Bait]*. It is an innovation *[bidʿa]*, albeit an excellent innovation, and it is surely one of the best practices that people have invented!"

Ibn Masʿūd (may Allāh be well pleased with him) used to say, on the subject of the ritual prayer of the forenoon *[ṣalāt aḍ-ḍuḥā]*: "O servants of Allāh, do not burden the people with something that Allāh has not required them to carry. If you insist on doing it regardless, perform it *[ṣallū-hā]* in your own houses."

None of this points to the negation of what we have mentioned previously, concerning the excellent merits traditionally ascribed to its performance. In making such remarks, they simply intended to emphasize that it should not be likened to the obligatory ritual prayer *[ṣalāt al-farḍ]*, in case people became convinced of its compulsory status. People are not all equal, in terms of the energy *[nashāṭ]* available for religious service *[ʿibāda]*, so they sought to lighten their load, and tried to make it easier for them to practice worshipful obedience *[ṭāʿa]*. This is borne out by the implicit significance of the report of ʿUtbān ibn Mālik (may Allāh be well pleased with him), who said:

"Allāh's Messenger (Allāh bless him and give him peace) performed the supererogatory prayer of the forenoon *[subḥat aḍ-ḍuḥā]* in his own

[128] ***Author's note***: This report has been related by Ibn al-Munādī, one of our own [Ḥanbalī] colleagues, who supplies a chain of transmission *[isnād]* from **Ibn ʿUmar** (may Allāh be well pleased with him and with his father).

apartment, so those who were present stood behind him and performed the prayer too."

Then again, whenever ʿĀʾisha (may Allāh be well pleased with her) intended to perform it, she would lock the door. As for Ibn ʿAbbās (may Allāh be well pleased with him and with his father), he would perform it one day, then leave it out for ten.

Concerning the third litany *[wird]* of the daytime.

As for the third litany *[wird]* of the daytime, it coincides with the [voluntary] ritual prayer *[ṣalāt]* before and after the [prescribed prayer of] noon *[qabla 'ẓ-ẓuhr wa ba'da-hā]*. According to the traditional report we have received from Shaikh Abū Naṣr Muḥammad ibn al-Bannā',[129] [the Prophet's wife] Umm Ḥabība (may Allāh be well pleased with her) once said:

"If a worshipper performs four [voluntary] cycles of ritual prayer *[raka'āt]* before the [prescribed prayer of] noon *[ẓuhr]*, and four after it, Allāh (Exalted is He) will make his flesh unlawful to the Fire of Hell."

It has been said that the gates of Heaven are held open, as are those of the Garden of Paradise, from just after the sun's decline from the meridian *[zawāl]*, until the noon prayer *[ẓuhr]* is performed. This explains why prayers of supplication *[da'awāt]*, as it has also been said, are sure to be answered at this hour. It also explains why one is recommended to make a constant practice, at this hour, of worshipful service *['ibāda]*, supplication *[du'ā']*, and remembrance *[dhikr]*.

Highly relevant, in this context, is the traditional report *[ḥadīth]* from Abū Ayyūb al-Anṣārī (may Allāh be well pleased with him), who said: "The Prophet (Allāh bless him and give him peace) used to devote himself assiduously to four cycles of prayer *[raka'āt]* before the [prescribed prayer of] noon *[ẓuhr]*. People were curious about this, so he explained (Allāh bless him and give him peace):

> The gates of the Garden of Paradise are held open at the moment of the sun's decline from the meridian *[zawāl]*, and they are not bolted shut until the ritual prayer *[ṣalāt]* is begun. So I like to be well to the fore!

129 ***Author's note:*** Shaikh Abū Naṣr Muḥammad ibn al-Bannā' narrates this report on the authority of his father, citing a chain of transmission *[isnād]* from **Umm Ḥabība** (may Allāh be well pleased with her).

ʿĀʾisha (may Allāh be well pleased with her) was once asked: "To which ritual prayer *[ṣalāt]* was Allāh's Messenger (Allāh bless him and give him peace) most fond of applying himself with special diligence?" To this she replied (may Allāh be well pleased with her): "He used to perform four [cycles of prayer] (Allāh bless him and give him peace) before the [prescribed prayer of] noon *[ẓuhr]*, prolonging the standing posture *[qiyām]* in each of them, and making the very best, in each of them, of the acts of bowing *[rukūʿ]* and prostration *[sujūd]*."

Concerning the fourth litany *[wird]* of the daytime.

As for the fourth litany *[wird]* of the daytime, it is performed in the interval between the [prescribed ritual prayers of] noon *[ẓuhr]* and afternoon *[ʿaṣr]*.

Shaikh Abū Naṣr Muḥammad ibn al-Bannāʾ has informed us, citing traditional authority for his report,[130] that Allāh's Messenger (Allāh bless him and give him peace) once said:

> If someone enlivens the interval between the [prescribed ritual prayers of] noon *[ẓuhr]* and afternoon *[ʿaṣr]*, Allāh will keep his heart alive, even on the day when [all other] hearts die.

Tradition tells us that Ibn ʿUmar (may Allāh be well pleased with him and with his father) used to enliven the interval between the [prescribed ritual prayers of] noon *[ẓuhr]* and afternoon *[ʿaṣr]*.

Ibrāhīm an-Nakhaʿī (may Allāh bestow His mercy upon him) is reported as having said: "They [the early believers] used to liken the [voluntary] ritual prayer *[ṣalāt]* performed between the two [prescribed] evening prayers *[al-ʿishāʾain]*,[131] and that performed between the [prescribed ritual prayers of] noon *[ẓuhr]* and afternoon *[ʿaṣr]*, to the ritual prayer of the nighttime *[ṣalāt al-lail]*.[132] That was the regular practice of many of the servants [of the Lord], for they used to perform their litany-prayers *[yuṣallūna awrāda-hum]* between the [prescribed ritual prayers of] noon *[ẓuhr]* and afternoon *[ʿaṣr]*. During this hour, they would isolate themselves from creatures *[khalq]*, and devote

[130] ***Author's note***: Shaikh Abū Naṣr Muḥammad ibn al-Bannāʾ cites the following chain of transmission *[isnād]* for this report: **His own father, Shaikh Abū ʿAlī ibn Aḥmad ibn ʿAbdi'llāh ibn al-Bannāʾ—ʿUmar ibn Aḥmad—ʿAbdu'llāh ibn Muḥammad—Ṣāliḥ ibn Mālik—Jaʿfar ibn ʿUmar—Yūnus ibn ʿAmra—ʿAṭāʾ—Ibn ʿAbbās** (may Allāh be well pleased with him and with his father)—**the Prophet** (Allāh bless him and give him peace).

[131] That is to say, between the prescribed prayers of sunset *[maghrib]* and late evening *[ʿishāʾ]*. (See pp. 27–30 above.)

[132] See pp. 68 and 82 above.

themselves exclusively to the Lord of Truth *[Ḥaqq]*. It is a noble hour, appropriately devoted to seclusion *[khalwa]* with the Lord (Almighty and Glorious is He), and to His remembrance *[dhikr]*. It is an hour when prayer is the antidote to heedlessness."

In the interval between the [prescribed ritual prayers of] noon *[ẓuhr]* and afternoon *[ʿaṣr]*, the worshipper is recommended to practice seclusion *[iʿtikāf]* in the mosque *[masjid]*, for the purpose of [voluntary] prayer *[ṣalāt]* and remembrance *[dhikr]*, in order to combine the practice of seclusion *[iʿtikāf]* with the anticipation of the [next prescribed] ritual prayer *[intiẓār li'ṣ-ṣalāt]*. Such was the regular practice of our righteous predecessors *[as-salaf]*. An exception must be made, however, in the case of someone who has failed to catch any sleep before the sun's decline from the meridian *[zawāl]*. He should sleep during this hour, so as to fortify himself in preparation for the night vigil *[qiyām al-lail]*. His sleeping should properly be done before the time of the noon prayer *[qabla 'ẓ-ẓuhr]*, to make up for the previous night, and after the time of the noon prayer *[baʿda 'ẓ-ẓuhr]*, in preparation for the night that lies ahead. He is not recommended to sleep for more than eight hours [all told], but anything less than this amount of sleep, it has been said, is likely to result in some kind of physical disturbance, because sleep is the nourishment and refreshment of the physical body.

Shaikh Abū Naṣr Muḥammad ibn al-Bannā' has also informed us, citing traditional authority for his report,[133] that the Prophet (Allāh bless him and give him peace) once said:

> If a worshipper performs twelve [voluntary] cycles of ritual prayer, every day, Allāh will have a house built for him in the Garden of Paradise. Two [of these twelve] should be performed before the [prescribed prayer of] daybreak *[qabla 'l-fajr]*, four of them before the [prescribed prayer of] noon *[qabla 'ẓ-ẓuhr]*, two of them after the [prescribed prayer of] noon *[baʿda 'ẓ-ẓuhr]*, two of them before the [prescribed prayer of the] afternoon *[qabla 'l-ʿaṣr]*, and two of them after the [prescribed prayer of] sunset *[baʿda 'l-maghrib]*.

As reported on the authority of Saʿīd ibn al-Musayyib, ʿĀ'isha (may Allāh be well pleased with her) said that Allāh's Messenger (Allāh bless him and give him peace) once said:

> As for those who perform four [voluntary] cycles of ritual prayer *[al-muṣallūna li-arbaʿ]*, before the [prescribed prayer of the] afternoon *[qabla 'l-ʿaṣr]*, they will not have time to finish before Allāh grants them forgiveness, quite definitely.

[133] ***Author's note***: Shaikh Abū Naṣr Muḥammad ibn al-Bannā' cites the following chain of transmission *[isnād]* for this report: **His own father, Shaikh Abū ʿAlī ibn Aḥmad ibn ʿAbdi'llāh ibn al-Bannā'—Sahl—his [Sahl's] father—Abū Huraira** (may Allāh be well pleased with him)—**the Prophet** (Allāh bless him and give him peace).

A traditional saying *[ḥadīth]* that refers in general to supererogatory devotions *[nawāfil]* at these times.

In one traditional saying *[ḥadīth]* that has come down to us, we find a general reference to all supererogatory devotions *[nawāfil]* at these particular times of the day. According to this report, which has been conveyed to us by Shaikh Abū Naṣr, with a list of transmitting authorities,[134] Allāh's Messenger (Allāh bless him and give him peace) once said:

> If a worshipper performs six cycles of [voluntary] ritual prayer *[ṣallā sitta raka'āt]*, after the [prescribed prayer of] sunset *[ba'da'l-maghrib]* and before he has talked to anybody, they will be raised up for him to the Highest Heaven *['Illiyūn]*. He will be just like someone who is present on the Night of Power *[Lailat al-Qadr]* in the Farthest Mosque *[al-Masjid al-Aqṣā]*,[135] and that is better than devoting half a night to vigil. These devotions are referred to in the words of Allāh (Blessed and Exalted is He):
>
> | | |
> |---|---|
> | They used to sleep only a little
during the night,
and with the dawning of each day
they would seek forgiveness.
(51:17,18) | *kānū qalīlan mina 'l-laili
mā yahja'ūn:
wa bi'l-asḥāri
hum yastaghfirūn.* |
>
> —and in the words of Allāh (Exalted is He):
>
> | | |
> |---|---|
> | Their sides shun their couches,
as they call on their Lord
in fear and hope. (32:16) | *tatajāfā junūbu-hum 'ani 'l-maḍāji'i
yad'ūna Rabba-hum
khawfan wa ṭama'ā.* |
>
> —and also in the words of Allāh (Exalted is He):
>
> | | |
> |---|---|
> | And he entered the city
at a time when its people
were unheeding, and there
he found two men fighting; | *wa dakhala 'l-madīnata
'alā ḥīni ghaflatin
min ahli-hā fa-wajada
fī-hā rajulaini yaqtatilāni* |

[134] ***Author's note***: Shaikh Abū Naṣr Muḥammad ibn al-Bannā' cites the following chain of transmission *[isnād]* for this report: **His own father, Shaikh Abū 'Alī ibn Aḥmad ibn 'Abdi'llāh ibn al-Bannā'—Muḥammad ibn Aḥmad al-Ḥāfiẓ—Muḥammad ibn Badr al-Ḥumārī—Ḥammād ibn Mudrik—'Uthmān ibn 'Abdi'llāh ash-Shāmī—Muḥammad ibn Ibrāhīm—'Abdu'llāh ibn Abī Sa'īd—Ṭāwūs—'Abdu'llāh ibn 'Abbās** (may Allāh be well pleased with him and with his father)—**the Prophet** (Allāh bless him and give him peace).

[135] ***Author's note***: That is to say, in the Mosque of the Temple [in Jerusalem] *[Masjid Bait al-Maqdis]*.

the one was of his own party,	*hādhā min shī'ati-hi*
and the other was of his enemies.	*wa hādhā min 'aduwwi-h:*
Then the one who was	*fa-'staghātha-hu 'lladhī*
of his own party appealed to him	*min shī'ati-hi*
for help against the other	*'ala 'lladhī min*
who was of his enemies.	*'aduwwi-hi*
So Moses struck him with his fist,	*fa-wakaza-hu Mūsā*
and dispatched him.	*fa-qaḍā 'alai-h:*
He said: "This is of Satan's doing;	*qāla hādhā min 'amali 'sh-shaiṭān:*
he is surely an enemy,	*inna-hu 'aduwwun*
an obvious misleader. (28:15)	*muḍillun mubīn.*

If a worshipper performs four [voluntary cycles], after the [prescribed] ritual prayer of late evening *[al-'ishā' al-ākhira]*, he will be just like one who arrives in time to experience the Night of Power *[Lailat al-Qadr]* in the Sacred Mosque *[Masjid al-Ḥarām]*."

If a worshipper performs four [voluntary cycles] before the [prescribed prayer of] noon *[ẓuhr]*, and four after it, Allāh (Exalted is He) will forbid the Fire of Hell ever to consume his physical body.

If a worshipper performs four [voluntary cycles] before the [prescribed prayer of the] afternoon *['aṣr]*, Allāh will record him as entitled to immunity from the Fire of Hell.

As reported by Nāfi', on the authority of Ibn 'Umar (may Allāh be well pleased with him and with his father), Allāh's Messenger (Allāh bless him and give him peace) also said:

The two cycles of the ritual prayer of daybreak *[rak'atā 'l-fajr]* are dearer to me than this world and all that it contains.

As we are reliably informed by Shaikh Abū Naṣr,[136] 'Alī [ibn Abī Ṭālib] (may Allāh ennoble his countenance) was once asked about the supererogatory worship *[taṭawwu']* of the Prophet (Allāh bless him and give him peace), so he said: "Who is capable of that? He used to wait until the sun was as far to his left as it would be to his right at the time of the [prescribed prayer of the] afternoon *['aṣr]*, at which point he would perform two cycles of [voluntary] ritual prayer *[rak'atain]*.[137] When it was as far to his left as it would to his right at the time of [the prescribed prayer of] noon *[ẓuhr]*, he would perform four [voluntary cycles of prayer]. When the sun declined from the meridian, he would perform four [prescribed cycles of prayer]. He would then perform two

[136] ***Author's note:*** Shaikh Abū Naṣr Muḥammad ibn al-Bannā' narrates this report on the authority of his father, citing a chain of transmission *[isnād]* from **'Alī** (may Allāh ennoble his countenance).

[137] When the Prophet (Allāh bless him and give him peace) was in Medina, and facing the *Qibla* [direction of the Ka'ba in Mecca], the sun would rise on his left and set on his right.

[voluntary] cycles *[rakʿatain]* after the [prescribed prayer of] noon *[ẓuhr]*, and four before the [prescribed prayer of the] afternoon *[ʿaṣr]*."

To put all this in a nutshell, the servant [of the Lord] should seize the opportunity, after the call to prayer *[adhān]* and at the time of the final announcement *[iqāma]* [immediately before the prescribed prayer],[138] to perform a [voluntary] prayer *[ṣalāt]*, and to offer supplication *[duʿāʾ]* and humble entreaty *[taḍarruʿ]*, for it is a moment when the supplicant can expect a positive response, as we have previously explained.

138 See notes 303 and 304 on p. 225 below.

Concerning the fifth litany *[wird]* of the daytime.

As for the fifth litany *[wird]* of the daytime, it is performed in the interval between the [prescribed] ritual prayer of the afternoon *[ṣalāt al-ʿaṣr]* and the setting of the sun. It consists entirely of remembrance *[dhikr]*, in the form of glorifying the Lord *[tasbīḥ]*,[139] affirming His Uniqueness *[tahlīl]*,[140] seeking His forgiveness *[istighfār]*, reflecting on the Heavenly Kingdom *[tafakkur fi 'l-Malakūt]*, and reciting the Qurʾān, because the performance of supererogatory ritual prayer *[ṣalāt an-nāfila]* is forbidden during this period of time.

Before the setting of the sun, the worshipper should recite [the Sūras that begin with]:

> By the sun and its brightness.... (91:1) — *wa 'sh-shamsi wa ḍuḥā-hā....*

—and:

> By the night when it is enshrouding.... (92:1) — *wa 'l-laili idhā yaghshā....*

Then he should recite the Two Pleas for Refuge *[al-Muʿawwidhatain]*,[141] thereby marking the end of his day. He should also begin his night by reciting the Qurʾān and seeking refuge *[istiʿādha]*.

As reported on the authority of al-Ḥasan (may Allāh be well pleased with him), the Prophet (Allāh bless him and give him peace) once said, while mentioning the mercy of his Lord (Almighty and Glorious is He):

> Allāh (Exalted is He) has said: "O son of Adam, remember Me after the ritual prayer of the daybreak *[ṣalāt al-fajr]*, for an hour, and after the ritual prayer of the afternoon *[ṣalāt al-ʿaṣr]*, for an hour, for then I shall protect you in the interval between the two."

[139] See n. 11 on p. 9 above.

[140] See n. 10 on p. 9 above.

[141] That is to say, the two Sūras that begin with:

> Say: "I take refuge with the Lord of the Daybreak." (113:1) — *qul aʿūdhu bi-Rabbi 'l-falaq.*

— and:

> Say: "I take refuge with the Lord of mankind." (114:1) — *qul aʿūdhu bi-Rabbi 'n-nās.*

CHAPTER EIGHT

Concerning the five daily ritual prayers *[aṣ-ṣalawāt al-khams]*, with an account of their times of performance, their customary elements *[sunan]*, and their special qualities.

1.
Concerning the number of cycles *[raka'āt]* to be performed in each of the prescribed ritual prayers.

The prescribed ritual prayers *[aṣ-ṣalawāt al-maktūba]* are five in number, namely:

1. The dawn prayer *[ṣalāt al-fajr]*, which consists of two cycles *[rak'atān]*.
2. The noon prayer *[ṣalāt aẓ-ẓuhr]*, which consists of four cycles *[arba' raka'āt]*.
3. The afternoon prayer *[ṣalāt al-'aṣr]*, which consists of four cycles *[arba' raka'āt]*.
4. The sunset prayer *[ṣalāt al-maghrib]*, which consists of three cycles *[thalāth raka'āt]*.
5. The late evening prayer *[ṣalāt al-'ishā']*, the last of the five, which consists of four cycles *[arba' raka'āt]*.

This adds up to a daily total of seventeen cycles *[sab' 'ashara rak'a]*.

Fifty prayers had been prescribed as obligatory on the Night of the Heavenly Ascension *[Lailat al-Mi'rāj]*, the night when the Prophet (Allāh bless him and give him peace) was transported on his Heavenly Journey *[Isrā']*. But then the number was brought back down to five, as a dispensation of wisdom *[ḥikma]* on the part of Allāh, so that the burden He still imposed would seem light and easy, in contrast with that from which He had exempted His believing servants. By a similar act of dispensation, He relieved them of the duty to stand firm in battle with the unbelievers *[kāfirīn]* when the ratio was ten to one against them, and reduced the ratio to that of two to one against them. He likewise canceled the prohibition of eating, drinking, and engaging in sexual intercourse after sleep during the nights of fasting [in the month of Ramaḍān], by His pronouncement:

It has been made lawful for you, on the night of the Fast, to go in to your wives; they are a garment for you, and you are a garment for them.	*uḥilla la-kum* *lailata 'ṣ-ṣiyāmi 'r-rafathu* *ilā nisā'i-kum:* *hunna libāsun la-kum* *wa antum libāsun la-hun:*
Allāh knows that you have been deceiving yourselves, and He has relented toward you and pardoned you.	*'alima 'llāhu anna-kum kuntum* *takhtānūna anfusa-kum* *fa-tāba 'alai-kum wa 'afā 'an-kum:*
So now have intercourse with them, and seek that which Allāh has prescribed for you.	*fa-'l-āna bāshirū-hunna* *wa 'btaghū mā* *kataba 'llāhu la-kum:*
And eat and drink until the white thread becomes distinct to you from the black thread of the dawn. (2:187)	*wa kulū wa 'shrabū ḥattā yatabayyana* *la-kumu 'l-khaiṭu 'l-abyaḍu* *mina 'l-khaiṭi 'l-aswadi mina 'l-fajr.*

All this had previously been declared unlawful for them.

2.
Qur'ānic verses *[āyāt]* and Prophetic traditions *[akhbār]* relating to the obligatory status *[wujūb]* of the five daily prayers, and to the proper times *[awqāt]* for their performance.

As far as the obligatory status *[wujūb]* of the five daily prayers is concerned, the principle is established on the basis of His imperative statement (Almighty and Glorious is He):

And perform the ritual prayer,	*wa aqīmu 'ṣ-ṣalāta*
and pay the alms-due,	*wa ātu 'z-zakāta*
and bow your heads with those	*wa 'rka'ū*
who bow [in worship]. (2:43)	*ma'a 'r-rāki'īn.*

When it comes to defining the correct times *[awqāt]* for the performance of the five daily prayers, the authoritative sources include both Qur'ānic verses *[āyāt]* and Prophetic traditions *[akhbār]*.[142]

1. As for the relevant Qur'ānic verses *[āyāt]*, they are as follows:[143]

a) The words of Allāh (Almighty and Glorious is He):

So proclaim the glory of Allāh	*fa-subḥāna 'llāhi*
when you enter upon	*ḥīna*
the evening time,	*tumsūna*
and when you enter upon	*wa ḥīna*
the morning time—	*tuṣbiḥūn*
and to Him belongs the praise,	*wa la-hu 'l-ḥamdu*
in the heavens and the earth—	*fi 's-samā'i wa 'l-arḍi*
and when the sun is well on the wane,	*wa 'ashiyyan*
and when you enter	*wa ḥīna*
upon the noontime hour.	*tuẓhirūn.*
(30:17,18)	

[142] As used by the narrators of tradition, the term *khabar* (of which *akhbār* is the plural form) is sometimes synonymous with *ḥadīth*, meaning a report than can be traced all the way back to the Prophet Muḥammad himself (Allāh bless him and give him peace), whether the substance of that report be a saying of his or a description of his behavior in a certain situation. In some cases, however, the term *khabar* is applied to a tradition that may well have originated with the Prophet (Allāh bless him and give him peace), but which can only be traced with certainty to one of his Companions, or to some other reliable early source.

[143] In view of the wide range of traditional interpretation applied to the original Arabic, no English translation of these Qur'ānic verses *[āyāt]* can be regarded as strictly precise!

That is to say: **"So proclaim the glory of Allāh** by performing the ritual prayers for the sake of Allāh:[144] **When you enter upon the evening time,** perform the sunset and late evening prayers *[ṣalāt al-maghrib wa 'l-'ishā']*; **when you enter upon the morning time,** perform the dawn prayer *[ṣalāt al-fajr]*; **when the sun is well on the wane,** perform the afternoon prayer *[ṣalāt al-'aṣr]*; **and when you enter upon the noontime hour,** perform the midday prayer *[ṣalāt aẓ-ẓuhr]*."

b) He has said (Almighty and Glorious is He):

Surely the ritual prayer is a timed prescription for the believers. (4:103)	*inna 'ṣ-ṣalāta kānat 'ala 'l-mu'minīna kitāban mawqūtā.*

c) He has said (Exalted is He):

And perform the ritual prayer	*wa aqimi 'ṣ-ṣalāta*
at the two ends of the day and	*ṭarafayi 'n-nahāri*
in some watches of the night. (11:114)	*wa zulafan mina 'l-lail.*

d) He has also said (Exalted is He):

Perform the ritual prayer	*aqimi 'ṣ-ṣalāta*
at the sinking of the sun. (17:78)	*li-dulūki 'sh-shamsi.*

In other words, at its setting *[ghurūb]*; or, according to some authorities, at the time of its decline from the meridian *[zawāl]*.

e) He has said (Magnificent is His Majesty Sublime):

And extol the praise of your Lord	*wa sabbiḥ bi-ḥamdi Rabbi-ka*
before the rising of the sun,	*qabla ṭulū'i 'sh-shamsi*
and before its setting, and extol [the praise of your Lord]	*wa qabla ghurūbi-hā:*
in the watches of the night,	*wa min ānā'i 'l-laili*
and at the ends of the day, so that	*fa-sabbiḥ wa aṭrāfa 'n-nahāri*
you may earn His good pleasure. (20:130)	*la'alla-ka tarḍā.*

Qatāda[145] (may Allāh bestow His mercy upon him) has offered the following interpretation of this Qur'ānic verse *[āya]*:

[144] During the Islāmic ritual prayer *[ṣalāt]*, the glorification of the Lord *[tasbīḥ]* is uttered each time the worshipper adopts the postures of bowing *[rukū']* and prostration *[sujūd]*. While adopting the bowing posture, one says: "*Subḥāna Rabbiya 'l-'Aẓīm* [Glory to my Lord, the Almighty!]" and when in prostration: "*Subḥāna Rabbiya 'l-A'lā* [Glory to my Lord, the Most High!]"

[145] Abu 'l-Khaṭṭāb Qatāda ibn Di'āma ibn Qatāda as-Sadūsī. Learned in Qur'ānic exegesis *[tafsīr]* and Islamic jurisprudence *[fiqh]*, he was also an authority on Arabic poetry. He died in A.H. 118 (may Allāh bestow His mercy upon him).

“**Before the rising of the sun** comes the dawn prayer *[ṣalāt al-fajr]*; **before its setting** comes the afternoon prayer *[ṣalāt al-ʿaṣr]*; **in the watches of the night** come the sunset and late evening prayers *[ṣalāt al-maghrib wa 'l-ʿishāʾ]*; **and at** the point between **the ends of the day** comes the midday prayer *[ṣalāt aẓ-ẓuhr]*.”

2. As for the relevant Prophetic traditions *[akhbār]*, it is sufficient to cite the report transmitted on the authority of Ibn ʿAbbās (may Allāh be well pleased with him and with his father). According to this report, Allāh's Messenger (Allāh bless him and give him peace) once said:

> Gabriel (peace be upon him) came to visit me beside the House [the House of Allāh; the Kaʿba]. There he led me in the midday prayer *[ṣallā biya 'ẓ-ẓuhr]*, as soon as the sun had declined from the meridian, just enough to lengthen a shadow by the width of the strap of a sandal *[shirāk]*. Then he led me in the afternoon prayer *[ṣallā biya 'l-ʿaṣr]*, when the length of every shadow had become equal to the height of the corresponding object. Then he led me in the sunset prayer *[ṣallā biya 'l-maghrib]*, at the time when the person who was fasting broke his fast. Then he led me in the late evening prayer *[ṣallā biya 'l-ʿishāʾ]*, at moment when the final glow of twilight disappeared. Then he led me in the dawn prayer *[ṣallā biya 'l-fajr]*, at the point when food and drink became unlawful for anyone who was fasting.
>
> Then he led me again in the midday prayer *[ṣallā biya 'ẓ-ẓuhr]*, but this time it was when the length of every shadow had become equal to the height of the corresponding object. Then he led me again in the afternoon prayer *[ṣallā biya 'l-ʿaṣr]*, but this time it was when the length of every shadow had become equal to twice the height of the corresponding object. Then he led me again in the sunset prayer *[ṣallā biya 'l-maghrib]*, and, as on the previous occasion, he did so at the time when the person who was fasting broke his fast. Then he led me again in the late evening prayer *[ṣallā biya 'l-ʿishāʾ]*, only this time it was near the end of the first third of the night. Then he led me again in the dawn prayer *[ṣallā biya 'l-fajr]*, only this time it was when the glow of daybreak was already shining bright.
>
> Then he turned to me and said: “O Muḥammad, this is the timing of the Prophets *[Anbiyāʾ]* who came before you, and the timing includes the interval between these two precise moments.”

This particular tradition *[khabar]* represents our basic source for the appointed times *[mawāqīt]* of the five daily prayers. With respect to this subject, several other Prophetic sayings *[aḥādīth]*[146] have been handed down to us, but, since they all convey exactly the same meaning as the one just cited, we have decided to refrain from quoting them here.

[146] See note 142 on p. 112 above.

3.
Concerning those who performed these prayers *[ṣalawāt]* before the time of our Prophet Muḥammad (Allāh bless him and give him peace).

As we learn from one of the Prophetic traditions *[akhbār]*[147] that have been transmitted to us, a man from among the Helpers *[Anṣār]*[148] once asked the Prophet (Allāh bless him and give him peace) about the dawn prayer *[ṣalāt al-fajr]*: "Who performed it for the very first time?" So he informed the man that the first person who ever performed it was Adam (peace be upon him). Then he went on to tell him:

"The midday prayer *[ṣalāt aẓ-ẓuhr]* was performed by Abraham *[Ibrāhīm]* (peace be upon him), when Allāh (Exalted is He) delivered him from Nimrod's fiery furnace.

"The afternoon prayer *[ṣalāt al-ʿaṣr]* was performed by Jacob *[Yaʿqūb]* (peace be upon him), when Gabriel gave him the news about Joseph *[Yūsuf]* (peace be upon them both).

"The sunset prayer *[ṣalāt al-maghrib]* was performed by David *[Dāwūd]* (peace be upon him), when Allāh relented toward him and accepted his repentance.

"The prayer of the first third of the night *[ṣalāt al-ʿatama]*[149] was performed by Jonah, the son of Amittai, *[Yūnus ibn Mattai]* (peace be upon him). When Allāh brought him forth from the belly of the whale, he was emaciated like a chicken that has had all its feathers plucked. It was then that Gabriel (peace be upon him) came to him and said: 'Allāh (Exalted is He) pronounces the greeting of peace upon you, and He says to you: "I ask you this with diffidence, in view of the torment I have inflicted on you in the realm of the lower world: Are you well pleased with Me?" So he stood up and performed four cycles *[rakaʿāt]* of ritual prayer, then he said: 'I am indeed well pleased with my Lord. Yes, I am truly well pleased with my Lord.'"

[147] See note 142 on p. 112 above.

[148] The *Anṣār* [the Helpers] were the citizens of Medina who had embraced Islām, and who welcomed and supported the Prophet (Allāh bless him and give him peace) and the *Muhājirūn* [the Emigrés] at the time of the *Hijra* from Mecca to Medina.

[149] Another name for the late evening prayer *[ṣalāt al-ʿishāʾ]*.

4.
Concerning the fact that the first two of the ritual prayers *[ṣalawāt]* to be enjoined upon our Prophet (Allāh bless him and give him peace) were the dawn prayer *[ṣalāt al-fajr]* and the sunset prayer *[ṣalāt al-maghrib]*.

The first two of the ritual prayers *[ṣalawāt]* that were enjoined upon our Prophet (Allāh bless him and give him peace), and that he was commanded to perform, were the dawn and sunset prayers *[ṣalāt al-fajr wa 'l-maghrib]*.

Allāh (Almighty and Glorious is He) had made the pronouncement:

And extol the praise of your Lord in the evening and early in the morning. (40:55)	*wa sabbiḥ bi-ḥamdi Rabbi-ka* *bi'l-ʿashiyyi* *wa 'l-ibkār.*

His Messenger therefore made it his regular practice (Allāh bless him and give him peace) to perform two cycles *[rakʿatain]* of ritual prayer in the early morning *[ghadāh]* and two cycles in the evening *[ʿashiyy]*. This continued until the Night of the Heavenly Ascension *[Lailat al-Miʿrāj]*, the night when the Prophet (Allāh bless him and give him peace) was transported on his Heavenly Journey *[Isrā']*, at which point five daily prayers *[ṣalawāt]* were prescribed for him.

The dawn prayer *[ṣalāt al-fajr]* is actually the first prayer of the daytime *[nahār]*, then comes the midday prayer *[ṣalāt aẓ-ẓuhr]*. It is customary, however, for the religious scholars *[ʿulamā']* to begin their listing and learned treatment of the prayers with the midday prayer *[ṣalāt aẓ-ẓuhr]*. This custom is based on the saying of the Prophet (Allāh bless him and give him peace), in the tradition *[ḥadīth]* reported by Ibn ʿAbbās (may Allāh be well pleased with him and with his father):

> Gabriel (peace be upon him) came to visit me beside the House [the House of Allāh; the Kaʿba]. There he led me in the midday prayer *[ṣallā biya 'ẓ-ẓuhr]*, as soon as the sun had declined from the meridian, just enough to lengthen a shadow by the width of the strap of a sandal *[shirāk]*.[150]

[150] See p. 114 above, where the author (may Allāh be well pleased with him) has already quoted this tradition *[ḥadīth]* in full.

This tradition *[ḥadīth]* begins with the definition of the timing of the midday prayer *[ṣalāt aẓ-ẓuhr]*. The scholars have therefore treated the timing *[waqt]* of that prayer as the first of the [five] appointed times *[mawāqīt]*, on the grounds that it was the first [of the five daily prayers] to be prescribed as an obligatory religious duty.

As we have already explained, however, the dawn prayer *[ṣalāt al-fajr]* was the one performed by Adam (peace be upon him), and he was the first Prophet *[Nabī]*, the first member of the human race to be sent on a mission to the earth. In the most general sense, therefore, the dawn prayer *[ṣalāt al-fajr]* is known to be the first ritual prayer that was ever prescribed as an obligatory religious duty.

5.
Concerning the correct time for the performance of the dawn prayer *[ṣalāt al-fajr]*.

The first moment of the time of the dawn prayer *[ṣalāt al-fajr]* is the crack of the second dawn *[al-fajr ath-thānī]*,[151] which presents itself as a gleam of light in the farthest east, extending beyond the Qibla [the direction of the Ka'ba in Mecca][152] until it rises and stretches across the horizon, then spreads itself over the peaks of the mountains and over the rooftops of the stately mansions and palaces. The final moment of its time is marked by the brilliant glow that immediately precedes the appearance of the eyebrow of the sun. Between these two points there is a fairly wide space of time.

It is considered commendable to refer to this prayer as the daybreak prayer *[ṣalāt aṣ-ṣubḥ]* or the dawn prayer *[ṣalāt al-fajr]*, and not to call it the early morning prayer *[ṣalāt al-ghadāh]*, because Allāh (Exalted is He) has told us:

And [perform] the recital of dawn; surely the recital of dawn is witnessed. (17:78)	*wa qur'āna 'l-fajr:* *inna qur'āna 'l-fajri* *kāna mashūdā.*

That is to say: "The dawn prayer *[ṣalāt al-fajr]* is witnessed by the angels of the night, as well as by the angels of the day, since it takes place during the last watch of the angels who are charged with keeping records through the night, and during the first watch of the angels who are charged with keeping records through the day (peace be upon them all)."

[151] The second dawn *[al-fajr ath-thānī]* is also known as the true dawn *[al-fajr aṣ-ṣādiq]*.

[152] The direction of Jerusalem was the first *Qibla*. According to tradition, it was in the second year of the *Hijra*, in Rajab or Sha'bān, that the Muslims were commanded to perform their ritual prayers *[ṣalāt]* thenceforth in the direction of the Sacred Mosque *[Masjid al-Ḥarām]* in Mecca, which thus became the second—and permanent—*Qibla*. In Vol. 3, p. 62, Shaikh 'Abd al-Qādir al-Jīlānī (may Allāh be well pleased with him) tells us:

> As it is said: "The Ka'ba is a *Qibla* [direction of prayer] for the people of the Mosque, the Mosque is a *Qibla* for the people of Mecca, Mecca is a *Qibla* for the people of the Sacred Precinct, and the Sacred Precinct is a *Qibla* for the people of the earth."

The most meritorious approach is to perform it in the early phase, the stage of semidarkness known as *ghalas*,[153] although this is contrary to the doctrine of Imām Abū Ḥanīfa,[154] who maintained that there is greater merit in performing it when the light of daybreak is more clearly visible. Our own [Ḥanbalī] doctrine is based on the traditional report transmitted from [the Prophet's wife] 'Ā'isha (may Allāh be well pleased with her), in which it is stated that she once said:

"During the lifetime of Allāh's Messenger (Allāh bless him and give him peace), the womenfolk used to go out [to the mosque] to perform the dawn prayer *[ṣalāt al-fajr]* in his company, then they would return to their homes, with their woolen wrappers draped over their heads, and nobody would recognize them, on account of the lingering darkness *[ghalas]*."

According to another account of his doctrine, however, our own Imām Aḥmad [ibn Ḥanbal][155] maintained that the most important factor to be considered is the state of those who attend the congregation *[al-ma'mūmīn]*.[156] If they tend to show up closer to daybreak, the time near daybreak is more meritorious, since it makes for an increase in both the size of the gathering and the amount of the spiritual reward.

As for the first dawn *[al-fajr al-awwal]*,[157] no significance should be attached to it, because it neither causes anything to become unlawful, nor causes anything to become obligatory. This assertion is based on the statement attributed to Ibn 'Abbās (may Allāh be well pleased with him and with his father), who is reported as having said:

"The dawn is actually two dawns *[al-fajr fajrān]*. As for the one that results in the performance of the [dawn] prayer becoming lawful, and in

[153] The text reads: *wa 'l-afḍalu 't-taghlīsu bihā*. The expression *at-taghlīs bi 'ṣ-ṣalāt* means "to perform the [dawn] prayer in the time called *ghalas*." According to the classical Arabic lexicographers, the term *ghalas* is applied to "the darkness of the last part of the night, when it becomes mixed with the light of dawn; or, the beginning of the dawn, until it spreads in the tracts of the horizon." (See: E.W. Lane, *Arabic-English Lexicon*, art. GH–L–S.)

[154] Imām Abū Ḥanīfa (may Allāh bestow His mercy upon him) is the eponymous founder of the Ḥanafī *madhhab*, which is one of the four Sunnī schools of Islāmic jurisprudence *[fiqh]*. He died in A.H. 150/767 C.E.

[155] See note 7 on p. 7 above.

[156] In Arabic, the term *ma'mūm* (of which *ma'mūmīn* is a plural form) is used to denote someone who performs the ritual prayer behind an *imām*. (Both words are derived from the same triconsonantal root <'–m–m> as the preposition *amāma*, which means "in front of.")

[157] The first dawn *[al-fajr al-awwal]* is also known as the false dawn *[al-fajr al-kādhib]*.

eating and drinking becoming unlawful [for someone who is keeping the fast], it is the one that spreads out over the peaks of the mountains; that is the one that makes it unlawful [for someone who is keeping the fast to do anything that would break his fast]."

The two dawns have also been described in astronomical terms by certain learned scholars, endowed by Allāh (Almighty and Glorious is He) with knowledge of the cosmos. These are the definitions they provide:

1. The first dawn *[al-fajr al-awwal]*. This is the manifestation of the dominant force *[sulṭān]* controlling the rays of the sun. When the sun appears from behind the fifth earth, that force allows its light to gleam in the middle of the sky—until it cuts it off—for the brief duration of the first dawn. That gleam of light, which becomes visible in the sky in the final third of the night, is the first dawn. Then the darkness of the night returns, just as it was before, because the sun sinks into the lowest inclining orbit, where it is screened by the sixth earth, with the result that the gleam of light disappears from the sky.
2. The second dawn *[al-fajr ath-thānī]*. This is the breaking of the sun's glow *[shafaq]*, which is the manifestation of its whiteness with an underlying redness. This is its second reddish glow, and the first real display of its power at the end of the night. It is followed by the rising of the sun's disk, which means that the sun has become visible over the surface of the earth of this world—the seventh earth, in other words—and that its rays have burst forth from the lowest celestial sphere. (The lowest sphere is the fringe of the sky.) Its eye had been concealed by the mountains, the oceans, and the regions of high elevation, but now its rays are clearly visible, as they spread out toward the middle of the sky, extending horizontally *[mustaṭīran]* as well as vertically.

The first dawn is described as extending vertically *[mustaṭīlan]*, because it makes only a vertical appearance in the sky, then disappears from view. The second dawn is different, in that it appears across a broad front, embracing the whole horizon and all the regions of the sky. (The sun has two reddish glows *[shafaqatān]* at the time of its setting, as well as two reddish glows at the time of its rising.)

6.
Concerning the time prescribed for the performance of the midday prayer *[ṣalāt aẓ-ẓuhr]*. On how to determine whether the sun has begun its decline *[zawāl]*, and on how to measure the shadows caused by the sun.

The correct timing *[waqt]* of the midday prayer *[ṣalāt aẓ-ẓuhr]*:

As for the midday prayer *[ṣalāt aẓ-ẓuhr]*, the first moment of the time prescribed for its performance is when the sun has begun to decline from the meridian. The last moment is reached when the length of every shadow has become equal to the height of the corresponding object.

The most meritorious approach is to perform the midday prayer *[ṣalāt aẓ-ẓuhr]* without delay, except in conditions of extremely intense heat, and only if the sky is overcast, in the case of a worshipper who intends to go out and join the congregation. This qualification is based on the saying of the Prophet (Allāh bless him and give him peace):

> Put off the midday prayer until the atmosphere gets cooler *[abridū bi'ẓ-ẓuhr]*, for extremely intense heat is caused by the festering pus of Hell *[qaiḥ Jahannam]*.

Bilāl[158] (may Allāh be well pleased with him) is reported as having said: "I gave Allāh's Messenger (Allāh bless him and give him peace) the call *[adhān]*[159] to the midday prayer, but he said: 'Wait till it gets a bit cooler *[abrid]*!' Then I gave him the call a second time, and again he said: 'Wait till it gets a bit cooler!' Then I gave him the call a third time, and this time he said: 'Wait till it gets a bit cooler—till you can see the

[158] Bilāl al-Ḥabashī, an Abyssinian slave who had been ransomed by Abū Bakr (may Allāh be well pleased with them both), was the first muezzin *[mu'adhdhin]* appointed by the Prophet (Allāh bless him and give him peace) to summon the Muslim community to the five daily prayers.

[159] For the words of the call to prayer *[adhān]*, see note 303 on p. 225 below.

afternoon shadow of the hills.' Then he went on to say: 'Extremely intense heat is caused by the festering pus of Hell [qaiḥ Jahannam], so whenever the heat becomes insufferably intense, you should all wait until the atmosphere gets cooler [before performing the midday prayer.'"

How to determine whether the sun has begun its decline from the meridian [zawāl]:

When the sun has reached the point where it comes to a momentary standstill,[160] we know that its decline is about to begin. As soon as it has in fact declined from the meridian, however slightly, the time pre-scribed for the midday prayer [waqt aẓ-ẓuhr] has arrived.

According to the Prophetic tradition [ḥadīth]:[161]

> When the sun has declined by the width of the strap of a sandal [shirāk], that is the beginning of the time prescribed for the midday prayer [waqt aẓ-ẓuhr]. Then, when the length of every shadow has become equal to the height of the corresponding object, it is the end of the time prescribed for the midday prayer, and the beginning of the time prescribed for the afternoon prayer [waqt al-'aṣr].

How to measure the length of the shadow caused by the sun:

If you wish to determine these moments exactly, you need to measure the length of the shadow caused by the sun. In order to make the necessary measurements, you should set up some kind of pillar or pole on a piece of open ground, making sure that it is perfectly straight and upright. Then you must draw a line to mark the point where the shadow ends. Then you must watch to see whether the shadow is getting shorter or longer. If you notice that it is getting shorter, you will realize that the sun is not yet in decline. If you notice that it is steady, neither extending itself nor shrinking, the reason can only be that the sun has reached its point of momentary standstill, exactly at the meridian. It is not

---

[160] This is a reference to the fact that the sun comes to a halt, when it reaches the center of the sky, and interrupts its progress for a brief moment. As Shaikh 'Abd al-Qādir al-Jīlānī (may Allāh be well pleased with him) has explained in Vol. 3, pp. 72–73:

> The expression ṣāma 'n-nahār [lit., the daytime has kept fast] may be used at the point of midday in summer, when the sun is at its height, and the shade has almost disappeared. In the words of the anonymous poet:
>
> > Until, when the day keeps fast [ṣāma 'n-nahār], having reached the point of noon,
> >   and gossamer threads [lu'āb] appear to fall, in the light of the summer sun....

[161] The use of this expression may suggest that the following statement (in the text above) is a paraphrase of the actual words attributed to the Prophet (Allāh bless him and give him peace) in the tradition [ḥadīth] quoted earlier. (See p. 114 above.)

permissible to perform the ritual prayer *[ṣalāt]* at that point in time.

As soon as the shadow starts to grow longer, that is a sure indication of the sun's decline *[zawāl]*. You must therefore measure the increase, and compare it with the height of the object you are using as your standard. When the increase in the length of the shadow coincides exactly with the height of the standard, that is the end of the time prescribed for the midday prayer *[waqt aẓ-ẓuhr]*. The slightest additional increase will mark the advent of the time prescribed for the afternoon prayer *[waqt al-ʿaṣr]*. This period will last until the shadow has lengthened by another distance equal to the height of the standard, at which point the time prescribed for the afternoon prayer *[waqt al-ʿaṣr]* will have come to its end. The remainder of the afternoon, until just before the setting of the sun, is called the time of dire necessity *[waqt aḍ-ḍarūra]*.[162]

Instead of using a pillar or post, you may use your own stature as your standard of measurement. You will have to mark the spot where your own shadow falls, then, if you see that it is getting shorter, you will know that the sun has not yet begun to decline. If you notice that the shadow is holding steady, will realize that the sun is poised at the meridian. If it starts to grow longer, the decline *[zawāl]* must be under way, [so you will realize that the time prescribed for the midday prayer *[waqt aẓ-ẓuhr]* has arrived].

When it comes to reckoning whether the length of your shadow is equal to your own stature and height, you need to know that your height is seven times the length of your own foot, not counting the length of the foot you are standing on. You should stand with your face toward the sun, then instruct some other person to mark the farthest point of your shadow with an unmistakable sign. Then you must measure the distance from your heel to that sign. If the distance between the two points is less than seven feet, apart from any shadow already caused by the sun at the moment of its decline, you will know for sure that you are within the time prescribed for the midday prayer *[waqt aẓ-ẓuhr]*, and that the time prescribed for the afternoon prayer *[waqt al-ʿaṣr]* has not yet arrived. But if the shadow has lengthened by more than seven feet, you will recognize the advent of the time prescribed for the afternoon prayer *[waqt al-ʿaṣr]*.

[162] In other words, it is a period during which the prayer may still be performed, but only as a last resort, provided that the worshipper can plead the excuse of dire necessity. As the author (may Allāh be well pleased with him) explains on p. 139 below, in connection with the time prescribed for the late evening prayer *[waqt al-ʿishāʾ al-ākhira]*, the period of true merit *[waqt al-faḍīla]* is followed by a similar period of excuse and dire necessity *[waqt al-ʿudhr wa 'ḍ-ḍarūra]*.

7.
Concerning the differing lengths of the shadows caused by the sun in winter and summer, and in various regions of the world.

In connection with our foregoing discussion, concerning the measurement of shadows by feet, and the setting up of pillars or posts, it is important to note the differing conditions that prevail in winter and in summer. Depending on the season, the shadow caused by the sun will be longer or shorter from one month to the next.

The progressive increase in shadow length takes place in the winter season, because the sun is then in a position diametrically opposite to the object that casts a shadow, since its progress is confined to the fringe of the sky, and it does not ascend into the upper reaches of the atmosphere.

The progressive decrease in shadow length takes place in the summer season, because it is then that the sun rises high into the atmosphere, to shine on terrestrial objects from an overhead position.

During the first phase of its ascent, the sun is rising from the edge of the sky, so it causes a lengthy shadow to be cast by any object facing its emerging disk. The higher it rises, the shorter the shadow becomes, until the sun reaches the end of its ascending journey, at which point it comes to a momentary halt in the middle of the sky, at the meridian or zenith *[kabid as-samā']*. Then the sun takes off on its "cruise *[sayarān]*," its descending journey toward its eventual setting in the west *[maghrib]*, and the shadow immediately starts to grow longer, for this is the point of decline from the meridian *[zawāl]*.

Just as it differs from season to season, so does the length of shadow vary from country to country and from town to town. In those areas that are situated directly beneath the center of the celestial sphere *[wasaṭ al-falak]*, like Mecca and its surrounding districts, any shadow caused by the sun is very slight indeed, to the point where the sun has no shadow at all. On the other hand, in regions that are remote from the center of the celestial sphere, like Khurāsān and its neighboring districts, the sun produces a very lengthy shadow in summer and winter alike.[163] As far as length of shadow is concerned, summer in such areas is just like winter elsewhere. Even in summer, at the point when the sun declines from the meridian, they may already have as much as one whole foot of shadow.

[163] The province of Khurāsān, on the borders of Iran, Afghanistan and Central Asia, must have seemed very remote and strange—almost "out of this world"—to the medieval inhabitants of Mecca or Baghdād.

8.
Concerning the length of the shadow, measured in feet, that is already cast, in each month of the solar year, at the point when the sun declines from the meridian.

According to the ancient scholars in this field of science, the minimum length of the shadow already cast, at the moment when the sun declines from the meridian, is two feet. That is at the summer solstice in the solar month of June *[Ḥazīrān]*.

The maximum length of the shadow already cast, at the moment of the sun's decline, is eight feet. That is at the winter solstice in the solar month of December *[Kānūn al-Awwal]*.

From September to September, the meridian shadow lengths are as follows:

- In September *[Aylūl]:* five feet.
- In October *[Tishrīn al-Awwal]:* six feet.
- In November *[Tishrīn al-Ākhir]:* seven feet.
- In December *[Kānūn al-Awwal]:* eight feet.

This brings us to the winter solstice, the point where the daytime is at its shortest, and the night at its longest.[164] An eight-foot shadow—the maximum for the entire year—is already cast at the moment when the sun declines from the meridian. Henceforth, the shadow decreases and the daytime increases. Thus:

- In January *[Kānūn al-Ākhir]:* seven feet.
- In February *[Shubāṭ]:* six feet.
- In March *[Ādhār]:* five feet.

This brings us to the vernal equinox, when the day and the night are exactly equal in duration.[165] Then:

164 According to modern works of reference, the winter solstice (in the northern hemisphere) occurs around December 22.

165 According to modern works of reference, the vernal equinox (in the northern hemisphere) occurs on March 20 or 21.

- In April *[Nīsān]*: four feet.
- In May *[Ayyār]*: three feet.
- In June *[Ḥazīrān]*: two feet.

This brings us to the summer solstice, the point where the daytime is at its longest, and the night at its shortest.[166] A two-foot shadow—the minimum for the entire year—is already cast at the moment when the sun declines from the meridian. The daytime lasts for fifteen hours, while the night lasts for nine hours. Then:

- In July *[Tammūz]*: three feet.
- In August *[Āb]*: four feet.
- In September *[Aylūl]*: five feet.

This bring us to the autumnal equinox, when the night and the day are exactly equal in duration.[167]

Sufyān ath-Thawrī[168] (may Allāh bestow His mercy upon him) is reported as having said:

"The maximum length of the shadow already cast, at the point when the sun declines from the meridian, is seven feet."

According to a traditional report, it was ʿAbdu'llāh ibn Masʿūd[169] (may Allāh be well pleased with him) who said:

"In the summer season, our performance of the midday prayer *[ṣalāt aẓ-ẓuhr]*, in the company of Allāh's Messenger (Allāh bless him and give him peace), would take place when the shadow was from three feet to five feet in length. In the winter season, it would take place when the shadow was from five feet to six feet in length."

[166] According to modern works of reference, the summer solstice (in the northern hemisphere) occurs around June 22.

[167] According to modern works of reference, the autumnal equinox (in the northern hemisphere) occurs on September 22 or 23.

[168] Abū ʿAbdi'llāh Sufyān ibn Saʿīd ath-Thawrī (may Allāh bestow His mercy upon him) was born in Kūfa in A.H. 97/715 C.E. He founded a school of Islāmic jurisprudence *[fiqh]* which survived for about two centuries after his death in Baṣra in A.H. 161/778 C.E.

[169] Abū ʿAbd ar-Raḥmān ʿAbdu'llāh ibn Masʿūd al-Hudhalī (may Allāh be well pleased with him) was one of the earliest and closest Companions of the Prophet (Allāh bless him and give him peace). A man of lowly antecedents, he became an authority on the recitation and interpretation of the Qurʾān, and an expert on Islamic law and the Prophetic tradition. He died in A.H. 32 or 33.

9.
Concerning a somewhat different view of this matter, adopted by certain experts in astronomy.

Certain experts in astronomy have stated these facts and figures in somewhat different terms, as follows:

On the nineteenth day of March *[Ādhār]*, the sun declines from the meridian when the shadow cast by a human being is three feet in length.[170] The same principle applies to any object a person may set up for the purpose of measurement, so that, at the moment when the sun declines on that day, the length of the shadow cast by the object will be equal to three sevenths of its height.

The length of the shadow will thenceforth decrease, at the rate of one foot for every thirty-six days that pass, until the summer solstice is reached on the nineteenth of June *[Ḥazīrān]*,[171] at which point the daytime is at its longest, and the night at its shortest. On that day, the sun will decline from the meridian when the shadow cast by a human being is one half of a foot in length.

From that point on, the length of the shadow will increase, at the rate of one foot for every thirty-six days that pass, until the autumnal equinox is reached on the nineteenth day of September *[Aylūl]*.[172] On that day, the sun will decline from the meridian when the shadow cast by a human being is three feet in length.

The length of the shadow will then continue to increase, but now at the rate of one foot for every fourteen days, until the winter solstice is reached on the nineteenth day of December *[Kānūn al-Awwal]*,[173] at which point the night is at its longest, and the daytime at its shortest.

[170] That is to say, three times the length of the actual foot of the individual concerned. (See p. 123 above.)

[171] See note 166 on p. 127 above.

[172] See note 167 on p. 127 above.

[173] See note 164 on p. 126 above.

On that day, the sun will decline from the meridian when the shadow cast by a human being is seven and a half feet in length. This is the maximum length attained by the meridian shadow.

Thenceforth, with every fourteen days that pass, the length of the shadow will decrease by one foot, until the vernal equinox is reached on the nineteenth day of March *[Ādhār]*.[174] On that day, the sun will decline from the meridian when the shadow cast by a human being is three feet in length.[175] This point marks the sun's entry into the spring season.

As we have mentioned above, the rate of increase or decrease in the length of the shadow is one foot for every thirty-six days in the seasons of spring and summer, and one foot for every fourteen days in the seasons of autumn and winter.

[174] See note 165 on p. 126 above.

[175] That is to say, three times the length of the actual foot of the individual concerned. (See p. 123 above.)

10.
Concerning yet another view of this matter, suggested by one of our own Shaikhs.

The following tabulation represents the view of this matter preferred by one of our own Shaikhs. For each of the solar months, he lists the length of the shadow cast by a human being: (a) at the beginning of the time prescribed for the midday prayer *[waqt aẓ-ẓuhr]*, and (b) at the beginning of the time prescribed for the afternoon prayer *[waqt al-ʿaṣr]*. The length of the shadow is measured in feet, on the understanding that one foot is equal to one seventh of [the height of] any given individual, standing in an upright posture. It should also be noted that, in each case, the figures apply to the whole of the month concerned.

Month:	Midday	Afternoon
June *[Ḥazīrān]*:	3 ft.	9 ft.
July *[Tammūz]*:	4 ft.	8 ft.
August *[Āb]*:	5 ft.	10 ft.
September *[Aylūl]*:	6 ft.	12 ft.
October *[Tishrīn al-Awwal]*:	7 ft.	13 ft.
November *[Tishrīn al-Ākhir]*:	8 ft.	14 ft.
December *[Kānūn al-Awwal]*:	10 ft.	17 ft.
January *[Kānūn ath-Thānī]*:[176]	9 ft.	15 ft.
February *[Shubāṭ]*:	7 ft.	14 ft.
March *[Ādhār]*:	6 ft.	12 ft.
April *[Nīsān]*:	4 ft.	11 ft.
May *[Ayyār]*:	3 ft.	10 ft.

[176] *Kānūn ath-Thānī* [January] is also known as *Kānūn al-Ākhir*.

These figures represent the distances by which the sun declines from the meridian during each of the months of the year. Allāh knows best, of course, for His knowledge goes beyond the reach of our perception, and transcends the limited scope of our sciences.

11.
Concerning the permissibility of using less objective methods in order to ascertain whether the sun has declined from the meridian.

In order to determine the moment of the sun's decline from the meridian *[zawāl]*, it is by no means absolutely necessary to apply the methods and definitive calculations described above. They represent only one of several valid approaches to ascertaining the point of decline, and not everyone is in a position to adopt that particular approach. The crux of the matter is simply this: Whenever someone is reasonably persuaded and convinced of the sun's decline from the meridian *[ghalaba ʿalā zanni-hi wa yaqīn-hi zawālu 'sh-shams]*, it is incumbent upon that person to perform the midday prayer *[ṣalāt az-zuhr]*.

In relation to the prescribed times *[awqāt]*, people fall into three distinct categories:

a. Those for whom certainty is a strict obligation *[farḍu-hu 'l-yaqīn]*. If a person belongs within this category, it means that he is familiar with the minutes and the hours, and with the movement of the stars. With this knowledge at his disposal, he is able to determine the exact time with certainty.

b. Those for whom it is a strict obligation either to exercise their independent judgment *[ijtihād]*,[177] by making the necessary calculations on the basis of their own practical experience, or to follow the example *[taqlīd]* set by someone who makes the required effort.

Included in this category are craftsmen who lack objective knowledge of the times of day. If they are to exercise their independent judgment, they must therefore base their calculations on the experience obtained in the practice of their craft. For example, a baker will know from

[177] As a technical term of Islāmic jurisprudence, *ijtihād* means the effort made by a qualified expert to reach an independent judgment on a point of law, through the interpretation and application of the four basic sources or principles *[uṣūl]*, namely the Qur'ān, the Sunna, the consensus *[ijmāʿ]* of the recognized authorities, and deduction by analogy *[qiyās]*. A person qualified to exercise *ijtihād* is called a *mujtahid*.

experience that he normally bakes two or three batches of kneaded dough in the time before noon; or a miller will know that it usually takes him till around noon to grind a bushel *[qafīz]* of grain. He will therefore take advantage of the break before his next round of work, and duly perform the ritual prayer.

Just as it is hard for anyone to ascertain the time on a day when the sky is overcast, due to the sun's invisibility, there may be special circumstances in which a person is prevented from watching the time, or is too busily preoccupied to do so.

People in this category may sometimes have another option, namely, to perform the ritual prayer *[ṣalāt]* in response to the call to prayer *[adhān]*, provided that the call is given by someone who has expert knowledge of the prescribed times, or at least by someone who would not give the call without the permission of such an expert.

c. Those for whom it is a strict obligation to consult their intuitive sense of what is right and proper *[at-taḥarrī]*, and to delay their performance of the prayer until they feel reasonably sure that the prescribed time has indeed arrived. This applies to anyone who finds himself in an underground situation, and to all those who are confined or imprisoned in places where it is impossible to ascertain the time, whether by external indication, reported information, or the sound of the call to prayer *[adhān]*.[178]

To establish the guiding principle in all of this, let us quote the saying of the Prophet (Allāh bless him and give him peace):

> Whenever I give you an order, you must carry it out to the best of your ability.

[178] See note 303 on p. 225 below.

12.
Concerning the subtle and difficult nature of the task of ascertaining the precise moment of the sun's decline from the meridian *[maʿrifat az-zawāl bi't-taḥqīq]*.

It is indeed a subtle and difficult task, to ascertain with precision the moment of the sun's decline from the meridian *[maʿrifat az-zawāl bi't-taḥqīq]*. This is clearly conveyed to us in the tradition *[ḥadīth]*, according to which the Prophet (Allāh bless him and give him peace) once asked Gabriel (peace be upon him): "Has the sun declined from the meridian?" He received the answer: "No..., yes," so he said: "How can that be?" and Gabriel (peace be upon him) explained: "In the time it took for me to say to you: 'No..., yes,' the sun covered a distance of fifty thousand leagues *[farsakh]*[179] in its orbit across the celestial sphere."

It would seem that the Prophet (Allāh bless him and give him peace) was asking Gabriel (peace be upon him) about the sun's decline *[zawāl]* with respect to the knowledge *[ʿilm]* of Allāh (Exalted is He). For your own practical purposes, however, you will find the following guidelines sufficient:

If you are facing the *Qibla* [the direction of the Kaʿba],[180] on a day in the summer season, and the sun is over your right eyebrow, it has already declined from the meridian, without a doubt. You should therefore perform the midday prayer *[fa-ṣalli 'ẓ-ẓuhr]*.

If the shadow cast by every object has reached the point where it is equal in length to the height of the corresponding object, you know for sure that the time prescribed for the afternoon prayer *[waqt al-ʿaṣr]* has arrived.

[179] According to the classical Arabic lexicographers, the *farsakh* [parasang, or league] is three miles of the Hāshimī measure, i.e. thirty bow-shots reckoning the bow-shot as four hundred cubits, or sixty bow-shots reckoning the bow shot as two hundred cubits. (See E.W. Lane, *Arabic-English Lexicon*, art. *F-R-S-KH*.)

[180] See note 152 on p. 118 above.

If the sun is over your left eyebrow, again in the summer season, while you are facing the *Qibla*, you must be aware that the sun has not yet declined from the meridian.

If the sun is directly between your eyes, it has reached the point where it comes to a momentary halt in the middle of the sky, at the meridian or zenith *[kabid as-samā']*. It may actually have begun its decline, if this happens at the beginning of the winter season, when the daytime is growing shorter.

If the winter season has begun, and the sun is over your right eyebrow, it has definitely declined from the meridian. This is true at all times of the year, because, when this happens in the summer season, it marks the beginning of the time prescribed for the midday prayer *[waqt aẓ-ẓuhr]*, and if it happens in the winter season, it marks the end of the time prescribed for the midday prayer.

If the sun is over your left eyebrow, this may also mean that it has already declined from the meridian, on account of the shortening of the daytime in the winter season. It is not possible at the beginning of the summer season, however, on account of the extension that then occurs in the length of the daytime.

If the sun is directly between your eyes, in the winter season, it must have declined from the meridian, without a doubt.

If the sun has moved over to the point where it appears above your right eyebrow, again in the winter season, this marks the end of the time prescribed for the midday prayer *[waqt aẓ-ẓuhr]*.

All of the foregoing information is relevant to the inhabitants of the geographical zone of 'Irāq and Khurāsān,[181] who perform their prayers while facing the Ka'ba in the direction of the Black Corner *[ar-Rukn al-Aswad]*[182] and the door of the House [of Allāh]. As for the people of Yemen *[al-Yaman]* and the West *[al-Maghrib]*, and those who inhabit the neighboring regions, the opposite holds true in their case, since they perform their prayers while facing toward the Yamānī Corner *[ar-Rukn al-Yamānī]* and the rear part of the Ka'ba. The calculations must differ accordingly.

[181] See note 163 on p. 125 above.

[182] The Black Corner *[ar-Rukn al-Aswad]*, which is sometimes called the Corner of the House *[Rukn al-Bait]*, is the angle of the Ka'ba in which the Black Stone *[ar-Ḥajar al-Aswad]* is lodged.

13.
On how to identify the *Qibla,* once you have ascertained the sun's decline from the meridian *[zawāl]*.

Once you have ascertained the sun's decline from the meridian *[zawāl]*, and wish to identify the *Qibla*[183] [direction of the Kaʿba], you must cast your shadow to your left, for then you will be facing toward the *Qibla*.

You will be relieved to know that this can be summed up so neatly, and that it can be learned without laborious effort. If I went on at such great length, in discussing the ascertainment of the sun's decline from the meridian *[zawāl]*, I only did so because it happens to be the most difficult and the most subtle of all the times prescribed for ritual prayer *[awqāt]*.

As for measuring the length of shadow in feet, this practice goes back to the time of the Prophet (Allāh bless him and give him peace), as we know from the traditional report *[khabar]*[184] of Ibn Masʿūd[185] (may Allāh be well pleased with him). We may conclude that the subject has received a sufficiently thorough explanation in the preceding pages, though we must acknowledge that Allāh knows best.

[183] See note 152 on p. 118 above.

[184] See note 142 on p. 112 above.

[185] See note 169 on p. 127 above.

14.
Concerning the time prescribed for the afternoon prayer *[waqt al-ʿaṣr]*.

As for the time prescribed for the afternoon prayer *[waqt al-ʿaṣr]*, it begins, as we have mentioned above, as soon as there is the slightest increase in the length of shadow, beyond the point where the shadow is equal in length to the height of the person or object by which it is cast. The end of its prescribed time is reached when the shadow has come to be twice as long as the corresponding object. As we have also mentioned above, the remainder of the afternoon, until just before the setting of the sun, is called the time of dire necessity *[waqt aḍ-ḍarūra]*.[186]

The most meritorious approach is to perform the afternoon prayer *[ṣalāt al-ʿaṣr]* with the least possible delay.

[186] See note 162 on p. 123 above.

15.
Concerning the time prescribed for the sunset prayer *[waqt al-maghrib]*.

As far the sunset prayer *[ṣalāt al-maghrib]* is concerned, once the sun has set *[gharabat ash-shams]*, that is to say, as soon the tip of the sun's eyebrow has sunk out of sight, its prescribed time has arrived.

It actually has two prescribed times, of course, [to mark both the beginning and the end of the period allowed for its performance]. One of these is the setting *[ghurūb]* of the sun, and the other is the final disappearance of the sun's afterglow *[shafaq]*. The latter refers to the lingering redness *[ḥumra]* in the western sky, according to the more authentic of the two traditionally reported doctrines *[aṣaḥḥ ar-riwāyatain]*.

16.
Concerning the time prescribed for the late evening prayer *[waqt al-ʿishāʾ al-ākhira]*.

As soon as the sun's final reddish afterglow *[shafaq]* has disappeared completely, the beginning of the time prescribed for the late evening prayer *[waqt al-ʿishāʾ al-ākhira]* has definitely arrived. Within the whole of the time allowed for its performance, the period of true merit *[waqt al-faḍīla]* lasts until one third of the night has elapsed, according to one of the two traditionally reported doctrines on the subject. According to the other version, it lasts until halfway through the night *[niṣf al-lail]*. The period of true merit *[waqt al-faḍīla]* is then followed by the period of excuse and dire necessity *[waqt al-ʿudhr wa 'ḍ-ḍarūra]*,[187] which remains in effect as long as the second dawn *[al-fajr ath-thānī]*[188] has not yet risen into view.

The time prescribed for this prayer has two Arabic names, one of them being *ʿatama* [the first third of the night, after the disappearance of the sun's reddish afterglow], while the other is *al-ʿishāʾ al-ākhira* [the late evening]. We know this because the Prophet (Allāh bless him and give him peace) once said:

> The Arabs of the desert *[al-Aʿrāb]* have gained the upperhand over you, as far as the name of this particular prayer *[ṣalāt]* of yours is concerned, since *ʿatama* is what they call it.

In other words, its proper name was *al-ʿishāʾ al-ākhira*, but the Arabs of the desert insisted on calling it *ʿatama*, so the townspeople came into line with them in this respect.

The most meritorious approach is to delay its performance until toward the latter part of its prescribed time, which may mean either the

[187] That is to say, the period of true merit *[waqt al-faḍīla]* is followed by an additional period, during which the prayer may still be performed, as a last resort, provided that the worshipper can plead the excuse of dire necessity. (For a similar period of dire necessity *[waqt aḍ-ḍarūra]*, following the time prescribed for the afternoon prayer *[waqt al-ʿaṣr]*, see p. 137 above.)

[188] For precise definitions of the second dawn *[al-fajr ath-thānī]*, which is also known as the true dawn *[al-fajr aṣ-ṣādiq]*, see p. 118 above.

end of the first third of the night, or the end of the first half of the night, as we have explained above.

To be even more precise, the best time to perform this prayer is when the western twilight *[al-bayāḍ al-gharbī]* has entirely disappeared, and pitch blackness has taken its place. (The technical term for the final glimmer of twilight is "the second reddish afterglow *[ash-shafaq ath-thānī]*.") In order to meet this requirement, the prayer may have to be postponed until one fourth of the night has elapsed, or one third, or one half.

All of this hinges on one important condition, namely, that the worshipper *[muṣallī]* must not go to sleep before performing the prayer, for it is considered reprehensible to let sleep intervene as the cause of its postponement. So, if the worshipper has reason to fear the irresistible onset of slumber, his best course is to perform the prayer at once, and then go off to sleep. This explains why, according to the doctrine of Imām al-Shāfi'ī[190] (may Allāh bestow His mercy upon him), it is preferable to perform the [late evening] prayer at the beginning of its prescribed time. When we [of the Ḥanbalī school] maintain that the most meritorious approach is to delay its performance, we do so because the Prophet (Allāh bless him and give him peace) once said:

> Perform the late prayer late *[a'timū bi'l-'atama]*!

We also know that he went out one night [to perform the prayer in the mosque], when it was very late and totally dark *[qad a'tama]*, and that he then said (Allāh bless him and give him peace):

> If it had not meant imposing undue hardship upon my Community, I would have commanded them to perform it [as I have just done].

It is clear, therefore, that the Prophet (Allāh bless him and give him peace) not only delayed his own performance of this prayer, but also encouraged others to postpone their performance of it.

[190] Imām Abū 'Abdi'llāh Muḥammad ibn Idrīs ash-Shāfi'ī (may Allāh bestow His mercy upon him) was the founder of one of the four schools *[madhāhib]* of Islamic jurisprudence. He died in the year A.H. 204/820 C.E. Imām al-Ghazālī (may Allāh bestow His mercy upon him) was one of the most notable professors of the Shāfi'ī school.

17.
Concerning the established customary observances *[as-sunan ar-rātiba]* that are regularly performed in conjunction with these five daily prayers *[aṣ-ṣalawāt al-khams]*.

As for the established customary observances *[as-sunan ar-rātiba]* that are regularly performed in conjunction with these five obligatory daily prayers *[aṣ-ṣalawāt al-khams]*, they consist of thirteen cycles *[rak'a]* of ritual prayer, distributed as follows:

a. Two cycles of voluntary ritual prayer performed before the obligatory dawn prayer *[rak'atān qabla 'l-fajr]*.[191]

b. Two cycles of voluntary ritual prayer performed before the obligatory midday prayer *[rak'atān qabla 'ẓ-ẓuhr]*.[192]

c. Two cycles of voluntary ritual prayer performed after the obligatory midday prayer *[rak'atān ba'da 'ẓ-ẓuhr]*.

d. Two cycles of voluntary ritual prayer performed after the obligatory sunset prayer *[rak'atān ba'da 'l-maghrib]*.[193]

e. Two cycles of voluntary ritual prayer performed after the obligatory late evening prayer *[rak'atān ba'da 'l-'ishā' al-ākhira]*.[194]

f. Three cycles of the odd-numbered ritual prayer called *witr*.[195] In performing this voluntary prayer, the worshipper has two options: If he so wishes, he may perform it with a single salutation *[taslīma]*[196]

[191] For a detailed account of the dawn prayer *[ṣalāt al-fajr]*, the first of the five obligatory daily prayers (which is also known as *ṣalāt aṣ-ṣubḥ* [the prayer of daybreak]), see pp. 110 and 118–20 above.

[192] For a detailed account of the midday prayer *[ṣalāt aẓ-ẓuhr]*, the second of the five obligatory daily prayers, see pp. 110 and 118–20 above.

[193] For a detailed account of the sunset prayer *[ṣalāt al-maghrib]*, the fourth of the five obligatory daily prayers, see pp. 110 and 118–20 above.

[194] For a detailed account of the late evening prayer *[ṣalāt al-'ishā' al-ākhira]*, the last of the five obligatory daily prayers (which is also known as *ṣalāt al-'atama* [the prayer of the first third of the night, after the disappearance of the sun's reddish afterglow]), see pp. 110 and 118–20 above.

[195] See note 50 on p. 42 above.

[196] The term *taslīma* [salutation] is applied to the act of turning the head to the right and saying: "*as-salāmu 'alaikum wa raḥmatu'llāh* [Peace be upon you, and the mercy of Allāh]," then turning the head to the left and repeating these same words.

[at the end of the third cycle], as in the case of the sunset prayer *[ṣalāt al-maghrib]*. If he prefers, he may split it into two parts, making one salutation *[taslīma]* after two cycles, and another after the single cycle that concludes the *witr*. There is greater merit in choosing the second of these two options.

In the first of the three [cycles of the *witr* prayer], the worshipper should follow his recitation of the Opening Sūra of the Qur'ān *[al-Fātiḥa]*[197] with the Sūra of the Most High *[Sūrat al-A'lā]*, which reads:

Glorify the Name	*sabbiḥi 'sma*
of your Lord the Most High	*Rabbi-ka 'l-A'lā*
who created, and then shaped,	*alladhī khalqa fa-sawwā*
and who determined, then guided;	*wa 'lladhī qaddara fa-hadā*
and who brought forth the pasturage,	*wa 'lladhī akhraja 'l-mar'ā*
then turned it	*fa-ja'ala-hu*
into rust-colored stubble.	*ghuthā'an aḥwā.*
We shall make you recite	*sa-nuqri'u-ka*
[O Muḥammad]	
so that you shall not forget	*fa-lā tansā*
save that which Allāh wills.	*illā mā shā'a 'llāh:*
He surely knows what is spoken aloud	*inna-hu ya'lamu 'l-jahra*
and that which is kept hidden;	*wa mā yakhfā*
and We shall ease your way	*wa nuyassiru-ka*
unto the state of ease.	*li'l-yusrā.*
Therefore remind,	*fa-dhakkir*
in case the reminder	*in nafa'ati 'dh-*
brings some benefit.	*dhikrā*
He who fears will remember,	*sa-yadhdhakkaru man yakhshā*
but the most wretched will flout it,	*wa yatajannabu 'l-ashqā*
he who will roast in the Great Fire,	*alladhī yaṣla 'n-nāra 'l-kubrā*
in which he then will	*thumma lā yamūtu*
neither die nor live.	*fī-hā wa lā yaḥyā.*
Successful is he who purifies	*qad aflaḥa man tazakkā*
himself, and remembers	*wa dhakara 'sma*
the Name of his Lord,	*Rabbi-hi.*
and then performs the prayer.	*fa-ṣallā*
But you prefer the life	*bal tu'thirūna 'l-ḥayāta 'd-*
of this lower world,	*dunyā*
although the Hereafter is better	*wa 'l-ākhiratu khairun*
and more lasting.	*wa abqā.*
Surely this is in the ancient scrolls:	*inna hādhā la-fi 'ṣ-Ṣuḥufi 'l-ūlā*
the scrolls of Abraham and Moses.	*Ṣuḥufi Ibrāhima wa Mūsā.*
(87:1–19)	

197 The recitation of the Opening Sūra of the Qur'ān *[al-Fātiḥa]* is an essential element *[rukn]* in every performance of the ritual prayer *[ṣalāt]*, which is rendered null and void by its omission.

In the second [cycle of the *witr* prayer], after *al-Fātiḥa,* he should recite the Sūra called "the Unbelievers" *[Sūrat al-Kāfirūn],* which reads:

Say: "O unbelievers,	*qul yā ayyuha 'l-kāfirūn*
I do not worship what you worship,	*lā aʿbudu mā taʿbudūn*
and you are not worshipping	*wa lā antum ʿābidūna*
that which I worship;	*mā aʿbud*
nor shall I worship	*wa lā ana ʿābidun*
what you have worshipped,	*mā ʿabadtum*
neither will you worship	*wa lā antum ʿābidūna*
that which I worship.	*mā aʿbud*
To you your religion,	*la-kum dīnu-kum*
and to me my religion!" (109:1–6)	*wa liya dīn.*

In the third [cycle of the *witr* prayer], again after *al-Fātiḥa,* he should recite the Sūra of Sincere Devotion *[Sūrat al-Ikhlāṣ],* which reads:

Say: "He is Allāh, One!	*qul Huwa 'llāhu Aḥad*
Allāh, the Everlasting Refuge!	*Allāhu 'ṣ-Ṣamad*
He does not beget,	*lam yalid*
nor was He begotten;	*wa lam yūlad*
and there is none	*wa lam yakun la-hu*
comparable unto Him." (112:1–4)	*kufuwan aḥad.*

In the first of the two cycles of the customary dawn prayer *[sunnat al-fajr],* after *al-Fātiḥa,* the worshipper should recite the Sūra called "the Unbelievers" *[Sūrat al-Kāfirūn],* then, in the second cycle, again after *al-Fātiḥa,* he should recite the Sūra of Sincere Devotion *[Sūrat al-Ikhlāṣ].* The worshipper is recommended to perform these two cycles of voluntary prayer in his private residence, and only then to go out [to join the congregation in the mosque]. He is also recommended to devote himself to the remembrance of Allāh (Exalted is He), and to refrain from any conversation that is not absolutely necessary, from the time of completing the two voluntary cycles until the moment when he embarks upon the performance of the prayer that is strictly obligatory *[farīḍa].*

In the two cycles [of customary prayer] after the obligatory sunset prayer *[ṣalāt al-maghrib],* the Qurʾānic recitation should be the same as in the two cycles preceding the obligatory dawn prayer *[ṣalāt al-fajr].*

Ibn ʿUmar (may Allāh be well pleased with him and with his father) is reported as having said:

"On more than twenty occasions, I heard Allāh's Messenger (Allāh bless him and give him peace) reciting:

'Say: "O unbelievers...,"'	*qul yā ayyuha 'l-kāfirūn...*

—and:

'Say: "He is Allāh, One!..."'	*qul Huwa 'llāhu Aḥad...*

—in the course of performing the two [cycles of customary prayer] after the obligatory sunset prayer *[ṣalāt al-maghrib]*."

In the case of Ṭāwūs (may Allāh bestow His mercy upon him), we know from a traditional report that he used to recite, in the first of the two cycles:

The Messenger believes in that which has been sent down to him from his Lord, and so do the believers.	*āmana 'r-Rasūlu bi-mā unzila ilai-hi wa 'l-muʾminūn:*
Each one believes in Allāh and His angels and His Books and His Messengers— we make no distinction between any of His Messengers—and they say: "We hear, and we obey."	*kullun āmana bi'llāhi wa malāʾikati-hi wa kutubi-hi wa rusulih: lā nufarriqu baina aḥadin min rusulih: wa qālū: samiʿnā wa aṭaʿnā.*
Grant us Your forgiveness, our Lord; and unto You is the homeward journey.	*ghufrāna-ka Rabba-nā wa ilai-ka 'l- maṣīr—*
Allāh does not charge any soul except to the extent of its capacity. To its credit is that which it has earned, and to its debit is what it has deserved.	*lā yukallifu 'llāhu nafsan illā wusʿa-hā: la-hā mā kasabat wa ʿalai-hā ma 'ktasabat:*
Our Lord, do not take us to task if we forget, or miss the mark.	*Rabbanā lā tuʾākhidh-nā in nasīnā aw akhṭaʾnā:*
Our Lord, do not lay upon us such a burden as You laid upon those before us.	*Rabbanā wa lā taḥmil ʿalai-nā iṣran ka-mā ḥamalta-hu ʿala 'lladhīna min qabli-nā:*
Our Lord, do not lay upon us more than we have the strength to bear.	*Rabbanā wa lā tuḥammil-nā mā lā ṭāqata la-nā bih:*
And pardon us, and forgive us, and have mercy on us. You are our Protector, so help us against the people of the unbelievers. (2:285–6)	*wa ' ʿfu ʿan-nā wa 'ghfir la-nā wa 'rḥam-nā: Anta Mawlā-nā fa-'nṣur-nā ʿala 'l-qawmi 'l-kāfirīn.*

—and in the second cycle:

Say: "He is Allāh, One!..."	*qul Huwa 'llāhu Aḥad...*

The worshipper is strongly recommended to perform these two cycles [of customary prayer] with the least possible delay, because, as we know from the traditional report transmitted on the authority of Ḥudhaifa (may Allāh be well pleased with him), the Prophet (Allāh bless him and give him peace) once said:

> Waste no time in performing the two [voluntary] cycles after the sunset prayer *[ar-rak'atain ba'da 'l-maghrib]*, so that the angels may carry them up to heaven, together with the prescribed prayer.

For the same reason, the worshipper is recommended to keep their performance fairly short.

In another tradition *[ḥadīth]*, the Prophet (Allāh bless him and give him peace) has told us:

> If someone performs two [voluntary] cycles after the sunset prayer *[ṣallā rak'atain ba'da 'l-maghrib]*, and before he has engaged in any talk, his prayer *[ṣalāt]* will be carried aloft to the uppermost heaven *['Illiyyūn]*.[199]

There is also evidence to support the view that it is commendable to prolong the performance of these two [voluntary cycles after the obligatory sunset prayer], inasmuch as Ibn 'Abbās (may Allāh be well pleased with him and with his father) is reported as having said:

"Allāh's Messenger (Allāh bless him and give him peace) used to prolong the Qur'ānic recitation in the two voluntary cycles after the sunset prayer, to the point where the people in attendance at the mosque would all have dispersed to their homes."

We have a similar account from Ḥudhaifa (may Allāh be well pleased with him), who is reported as having said:

"I once came [to the mosque] to join Allāh's Messenger (Allāh bless him and give him peace), and I performed the sunset prayer *[ṣallaitu ṣalāta 'l-maghrib]* together with him. He then proceeded to perform the voluntary prayer, until the time prescribed for the obligatory late evening prayer *[al-'ishā' al-ākhira]*. Then he left the mosque and went back to his house."

There is also traditional evidence to suggest that the commendable course is for the worshipper to perform these two [voluntary cycles after the sunset prayer] in his private residence.

[199] In the words of Allāh (Almighty and Glorious is He):

> The register of the righteous is in *'Illiyyūn*. Ah, what will convey to you what *'Illiyyūn* is? A written record, attested to by those who are brought near [unto their Lord] (83:18–21).

For instance, ʿĀʾisha (may Allāh be well pleased with her) is reported as having said that [her husband] the Prophet (Allāh bless him and give him peace) used to perform the two voluntary cycles after the sunset prayer *[baʿda 'l-maghrib]* in his own apartment. A similar report has come down to us from Umm Ḥabība[200] (may Allāh be well pleased with her).

Ibn ʿUmar (may Allāh be well pleased with him and with his father) is reported as having said:

"Allāh's Messenger (Allāh bless him and give him peace) would never perform the two voluntary cycles after the sunset prayer *[baʿda 'l-maghrib]*, except in his own apartment."

Let us give the last word on this subject to Sahl ibn Saʿd as-Sāʿidī (may Allāh be well pleased with him), who is reported as having said:

"By the time I had attained to manhood, I found myself living in the age of [the Caliph] ʿUthmān ibn ʿAffān (may Allāh be well pleased with him), and I noticed that, as soon as the obligatory sunset prayer had ended with the salutation *[taslīma]*,[201] there would not be one single member of the congregation performing the two—meaning the two voluntary cycles after the sunset prayer *[ar-rakʿatain baʿda 'l-maghrib]*—in the mosque *[masjid]*. They would all be jostling toward the door of the mosque, departing in haste to perform the customary prayer in their own homes."

[200] Like ʿĀʾisha, Umm Ḥabība (may Allāh be well pleased with them both) is revered as one of the "Mothers of the Believers *[Ummahāt al-Muʾminīn]*," the wives of the Prophet (Allāh bless him and give him peace).

[201] See note 196 on p. 141 above.

18. Concerning the special qualities of the five daily prayers *[aṣ-ṣalawāt al-khams]*.

According to a traditional report transmitted by Abū Salama ibn ʿAbd ar-Raḥmān, on the authority of Abū Huraira (may Allāh be well pleased with him), Allāh's Messenger (Allāh bless him and give him peace) once said:

> If one of you had a stream flowing by his door, in which he bathed himself five times every day, do you suppose that any trace of his physical dirt would be left behind?

"No!" was the unanimous response, so he went on to say:

> Well, that is just how it is in the case of the five daily prayers *[aṣ-ṣalawāt al-khams]*. Allāh (Exalted is He) uses them to wipe away sins.

Abū Thaʿlaba al-Quraẓī is reported as having said: "I heard [the Caliph] ʿUmar ibn al-Khaṭṭāb (may Allāh be well pleased with him) say: 'Allāh's Messenger (Allāh bless him and give him peace) once said:

> ""They [the sinners] feel the scorching heat, but then, when they perform the prayer of daybreak *[ṣallaw aṣ-subḥ]*, the prayer *[ṣalāt]* washes off whatever sin preceded it. Then they feel the scorching heat again, until they perform the midday prayer *[ṣallaw aẓ-ẓuhr]*, and the prayer *[ṣalāt]* washes off whatever sin preceded it. Then they feel the scorching heat yet again, until the time of the afternoon prayer *[ṣalāt al-ʿaṣr]* is at hand, so they perform it, and the prayer washes off whatever sin preceded it."

"'The Prophet (Allāh bless him and give him peace) continued in this vein, until he had mentioned each of the five daily prayers *[aṣ-ṣalawāt al-khams]*.'"

Al-Ḥarth, the freedman *[mawlā]* of ʿUthmān ibn ʿAffān, (may Allāh bestow His mercy upon him), is reported as having said:

"On one occasion, [the Caliph] ʿUthmān ibn ʿAffān (may Allāh be well pleased with him) had taken his seat, then called for some water and used it to perform his ritual ablution. Then he said: 'I saw Allāh's

Messenger (Allāh bless him and give him peace) perform this ritual ablution of mine *[tawaḍḍa'a wuḍū'ī hādhā]*.'[202]

"Then he went on to say: 'So, if anyone else performs this ritual ablution of mine, then duly proceeds to perform the midday prayer *[ṣalla'ẓ-ẓuhr]*, he will be granted forgiveness for whatever sins he may have committed between that point and the prayer of daybreak *[ṣalāt aṣ-subḥ]*.

"'Then, if he duly proceeds to perform the afternoon prayer *[ṣalla 'l-'aṣr]*, he will be granted forgiveness for whatever sins he may have committed between that point and the midday prayer *[ṣalāt aẓ-ẓuhr]*.

"'Then, if he duly proceeds to perform the sunset prayer *[ṣalla 'l-maghrib]*, he will be granted forgiveness for whatever sins he may have committed between that point and the afternoon prayer *[ṣalāt al-'aṣr]*.

"'Then, if he duly proceeds to perform the late evening prayer *[ṣalla 'l-'ishā' al-ākhira]*, he will be granted forgiveness for whatever sins he may have committed between that point and the sunset prayer *[ṣalāt al-maghrib]*. Then maybe he will go to bed and spend his night tossing and turning.

"'Then, if he duly proceeds to perform the daybreak prayer *[ṣalla 'ṣ-ṣubḥ]*, he will be granted forgiveness for whatever sins he may have committed between that point and the late evening prayer *[ṣalāt al-'ishā' al-ākhira]*. For:

Surely the good deeds will drive away the evil deeds. (11:114)'	*inna 'l-ḥasanāti* *yudhhibna 's-sayyi'āt.*

"His listeners then said to him: 'So, these [five daily prayers] are the "good deeds *[ḥasanāt]*," but what are the "abiding deeds of righteousness *[al-bāqiyātu 'ṣ-ṣāliḥāt]*?"[203] To this he replied: 'They are the affirmations:

• Glory be to Allāh!	*subḥāna 'llāh!*
• Praise be to Allāh!	*al-ḥamdu li'llāh!*
• There is no god but Allāh!	*la ilāhā illa 'llāh!*
• Allāh is Supremely Great!	*Allāhu Akbar!*
• There is no power, nor is there any strength, except through Allāh, the All-High, the Almighty!	*lā ḥawla* *wa lā quwwata* *illā bi'llāhi 'l-* *'Aliyyi 'l-'Aẓīm!* '"

[202] The verb *tawaḍḍa'a* and the noun *wuḍū'* are both derived from the three-consonant root *w–ḍ–'*. The ablution called *wuḍū'* is actually the minor ritual cleansing, as distinguished from *ghusl*, the major ritual cleansing, which requires the washing of the whole body.

[203] Allāh (Almighty and Glorious is He) has spoken of "the abiding deeds of righteousness *[al-bāqiyātu 'ṣ-ṣāliḥāt]*" in Q. 18:46 and 19:76.

According to a traditional report from Jaʿfar ibn Muḥammad, his father told him that his grandfather (may Allāh be well pleased with him) once told him that Allāh's Messenger (Allāh bless him and give him peace) had said:

> The ritual prayer *[ṣalāt]* is the means of pleasing the Lord and the angels *[marḍāt ar-Rabb wa 'l-malā'ika]*; the exemplary custom of the Prophets *[sunnat al-Anbiyā']* (may Allāh's blessings be upon them all); the light of spiritual experience *[maʿrifa]* and the root of faith *[īmān]*; the response to supplication and the acceptance of good deeds; a blessing upon sustenance; the comfort of physical bodies; a weapon against hostile forces; the means of displeasing the Devil *[Shaiṭān]*; an intercessor between the worshipper and the Owner of the Heavens *[Mālik as-Samāwāt]*; a lamp in his tomb and a cushion beneath his side; his response to Munkar and Nakīr;[204] and a friendly companion to visit with him in his tomb, until the Day of Resurrection *[Yawm al-Qiyāma]*.
>
> Then, when the Day of Resurrection has arrived, the ritual prayer *[ṣalāt]* will be a cooling shade above him, a crown upon his head, a garment upon his body, a guiding light in front of him, a screen between him and the Fire of Hell, the proof in the presence of the Lord (Almighty and Glorious is He) that he is one of the true believers *[mu'minīn]*, a weight in the Balance *[al-Mīzān]*,[205] a passport across the Bridge over Hell *[aṣ-Ṣirāṭ]*,[206] and a key to the Garden of Paradise.
>
> This is all because the ritual prayer *[ṣalāt]* is a glorification of the Lord *[tasbīḥ]*,[207] a declaration that all praise belongs to Him *[taḥmīd]*,[208] a proclamation of His Sanctity *[taqdīs]*,[209] an exaltation of His Might and Majesty *[taʿẓīm]*,[210] a recitation of His Book *[qirā'a]*,[211] and a personal supplication *[duʿā']*. The most meritorious of all good deeds is surely the ritual prayer, duly performed at the time prescribed for it *[aṣ-ṣalāt li-waqti-hā]*.

[204] Munkar and Nakīr are the two angels charged with the interrogation of the dead. Their names do not occur in the Qur'ān, but they are mentioned in a saying of the Prophet (Allāh bless him and give him peace), in which their work is described in some detail.

[205] For a detailed account of the Balance *[Mīzān]*, see Vol. 1, pp. 242–46.

[206] For a minutely detailed description of the Bridge over Hell *[aṣ-Ṣirāṭ]*, in a traditional account attributed to the Prophet (Allāh bless him and give him peace), see Vol. 2, p. 251.

[207] The verbal noun *tasbīḥ* is derived from the three-consonant root *s–b–ḥ*, which occurs in the expression "*subḥāna 'llāh* [Glory be to Allāh]!"

[208] The verbal noun *taḥmīd* is derived from the three-consonant root *ḥ–m–d*, which occurs in the expression "*al-ḥamdu li'llāh* [Praise be to Allāh]!" Also derived from this root are Muḥammad and Aḥmad, the names of the Prophet (Allāh bless him and give him peace), which mean "Highly Praised" and "Praiseworthy."

[209] The verbal noun *taqdīs* is derived from the three-consonant root *q–d–s*, which conveys the basic idea of "holiness, sanctity." The verb *taqaddasa* is used in the expression "*taqaddasa'llāh* [Sanctified is Allāh]!" This same root occurs in the words *Maqdis* and *Muqaddas*, which are applied to the Temple of Jerusalem.

[210] The verbal noun *taʿẓīm* is derived from the three-consonant root *ʿ–ẓ–m*, which occurs in *al-ʿAẓīm* [the Almighty; the Sublime], which is one of the Most Beautiful Names of Allāh (Exalted is He).

[211] The word *qirā'a* [reading; recitation] is derived from the same three-consonant root—*q–r–'*—as Qur'ān. In certain contexts, notably that of the ritual prayer, *qirā'a* means specifically "the recitation of the Qur'ān."

Ibn ʿUmar (may Allāh be well pleased with him and with his father) is reported as having said: "I once heard Allāh's Messenger (Allāh bless him and give him peace) say:

> 'The five daily prayers *[aṣ-ṣalawāt al-khams]* are the supporting pillar of the true religion *[ʿimād ad-dīn]*. Allāh does not accept faith *[īmān]* without the ritual prayer *[ṣalāt]*.'"

Anas ibn Mālik (may Allāh be well pleased with him) is reported as having said:

"A man once asked: 'O Messenger of Allāh, how many ritual prayers *[ṣalawāt]* has Allāh (Almighty and Glorious is He) enjoined upon His servants as obligatory religious duties?' When he received the reply: 'Five ritual prayers *[khams ṣalawāt]*,' the man went on to ask: 'And is there anything [obligatory] before them or after them?' So the Prophet (Allāh bless him and give him peace) told him:

> "'As obligatory religious duties, Allāh has enjoined upon His servants a total of five ritual prayers *[ṣalawāt khams]*. There is nothing [obligatory] before them or after them.'

"The man then swore by Allāh that he would perform all five, neither adding to them nor subtracting from them, whereupon Allāh's Messenger (Allāh bless him and give him peace) said: 'If he is true to his oath, he will enter the Garden of Paradise!'"

Tamīm ad-Dārī (may Allāh be well pleased with him) is reported as having said: "Allāh's Messenger (Allāh bless him and give him peace) once said:

> "'The first item for which the servant [of the Lord] will be called to account, on the Day of Resurrection *[Yawm al-Qiyāma]*, will be his performance of the obligatory ritual prayer *[ṣalāt]*. If he has carried it out completely, it will be recorded as perfect in his credit column. If he has not carried it out completely, Allāh (Almighty and Glorious is He) will say to the angels: "See if you can find any voluntary observances *[taṭawwuʿ]* to My servant's credit, then apply them in order to make up for what he has omitted in this area."'"

Anas ibn Ḥakīm aḍ-Ḍabīʾ is reported as having said: "Abū Huraira (may Allāh be well pleased with him) once said: "'When you get back home to your family, be sure to let them know that I heard Allāh's Messenger (Allāh bless him and give him peace) say:

> ""'The first item for which the servant [of the Lord] will be called to account, on the Day of Resurrection *[Yawm al-Qiyāma]*, will be his performance of the prescribed ritual prayer *[aṣ-ṣalāt al-maktūba]*. If he has carried it out completely,

> [well and good]. If not, an investigation will be undertaken [by the angels], and if he has any voluntary observances *[taṭawwuʿ]* to his credit, they will be applied in order to complete his record of obligatory performance *[farīḍa]*. The same procedure will then be followed when it comes to assessing his achievements in other spheres of duty.'""

Anas ibn Mālik (may Allāh be well pleased with him) is also reported as having said: "Allāh's Messenger (Allāh bless him and give him peace) once said:

> "'The first item for which the servant [of the Lord] will be called to account [on the Day of Resurrection] will be his performance of the ritual prayer *[ṣalāt]*, and the first obligatory religious duty to be enjoined upon this Community *[Umma]* by Allāh (Exalted is He) was none other than the ritual prayer *[ṣalāt]*.'"

19.
Concerning the practice of going out to the mosque *[masjid]*, the special merit of worshipping in congregation *[jamāʿa]*, and the virtue of a humble attitude toward the ritual prayer *[ṣalāt]*.

According to a traditional report transmitted by Nāfiʿ, on the authority of Ibn ʿUmar (may Allāh be well pleased with him and with his father), Allāh's Messenger (Allāh bless him and give him peace) once said:

> Between the ritual prayer performed in congregation *[ṣalāt al-jamāʿa]* and that performed individually *[al-fadhdh]*, the difference [on the scale of merit] is one of twenty-seven degrees.

According to a traditional report transmitted on the authority of Abū Huraira (may Allāh be well pleased with him), Allāh's Messenger (Allāh bless him and give him peace) also said:

> When the servant [of the Lord] performs his ritual ablution *[tawaḍḍaʾa]*, then goes out to join the congregation in the mosque *[masjid]*, for every step he takes, Allāh (Almighty and Glorious is He) records a good deed in his credit column, deletes a bad deed from his debit column, and raises his spiritual status by one degree. The welcome he receives from Allāh (Exalted is He) is just like the joyful welcome accorded to a long-absent relative, when he finally comes home to his family.

According to another traditional report, this one transmitted by Abū ʿUthmān an-Nahdī, on the authority of Salmān [al-Fārisī] (may Allāh be well pleased with him), Allāh's Messenger (Allāh bless him and give him peace) once said:

> Allāh (Almighty and Glorious is He) says: "When someone performs his ritual ablution *[tawaḍḍaʾa]* in his own house, and does his ablution really well *[aḥsana 'l-wuḍūʾ]*, then visits Me in one of My houses, he is coming to Me as a guest *[zāʾir]*, and it is a duty *[ḥaqq]* incumbent upon the host *[mazūr]* to offer his guest an honorable and generous reception."[212]

[212] This Divine Saying is a Sacred Tradition *[Ḥadīth Qudsī]*, not a verse *[āya]* of the Qurʾān.

According to yet another traditional report, this one transmitted on the authority of Sālim ibn ʿAbdi'llāh, [the Caliph] ʿUmar ibn al-Khaṭṭāb (may Allāh be well pleased with him) once said:

"Gabriel came to the Prophet (peace be upon them both) and said to him: 'To those who walk to the mosques *[masājid]* on foot, in the darkness of the night, you must convey the good news that they will be granted perfect light on the Day of Resurrection *[Yawm al-Qiyāma]*!'"

From a similar traditional report, this one transmitted on the authority of Abu'd-Dardā' (may Allāh be well pleased with him), we learn that the Prophet (Allāh bless him and give him peace) once said:

> If a person walks to the mosques *[masājid]* on foot, in the darkness of the night, Allāh (Exalted is He) will grant him light on the Day of Resurrection *[Yawm al-Qiyāma]*.

It is reported on the authority of Saʿīd al-Khudrī (may Allāh be well pleased with him) that he once heard Allāh's Messenger (Allāh bless him and give him peace) say:

> The ritual prayer performed in congregation *[ṣalāt al-jamāʿa]* is more meritorious, by twenty-five degrees, than the ritual prayer performed in private *[ṣalāt al-fadhdh]*.

According to a traditional report transmitted by Nāfiʿ, on the authority of Ibn ʿUmar (may Allāh be well pleased with him and with his father), Allāh's Messenger (Allāh bless him and give him peace) once said:[213]

> Between the ritual prayer performed in congregation *[ṣalāt al-jamāʿa]* and that performed individually *[al-fadhdh]*, the difference [on the scale of merit] is one of twenty-seven degrees.

From another traditional report, this one transmitted on the authority of Anas ibn Mālik (may Allāh be well pleased with him), we learn that Allāh's Messenger (Allāh bless him and give him peace) once said:

> O ʿUthmān ibn Maẓʿūn,[214] if someone performs the daybreak prayer as a member of a congregation *[ṣalla 'ṣ-ṣubḥ fī jamāʿa]*, he will be credited with a Pilgrimage *[Ḥijja]* that has been blessed, and a Visitation *[ʿUmra]* that is worthy of acceptance.[215]

[213] The author (may Allāh be well pleased with him) has already quoted this saying of the Prophet (Allāh bless him and give him peace) at the beginning of this subsection.

[214] ʿUthmān ibn Maẓʿūn should not be confused with the Caliph, ʿUthmān ibn ʿAffān, (may Allāh be well pleased with them both). The former was a talented poet, and a staunch supporter of the Prophet (Allāh bless him and give him peace).

[215] The term *Ḥijja* is applied to a specific performance of the *Ḥajj* [Pilgrimage]. For a full account of the rites of the *Ḥajj* [Pilgrimage] and the *ʿUmra* [Visitation; Lesser Pilgrimage], see Vol. 1, pp. 26–52.

> O ʿUthmān, if someone performs the midday prayer as a member of a congregation *[ṣalla 'ẓ-ẓuhr fī jamāʿa]*, he will be credited with twenty-five ritual prayers, each and every one of them just like it, and he will be awarded seventy degrees in the Garden of Paradise *[Jannat al-Firdaws]*.
>
> O ʿUthmān, if someone performs the afternoon prayer as a member of a congregation *[ṣalla 'l-ʿaṣr fī jamāʿa]*, then practices the remembrance of Allāh (Exalted is He) until the sun goes down, it will be to his credit as if he had emancipated a band of the offspring of Ishmael *[Ismāʿīl]* from slavery, together with twelve thousand others for every man amongst them.
>
> O ʿUthmān, if someone performs the sunset prayer as a member of a congregation *[ṣalla 'l-maghrib fī jamāʿa]*, he will be credited with twenty-five ritual prayers, each and every one of them just like it, and he will be awarded seventy degrees in the Garden of Eden *[Jannat ʿAdn]*.
>
> O ʿUthmān, if someone performs the late evening prayer as a member of a congregation *[ṣalla 'l-ʿishā' al-ākhira fī jamāʿa]*, it will be just as if he had kept vigil on the Night of Power *[Lailat al-Qadr]*.[216]

When a man sets out for the mosque *[masjid]*, he is strongly recommended to approach it with a feeling of dread, a sense of apprehension, and an attitude of humility and submissiveness. He is also recommended to maintain a bearing of calm serenity and solemn dignity. He should persuade himself that he needs to improve his patterns of thought and behavior, by detaching himself from his recent involvement in the conditions and concerns of this lower world. He should set out in a spirit of hope and fear, self-abasement, humility and contrition, free from vain conceit, arrogant pride, boastfulness, and the desire to impress other people and win the admiration of his fellow creatures. He should set out with the intention of turning himself in the direction of Allāh (Almighty and Glorious is He), by making his way to one of those houses of worship of His, which:

Allāh has allowed to be raised up,	*adhina 'llāhu an turfaʿa*
and in which [He has allowed]	*wa yudhkara*
His Name to be commemorated;	*fī-ha 'smu-hu*
glorifying Him therein,	*yusabbiḥu la-hu*
in the mornings and the evenings,	*fīhā bi'l-ghuduwwi wa 'l-āṣāl—*
are men whom neither commerce	*rijālun lā tulhī-him tijāratun*
nor trafficking diverts	*wa lā baiʿun*
from the remembrance of Allāh.	*an dhikri 'llāhi.*
(24:36,37)	

[216] For a detailed account of the practice of keeping vigil during the nights of the month of Ramaḍān, especially the Night of Power *[Lailat al-Qadr]*, see Vol. 3, pp. 126–35.

If the worshipper finds, on arriving at the mosque *[masjid]*, that the congregational prayer is already in progress, he must join the congregation in performing whatever remains of the ritual prayer *[mā adraka mina 'ṣ-ṣalāti ṣallā ma'a 'l-jamā'a]*. Then he must make up [separately] for what he has missed. This is in accordance with the tradition *[ḥadīth]* reported on the authority of Abū Huraira (may Allāh be well pleased with him), who stated that Allāh's Messenger (Allāh bless him and give him peace) once said:

> If one of you arrives when the ritual prayer has already begun *[qad uqīmati 'ṣ-ṣalāt]*, he should move forward unobtrusively [and join the ranks of the congregation]. He must perform as much of the congregational prayer as he is in time for, and then make up [separately] for the part that he has missed by arriving late.

In another version of this same tradition *[ḥadīth]*, the wording is:

> He should move forward with a bearing of calm serenity *[sakīna]* and solemn dignity *[waqār]*.

The worshipper must be on his guard against vain conceit, in case it should come to be his motive for extraordinary diligence and unremitting perseverance in the performance of acts of worship *['ibādāt]*, because that would cause him to fall from the approving eye of Allāh (Almighty and Glorious is He). It would remove him from His nearness. It would make him blind to his true spiritual condition. It would deprive him of the light of his faculty of insight, and of the sweetness he used to discover in his worship. It would obscure the pure clarity of his spiritual experience *[ma'rifa]*. It might even result in his work being rejected and shattered, because we are traditionally informed that Allāh (Blessed and Exalted is He) will not accept any deed from those who give themselves airs, unless and until they repent. According to one traditional account *[ḥadīth]*:

> Abraham *[Ibrāhīm]*, the Bosom Friend of the All-Merciful *[Khalīl ar-Raḥmān]*,[217] (peace be upon him), once devoted a whole night to vigil and worship *[aḥyā laila]*.[218] Then, when day dawned, he took pride in the fact that he had kept vigil throughout the night. He said: "Good indeed is the Lord, the Lord of Abraham, and good indeed is His servant, Abraham!"

[217] The Prophet Abraham *[Ibrāhīm]* (peace be upon him) is more usually called *Khalīlu'llah* [the Bosom Friend of Allāh]. The meaning, of course, is essentially the same, since *ar-Raḥmān* [the All-Merciful] is one of the Names of Allāh (Exalted is He).

[218] The noun corresponding to the verb *aḥyā* is *iḥyā'*. In non-religious contexts, the Arabic expression *iḥyā' al-lail* (literally, enlivening the night, or bringing the night to life) means simply "to stay awake throughout the night." In a religious context, it refers to the practice of keeping vigil in order to enliven the night with religious service, worship, adoration and devotion.

> But then, when it was time for his early morning meal, he found that no one would eat with him, although he (may Allāh bless him and give him peace) was fond of having other people eat with him. So he took his meal outside on the street, in the hope that someone passing by might stop and share it with him.
>
> At this point, a pair of angels descended from heaven above. When they came toward him [in human form], Abraham (peace be upon him) invited them to eat breakfast with him. They accepted his invitation, so he said to them: "Come, let us go to this garden over here, for in it there is a fountain of water, so we can enjoy our breakfast beside it."
>
> So they went together into the garden, but only to find that the fountain had dried up, and there was not a drop of water in it. This was a very distressing experience for Abraham (peace be upon him), and he was terribly embarrassed about what he had said, since there was actually no water to be found. But the angels said to him: "O Abraham, offer a supplication to your Lord, and ask Him to restore the water to the fountain."
>
> Abraham (peace be upon him) accepted their advice and made his entreaty to Allāh (Almighty and Glorious is He), but he received no response whatsoever. This troubled him greatly, so he said to the angels: "You two had better appeal to Allāh!" One of them thereupon offered a supplication, and the water returned to the fountain. Then the other angel made his supplication, and the fountain began to spout abundantly. Only then did they let him know that they were angels [in human form]. They explained to him that his vainglorious pride in his night of vigil had caused his supplication to be rejected, so that he received no response to his plea.

If this was how Allāh (Almighty and Glorious is He) treated His Bosom Friend, Abraham (peace be upon him), how can He be expected to deal with others?

Far from taking pride in his devout observance of religious duties, the servant [of the Lord] must be firmly convinced that all his commitment to worshipful obedience *[ṭāʿa]*, and his zealous dedication to it, can only be attributed to helpful guidance *[tawfīq]* from Allāh, and to His blessing, favor, mercy and grace. He must therefore stand in His presence (Almighty and Glorious is He) with an attitude of reverence, humility and self-abasement, as if he could witness Him directly with his ordinary eyes. As the Prophet (Allāh bless him and give him peace) has told us:

> You must worship Allāh as if you could see Him, for, even if you do not see Him, he surely does see you.

According to the Sacred Tradition *[Ḥadīth Qudsī]* that has been transmitted to us, Allāh (Almighty and Glorious is He) told Jesus, the son of Mary *[ʿĪsā 'bnu Maryam]* (peace be upon them both), by way of inspiration:

> When you stand in My presence, you must stand there with the attitude of one who is fearful, humble, and reproachful toward his own lower self *[nafs]*, for it is surely deserving of reproach. And if you appeal to Me in supplication, your limbs must be trembling while you offer Me your supplication.

As we also know from traditional sources, Allāh (Exalted is He) conveyed the same message to Moses *[Mūsā]* (peace be upon him), likewise by way of inspiration.

From a report concerning Ibn Sīrīn (may Allāh bestow His mercy upon him), we learn that whenever he stood up to perform the ritual prayer *[ṣalāt]*, his face would turn ghastly pale, from fear and dread of Allāh (Almighty and Glorious is He).

In the case of Muslim ibn Yasār (may Allāh bestow His mercy upon him), as soon as he had embarked upon the ritual prayer *[ṣalāt]*, he became completely deaf to the sound of a human voice, or to any other sound for that matter, due to intense concentration on the prayer, and from fear of Allāh (Almighty and Glorious is He).

ʿĀmir ibn ʿAbd Qais once said: "I would prefer to have daggers at odds between my shoulder blades, rather than be thinking of any worldly matter, while I am engaged in performing the ritual prayer *[ṣalāt]*."

It was Saʿd ibn Muʿādh (may Allāh be well pleased with him) who said: "It has never once happened, while I was performing the ritual prayer *[ṣalāt]*, that I talked to myself about any worldly matter, until I got up and left [the place of worship]."

Mujāhid (may Allāh bestow His mercy upon him) once said:

"Whenever [ʿAbdu'llāh] ibn az-Zubair (may Allāh be well pleased with him and with his father) was engaged in performing the ritual prayer *[ṣalāt]*, he seemed like a very old man, on account of his great humility.

"As for Wahb (may Allāh bestow His mercy upon him), when he stood up to perform the ritual prayer *[ṣalāt]*, he looked like someone who was catching a glimpse of Hell *[Jahannam]*.

"In the case of ʿUtbat al-Ghulām, while he was engaged in performing the ritual prayer *[ṣalāt]*, even in the season of winter, the sweat would be pouring from his skin. When people asked him why this was so, he explained: 'It is because of my acute sense of shame in the presence of Allāh (Almighty and Glorious is He).'

"A fire once broke out in the house of Muslim ibn Yasār (may Allāh bestow His mercy upon him), while he was praying *[yuṣallī]* in one of its rooms. The people of Baṣra become alarmed, so they dashed out and extinguished the blaze. Muslim himself was quite unaware of the fire, until they had already put it out, and he had finished performing his ritual prayer *[ṣalāt]*. On another occasion, it is said, he was praying in a large congregational mosque *[jāmiʿ]*, when a column of the building collapsed and fell right by his side. This caused a panic among the folk in the adjoining marketplace, but Muslim himself had no idea that it had happened."

From a report concerning ʿAmmār ibn az-Zubair (may Allāh bestow His mercy upon him), we learn that he was once engaged in performing his ritual prayer *[yuṣallī]*, having placed his sandals on the ground in front of him. He had recently repaired those sandals of his, and his attention wandered to the brand new straps. So, when he had finished his ritual prayer *[ṣalāt]*, he threw his sandals away, and he never wore sandals again, from then until the day he died (may Allāh bestow His mercy upon him).

According to the story that is told about ar-Rabīʿ ibn Khaitham (may Allāh bestow His mercy upon him), he was once performing the ritual prayer [at night] as an act of voluntary devotion *[yuṣallī taṭawwuʿan]*, having tethered in front of him a horse worth twenty thousand dirhams [silver coins]. Along came a thief, who untethered the horse and made off with it. Early the next morning, people came to commiserate with the unfortunate victim, so he told them: "As a matter of fact, I did happen to see the person unhitching it, but I was engaged at the time in something far dearer to me than my horse." Later that same day, lo and behold, the horse came trotting out of nowhere, until it halted right in front of him!

According to a traditional report, the Prophet (Allāh bless him and give him peace) once performed the ritual prayer *[ṣallā]* while wearing a black shawl, in which there was a thread of red fiber. As soon as he had concluded the prayer by pronouncing the final salutation *[sallama]*,[219] he complained: "This thread distracted me from my ritual prayer *[alhā-nī ʿan ṣalātī]*!"

[219] The verb *sallama* means "he pronounced the *taslīma* [salutation]." In other words, the Prophet (Allāh bless him and give him peace) concluded his prayer by turning his head to the right and saying: "*as-salāmu ʿalaikum wa raḥmatu'llāh* [Peace be upon you, and the mercy of Allāh]," then turning his head to the left and repeating these same words.

Allāh (Exalted is He) has extolled the virtue of those who are humble in their attitude toward the ritual prayer *[ṣalāt]*, for He has told us (Exalted is He):

Successful indeed are the believers,	*qad aflaḥa 'l-mu'minūn:*
who are humble	*alladhīna hum*
in their prayers. (23:1,2)	*fī ṣalāti-him khāshi'ūn.*

As explained by az-Zuhrī (may Allāh bestow His mercy upon him), this attitude of humility signifies a person's calm and complete commitment to his ritual prayer *[sukūn al-mar'i fī ṣalāti-hi]*.

When a person is in this state, it has been said, he knows neither who is to his right, nor who is to his left, during the ritual prayer *[ṣalāt]*, on account of his total preoccupation with the prayer itself. It is for this very reason that the Prophet (Allāh bless him and give him peace) once said:

> In the ritual prayer, there must truly be a focus of concentration *[inna fi 'ṣ-ṣalāti la-shughlan]*.

20.
Concerning the importance of performing the five daily prayers *[aṣ-ṣalawāt al-khams]* with all due care and attention to detail, and on what we know from traditional sources about the punishment awaiting those who neglect to perform them correctly.

According to a report transmitted by al-Aʿmash, on the authority of Shaqīq ibn Salama, it was related by Ibn Masʿūd (may Allāh be well pleased with him) that Allāh's Messenger (Allāh bless him and give him peace) once said:

> If the servant [of the Lord] performs the ritual prayer *[ṣalāt]* during the first part of the time prescribed for it, his prayer will rise up into the sky above, and it will have a light to guide it all the way to the Heavenly Throne *[ʿArsh]*. It will seek forgiveness on behalf of its owner until the Day of Resurrection *[Yawm al-Qiyāma]*, and it will say: "May Allāh take good care of you, as you took good care of me!"
>
> If the servant [of the Lord] performs the ritual prayer *[ṣalāt]*, but not at the time prescribed for it, his prayer will rise up toward the sky, but without a light to to guide it. So, when it reaches a certain point in the air above, it will flap about like an article of clothing, or a tattered rag, and he will feel it slapping him in the face. Then it will say: "May Allāh neglect you, as you neglected me!"

According to the tradition *[ḥadīth]* narrated by ʿUbāda ibn aṣ-Ṣāmit (may Allāh be well pleased with him), the Prophet (Allāh bless him and give him peace) once said:

> If someone performs the ritual ablution *[tawaḍḍaʾa]*, and does the ablution *[wuḍūʾ]* with the utmost care and attention to detail, then proceeds to perform the ritual prayer *[ṣalāt]*, and does every part of it perfectly, whether it be the bowing posture *[rukūʿ]*, the prostration *[sujūd]*, or the Qurʾānic recitation *[qirāʾa]*, the prayer *[ṣalāt]* will say to him: "May Allāh take good care of you, as you took good care of me!"
>
> Then it will be raised up into the sky above, accompanied by a radiance and a guiding light. The gates of heaven will therefore be opened to let it pass through

> so that it can travel all the way to Allāh (Almighty and Glorious is He), and then intercede with Him on behalf of its owner.
>
> If, on the other hand, the worshipper is negligent in his performance of the bowing posture *[rukū']*, the prostration *[sujūd]*, or the Qur'ānic recitation *[qirā'a]*, the prayer *[ṣalāt]* will say to him: "May Allāh neglect you, as you neglected me!" Then it will be raised up in darkness toward heaven, so the gates of heaven will be shut to keep it out. It will then flap about in the air like a tattered piece of clothing, and its owner will feel it slapping him in the face.

Ibn Mas'ūd (may Allāh be well pleased with him) is also reported as having said:

"I once asked Allāh's Messenger (Allāh bless him and give him peace): 'Which deeds are the most meritorious?' and he replied: 'The ritual prayers performed at the times prescribed for them *[aṣ-ṣalawāt li-waqti-hinna]*, the dutiful treatment of one's parents *[birr al-wālidain]*,[220] and the sacred struggle waged in the cause of Allāh (Almighty and Glorious is He) *[al-jihād fī sabīli 'llāh ('azza wa jall)]*.'"[221]

According to a traditional report from Ibrāhīm ibn Abī Maḥdhūra, the muezzin *[mu'adhdhin]*, his father told him that his grandfather (may Allāh be well pleased with him) once told him that Allāh's Messenger (Allāh bless him and give him peace) had said:

> The first part of the time prescribed [for the ritual prayer] is Allāh's good pleasure *[Riḍwānu'llāh]*. The middle section of the prescribed time is Allāh's mercy *[Raḥmatu'llāh]*. The last part of the prescribed time is Allāh's pardon *['Afwu'llāh]*.[222]

Allāh (Exalted is He) has warned us:

So woe to those who pray,	*fa-wailun li'l-muṣallīn:*
but are heedless	*alladhīna hum 'an*
of their prayers,	*ṣalāti-him sāhūn:*
and to those who make a show,	*alladhīna hum yurā'ūn:*
yet withhold the smallest charity.	*wa yamna'ūna 'l-mā'ūn.*
(107:4,5)	

220 For a detailed account of filial piety *[birr]*, see Vol. 1, pp. 96–99.

221 The Islāmic term *jihād* [sacred struggle or holy war] is all too frequently misunderstood, especially but not only by non-Muslims. Sometimes, alas, its meaning is willfully misrepresented—by polemicists hostile to Islām, as well as by misguided zealots within the Islāmic Community itself. Fortunately for us, the works of Shaikh 'Abd al-Qādir al-Jīlānī (may Allāh be well pleased with him) contain many valuable explanations of the true significance of the term *jihād*. (See, for instance, Vol. 2, pp. 44–45.)

222 This is reminiscent of the well-known saying of the Prophet (Allāh bless him and give him peace) concerning the month of Ramaḍān:

> It is a month the beginning of which is a mercy, the middle of which is a forgiveness, and the last part of which is a deliverance from the Fire of Hell.

Ibn ʿAbbās (may Allāh be well pleased with him and with his father) was commenting on these words, when he said: "By Allāh, it is not that they abandon their prayers altogether, but rather that they postpone them beyond the times prescribed for their performance."

Saʿd (may Allāh be well pleased with him) once said: "I asked the Prophet (Allāh bless him and give him peace) about His words (Almighty and Glorious is He):

So woe to those who pray, but are heedless of their prayers.	*fa-wailun li'l-muṣallīn:* *alladhīna hum ʿan* *ṣalāti-him sāhūn.*

—and he said (Allāh bless him and give him peace):

"'They are those who postpone the ritual prayer *[ṣalāt]* beyond the time prescribed for its performance.'"

Al-Barāʾ ibn ʿĀzib al-Awsī al-Anṣārī [223] (may Allāh be well pleased with him and with his father) is reported as having said, when commenting on the words of Allāh (Exalted is He):

So now there has succeeeded them a later generation, who have wasted the prayer and followed the desires of the flesh. So they will meet with temptation. (19:59)	*fa-khalafa-hum min baʿdi-him* *khalfun aḍāʿu 'ṣ-ṣalāta* *wa 'ttabaʿu 'sh-* *shahawāti* *fa-sawfa yalqawna ghayyā.*

—"'Temptation *[Ghayy]*' is the name of a valley in Hell *[Jahannam]*."

Ibn ʿAbbās (may Allāh be well pleased with him and with his father) was also commenting on these words, when he said: "The only person to enter it will be someone who wastes the times prescribed for his performance of the ritual prayer *[ṣalāt]*."

According to a traditional report transmitted on the authority of ʿAbdu'llāh ibn ʿAmr ibn al-ʿĀṣ (may Allāh be well pleased with him and with his father), Allāh's Messenger (Allāh bless him and give him peace) was speaking about the ritual prayer *[ṣalāt]* one day, and he said:

> For someone who observes it [i.e., the ritual prayer] with all due care, it will be a guiding light, a proof [of righteousness], and a means of salvation on the Day of Resurrection *[Yawm al-Qiyāma]*. But for someone who fails to observe it with all due care, it will not be a guiding light, and it will be neither a proof [of

[223] Al-Barāʾ ibn ʿĀzib al-Awsī al-Anṣārī (may Allāh be well pleased with him and with his father) was a Companion of the Prophet (Allāh bless him and give him peace) and a devoted follower of ʿAlī (may Allāh ennoble his countenance). He died in A.H. 71 or 72.

righteousness] nor a means of salvation from the Fire of Hell. On the Day of Resurrection *[Yawm al-Qiyāma]*, he will be in the company of Qārūn, Pharaoh, Hāmān[224] and Ubayy ibn Khalaf.[225]

According to a traditional report transmitted by al-Ḥarth, on the authority of the Commander of the Believers *[Amīr al-Mu'minīn]*, 'Alī ibn Abī Ṭālib (may Allāh be well pleased with him), the Prophet (Allāh bless him and give him peace) once said:

> If someone treats his ritual prayer *[ṣalāt]* with disrespect, Allāh (Almighty and Glorious is He) will subject that person to fifteen different punishments, six of them before death, three at the time of death, three in the grave, and three when he emerges from the grave [at the Resurrection].
>
> As for the six punishments to be inflicted on him before death, they are the following:
>
> 1. He will be deprived of his reputation as one of the righteous *[ṣāliḥīn]*.
> 2. He will be deprived of the blessed quality *[baraka]* of life.
> 3. He will be deprived of the blessed quality *[baraka]* of sustenance.
> 4. He will receive no credit whatsoever for any deeds of goodness, until he perfects his ritual prayer *[ṣalāt]*.
> 5. His supplication *[du'ā']* will not be answered.
> 6. No plea on his behalf will be included in the supplication of the righteous *[du'ā' aṣ-ṣāliḥīn]*.
>
> As for the three punishments to be inflicted on him at the time of death, they are the following:
>
> 1. He will die so thirsty that, even if seven oceans were poured into his throat, his thirst could not be quenched.
> 2. He will die suddenly and without warning.
> 3. The weight of all the iron in this world, and of all its wood and stones, will be heaped upon his neck and shoulders.
>
> As for the three punishments to be inflicted on him in the grave, they are the following:
>
> 1. His grave will be too narrow and cramped for him to lie in comfort.
> 2. His grave will be dark and gloomy place for him.
> 3. He will become incapable of articulate speech.
>
> Finally, as for the three punishments to be inflicted on him when he emerges from the grave [at the Resurrection], they are the following:
>
> 1. When he meets Allāh (Almighty and Glorious is He), he will find that He is angry with him.
> 2. When he is called to account, his reckoning will be very harsh and severe.
> 3. He will be banished from the presence of Allāh (Almighty and Glorious is He), and cast into the Fire of Hell, unless Allāh pardons him.

[224] Qārūn (who is called Korah in the Hebrew scriptures) and Pharaoh and Hāmān (Pharaoh's prime minister) are mentioned together in the Qur'ān (40:23,24).

[225] Ubayy ibn Khalaf was a treacherous enemy of the Prophet Muḥammad (Allāh bless him and give him peace). According to some of the traditional commentators, he is referred to in Q. 25:27.

21.
Concerning the tremendous importance and the enormous significance of the ritual prayer *[ṣalāt]*.

Allāh (Blessed and Exalted is He) commanded His Messenger Muḥammad (Allāh bless him and give him peace) to perform the ritual prayer *[ṣalāt]*. In many Qur'ānic verses *[āyāt]*, Allāh first of all revealed his Prophetic mission *[awḥā bi'n-Nubuwwa]*, then his duty to perform and establish the ritual prayer *[ṣalāt]*, before any other good practice *['amal]*, and before any other obligatory religious duty *[farīḍa]*. For instance, consider His words (Exalted is He):

Recite what has been revealed to you of the Book, and establish the ritual prayer. (29:45)	*utlu mā ūḥiya ilai-ka* *mina 'l-kitābi* *wa aqimi 'ṣ-ṣalāh.*

To this He then added (Almighty and Glorious is He):

The ritual prayer helps to prevent indecency and reprehensible behavior. (29:45)	*inna 'ṣ-ṣalāta tanhā* *'ani 'l-faḥshā'i* *wa 'l-munkar.*

Allāh (Glorious and Exalted is He) also said [to His Messenger (Allāh bless him and give him peace)]:

And instruct your family to pray, and be patient in it. We ask of you no provision; We provide for you. (20:132)	*wa 'mur ahla-ka bi'ṣ-ṣalāti* *wa 'ṣṭabir 'alai-hā:* *lā nas'alu-ka rizqā:* *naḥnu narzuqu-k.*

Allāh (Almighty and Glorious is He) has also addressed all the believers *[mu'minīn]*, commanding them to turn to patience *[ṣabr]* and the ritual prayer *[ṣalāt]*, for help with all their efforts to serve Him through acts of worshipful obedience *[ṭā'āt]*, for He has said:

O all you who believe, seek help in patience and prayer; surely Allāh is with those who are patient.	*yā ayyuha 'lladhīna āmanu 'sta'īnu* *bi'ṣ-ṣabri wa 'ṣ-ṣalāh:* *inna 'llāha ma'a 'ṣ-ṣābirīn.*

He has also said (Exalted is He):

And We appointed them to be leaders	*wa ja'alnā-hum a'immatan*
guiding by Our command,	*yahdūna bi-amri-nā*
and We revealed to them	*wa awḥainā ilai-him*
the doing of good deeds,	*fi'la 'l-khairāti*
and the performance of the prayer,	*wa iqāma 's-ṣalāti*
and the payment of the alms-due,	*wa ītā'a 'z-zakāh:*
and Us they served. (21:73)	*wa kānū la-nā 'ābidīn.*

Here he has mentioned all good deeds in general, they being all acts of worshipful obedience *[ṭā'āt]*, together with the avoidance of all acts of sinful disobedence *[ma'āṣī]*. Then He has singled out the performance of the ritual prayer *[ṣalāt]* for special mention, and enjoined it upon them in particular.

The Prophet (Allāh bless him and give him peace) bequeathed the ritual prayer *[ṣalāt]* to his Community, at the point of his departure from this world, for he said:

> Allāh, Allāh, Allāh! In [your dutiful performance of] the ritual prayer, and in [your treatment of] what your right hands possess *[fi 's-ṣalāti wa fī-mā malakat aimānu-kum]*.[226]

This was his final bequest (Allāh bless him and give him peace), and indeed, we are told in the tradition *[ḥadīth]* that this was the last bequest of every Prophet *[Nabī]* to his Community *[Umma]*, and his final testament to them at the point of his departure from this world.

The ritual prayer *[ṣalāt]* was thus the first obligatory religious duty *[farīḍa]* to be made incumbent upon the Prophet Muḥammad (Allāh bless him and give him peace) and upon his Community *[Umma]*, and the dutiful performance thereof was the last injunction bequeathed by him to his Community. It will be the final element to be taken away from Islām, and the first item about which the servant [of the Lord] will be questioned on the Day of Resurrection *[Yawm al-Qiyāma]*, when he is called to account for his religious practice. It is the supporting pillar *['amūd]* of Islām, and once it has gone, there will no longer be either any such thing as religion *[dīn]* or any such thing as Islām. According to the tradition *[ḥadīth]*, the Prophet (Allāh bless him and give him peace) once said:

> The first element of your religion *[dīn]* that you lose will be fidelity *[amāna]*, and the last element of it that you lose will be the ritual prayer *[ṣalāt]*. The time will come when only good-for-nothing types will still be performing the ritual prayer *[la-yuṣalliyanna aqwāmun lā khalāqa la-hum]*.

[226] The Qur'ānic expression "what your right hands possess *[mā malakat aimānu-kum]*" means "your slaves."

According to the doctrine of our Imām, Aḥmad [ibn Ḥanbal][227] (may Allāh bestow His mercy upon him), a person who abstains from the ritual prayer *[ṣalāt]* should be condemned as an unbeliever *[yukaffar]*, if he abstains from it deliberately, denying its obligatory status *[jāḥidan li-wujūbi-hā]*, in which case he is subject to the penalty of death. On this point there is no difference of opinion within the Ḥanbalī school of Islāmic jurisprudence *[madhhab]*.

As for the case where a person abstains from the ritual prayer *[ṣalāt]* out of careless neglect and laziness, although he does maintain his belief in its obligatory status, he must be summoned to perform it within a certain time. Then, if he does not perform the ritual prayer *[ṣalāt]* before the time allowed for it has expired, he should be condemned as an unbeliever *[yukaffar]*, and he should be put to death by the sword for his unbelief *[kufr]*.

In each of the two cases described above, the execution should be carried out three days after the guilty individual has been called upon to repent [and has refused to do so], as in the essentially similar case of the apostate *[murtadd]*. The offender's property should then be confiscated as *fai'* [booty obtained without fighting], and deposited in the public treasury *[bait al-māl]* of the Muslims. No funeral prayer should be performed over him *[lā yuṣallā ʿalai-hi]*, nor should he be buried in any of the cemeteries in which Muslims are interred.

According to one account of his doctrine, however, our Imām, Aḥmad ibn Ḥanbal (may Allāh bestow His mercy upon him), maintained that the death sentence should not be imposed, in the case of careless neglect, unless and until the offender has failed to perform three [consecutive] ritual prayers *[ṣalawāt]*, and there is not enough time to spare before the fourth becomes due. He should then be put to death in the execution of a penalty specifically prescribed by the sacred law *[ḥadd]*,[228] as in the case of a respectably married man who has been

[227] See note 7 on p. 7 above.

[228] The specific punishments prescribed by Islāmic law *[ḥudūd*, plural of *ḥadd]*, and the offenses for which they are prescribed, are as follows: (1) For *zinā* in the sense of adultery: death by stoning *[rajm]*. (2) For *zinā* in the sense of fornication: one hundred lashes. (3) For *qadhf* [falsely accusing a married person of adultery]: eighty lashes. (4) For apostasy *[irtidād]*: death. (5) For drinking intoxicating beverages *[shurb]*: eighty lashes. (6) For theft *[sariqa]*: amputation of the right hand. (7) For highway robbery *[qaṭʿ aṭ-ṭarīq]*: (a) amputation of hands and feet (for robbery only) or (b) death by the sword or crucifixion (for robbery with murder).

convicted of unlawful sexual intercourse *[az-zānī al-muḥṣan]*.[229] His legal status *[ḥukm]* should be that of the Muslim dead, which means that his Muslim heirs *[waratha]* are entitled to inherit his estate.[230]

According to the doctrine of Imām Abū Ḥanīfa (may Allāh bestow His mercy upon him), the offender should not be put to death. Instead, he should be held in prison until he performs the ritual prayer *[yuṣallī]*. That is to say, he must either repent, or languish in prison until he dies.

According to the doctrine of Imām ash-Shāfiʿī (may Allāh bestow His mercy upon him), the offender should be put to death by the sword, in the execution of a penalty specifically prescribed by the sacred law *[ḥadd]*, and should not be treated as an unbeliever *[lā yukaffar]*.

We have already presented the evidence that points to this offender's unbelief *[kufr]*, since it is contained within the Qurʾānic verses *[āyāt]* and Prophetic traditions *[akhbār]* cited above. For the purpose of further substantiating that evidence, let us conclude this subsection by adding the following citations:

According to a traditional report transmitted on the authority of Jābir ibn ʿAbdi'llāh (may Allāh be well pleased with him and with his father), Allāh's Messenger (Allāh bless him and give him peace) once said:

> To close the gap between a man on the one side, and unbelief *[kufr]* and associating partners with Allāh *[shirk]* on the other, all it takes is the abandonment of the ritual prayer *[ṣalāt]*.

According to a traditional report transmitted on the authority of ʿAbdu'llāh ibn Zaid, who passed it on from his father (may Allāh be well pleased with him), Allāh's Messenger (Allāh bless him and give him peace) once said:

> Between us [the believers] and them [the unbelievers] lies the abandonment of the ritual prayer *[ṣalāt]*. If a person ceases to observe it, he is thereby guilty of unbelief *[kafara]*.

According to a traditional report from Jaʿfar ibn Muḥammad, who transmitted it on the authority of his father (may Allāh be well pleased

229 Before a respectably married man *[muḥṣan]* can be convicted of unlawful sexual intercourse *[zinā]*, Islāmic law requires his accuser to produce four male witnesses of impeccable character, each of whom must be prepared to testify that he had actually seen "the pen in the pen-holder." Failing such testimony, the person making the accusation is himself subject to a penalty of eighty lashes.

230 In other words, according to this version of the Ḥanbalī doctrine, this offender should be punished as a guilty Muslim, not as an unbeliever.

with him), Allāh's Messenger (Allāh bless him and give him peace) once noticed that a man, during the performance of his ritual prayer *[ṣalāt]*, was bobbing his head, with the kind of pecking motion made by crows, so he said:

> If this creature were to die [at his moment], he would die beyond the pale of the religion *[dīn]* of Muḥammad (Allāh bless him and give him peace).

According to a traditional report from ʿAṭiyya al-ʿAwfī, who transmitted it on the authority of Abū Saʿīd al-Khudrī (may Allāh be well pleased with him), Allāh's Messenger (Allāh bless him and give him peace) once said:

> If a man abandons his ritual prayer *[ṣalāt]* deliberately, his name will be inscribed on the gate of the Fire of Hell, in the list of those who are doomed to enter it.

According to a traditional report transmitted on the authority of Anas ibn Mālik (may Allāh be well pleased with him), Allāh's Messenger (Allāh bless him and give him peace) once said:

> Oh yes indeed, if someone forgets about the prayer of the first third of the night *[ṣalāt al-ʿatama]*, and lies down to sleep without having performed it, the angels will say to him: "May your eyes neither sleep nor rest! May Allāh keep you in suspense between the Garden of Paradise and the Fire of Hell, as you have kept us in suspense!"

22.
Concerning forty-five bad habits that should be outlawed from the performance of the obligatory ritual prayer *[ṣalāt al-farīḍa]*.

According to a traditional report, transmitted on the authority of al-Ḥasan al-Baṣrī (may Allāh bestow His mercy upon him), the learned scholars *[ʿulamāʾ]* among the Companions *[Aṣḥāb]* of Allāh's Messenger (Allāh bless him and give him peace) used to maintain that forty-five habits are reprehensible, and should be outlawed from the performance of the obligatory ritual prayer *[ṣalāt al-farīḍa]*, namely:

1. Grunting *[tanaḥnuḥ]* with deliberate intent.
2. Fidgeting *[tashāghul]* with deliberate intent.
3. Sneezing *[taʿāṭus]* with deliberate intent.
4. Raising one's head and gazing up toward the sky.

In this case, the reason for disapproval can best be explained by citing the following traditional report:

"The Prophet (Allāh bless him and give him peace) used to turn his gaze toward the sky above, but then he received the Qurʾānic revelation:

Successful indeed are the believers,	*qad aflaḥa 'l-muʾminūn:*
who are humble	*alladhīna hum fī*
in their prayers. (23:1,2)	*ṣalāti-him khāshiʿūn.*

—so Allāh's Messenger (Allāh bless him and give him peace) kept his head bowed down *[ṭaʾṭaʾa raʾsa-hu]*."

This became the basis for the recommendation that a man should not extend his gaze beyond the edge of his prayer mat *[muṣallā]*.

5. Pressing the flesh beneath the chin against the upper part of the chest *[ilṣāq al-ḥanak bi'ṣ-ṣadr]*.
6. Inspecting one's clothes in search of lice and fleas *[faly ath-thawb]*.
7. Wearily stretching one's limbs *[tamaṭṭī]*.
8. Heaving a deep sigh *[tanaffus aṣ-ṣuʿadāʾ]*.

9. Shutting one's eyes *[taghmīḍ al-ʿainain]*.

10. Turning and glancing around during the prayer *[al-iltifāt fi 'ṣ-ṣalāt]*.

According to a traditional report, ʿUtba ibn ʿĀmir (may Allāh be well pleased with him) referred to this when he said, in commenting on the words of Allāh (Exalted is He):

Those who are constant in their prayer. (70:23)	*alladhīna hum ʿalā ṣalāti-him dā'imūn.*

—"While they are performing the prayer, they turn neither to the right nor to the left."

ʿĀʾisha (may Allāh be well pleased with her) is reported as having said: "I once asked Allāh's Messenger (Allāh bless him and give him peace) about the case of a man who turns and glances around during the ritual prayer *[ṣalat]*, and he replied:

> "'That is nothing but a crooked trick, by which the Devil *[ash-Shaiṭān]* contrives to steal from the prayer performed by My servant.'"

It is said that Ṭalḥa (viz., the son of Muṣrif) once came to visit ʿAbd al-Jabbār ibn Wāʾil. He found the latter involved with a group of people, so he whispered something to him, and took his leave. ʿAbd al-Jabbār then said to his companions: "Do you know what he said? He said: 'When I saw you yesterday, I noticed that you were turning and glancing around, while you were performing the ritual prayer *[wa anta tuṣallī]*.'"

From the following tradition *[ḥadīth]*, we learn that Allāh's Messenger (Allāh bless him and give him peace) once said:

> When the servant [of the Lord] begins the ritual prayer *[fataḥa 'ṣ-ṣalāt]*, Allāh confronts him with His face, and He does not turn it away, unless the servant is the one who turns aside, or glances to right and left.

To quote another tradition *[ḥadīth]*:

> As long as the servant [of the Lord] is constant in the performance of his ritual prayer *[ṣalāt]*, he possesses three characteristics, namely: (1) Righteousness *[birr]* is steadily showering down upon him, from the clouds in the sky onto the parting of the hair on his head. (2) Angels are flying to and fro, between a spot next to his feet and the clouds in the sky. (3) An angelic herald is crying: "If the person at prayer *[al-muṣallī]* only knew with Whom he is intimately conversing *[yunājī]*, he would not move away *[ma 'ntaqal]*.

That is to say, he would not turn around and leave.

The habit of turning and glancing around *[iltifāt]* is very reprehensible indeed. It has even been said that it cuts off the prayer *[ṣalāt]* completely. It certainly indicates a serious lack of respect for the prayer *[ṣalāt]*, and for its rules of conduct *[ādāb]*.

11. Adopting the canine squatting posture known as *iq'ā'*,[231] when in the sitting position *[qu'ūd]* during [the final stage of] the ritual prayer.[232]

12. Refusing to follow the leader of the prayer *[imām]*.

13. Spreading the forearms wide, while in the posture of prostration *[sujūd]*.

14. Placing the chest on the thighs, while in the posture of prostration *[sujūd]*.

15. Pressing the armpits close to the sides of the body, while in the posture of prostration *[sujūd]*.

The worshipper must keep a space between his armpits and the sides of his body, and not squeeze the former close against the latter. We know this from the traditional report concerning the example set by the Prophet (Allāh bless him and give him peace), in which it is stated:

"If a little lamb had tried to pass beneath his arms, when he was performing the act of prostration *[idhā sajada]*, it would have been able to get through."

This was due to the fact that he went to great lengths in raising his elbows away from the sides of his body, as we are told in another tradition *[ḥadīth]*:

"When Allāh's Messenger (Allāh bless him and give him peace) was performing the act of prostration *[idhā sajada]*, he used to keep his upper arms well apart from the sides of his body."

16. Keeping the fingers spread apart, while in the posture of prostration *[sujūd]*, when they should actually be kept close together.

[231] As Shaikh 'Abd al-Qādir al-Jīlānī (may Allāh be well pleased with him) has explained in Vol. 1, p. 353:

> Subject to disapproval during the ritual prayer is the squatting posture known as *iq'ā'*, which means that a person stretches the upper sides of his feet out on the ground and sits on his heels, or that he sits with both his buttocks on the ground while keeping both his feet erect. In the words of the Prophet (Allāh bless him and give him peace):
>
> > It is a way of squatting that is like the squatting posture of the dog; it is forbidden to adopt it.

[232] It is while in the sitting position *[qu'ūd]* that the worshipper concludes his performance of the ritual prayer *[ṣalāt]*, by pronouncing the greetings *[taḥiyyāt]*, the testimony *[tashahhud]*, and the salutation *[taslīma]*.

17. Placing the hands short of the knees, while in the posture of bowing *[rukū']*.

18. Planting one foot on top of the other.

19. Keeping either foot dangling off the ground.

20. Allowing one's waist-wrapper *[izār]* or trouser pants *[sarāwīl]* to hang loosely suspended.[233]

21. Picking one's teeth *[takhlīl]*.

22. Licking one's lips *[talammuẓ]*.

23. Swallowing food amounting to a grain or a couple of grains.

24. Belching up undigested food, and then swallowing it down again.

25. Expelling saliva with the tongue, while in the posture of prostration *[sujūd]*.

26. Blowing wind, while in the posture of prostration *[sujūd]*.

27. Arranging pebbles [on the ground in front of you].

28. Stepping sideways.

29. Raising your voice above that of the person sitting next to you, when pronouncing the testimony *[tashahhud]*.[234]

[233] According to a traditional report, the Prophet (Allāh bless him and give him peace) once said:

> The Muslim's mode of wearing the *izār* [waist-wrapper] is to have it reaching the middle of the shank. There is no offense and no sin with respect to what is between that point and the ankles, but if anything is lower than the ankles, it is in the Fire of Hell. If anyone trails his *izār* out of vain conceit, Allāh (Exalted is He) will pay no attention to him. (See Vol. 1 p. 352.)

[234] The testimony *[tashahhud]* is pronounced after two cycles of prayer *[rak'atain]* and, in a prayer consisting of more than two cycles, in the final stage of the last cycle. While in the sitting position *[qu'ūd]*, the worshipper recites:

Greetings, prayers and good deeds	*at-taḥiyyātu li'llāhi wa 'ṣ-ṣalawātu*
are due to Allāh. Peace be upon you,	*wa 'ṭ-ṭayyibāt—as-salāmu 'alai-ka*
O Prophet, and the mercy of Allāh	*ayyuha 'n-nabiyyu wa raḥmatu'llāhi*
and His blessings! Peace be on us,	*wa barakātuh—as-salāmu 'alai-nā*
and on all the righteous servants of Allāh.	*wa 'alā 'ibādi 'llāhi 'ṣ-ṣāliḥīn.*

Then, while raising the index finger of the right hand, and pointing it to emphasize the affirmation of Divine Oneness, the worshipper continues:

I bear witness that there is no god but Allāh,	*ashhadu an lā ilāha illa 'llāh—*
and I bear witness that Muḥammad	*wa ashhadu anna Muḥammadan*
is His servant and His Messenger.	*'abdu-hu wa rasūluh.*

Such is the wording preferred by Imām Aḥmad ibn Ḥanbal and Imām Abū Ḥanīfa (may Allāh bestow His mercy upon them). There are slight differences in the version adopted by followers of the school *[madhhab]* of Imām ash-Shāfi'ī (may Allāh bestow His mercy upon them), who recite:

Blessed greetings	*at-taḥiyyātu 'l-mubārakatu*
and good prayers are due to Allāh.	*wa 'ṣ -ṣalawātu 'ṭ-ṭayyibātu li'llāh—*
Peace be upon you,	*as-salāmu 'alai-ka*
O Prophet, and the mercy of Allāh	*ayyuha 'n-nabiyyu wa raḥmatu'llāhi*
and His blessings! Peace be on us,	*wa barakātuh—as-salāmu 'alai-nā*
and on all the righteous servants of Allāh.	*wa 'alā 'ibādi 'llāhi 'ṣ-ṣāliḥīn.*
I bear witness that there is no god but Allāh.	*ashhadu an lā ilāha illa 'llāh—*
And I bear witness that Muḥammad	*wa ashhadu anna Muḥammadan*
is the Messenger of Allāh.	*rasūlu 'llāh.*

30. Recognizing the identity of the person to your right, and that of the person to your left.

31. Nodding and winking *[īmā']*.

32. Making pointed gestures *[ishāra]*.

33. Swallowing vomit *[jashā']*, or anything that emerges from the throat.

34. Deliberate coughing *[isti'āl]*.

35. Blowing one's nose *[tamakhkhuṭ]*.

36. Spitting *[tabazzuq]*.

37. Paying attention to clothes.

38. Rubbing the dust from one's brow, before leaving [at the end of the prayer].

39. Arranging pebbles more than one single time.

40. Dusting the spot where the forehead will be placed in the act of prostration *[sujūd]*.

41. Inserting the supplication *[du'ā']* after the testimony *[tashahhud]*, if you are acting as a prayer leader *[imām]*.

42. Sitting in the prayer-niche *[miḥrāb]*, after the final salutation *[taslīm]*, but before the prayer leader *[imām]* has shifted from his place and moved over to his left.

43. Knotting the fingers with the hand during the performance of the ritual prayer *[ṣalāt]*.

44. Fiddling with one's beard.

45. Fiddling with one's gown.

The Prophet (Allāh bless him and give him peace) is reported as having said:

> Allāh pays no attention to the ritual prayer *[ṣalāt]* performed by a man whose heart is not in it, as well as his body.

Allāh's Messenger (Allāh bless him and give him peace) once noticed a man fiddling with his beard, so he said:

> If only this man's heart would be humbly submissive, his physical limbs and organs would also be humbly submissive.

Al-Ḥasan [al-Baṣrī] (may Allāh bestow His mercy upon him) once noticed that a man was playing with the pebbles [on the ground in front of him], and that he was saying as he did so: "O Allāh, marry me to one of those maidens of Paradise with such lovely eyes *[al-ḥūr al-ʿīn]*!"[235] So al-Ḥasan said: "It must be hard for the Matchmaker to take your marriage proposal seriously, since you offer it while playing a silly game!"

According to ʿAbd ar-Raḥmān ibn ʿAbdi'llāh, [his father] ʿAbdu'llāh [ibn Masʿūd] (may Allāh be well pleased with him) once said:

"If people will insist on raising their eyes toward the sky above, the outcome may well be that their eyesight does not come back to them!"

That is to say, in the course of the ritual prayer *[ṣalāt]*.

It was al-Awzāʿī (may Allāh bestow His mercy upon him) who said:

"Although two men are both engaged in the ritual prayer *[ṣalāt]*, the difference between them is as great as the difference between heaven and earth. One of them is dedicated to Allāh (Exalted is He) with his heart, while the other is heedless and inattentive *[lāh wa sāh]*."

From one authentic traditional report *[khabar]*, we learn that Allāh's Messenger (Allāh bless him and give him peace) once said:

> The worshipper *[muṣallī]* will be rewarded for half of his ritual prayer *[ṣalāt]*, provided that he remembers [what he is doing] for one tenth of it.

That is to say, provided that he is consciously aware of it, and that his heart is present in it.

According to another tradition *[ḥadīth]*, he also said (Allāh bless him and give him peace):

> [For the performance of one prayer] a worshipper *[muṣallī]* may be credited with four hundred ritual prayers *[ṣalāt]*; another worshipper may be credited with two hundred ritual prayers; another worshipper may be credited with one hundred and fifty ritual prayers; and yet another worshipper may be credited with seventy ritual prayers.
>
> One ritual prayer *[ṣalāt]* may be equal in value to fifty ritual prayers; another ritual prayer may be equal in value to twenty-seven ritual prayers; another ritual prayer may be equal in value to ten ritual prayers; and yet another ritual prayer may have the value of just one single ritual prayer *[ṣalāt wāḥida]*.
>
> As for the worshipper who is credited with four hundred ritual prayers *[ṣalāt]*, he is the one who performs the prayer *[yuṣallī]* at Mecca, in the Sacred House *[al-Bait al-Ḥarām]*, together with the prayer leader *[imām]*, as a member of the congregation, without having missed the initial declaration of Allāh's Supreme Greatness *[at-takbīrat al-ūlā]*.[236]

[235] See note 9 on p. 9 above.

[236] This initial declaration is often called the consecratory declaration of Allāh's Supreme Greatness *[takbīrat al-iḥrām]*. It is the affirmation "*Allāhu Akbar* [Allāh is Supremely Great!]," which is pronounced as an act of consecration *[iḥrām]* at the beginning of the performance of the ritual prayer *[ṣalāt]*.

As for the worshipper who is credited with two hundred ritual prayers *[ṣalāt]*, he is the prayer leader *[imām]*, the one who leads the people in prayer *[ya'ummu 'n-nās]*, but only after he has made himself thoroughly familiar with all the rules that govern the correct performance of the ritual prayer *[aḥkām aṣ-ṣalāt]*.

As for the worshipper who is credited with one hundred and fifty ritual prayers *[ṣalāt]*, he is the muezzin *[mu'adhdhin]*, meaning someone who gives the call to prayer *[adhān]*.

As for the worshipper who is credited with seventy ritual prayers *[ṣalāt]*, he is the one who brushes his teeth *[yastāku]*[237] and performs his ritual ablution *[wuḍū']* correctly in every detail, then performs the ritual prayer in the large congregational mosque, as a member of the congregation *[yuṣallī fi 'l-jāmi' fi 'l-jamā'a]*.

As for the worshipper who is credited with fifty ritual prayers *[ṣalāt]*, he is the man who performs the ritual prayer in the large congregational mosque, together with the prayer leader, as a member of the congregation *[yuṣallī fi 'l-jāmi' ma'a 'l-imām fi 'l-jamā'a]*, even though he may have missed the consecratory declaration of Allāh's Supreme Greatness *[takbīrat al-iḥrām]*.

As for the worshipper who is credited with twenty-seven ritual prayers *[ṣalāt]*, he is the man who performs his ritual ablution *[wuḍū']* correctly in every detail, then performs the ritual prayer in a small mosque *[masjid]*, as a member of the congregation, and without without having missed the consecratory declaration of Allāh's Supreme Greatness *[takbīrat al-iḥrām]*.

As for the worshipper who is credited with ten ritual prayers *[ṣalawāt]*, he is the man who joins the congregation *[jamā'a]*, although he arrives after the consecratory declaration of Allāh's Supreme Greatness *[takbīrat al-iḥrām]* has already been pronounced [by the prayer leader].

As for the worshipper who is credited with one single ritual prayer *[ṣalāt]*, he is the one who performs the prayer *[yuṣallī]* by himself, not as a member of a congregation.

As for the worshipper who is not credited with any ritual prayer *[ṣalāt]* at all, he is the one who keeps bobbing his head like a rooster, and does not properly perform the acts of bowing *[rukū']* and prostration *[sujūd]*. This is the person whose ritual prayer *[ṣalāt]* will be draped in the air like a tattered rag, so that its owner will feel it slapping him in the face. He will be told: "May Allāh not take care of you, as you have failed to take care of your ritual prayer *[ṣalāt]*!"

[237] The verb *yastāku* is derived from the same three-consonant root—*s–w–k*—as the noun *siwāk*, which denotes a small stick, softened at the tip by chewing or beating to form a kind of toothbrush.

23.
Concerning the intention *[niyya]* that must be formulated by every worshipper *[muṣallī]* before he begins his ritual prayer *[ṣalāt]*. A detailed account of the movements, postures and utterances that constitute the performance of the ritual prayer *[ṣalāt]*.

It is incumbent upon every worshipper *[muṣallī]* to formulate the intention *[niyya]*,[238] before proceeding to perform his ritual prayer *[ṣalāt]*.

He should picture the Kaʿba, the Sacred House *[al-Bait al-Ḥarām]*, in front of him, and keep his eyes fixed steadily upon it, as we have already explained in the early part of this book.[239]

He should be absolutely convinced *[yatayaqqan]* that he is standing in the presence of Allāh (Exalted is He), and he should not doubt that he is holding himself erect in the sight of Allāh, so that He is really seeing him. This certitude is fully justified, because Allāh (Exalted is He) has said:

Put your trust in the All-Glorious,	*wa tawakkal ʿala 'l-ʿAzīzi 'r-*
the All-Compassionate,	*Raḥīm:*
who sees you when	*alladhī yarā-ka*
you stand and [who sees]	*ḥīna taqūm:*
your bowing down	*wa taqalluba-ka*
among those who prostrate	*fi 's-sājidīn.*
themselves. (26:217–9)	

[238] At the very beginning of his famous *Ṣaḥīḥ*, Imām al-Bukhārī has prefaced his vast compilation of authentic Prophetic traditions *[aḥādīth]* with the saying of Allāh's Messenger (Allāh bless him and give him peace):

> Actions derive their value from the intentions [on the strength of which they are performed], and every man is credited with what he actually intended *[innama 'l-aʿmālu bi-'n-niyyāti wa innamā li-kulli 'mri'in bi-mā nawā]*.

[239] See Vol. 1, p. 10, where the author (may Allāh be well pleased with him) has explained:

> As for facing the *Qibla*, this means facing the actual Kaʿba if one is in Mecca or any place in its vicinity. If one is at a distance from it, however, it means facing in its direction, [as nearly as this can be ascertained] by the exercise of judgment *[ijtihād]* and by making the effort to deduce it from all available evidence, such as that provided by the stars, the sun, the winds, etc.

It is also confirmed by the words of the Messenger (Allāh bless him and give him peace):

> You must worship Allāh as if you could see Him, for, even if you do not see Him, he surely does see you.

When he formulates his intention *[yanwī]* to perform the obligatory ritual prayer *[aṣ-ṣalāt al-farīḍa]*, it is more appropriate [though not absolutely essential] for the worshipper to state specifically whether it is to be performed as a prompt fulfillment *[adā']* [i.e., within the prescribed time], or as an overdue fulfillment *[qaḍā']* [i.e., to make up for his having failed to perform it during the prescribed time].[240]

The worshipper should then raise his hands to the lobes of his ears, or to a position level with his shoulders. (We have given a detailed description of this in the early part of this book.)[241] As to whether he should keep his fingers close together, or whether he should spread them apart, there are two conflicting traditional accounts [of the Ḥanbalī doctrine on this point].

When he raises his hands, and proclaims the Supreme Greatness of Allāh by saying "*Allāhu Akbar*!" it is as if the worshipper is removing the veil between him and Allāh (Exalted is He). He has now arrived at the place where it is not permissible to turn and glance around, and where no distraction is allowed, because he must realize that he is in the sight of One who sees his every movement, and who knows what is churning in his lower self *[nafs]*, as well as all that is concealed within his innermost being *[sirr]* and his heart *[qalb]*.

[240] The verb *yanwī* [he intends; he is intending to...], like the corresponding noun *niyya* [intention], is derived from the three-consonant root *n–w–y*. The basic form of the verb is *nawā* [he has intended; he has made it his intention to...]. The form *nawaitu* [I have intended; I have made it my intention to...] is used by the worshipper when he formulates his intention in Arabic.

[241] Thus, a typical formulation of the intention *[niyya]* to perform an obligatory prayer, within the prescribed time, would be:

I have made it my intention	*nawaitu*
to perform the obligatory sunset prayer,	*uṣallī farḍa 'l-maghrib—*
[consisting of] three cycles,	*thalātha raka'ātin*
within the prescribed time,	*adā'an*
for the sake of Allāh (Exalted is He).	*li'llāhi (ta'ālā).*

If the same prayer is to be performed, but after the prescribed time has elapsed, the word *qaḍā'an* should be substituted in place of *adā'an*.

[281] See Vol. 1, p. 15, where Shaikh 'Abd al-Qādir al-Jīlānī (may Allāh be well pleased with him) has explained:

> This means that one's hands are brought up close to the shoulders, the thumbs are held beside the lobes of the ears, and the tips of the fingers next to upper parts of the ears. Then the hands are lowered again.

The worshipper must therefore fix his gaze on the spot where he will shortly place his forehead in the act of prostration *[sujūd]*. He must not turn and glance to right and left, nor raise his head toward the sky above, and when he says:

"Glory be to You, O Allāh,	*subḥāna-ka 'llāhumma*
and praise be to You!	*wa bi-ḥamdi-ka*
Blessed is Your Name,	*wa tabāraka 'smu-ka*
and Exalted is Your Majesty.	*wa taʿālā jaddu-ka*
There is no god other than You."	*wa lā ilāha ghairu-k.*

—he must be aware that he is addressing One who is hearing him, attending to him, and watching him, and from Whom nothing is hidden, not even the position of a single hair, nor the slightest movement made by any limb or organ of his body.

The same must hold true when he says [in his recitation of *al-Fātiḥa*, the Opening Sūra of the Qur'ān]:

You alone do we worship,	*iyyā-ka naʿbudu*
and of You alone do we seek help.	*wa iyyā-ka nastaʿīn—*
Guide us in the straight path. (1:4,5)	*ihdina 'ṣ-ṣirāṭa 'l-mustaqīm.*

—for he must grasp the meaning of what he is saying, and realize to Whom he is addressing this recitation.

At the same time, the worshipper must not forget to maintain an attitude of humility, and to be constantly on his guard against fits of absentmindedness, which could make him lose track of the stage he has reached in the performance of his prayer.

In his recitation of *al-Fātiḥa*, he must be careful to observe the eleven instances where an intensified pronunciation *[tashdīd]*[242] is required,[243] namely:

1,2. – ***ll*** – and – ***bb*** – in the first verse *[āya]*:

al-ḥamdu li'LLāhi	Praise be to Allāh,
raBBi 'l-ʿālamīn.	Lord of All the Worlds,

[242] As a term of Arabic grammar, *tashdīd* denotes the doubling of a consonant, the occurrence of which is indicated (in some texts, especially that of the Qur'ān) by a special superscript mark. The intensified pronunciation of doubled consonants comes naturally to the native speakers of certain languages, notably Italian, but not to many others, including those whose mother tongue is English!

[243] The recitation of *al-Fātiḥa* is preceded by the invocation *[basmala]*: "*Bismi 'llāhi 'r-Raḥmāni 'r-Raḥīm* [In the Name of Allāh, the All-Merciful, the All-Compassionate]." This is not counted, however, as one of its verses *[āyāt]*, the first of which is therefore:

Praise be to Allāh, Lord of All the Worlds.	*al-ḥamdu li'llāhi Rabbi 'l-ʿālamīn.*

3,4. – **r-r** – twice in the second verse *[āya]*:

aR-Raḥmāni 'R-Raḥīm.	the All-Merciful, the All-Compasionate,

5. – **d-d** – in the third verse *[āya]*:

māliki yawmi 'D-Dīn.	Master of the Day of Reckoning.

6,7. – **yy** – twice in the fourth verse *[āya]*:

iYYā-ka na'budu	You alone do we worship,
wa iYYā-ka nasta'īn.	and of You alone do we seek help.

8. – **ṣ-ṣ** – in the fifth verse *[āya]*:

ihdina 'Ṣ-Ṣirāṭa 'l-mustaqīm.	Guide us in the straight path,

9. – **ll** – in the sixth verse *[āya]*:

ṣirāṭa 'LLadhīna an'amta 'alai-him.	the path of those whom You have blessed,

10,11. – **ḍ–ḍ** – and – **ll** – in the seventh and final verse *[āya]*:

ghairi 'l-maghḍūbi 'alai-him	not of those who earn Your wrath,
wa la 'Ḍ-ḌāLLīn.	nor of those who go astray.

The worshipper must also be very careful to avoid any mispronunciation or grammatical mistake *[laḥn]* that would alter the meaning, because the recitation of *al-Fātiḥa* is an obligatory requirement *[farīḍa]*. It is a basic essential *[rukn]*,[244] by the omission of which the ritual prayer *[ṣalāt]* is rendered null and void.

In all of this, the worshipper should feel as if he is standing on the Narrow Bridge *[Ṣirāṭ]*, with the Garden of Paradise and its blissful attributes to his right, and the Fire of Hell and its terrible contents to his left. He should regard himself as making an application, by offering his ritual prayer *[ṣalāt]*, for what Allāh (Almighty and Glorious is He) has promised, which is the reward of the Garden of Paradise, provided that his prayer *[ṣalāt]* meets all the standards of validity. He should also have the feeling that he is presenting it in order to obtain immunity from Allāh's threat, which is the torment of the Fire of Hell. All of this

[244] As explained by Shaikh 'Abd al-Qādir al-Jīlānī (may Allāh be well pleased with him) in an earlier Chapter of the present work:

The ritual prayer *[ṣalāt]* has some elements that are basic essentials *[arkān*, plural of *rukn]*, some that are necessities *[wājibāt]*, others that are recommended practices *[masnūnāt]*, and yet others that are formal refinements *[hai'āt]*. (See Vol. 1, pp. 13–16.)

should be infused with a sense of certainty from his heart, and a present awareness on the part of his conscious understanding.

Furthermore, the worshipper should be firmly convinced that he is performing the prayer as a consignor *[yuṣallī ṣalāt mūdiʿ]*, that his consignment will undoubtedly be delivered to Allāh (Exalted is He) for His review, and that the only credit he gets for it will be whatever, in the sight of Allāh, he is entitled to receive.

Next, after he has completed his recitation of *al-Fātiḥa*, the worshipper should go on to recite as many complete Sūras of the Qurʾān as he can easily manage.[245] It is better to recite Sūras from beginning to end, rather than their final or middle sections.

He should listen carefully to what he is reciting, and try to grasp the meaning of the words he is uttering and pronouncing. Likewise, if he is being led *[maʾmūm]*, he should listen carefully to the recitation of the prayer leader *[imām]* and try to understand its meaning. He should take note of the exhortations and admonitions it contains, and resolve to carry out its commandments and comply with its prohibitions. His attention to these points should be maintained until the end of the Sūra is reached.

Having completed the Qurʾānic recitation, the worshipper must stand still and keep silent, long enough to catch his breath, before he proceeds to adopt the bowing posture *[qabla an yarkaʿa]*.[246] He must not combine his Qurʾānic recitation uninterruptedly with the affirmation of Allāh's Supreme Greatness that precedes the adoption of the bowing posture *[takbīrat ar-rukūʿ]*.

Then, after this brief pause for breath, the worshipper must say:

Allāh is Supremely Great!	*Allāhu Akbar!*

—while raising his hands to the lobes of his ears, or to a position

[245] In the words of Allāh (Almighty and Gorious is He):

Therefore recite of the Qurʾān that which is easy for you. (73:20)	*fa-'qraʾū mā tayassara mina 'l-Qurān.*

[246] The basic verb *rakaʿa* (of which *yarkaʿa* is a subjunctive form) is derived from the same three-consonant root <*r–k–ʿ*> as the noun *rukūʿ* [bowing; the bowing posture]. The term *rakʿa* [an act of bowing] which is also derived from this root, has acquired an extended meaning, since it is generally used to denote the whole series of movements and postures—including the *rukūʿ*—that constitute one cycle of the ritual prayer *[ṣalāt]*. (The dual and plural forms, corresponding to the singular form *rakʿa*, are *rakʿatān/-ain* and *rakaʿāt*, respectively.)

level with his shoulders. (We have given a detailed description of this in the early part of this book.)[247]

As soon as the declaration of Allāh's Supreme Greatness *[takbīr]*[248] has been accomplished, the worshipper must lower his hands. Then he must bend down from his upright stance *[qiyām]* in order to perform the act of bowing *[rukū']*.

The palms of his hands must now be cupped over his knees, while his fingers are slightly separated. He should support his weight by leaning on the full length of his arms [lit., on his upper arms and his forearms]. He must keep his back straight, neither raising his head, nor tilting it so low that it causes him to lose his balance.

According to one traditional account:

> When the Prophet (Allāh bless him and give him peace) performed the act of bowing *[raka'a]*, if there had been a drop *[qaṭra]* of water on his back, it would not have moved from its place.

In a slightly different version, the wording is:

> When the Prophet (Allāh bless him and give him peace) performed the act of bowing *[raka'a]*, if there had been a glass *[qadaḥ]* of water on his back, it would not have moved from its place.

That was because he kept his back so perfectly straight and level (Allāh bless him and give him peace).

While he is holding this posture, the worshipper must say, three times:

Glory to my Lord, the Almighty!	*Subḥāna Rabbiya 'l-'Aẓīm.*

A threefold repetition is actually the minimum of perfection, for, as al-Ḥasan al-Baṣrī (may Allāh bestow His mercy upon him) once said: "The most complete glorification *[tasbīḥ]* is seven repetitions, the average is five, and the minimum is three."

[247] See note 241 on p. 177 above.

[248] In this instance, the verbal noun *takbīr* is used without the termination *-a/-at*, which is added when a single instance of this affirmation is specified, e.g., *takbīra wāḥida* [one affirmation of Allāh's Supreme Greatness], or when the term is grammatically linked to a qualifying noun, e.g., *takbīrat ar-rukū'* [the-affirmation-of-Allāh's-Supreme-Greatness of-the-bowing-posture] and *takbīrat al-iḥrām* [the-affirmation-of-Allāh's-Supreme-Greatness of-the-initial-consecration].

The worshipper must then raise his head [and his hands as before], saying *[musammiʿan]*:[249]

May Allāh hear and accept the praise of one who praises Him!	*samiʿa 'llāhu li-man ḥamidah.*

Then, having resumed an upright posture, he must stand calmly composed *[yaṭma'innu]*, allowing his hands to hang freely by his sides.[250]

Next, the worshipper must sink down into the posture of prostration *[sujūd]*. He must place his knees on the ground first of all, then his hands, then his forehead and his nose. He must settle himself firmly on the ground, and maintain a state of calm composure *[yaṭma'innu]* in his prostration *[sujūd]*. He must align himself so that he is pointing toward the *Qibla* [direction of the Kaʿba] with every member and part of his body.

From the following tradition *[ḥadīth]*, we learn that the Prophet (Allāh bless him and give him peace) once said:

> I have been commanded to perform the act of prostration *[sujūd]* by resting on seven bones.[251]

In the words of another tradition *[ḥadīth]*:

> The servant [of the Lord] is supposed to prostrate himself *[yasjudu]* by resting on seven members of his body, so if he leaves any one of those members out of the act, that member will curse him.

In his posture of prostration *[sujūd]*, the worshipper should be neatly compact, not sprawled out over the ground. Far from spreading his forearms wide, he must place his fingers on the ground in the same position, relative to his ears or his shoulders, as the one recommended when the hands are raised in the upright posture *[qiyām]*, in conjunction

[249] In the Arabic text, the participle *musammiʿan* is sufficient, all by itself, to signify: "saying: '*samiʿa 'llāhu li-man ḥamidah* [May Allāh hear and accept the praise of one who praises Him!]" (Like the verb *samiʿa*, it is derived from the three-consonant root *s–m–ʿ*.)

[250] At this point, as Shaikh ʿAbd al-Qādir al-Jīlānī (may Allāh be well pleased with him) has mentioned in Vol. 1, p. 14, it is necessary—though not absolutely essential—for the worshipper to utter a declaration of praise *[taḥmīd]*, by saying:

Our Lord, and to You be the praise!	*Rabba-nā wa la-ka 'l-ḥamd.*

The worshipper is also recommended, as a customary practice, to add the words:

Enough [praise] to fill the heavens and the earth, and to fill anything beyond them, as You wish.	*mil'u 's-samāwāti wa mil'u 'l-arḍ: wa mil'u mā shi'ta min shai'in baʿd.*

[251] That is to say: (1) the skull bone in the forehead, (2,3) the bones in the two hands, (4,5) the two kneecaps, and (6,7) the bones in the two feet.

with the declaration of Allāh's Supreme Greatness *[takbīr]*. He must not place his hands in line with top of his head.

He must keep his fingers close together, and point them toward the *Qibla* [direction of the Ka'ba]. As we have previously explained,[252] he must keep his upper arms well clear of the sides of his body, his thighs from touching the calves of his legs, and his stomach from coming in contact with the ground.

While he is in the posture of prostration *[sujūd]*, the worshipper must say:

Glory to my Lord, the Most High! *Subḥāna Rabbiya 'l-A'lā.*

He should utter this glorification three times, as in the posture of bowing *[rukū']*.

Then he must raise his head, saying *[mukabbiran]*:[253]

Allāh is Supremely Great! *Allāhu Akbar!*

He must now sit on his left leg, while placing his right leg so that the right foot is in an upright position [i.e., with the heel raised], and so that his toes are pointing toward the *Qibla* [direction of the Ka'ba]. While sitting in this posture, he must say:

My Lord, forgive me! *Rabbi 'ghfir lī*

He should say this three times, while glancing at his breast.

Next, he must prostrate himself *[yasjudu]* a second time, in the same manner as before. Then he must raise his head from the ground, saying *[mukabbiran]*:

Allāh is Supremely Great! *Allāhu Akbar!*

Then he must raise his hands from the ground, and then his knees, relying on his knees to lift his weight. As he rises to stand on the soles of his feet, he should not put one foot ahead of the other, for that is considered reprehensible. It has even been said that it cuts off the ritual prayer *[ṣalāt]*, and there is a traditional report to that effect, transmitted on the authority of Ibn 'Abbās (may Allāh be well pleased with him and with his father).

[252] See the list of forty-five bad habits, on pp. 169–73 above.

[253] In the Arabic text, the participle *mukabbiran* is sufficient, all by itself, to signify: "saying: '*Allāhu Akbar* [Allāh is Supremely Great!]" Like the superlative adjective *akbar*, the verb *kabbara*, and the verbal noun *takbīr*, it is derived from the three-consonant root *k–b–r*.

The worshipper must now perform the second cycle *[rakʿa]* in the same manner as the first, until [after the second prostration] he adopts a sitting posture, in order to perform the first testimony *[at-tashahhud al-awwal]*. He must sit on his left leg, while placing his right leg so that the right foot is in an upright position [i.e., with the heel raised], and so that his toes are pointing toward the *Qibla* [direction of the Kaʿba]. He must place his left hand on his left thigh, and his right hand on his right thigh.

While pointing with the finger next to the thumb, i.e., the index finger *[sabbāba]* [of his right hand], he should join the thumb *[ibhām]* and the middle finger *[wusṭā]* to form a circle, and hold the little finger *[khinṣir]* and the ring finger *[binṣir]* in the grip of his hand. He must keep a watchful eye on his finger from the beginning of his testimony *[tashahhud]* to the end, because the Prophet (Allāh bless him and give him peace) is reported as having said:

> When one of you is in the sitting posture, in the course of performing the ritual prayer *[ṣalāt]*, he must not fiddle with anything, for he is engaged in intimate converse with his Lord *[yunājī Rabba-hu]*. He must place his left hand on his left thigh, and his right hand on his right thigh, then focus his heart and his eyes on his finger, for it can serve as a swatter to whisk away the Devil *[midhabba li'sh-Shaiṭān]*.

The worshipper must now perform the testimony *[tashahhud]*, by saying:

Greetings, prayers and good deeds are due to Allāh.	*at-taḥiyyātu li'llāhi wa 'ṣ-ṣalawātu wa 'ṭ-ṭayyibāt—*
Peace be upon you, O Prophet, and the mercy of Allāh and His blessings!	*as-salāmu ʿalai-ka ayyuha 'n-nabiyyu wa raḥmatu'llāhi wa barakātuh—*
Peace be on us, and on all the rightesous servants of Allāh.	*as-salāmu ʿalai-nā wa ʿalā ʿibādi 'llāhi 'ṣ-ṣāliḥīn.*
I bear witness that there is no god but Allāh, and I bear witness that Muḥammad is His servant and His Messenger.	*ashhadu an lā ilāha illa 'llāh— wa ashhadu anna Muḥammadan ʿabdu-hu wa rasūluh.*

Next, the worshipper must stand up,[254] saying *[mukabbiran]*:

Allāh is Supremely Great!	*Allāhu Akbar.*

[254] That is to say, in order to perform the third cycle *[rakʿa]*.

He must recite *al-Fātiḥa* only, with no additional Qur'ānic recitation, and then go on to perform the acts of bowing *[rukū']* and prostration *[sujūd]*, in the same manner as before.

The worshipper must then perform the fourth cycle *[rak'a]* in the same manner as the third [i.e., reciting *al-Fātiḥa* only]. Then he must adopt the sitting posture in order to perform the testimony *[tashahhud]*, which he must carry out in the manner we have described above. This time, however, when he reaches the words:

His servant and His Messenger.	*'abdu-hu wa rasūluh.*

—he must go on to say:

O Allāh, bless Muḥammad, and the family of Muḥammad, as You have blessed Abraham!	*Allāhumma ṣallī 'alā Muḥammadin* *wa 'alā āli Muḥammadin* *ka-mā ṣallaita 'alā Ibrāhīm.*
Surely You deserve to be praised and extolled!	*inna-ka* *Ḥamīdun Majīd.*
And bestow Your grace upon Muḥammad, and upon the family of Muḥammad, as You have bestowed Your grace upon Abraham!	*wa bārik* *'alā Muḥammadin* *wa 'alā āli Muḥammadin* *ka-mā bārakta* *'alā Ibrāhīm.*
Surely You deserve to be praised and extolled!	*inna-ka* *Ḥamīdun Majīd.*

According to another account of the doctrine of our Imām Aḥmad [ibn Ḥanbal], the mention of Abraham *[Ibrāhīm]* should be followed by a reference to his family, so the worshipper must say:

as You have blessed Abraham, and the family of Abraham.	*ka-mā ṣallaita 'alā Ibrāhīma* *wa 'alā āli Ibrāhīm.*

—and:

as You have bestowed Your grace upon Abraham, and the upon family of Abraham.	*ka-mā bārakta* *'alā Ibrāhīm.* *wa 'alā āli Ibrāhīm.*

At this point, which marks the conclusion of the testimony *[tashahhud]*, the worshipper is recommended to seek refuge from four perils. He should therefore say:

O Allāh, I take refuge with You from the torment of Hell, and from the torment of the grave,	*Allāhumma innī a'ūdhu bi-ka* *min 'adhābi jahannam:* *wa min 'adhābi 'l-qabr:*

and from the mischief of the False Messiah, and from the mischief of life and death.	*wa min fitnati 'l-* *masīḥi 'd-dajjāl:* *wa min fitnati 'l-maḥyā* *wa 'l-mamāt.*

He should then offer the following supplications:

O Allāh, I beg You to grant me all that is good, both what I know of it and that which I do not know,	*Allāhumma innī as'alu-ka 'l-khaira* *ulla-hu mā 'alimtu min-hu* *wa mā lam a'lam.*
and I take refuge with You from all that is evil, both what I know of it and that which I do not know.	*wa a'ūdhu bi-ka mina 'sh-sharri* *kulli-hi mā 'alimtu min-hu* *wa mā lam a'lam.*
O Allāh, I beg You to grant me the goodness of that which Your righteous servants have asked of You,	*Allāhumma innī as'alu-ka* *min khairi mā sa'ala-ka* *'ibādu-ka 'ṣ-ṣāliḥūn.*
and I take refuge with You from the evil of that from which Your righteous servants have sought refuge with You.	*wa a'ūdhu bi-ka* *min sharri* *ma 'sta'ādha bi-ka minhu* *'ibādu-ka 'ṣ-ṣāliḥūn.*
O Allāh, I beg You to grant me the Garden of Paradise, and whatever brings one close to it, by word and by deed.	*Allāhumma innī* *as'alu-ka 'l-jannata wa mā* *qarraba ilai-hā* *min qawlin wa 'amal.*
Our Lord, give us in this world good, and good in the hereafter, and guard us against the torment of the Fire [of Hell]! (2:201)	*Rabba-nā āti-nā* *fi 'd-dunyā ḥasanatan* *wa fi 'l-ākhirati ḥasanatan* *wa qinā* *'adhāba 'n-nār.*
Our Lord, forgive us our sins, and grant us remission for our evil deeds, and let us end our earthly lives in the company of the righteous.	*Rabba-nā fa-'ghfir* *la-nā dhunūba-nā* *wa kaffir 'an-nā sayyi'āti-nā* *wa tawaffa-nā* *ma'a 'l-abrār.*
Our Lord, give us that which You have promised us through Your Messengers, and do not put us to shame on the Day of Resurrection. Surely You will not fail to keep the tryst! (3:194)	*Rabba-nā wa āti-nā* *mā wa'adta-nā* *'alā Rusuli-ka* *wa lā tukhzi-nā* *yawma 'l-qiyāmah:* *inna-ka* *lā tukhlifu 'l-mī'ād.*

If the worshipper wishes to add further supplications to these, it is permissible for him to do so, unless he is acting as a prayer leader *[imām]*, in which case it would make the proceedings unduly lengthy for those who are following his lead *[ma'mūmīn]*. For one who is leading others in prayer, brevity is the recommended practice *[mustaḥabb]*, out of consideration for their feelings, and because there may be someone amongst them who has a pressing need to attend to.

The worshipper must then conclude the ritual prayer *[ṣalāt]* by performing the salutation *[taslīma]*,[255] after which he should offer supplications for his own sake, for the sake of his parents, and on behalf of all the Muslims.

At every stage in all of this, the worshipper must be timidly apprehensive about its ultimate outcome, wondering how his prayer may be received in the sight of Allāh (Exalted is He), the One who summons us to it, the One who commands us to perform it, the One who rewards us for it [if it is acceptable], and the One who punishes us for it, if it is done badly. So, when he finally emerges from the process, he should undertake a conscious review of his performance. Then, if he can honestly give it a clearance and a clean bill of health, he must offer grateful praise to Allāh (Exalted is He), since He is the One who made him capable of such an achievement. If, on the other hand, he finds it marred by deficiency and imperfection, he must repent to Allāh (Almighty and Glorious is He) and seek Allāh's forgiveness. He must prepare himself to do better, and make a serious effort to be more careful in future.

There is a clear indication to prove that a ritual prayer *[ṣalāt]* has been accepted, and an equally clear indication to prove that it has been rejected. The sure sign of its acceptance is that it has been effective in deterring and preventing its owner from indulging in immoral behavior and reprehensible conduct, while encouraging him to do better, renewing his intention to strive after righteousness, increasing his acts of worshipful obedience, his charitable deeds, his eagerness for spiritual rewards, his resistance to bad influences, and his disapproval of sinful acts of disobedience and misconduct. For, as Allāh (Almighty and Glorious is He) has told us:

The ritual prayer helps to prevent	*inna 'ṣ-ṣalāta tanhā*
indecency and reprehensible behavior.	*'ani 'l-faḥshā'i wa 'l-munkar:*
The remembrance of Allāh is greater;	*wa la-dhikru 'llāhi akbar:*
and Allāh knows the things you do.	*wa 'llāhu ya'lamu mā taṣna'ūn.*
(29:45)	

[255] In other words, he must turn his head to the right and say:

Peace be upon you, and the mercy of Allāh.	*as-salāmu 'alaikum wa raḥmatu'llāh.*

—then turn his head to the left and repeat these same words.

Our treatment of this subject is equally applicable to the prayer leader *[imām]*, the worshipper who follows his lead *[ma'mūm]*, and the worshipper who prays by himself *[munfarid]*.

As for the essential prerequisites of the ritual prayer *[sharā'iṭ aṣ-ṣalāt]*, its necessary elements *[wājibāt]*, and its customarily recommended practices *[masnūnāt]*, we have provided a detailed account of these in the first part of this book.[256]

Allāh is the One who enables us to do what is right and proper *[al-Muwaffiq li'ṣ-ṣawāb]*.

[256] See Vol. 1, pp. 13–16.

24.
Concerning the qualifications and responsibilities of the prayer leader *[imām]*.

It is not appropriate for a man to act as a prayer leader *[imām]* unless or until he possesses all the attributes we are about to mention, namely:

1. He should not be keen to put himself forward, as long as he can find someone sufficiently qualified to spare him from having to do so, and on no account should he put himself forward in the presence of someone better qualified than he.

This is most important, because, as we know from the tradition *[ḥadīth]*, the Prophet (Allāh bless him and give him peace) is reported as having said:

> If a man leads *[amma]* the people in prayer, when there is someone better qualified in the congregation behind him, they will suffer constant ignominy.

[The Caliph] ʿUmar ibn al-Khaṭṭāb (may Allāh be well pleased with him) once said:

"That I should charge to the battlefront and get my head cut off, without incurring any sin thereby, would be far better than putting myself forward to lead a congregation that included Abū Bakr, the Champion of Truth *[aṣ-Ṣiddīq]*, (may Allāh be well pleased with him)."

2. He must be a competent reciter *[qāriʾ]* of the Book of Allāh, a trained expert *[faqīh]* in the religion *[dīn]* of Allāh, and a proficient student of the exemplary practice *[sunna]* of Allāh's Messenger (Allāh bless him and give him peace), because the latter said, as reported in the tradition *[ḥadīth]*:

> Entrust the oversight of your religion to your experts in Islāmic jurisprudence *[fuqahāʾ]*, and let your prayer leaders *[aʾimma]* be the Qurʾān-reciters *[qurrāʾ]* among you.

The Prophet (Allāh bless him and give him peace) also said:

> Those who lead you in prayer are your finest élite *[yaʾummu-kum khiyāru-kum]*, for they are your ambassadorial delegates *[wufūd]* to Allāh (Almighty and Glorious is He).

By according them this special accolade, the Prophet (Allāh bless him and give him peace) was simply drawing attention to the fact that they are people distinguished by religious faith and virtue, knowledge of Allāh (Almighty and Glorious is He), and fear of Allāh (Exalted is He), who are concerned not only with their own prayer *[ṣalāt]*, but also with the prayer performed by those behind them. They are keenly aware of the responsibility they must bear, both for themselves and for those behind them, if they are guilty of any impropriety in their performance of the ritual prayer *[ṣalāt]*.

When he mentioned the Qur'ān-reciters *[qurrā']*, the Prophet (Allāh bless him and give him peace) was not referring to those who have merely memorized the text of the Qur'ān, without putting it into practice. What he meant to emphasize (Allāh bless him and give him peace) was the importance of acting on the message of the Qur'ān, as well as learning it by heart. As we are told in the tradition *[ḥadīth]*:

> The person most worthy of this Qur'ān is someone who puts it into practice, even if he does not read it.

It is quite possible for the Qur'ān to be memorized by someone who fails to put it into practice, and who makes not the slightest effort to abide by the rules it lays down, neither implementing the prescriptions enjoined upon him by Allāh, nor observing the prohibitions He has imposed upon him. We are not interested in such a person, and he deserves no respect. Allāh's Messenger (Allāh bless him and give him peace) has told us:

> A person can hardly believe in the Qur'ān, if he considers it permissible to do the things it has declared unlawful.

It is not permissible, therefore, for people to set anyone in front of them in their ritual prayer *[ṣalāt]*, as a leader *[imām]*, other than the individual amongst them who knows Allāh best, and fears him the most. If they go against this instruction, and appoint someone less qualified, they will suffer constant ignominy, backwardness and deficiency in their religion, and remoteness from Allāh (Exalted is He), from His good pleasure *[riḍwān]*,[257] and from His Garden of Paradise.

[257] As an ordinary noun, the Arabic word *riḍwān* means "approval; consent; good pleasure." In the standard works of reference, the angel called Riḍwān is variously described as the porter, the gardener, the doorkeeper, the keeper, the guardian, the treasurer, or the custodian of Paradise.

May Allāh bestow His mercy upon any group of people who take a serious interest in their religion *[dīn]* and their ritual prayers *[ṣalawāt]*, so that they appoint their finest élite *[khiyār]* to lead them. In so doing, they will be following the exemplary practice *[sunna]* of their Prophet (Allāh bless him and give him peace), and thereby seeking nearness to their Lord (Blessed and Exalted is He).

3. It is also important that the prayer leader *[imām]* should be someone who is careful to guard his tongue from responding, when people engage in faultfinding and backbiting at his expense, unless he has something good to say.

4. He must not only enjoin what is right and fair *[maʿrūf]*, but also practice it himself, and he must not only forbid what is wrong and unfair *[munkar]*, but also avoid committing it himself.[258]

5. He must love goodness and those who practice it, and he must hate evil and those who practice it.

6. He must be thoroughly familiar with the exact times prescribed for the ritual prayer *[mawāqīt aṣ-ṣalāt]*, and meticulous in observing them.

7. He must fully appreciate the significance and the serious importance of his rôle.

8. He must be chaste with regard to his stomach and his sexual organs *[ʿafīf al-baṭn wa 'l-farj]*, and keep his hand withdrawn from contact with things that are unlawful *[maḥārim]*.

9. He must expend little energy for any purpose other than seeking to obtain the approval of Allāh (Almighty and Glorious is He).

10. He must be mild-tempered, long-suffering, and patient in the face of injury and insult. This means that he must turn a blind eye to mischievous provocation, be tolerant of those who speak ill of him, be patient with those who treat him foolishly, and behave well toward those who behave badly toward him.

11. He must beware of taking a prurient interest in things that are unlawful *[maḥārim]*. If he sees that a private part *[ʿawra]* is exposed to view, he must cover it up, and if he happens to notice something shameful, he must conceal it.

[258] Shaikh ʿAbd al-Qādir al-Jīlānī (may Allāh be well pleased with him) has devoted an entire Chapter, earlier in the present work, to the duty to enjoin what is what is right and fair and to forbid what is wrong and unfair *[al-amr bi'l-maʿrūf wa 'n-nahy ʿani 'l-munkar]*. (See Vol. 1, pp. 151–70.)

12. He must shun altercation with ignorant fools, and respond to their nonsense by saying: "O Allāh, let there be peace! *[Allāhumma salāmā]*."[259]

13. While other people should find him to be a reassuring source of comfort, his feeling about himself must be one of grave concern, as he yearns for deliverance and strives for his personal salvation.

14. He must acknowledge that he is being put to the test, recognize the magnitude of the challenge he faces, and understand the momentous significance and enormous importance of the task assigned to him. His overriding concern must therefore be to discharge the solemn responsibility laid upon him, by proving himself worthy of the great dignity of the prayer leader's rôle *[imāma]*, its tremendous value, and its beneficial quality.

15. He must be a man of few words, except when he needs to speak about matters relating to his sphere of interest.

16. [He must be aware that] there is a state of being *[ḥāl]* that is appropriate for him [as prayer leader], and a state of being that is appropriate for the people [who follow his lead].

17. When he stands in his prayer-niche *[miḥrāb]*, he must realize that he is standing in the station of the Prophets *[maqām an-Nabiyyīn]* and of the Caliph of the Chief of the Messengers *[Khalīfa Sayyid al-Mursalīn]*, and that he is communing with the Lord of All the Worlds *[yunājī Rabb al-ʿĀlamīn]*.

18. He must exercise his independent judgment *[ijtihād]*,[260] in order to ensure the complete performance of the ritual prayer *[ṣalāt]*, and also to ensure the well-being of those behind him, meaning those who are following his leadership *[imāma]*.

19. He must keep the performance of the ritual prayer *[ṣalāt]* as short and simple as possible, without prejudice to its completeness.

20. He must conduct the ritual prayer *[ṣalāt]* in a way that accommodates the weakest member of the congregation. This means that he must regard himself as inferior to those who pray behind him, recognizing that their leadership *[imāma]* has been assigned to him as a test, and realizing that Allāh (Exalted is He) will hold him responsible for the performance of the obligatory duties *[farāʾiḍ]*, not just on his own account, but also on that of the weakest member of the congregation.

[259] This is a clear allusion to Q. 25:63.

[260] See note 177 on p. 132 above.

21. When putting himself forward to lead the congregation, he should do so as one who is tearfully lamenting his mistakes, feeling remorse for his previous negligence and his former sins, and regretting his lost opportunities.

22. He must not adopt a proud and haughty attitude toward those who pray behind him, nor assume an air of superiority over those to whom he is actually subordinate.

23. He must not become a fanatical champion of his own cause, when comments are made about his positive qualities and his shortcomings. He should neither like it when people praise him, nor dislike it when they blame him. His attitude toward the congregation should be the same in either case.

24. He must be someone to whom no falsehood can be imputed.

25. He must be well-mannered in his eating habits.

26. He must be someone who keeps his clothes clean and tidy.

27. He must be modest in his style of dressing, and unassuming in the way he sits in company.

28. He must not be someone who has been punished *[maḥdūd]* for a serious offense against the law of Islām.[261]

29. He must not be the kind of person who arouses misgivings in people.

30. He must not be the kind of person who would denounce his brother to the political authority *[sulṭān]*.

31. He must not be someone who divulges people's secrets. (That is to say, he must not be someone who broadcasts them.)

32. He must not be someone who goes looking for the worst in people.

33. He must not be the kind of person who harbors feelings of hatred and resentment toward his brother.

34. He must not be the kind of person who would cheat in his management of funds entrusted to him, in his commercial dealings, or in the repayment of a loan.

35. He must not put himself forward [to lead the prayer] as long as his diet and his means of livelihood are unclean.

36. He must not put himself forward as long as he feels a craving to occupy the prayer leader's position *[imāma]*.

37. He must not put himself forward as long as he recognizes that he

[261] The term *maḥdūd* is applied to a person who has suffered the penalty *[ḥadd]* prescribed by Islāmic law for one of the offenses listed in note 228 on p. 166 above.

still harbors some feeling of envy, or resentment, or malice, or hatred, or spite, or grievance, or vindictiveness.

38. He must not be seeking blood revenge *[tha'r]*.

39. He must not be trying to win support for himself.

40. He must not be trying to satisfy a grudge.

41. He must not be chasing the wife of a Muslim.

42. He must not be cheating anyone belonging to the Community of Muḥammad (Allāh bless him and give him peace).

43. He must not talk about a seditious conspiracy *[fitna]*, and he must neither get involved in it nor do anything to encourage it.

44. Far from engaging in such negative activity, he must positively assist the upholders of the truth *[ahl al-ḥaqq]* against the supporters of falsehood *[ahl al-bāṭil]*, with his hand, his tongue and his heart.

45. He must always speak the truth, even if it is bitter.

46. He must not be affected, in his commitment to Allāh, by criticism from any quarter.

47. He should neither like it when people praise him, nor dislike it when they blame him.

48. When offering the supplication *[du'ā']*, immediately after the ritual prayer *[ṣalāt]* in which he has led the congregation, he should not make any request for himself in particular. He should rather couch the supplication in general terms, applicable to them as well as to himself, for it would amount to a breach of trust on his part, if he were to single himself out at their expense.

49. He should not accord preferential respect to certain members of the congregation over others,[262] except to those who are endowed with knowledge and understanding. As the Prophet (Allāh bless him and give him peace) once said:

> Let those who follow me closely [in the ritual prayer] be persons endowed with understanding and restraint *[ulu 'l-aḥlām wa 'n-nahy]*.

They should be treated with the same respect by those who line up next to them behind the leader's back.

50. He must not invite the rich man to move close to him, while treating the poor man with disdain.

51. It is not appropriate for him to step forward to lead a congregation that includes people who disapprove of his leadership *[imāma]*. If there

[262] That is to say, by inviting them to occupy the positions immediately behind him, in front of the rest of the congregation.

are some amongst them who disapprove of him, and some who do not disapprove of him, he must investigate the situation thoroughly. Then, if he discovers that those who disapprove of him are in the majority, he must vacate the prayer-niche *[miḥrāb]* and decline to approach it again.

This only applies if their disapproval of him is based on sound knowledge and a true assessment of his character. If it is due to ignorance, falsehood and stupidity, or to fanatical adherence to a particular doctrine *[ʿaṣaba li-madhhab]*, or to some heretical tendency *[hawā]*, he should pay no attention to their disapproval. If such is the case, he should not refrain from leading them in the performance of the ritual prayer *[ṣalāt]*, unless he has reason to fear that an outbreak of public disorder could be sparked by his failure to withdraw. Under these circumstances, he should step aside and vacate the prayer-niche *[miḥrāb]*, until such time as the people have become reconciled with one another, and are content to accept his leadership.

52. He must not be the kind of person who is always getting into arguments, or who is constantly swearing and cursing.

53. He must not be someone who finds pretexts for dabbling in matters that are unsavory and highly suspect.

56. He must not be on intimate terms, or engage in social intercourse, with people other than the righteous *[ṣāliḥīn]*.

57. It is not appropriate for him to serve as a prayer leader *[imām]* as long as he is still has a fondness for mischievous intrigue *[fitna]* and those who practice it, and even worse, for sinful disobedience *[maʿṣiya]* and those who practice it, and for political leadership *[riyāsa]* and those who are interested in pursuing it.

58. In order to qualify, he must be very patient in coping with the injuries and insults people can inflict, lovingly disposed toward them, eager to secure their welfare, and dedicated to providing them with constructive advice.

59. He must not quarrel over the position of prayer leader *[imāma]*, and he certainly must not come to blows over it, with someone who is just as well qualified to carry out the task.

As we know from traditional reports concerning the great figures of the past, our righteous forebears had a strong aversion to assuming the prayer leader's rôle *[imāma]*, so much so that they would put forward some who was less than their equal in nobility and religious stature, in their eagerness to offload the burden and obtain relief, and from fear of incurring the liability for some shortcoming.

60. When an officer of the government *[dhū sulṭān]* is present in his company, it is not appropriate for the usual prayer leader *[imām]* to put himself out in front of him in the ritual prayer *[ṣalāt]*, except with his permission. By the same token, he should not sit down in the presence of such a person, except with his permission.

61. If he stays for some time in a village, or a way station, or an encampment belonging to a clan *[qabīla]* or tribe of the Arabs of the desert *[ḥayy min aḥyā' al-'Arab]*, he must not act as their prayer leader *[lā ya'ummu-hum]* without their permission. By the same token, if he happens to find himself in the company of people in a caravan, a group of travelers who represent a potential congregation, he must not take it upon himself to act as their prayer leader *[lā ya'ummu-hum]* without their permission.

62. Far from prolonging the performance of the ritual prayer *[ṣalāt]*, the prayer leader *[imām]* is under an obligation to keep it as short as possible, without detriment to its essential completeness. If this needs any further explanation, we have only to cite the following traditional reports:

According to Abū Huraira (may Allāh be well pleased with him), Allāh's Messenger (Allāh bless him and give him peace) once said:

> Whenever one of you is acting as a prayer leader *[imām]*, he should keep it short and easy, for standing behind him are the young and the old, and those who have pressing needs. When he is performing the ritual prayer on his own behalf, that is when he may prolong it as much as he wishes.

Abū Wāqid (may Allāh be well pleased with him) is reported as having said:

"Allāh's Messenger (Allāh bless him and give him peace) was one of the speediest of them all when it came to leading the people in the ritual prayer *[ṣalāt]*, and the most long-drawn-out of them all when it came to his personal performance."

25.
Concerning the intention *[niyya]* of the prayer leader *[imām]*, his instructions to the congregation, and how he ought to station himself in the prayer-niche *[miḥrāb]*.

The prayer leader *[imām]* must not embark upon the performance of the ritual prayer *[ṣalāt]*, nor should he pronounce the declaration of Allāh's Supreme Greatness *[lā yukabbir]*,[263] until he has made the intention, at least with his heart, to carry out the task of leadership *[imāma]*. If he also expresses his intention with his tongue, so much the better.

[Before starting the prayer] he should turn and look to right and left, for he must make sure that the worshippers are lined up in perfectly straight rows. He should then say:

Hold yourselves erect!	*istaqīmū*
May Allāh bestow His mercy upon you!	*yarḥamu-kumu 'llāh.*
Straighten your ranks!	*i'tadilū*
May Allāh be well pleased with you!	*raḍiya 'llāhu 'an-kum.*

He should instruct them to fill the gaps in their ranks, to hold their shoulders in an even line, and to move closer to one another until their shoulders are actually touching. This is very important, because any crookedness of the shoulders and unevenness of the ranks will represent a diminution of the value of the ritual prayer *[ṣalāt]*, and will provide a opportunity for the devils *[shayāṭīn]* to come and stand alongside the people in the rows. As we learn from the tradition *[ḥadīth]*, the Prophet (Allāh bless him and give him peace) is reported as having said:

> Align the rows tightly, keep the shoulders straight, and fill the gaps, so as to leave no space for the likes of the offspring of the *ḥadhaf*[264] to stand between you.

[263] That is to say, [until he has formulated his intention...] he should not utter the *takbīra*, meaning the affirmation: "*Allāhu Akbar* [Allāh is Supremely Great!]," which is pronounced as an act of consecration *[iḥrām]* at the beginning of the performance of the ritual prayer *[ṣalāt]*.

[264] According to the classical Arabic lexicographers, the term *ḥadhaf* is applied to small, black sheep or goats, with short and fine wool or hair, without tails and without ears; or to the young ones of sheep or goats, in general; or, metaphorically, to various other creatures. (See: E.W. Lane, *Arabic-English Lexicon*, art. Ḥ-DH-F.)

That is to say, the likes of the offspring of sheep and goats *[ghanam]*, meaning the devils *[shayāṭīn]*.

According to one traditional report:

"When the Prophet (Allāh bless him and give him peace) stood ready to lead the ritual prayer *[ṣalāt]*, he would not pronounce the declaration of Allāh's Supreme Greatness *[lam yukabbir]* until he had turned and looked to right and left. He would instruct the members of the congregation to hold their shoulders in an even line, and he would say: 'Do not stand at odds, for then your hearts will be at odds!'"

According to another traditional report:

"One day, the Prophet (Allāh bless him and give him peace) noticed that a man was holding himself in such a way that his chest was sticking out from the row in which he was standing, so he said: 'All of you had better hold your shoulders in an even line, otherwise Allāh (Exalted is He) will surely cause your hearts to be out of harmony.'"

The following traditional report is one of those accepted as authentic by both Imām Muslim and Imām al-Bukhārī (may Allāh bestow His mercy upon them).[265] It informs us that Sālim ibn Abi 'l-Ja'd (may Allāh bestow His mercy upon him) once heard an-Nu'mān ibn Bashīr (may Allāh be well pleased with him) say that Allāh's Messenger (Allāh bless him and give him peace) used to say:

> You had better straighten your ranks, otherwise Allāh (Exalted is He) will surely cause your faces to be out of harmony.

According to yet another traditional report, this one transmitted on the authority of Qatāda (may Allāh bestow His mercy upon him) from Anas ibn Mālik (may Allāh be well pleased with him), the latter stated that Allāh's Messenger (Allāh bless him and give him peace) once said:

> You must keep your ranks straight, for the straightness of the ranks is part of what makes the ritual prayer complete *[taswiyat aṣ-ṣufūf min tamām aṣ-ṣalāt]*.

In the case of [the Caliph] 'Umar ibn al-Khaṭṭāb (may Allāh be well pleased with him), it is reported that, whenever he acted in the capacity of prayer leader *[imām]*, he would not pronounce the declaration of Allāh's Supreme Greatness *[kāna lā yukabbiru]* until a man, to whom he

[265] These are the compilers of the two most famous collections of Prophetic traditions, under the titles *Ṣaḥīḥ al-Bukhārī* and *Ṣaḥīḥ Muslim*. (The term *ṣaḥīḥ* means "correct; authentic.")

had assigned the task of drawing up the ranks, came and informed him that they had been properly aligned. Only at that point would he pronounce the declaration of Allāh's Supreme Greatness. The same practice was later implemented by [the pious Umayyad Caliph] ʿUmar ibn ʿAbd al-ʿAzīz (may Allāh bestow His mercy upon him).

It is related that Bilāl the Muezzin *[al-Muʾaddhin]* (may Allāh be well pleased with him) had a special method of his own for persuading the members of the congregation to straighten their ranks: He used to thrash them on their Achilles' tendons *[ʿarāqīb]* with a kind of whip called the *dirra*, until they aligned themselves in proper order. As one of the learned scholars *[ʿulamāʾ]* has pointed out:

"The obvious conclusion to be drawn, in considering the implications of this report, is that Bilāl (may Allāh be well pleased with him) must have followed that practice during the lifetime of Allāh's Messenger (Allāh bless him and give him peace), whenever he was about to make the announcement of readiness *[iqāma]*,[266] just before he [the Prophet (Allāh bless him and give him peace)] embarked on the performance of the ritual prayer *[ṣalāt]*. It must have been during that period, because Bilāl (may Allāh be well pleased with him) did not act as muezzin *[lam yuʾaddhin]* for anyone after the Prophet (Allāh bless him and give him peace), except on one particular day, after his return from Syria during the time of [the Caliph] Abū Bakr, the Champion of Truth *[aṣ-Ṣiddīq]*, (may Allāh be well pleased with him).

"On that one occasion, he responded to the request of Abū Bakr and the other Companions *[Ṣaḥāba]* (may Allāh be well pleased with them all), for they all shared a sense of longing for Allāh's Messenger (Allāh bless him and give him peace) and for his era. But when Bilāl (may Allāh be well pleased with him) reached the words:

I bear witness that Muḥammad is the Messenger of Allāh.	*ashhadu anna Muḥammadan Rasūlu'llāh.*

—he suddenly desisted from giving the call to prayer *[adhān]*, because he was simply unable to continue with it any further. He swooned and fell down in a faint, overwhelmed by love for the Prophet (Allāh bless him and give him peace) and yearning for his company. At that point, the mournful lamentation of those senior citizens of Medina, the

[266] See note 304 on p. 225 below.

Emigrés *[Muhājirūn]* and the Helpers *[Anṣār]*,[267] became extremely loud and intense, so much so that the elderly widows and spinsters *[ʿawātiq]*[268] emerged from their private quarters, moved by a nostalgic longing for the Prophet (Allāh bless him and give him peace).

"It is therefore definitely established, on the basis of these historical facts, that his practice of thrashing the members of the congregation on their Achilles' tendons *[ʿarāqīb]* was put into effect during the lifetime of Allāh's Messenger (Allāh bless him and give him peace)."

It is not appropriate for the prayer leader *[imām]* to station himself inside the inner niche *[ṭāq]* of the *Qibla*, thereby blocking the view of it that would otherwise be available to the members of the congregation behind him. He should rather stand back from it a little way. [According to another account of his doctrine, however, our Imām Aḥmad ibn Ḥanbal (may Allāh bestow His mercy upon him) maintained that it is actually commendable for the prayer leader *[imām]* to station himself inside the inner niche.]

He must not station himself on a spot that would place him on a higher level than those who are following his lead *[maʾmūmīn]*. If he does this, some experts have argued, his ritual prayer *[ṣalāt]* will be rendered null and void.

Once he has concluded his performance of the ritual prayer *[sallama min ṣalāti-hi]*,[269] it is not appropriate for him to linger in his niche *[miḥrāb]*. He should get up promptly and move over to his left, then perform his supererogatory devotions *[tanafful]* on that side of the niche *[miḥrāb]*. This is based on the traditional report of al-Mughīra ibn Shuʿba[270] (may Allāh be well pleased with him), who stated that the Prophet (Allāh bless him and give him peace) once said:

[267] See note 148 on p. 115 above.

[268] The term *ʿātiq* (of which *ʿawātiq* is the plural form) is applied to a woman who is her own mistress, in the sense of having outlived her parents, and being beyond the normal age for marriage (or remarriage, in the case of a widow or divorcée). The Arabic root *ʿ–t–q* conveys the basic idea of "emancipation." (See: E.W. Lane, *Arabic-English Lexicon*, art. *ʿ–T–Q*.)

[269] See note 255 on p. 187 above,

[270] Al-Mughīra ibn Shuʿba (may Allāh be well pleased with him) is often referred to by the nickname Mughīrat ar-Raʾy ["Quick-witted"], which he acquired in recognition of his proverbial ingenuity. He claimed that he was the last man to be with the Prophet (Allāh bless him and give him peace), and he used to say: "I took my ring and let it fall into the grave, then I said: 'My ring has dropped.' But I had actually thrown it in on purpose, so that I might touch the Messenger (Allāh bless him and give him peace), and be the last man to be with him." At the time of his death, in A.H. 49., he held the important post of Governor of Kūfa.

The prayer leader *[imām]* must not go on to perform voluntary devotions *[lā yataṭawwaʿ]* in the place he occupies while leading the people in the prescribed prayer *[maktūba]*.

In the case of the follower *[maʾmūm]*, on the other hand, the equivalent of this is quite permissible. Since he is allowed the option, he may either perform his [voluntary] prayers on the same spot, if he wishes to do so, or he may choose to move back from it a little way.

The prayer leader *[imām]* must observe two moments of silent pause: (1) at the very beginning of the prayer *[iftitāḥ aṣ-ṣalāt]*, and (2) when he has finished the Qurʾānic recitation *[qirāʾa]*, just before he adopts the bowing posture *[qabla an yarkaʿa]*, so that he may catch his breath and calm the intense vibration experienced during his recitation. He must not combine his Qurʾānic recitation uninterruptedly with the affirmation of Allāh's Supreme Greatness that precedes the adoption of the bowing posture *[takbīrat ar-rukūʿ]*, because an instruction to this effect is attributed to the Prophet (Allāh bless him and give him peace), in the tradition *[ḥadīth]* reported by Samura ibn Jundab (may Allāh be well pleased with him).

When he performs the prayer with a screening object in front of him *[ṣallā ilā sutra]*,[271] he must position himself very close to it. If he leaves any gap at all between himself and the object used as a screen, it must not be wide enough to allow a wild black dog, or a donkey, or a woman, to pass through. Should any of these come in between, his ritual prayer *[ṣalāt]* will be cut off at that point, according to the doctrine of Aḥmad ibn Ḥanbal, our Imām, (may Allāh bestow His mercy upon him). As far as the donkey and the woman are concerned, however, there is another account of his doctrine, according to which these two are harmless in this respect.[272]

[271] According to E.W. Lane (*Arabic-English Lexicon*, art. *S–T–R*), the predominant application of the term *sutra* [screening object] is to "a thing which a person praying sets up before him; [sticking it in the ground, or laying it down if the ground be hard, in order that no living being or image may be the object next before him;] such as a whip, and a staff having a pointed iron at its lower extremity."

At various times, according to traditions *[aḥādīth]* recorded by Imām al-Bukhārī (may Allāh bestow His mercy upon him), the Prophet (Allāh bless him and give him peace) used a wide range of creatures and articles as *sutra* objects, including baggage-camels, horses, trees, saddles, a couch, a lance, a stick, and the pillars of a mosque.

[272] According to a traditional report recorded by Imām al-Bukhārī, ʿĀʾisha (may Allāh be well pleased with her) once exclaimed: "Would you place us women on the same level as donkeys and dogs? By Allāh, the Prophet (Allāh bless him and give him peace) used to perform the ritual prayer *[ṣalāt]* while I was lying on the couch between him and the *Qibla*."

When the prayer leader *[imām]* adopts the bowing posture *[idhā raka'a]*, he must utter three glorifications *[tasbīḥāt]*,[273] in the manner we have previously described. He must be careful not to utter them too rapidly or too soon, and they should be fully pronounced, in a calm, deliberate, and clearly audible voice. This is very important because, if he utters the glorification *[tasbīḥ]* too quickly, the people behind him will not be able to keep pace with him. This may result in a situation where the members of the congregation *[ma'mūmīn]* start to anticipate his movements. Their prayer will thus be spoiled, and he will incur the liability for their sin.

The same considerations apply when he raises his head from the bowing posture *[rukū']*, and says:

May Allāh hear and accept the praise of one who praises Him!	*sami'a 'llāhu li-man ḥamidah.*

—then stands quite still in an upright posture, while he says:

Our Lord, and to You be the praise!	*Rabba-nā wa la-ka 'l-ḥamd.*

He must pronounce these words in an unhurried voice, so that the members of the congregation *[ma'mūmūn]* can easily keep up with him. If he goes on to add the words:

Enough [praise] to fill the heavens and the earth, and to fill anything beyond them, as You wish.	*mil'u 's-samāwāti wa mil'u 'l-arḍ: wa mil'u mā shi'ta min shai'in ba'd.*

—this is quite permissible, because the practice is reliably attributed to the Prophet (Allāh bless him and give him peace).

Anas ibn Mālik (may Allāh be well pleased with him) is reported as having said:

"When Allāh's Messenger (Allāh bless him and give him peace) raised his head from the bowing posture *[rukū']*, he used to stand upright for such a long time [before making the prostration], that people would say: 'He seems to have forgotten [what comes next].'"

In the posture of prostration *[sujūd]*, and when he adopts the sitting posture *[jalsa]* between the two acts of prostration *[sajdatain]*, he must

[273] In other words, he must say, three times:

Glory to my Lord, the Almighty!	*Subḥāna Rabbiya 'l-'Aẓīm.*

likewise hold himself still for a while, so that those behind him can keep up with him in the performance of each essential element *[rukn]*.[274]

No serious attention need be paid to the assertion of those who say: "If he does that [i.e., if he holds his posture for a considerable length of time], someone who is supposed to be following his lead *[ma'mūm]* may anticipate his next move, and that person's ritual prayer *[ṣalāt]* will thus be rendered null and void." The reasoning here is faulty, if we are assuming that he does that on a regular basis, because people will realize, when they notice that he does it constantly and persistently, that holding a steady posture is his normal practice. They will therefore keep pace with him, and not move prematurely.

The prayer leader *[imām]* should also be given the following advice: "It is recommended that you should instill some fear in them, before embarking on the performance of the ritual prayer *[ṣalāt]*, and that you should warn them against anticipating your movements, as we shall explain in the following subsection. Far from having a negative effect, this will be conducive to the common good, and to the completeness of everyone's ritual prayer *[ṣalāt]*."

As we are informed in the words of the tradition *[ḥadīth]*:

> Every performer of the ritual prayer is a shepherd, and he will be held responsible for his flock *[kullu muṣallin rā'in wa mas'ūlun 'an ra'iyyati-hi]*.

It has also been said that the prayer leader *[imām]* is a shepherd in relation to those whom he leads in the prayer.

It is therefore incumbent upon the prayer leader *[imām]* to give wise advice to those pray behind him. He must warn them against premature movement in the stages of bowing *[rukū']* and prostration *[sujūd]*. He must do what he can to improve their behavior, since he is a shepherd to them now, and he will be held responsible for them tomorrow [on the Day of Resurrection].

[274] As explained by the author (may Allāh be well pleased with him) in Vol. 1, pp. 13–14:

> The ritual prayer *[ṣalāt]* has some elements that are essential *[arkān*, pl. of *rukn]*, some that are necessities *[wājibāt]*, some that are recommended *[masnūnāt]*, and yet others that are formal refinements *[hai'āt]*. As for the basic essentials *[arkān]* these are fifteen in number: (1) Standing in an upright posture *[qiyām]*. (2) The consecratory declaration of Allāh's Supreme Greatness *[takbīrat al-iḥrām]*. (3) Recitation of *al-Fātiḥa*. (4) Bowing *[rukū']*. (5) Calm composure in the bowing posture. (6) Straightening up from the bowing posture. (7) Calm composure in the erect posture. (8) Prostration *[sujūd]*. (9) Calm composure in the posture of prostration. (10) Sitting between the two acts of prostration. (11) Calm composure in the sitting posture. (12) The final testimony *[tashahhud]*. (13) Adopting a sitting posture in order to make the final testimony. (14) Invocation of blessing *[ṣalāh]* on the Prophet (Allāh bless him and give him peace). (15) The salutation *[taslīm]*.

He must also strive to perfect his own ritual prayer *[ṣalāt]*, to master its performance and improve it, in order that he may be entitled to receive the same reward as those who pray behind him. Failure to do so will result in his being charged with the weight of their sins, whenever he acts badly and falls short.

26.
Concerning the *maʾmūm*, i.e., the worshipper who follows a leader *[imām]* when performing his ritual prayer *[ṣalāt]*, either singly or as a member of a congregation *[jamāʿa]*.

As for the *maʾmūm*, i.e., the worshipper who follows a leader *[imām]* when performing his ritual prayer *[ṣalāt]*, it is incumbent upon him to formulate the intention to pray in that capacity *[an yanwiya 'l-iʾtimām]*.

[If there is only one *maʾmūm* present] he must station himself to the right of the prayer leader *[imām]*; he must not stand in front of him, and he must not stand to his left.

If they are a congregation *[jamāʿa]*,[275] however, the customary practice *[sunna]* is for them to stand behind the prayer leader *[imām]*. So, if only one *maʾmūm* is present at the outset, standing to the leader's right as he utters the initial declaration of Allāh's Supreme Greatness *[kabbara]*, and another worshipper arrives at that point, the newcomer should join him in saying "*Allāhu Akbar*," while squeezing into line beside him. Then the two of them should move back together, to form a row behind the prayer leader *[imām]*. If there is not enough space to accommodate the second person, the prayer leader *[imām]* should push the pair of them back with his hand. He should not move forward from his own spot, unless there is a severe shortage of space behind him.

If a worshipper arrives when the congregation *[jamāʿa]* is already assembled, and he can find a gap in the row, he should insert himself into it. If he cannot find any gap to occupy, he must station himself to the right of the prayer leader *[imām]*. He must not pull a man back abruptly, to stand beside him and form a new row, because that is likely to result in confusion and disharmony, and may stir up feelings of hatred and hostility. It will also have the effect of invalidating the prayer *[ṣalāt]*

[275] That is to say, if there is more than one *maʾmūm* present.

performed by the one who is pulled out of his row, because he will become a solitary individual *[fadhdh]* in the process, and that [detachment from the ranks of the congregation] invalidates the ritual prayer *[ṣalāt]*, according to our doctrine *[ʿinda-nā]*.[276]

The late arrival should make a serious effort to squeeze his shoulders into the row, so that he can utter the declaration of Allāh's Supreme Greatness *[yukabbiru]* and enter into the ritual prayer in a state of consecration *[yuḥrimu bi'ṣ-ṣalāt]*.[277] He may then step back, together with one of the other worshippers, to form a new row.

If he enters the mosque *[masjid]* at the stage where the prayer leader *[imām]* is already in the bowing posture *[rukūʿ]*, the latecomer should pronounce two declarations of Allāh's Supreme Greatness *[kabbara takbīratain]*: one of them for the purpose of consecration *[li'l-iḥrām]*, and the other in connection with the act of bowing *[li'r-rukūʿ]*.[278] It is permissible, however, for him to utter only one such declaration, while intending them both *[in kabbara wāḥida wa nawā-humā]*.

If he enters at the stage where the prayer leader *[imām]* is already pronouncing the final testimony *[at-tashahhud al-akhīr]*,[279] his recommended course is to formulate the intention to perform the prayer *[an yanwiya 'ṣ-ṣalat]*, to pronounce the [consecratory] declaration of Allāh's Supreme Greatness *[yukabbira]*, and to sit down next to the prayer leader *[imām]*, so that he will still be in time to share the merit of the congregation *[jamāʿa]*. Then, when the leader concludes the congregational prayer with the salutation *[idhā sallama 'l-imām]*, the late arrival should build on his [consecratory] declaration of Allāh's Supreme Greatness, and go on to perform a complete ritual prayer by himself *[banā ʿalā takbīrati-hi wa ṣallā]*.

[276] When he uses the expression *ʿinda-nā* [in our opinion; according to our doctrine], Shaikh ʿAbd al-Qādir al-Jīlānī (may Allāh be well pleased with him) is referring to the doctrine of the Ḥanbalī school *[madhhab]* of Islāmic jurisprudence *[fiqh]*.

[277] In other words, he must insert himself sufficiently to be counted as a member of the congregation, at which point he can validly pronounce the consecratory declaration of Allāh's Supreme Greatness *[takbīrat al-iḥrām]*, by saying: "*Allāhu Akbar* [Allāh is Supremely Great!]."

[278] See the description of *takbīrat ar-rukūʿ* on pp. 180–81 above.

[279] That is to say, when the performance of that particular ritual prayer *[ṣalāt]* is within a few moments of being concluded. (For the wording of the final testimony *[at-tashahhud al-akhīr]*, see pp. 184 and 185 above.)

27.
Traditional sayings *[aḥādīth]* attributed to the Prophet (Allāh bless him and give him peace) and his Companions *[Ṣaḥāba]* (may Allāh's good pleasure be upon them all) concerning the proper conduct of the *ma'mūm*.

The following requirements must also be observed by the *ma'mūm*, i.e., the worshipper who follows a leader *[imām]* when performing his ritual prayer *[ṣalāt]*:

He must not anticipate the utterances and movements of prayer leader *[imām]*, especially when it comes to pronouncing the declaration of Allāh's Supreme Greatness *[takbīr]*, adopting the postures of bowing *[rukū']* and prostration *[sujūd]*, and rising up from these two postures.

While he must be extremely careful to avoid acting prematurely at these stages in particular, he must also spare no effort in striving to ensure that every single one of his actions in the ritual prayer *[ṣalāt]* is subsequent to the corresponding action of the leader *[imām]*. We have inherited many traditional sayings *[aḥādīth]* to that effect, some attributed to the Prophet (Allāh bless him and give him peace), and others to his Companions (may Allāh's good pleasure be upon them all).

For instance, the Prophet (Allāh bless him and give him peace) is reported as having said:

> How dare a person raise his head in advance of the prayer leader *[imām]*? Is he not afraid that Allāh may transform his head into the head of an ass?

According to another tradition *[ḥadīth]*, he once said (Allāh bless him and give him peace):

> The prayer leader *[imām]* bows down *[yarka'u]* before you do, prostrates himself *[yasjudu]* before you do, and raises his head before you do.

It was al-Barā' ibn 'Āzib[280] (may Allāh be well pleased with him and with his father) who said:

[280] See note 223 on p. 162 above.

"We used to pray behind the Prophet (Allāh bless him and give him peace), and whenever he sank down from his upright posture [to perform the act of prostration], not one of us would bend his back until Allāh's Messenger (Allāh bless him and give him peace) had placed his forehead on the ground."

In other words, the Companions of Allāh's Messenger (Allāh bless him and give him peace) used to stand quite still behind him, maintaining an upright posture, until the Prophet (Allāh bless him and give him peace) sank down, pronounced the declaration of Allāh's Supreme Greatness *[ḥattā yanḥaṭṭa wa yukabbira]*, and placed his forehead on the ground. Only then did they follow him [in performing the act of prostration].

Several of the Companions *[Ṣaḥāba]* (may Allāh be well pleased with them) are reported as having said:

"Allāh's Messenger (Allāh bless him and give him peace) would [have risen from his prostration and] be standing up straight, while we were still prostrating ourselves *[sujjad]*."

According to one traditional report, transmitted on the authority of Anas ibn Mālik (may Allāh be well pleased with him), Allāh's Messenger (Allāh bless him and give him peace) once said:

> How dare a person raise his head in advance of the prayer leader *[imām]*? Is he not scared that Allāh may transform his head into the head of an ass, or into the head of a pig?

Abū Huraira (may Allāh be well pleased with him) is reported as having said: "I once heard Abu'l-Qāsim[281] (Allāh bless him and give him peace) say:

> "'How dare a person raise his head in advance of the prayer leader *[imām]*? Is he not scared that Allāh may transform his head into the head of an ass?'"

It is related that Ibn Mas'ūd (may Allāh be well pleased with him) once noticed that a man was anticipating the movements of the prayer leader *[imām]*, so he said to him:

"You have neither performed the prayer by yourself, nor have you performed it while following your leader *[mā ṣalaita waḥda-ka wa lā bi-imāmi-ka 'qtadaita]*. He who has neither prayed by himself, nor followed his prayer leader, that is someone who has no prayer at all to his credit *[lā ṣalāta lah]*."

[281] Abu'l-Qāsim [father of al-Qasim] is the *kunya* [surname of relationship] of the Prophet Muḥammad (Allāh bless him and give him peace), whose son al-Qāsim died in infancy. (See Vol. 1, p. 100.)

It is also related that Ibn ʿUmar[282] (may Allāh be well pleased with him and with his father) once noticed that a man was anticipating the movements of the prayer leader *[imām]*, so he said to him: "You have neither performed the prayer by yourself, nor have you performed it with the prayer leader *[mā ṣalaita waḥda-ka wa lā ṣalaita maʿa 'l-imām]*." He then gave the culprit a beating, and ordered him to perform the ritual prayer *[ṣalāt]* all over again.

According to another traditional report, this one transmitted on the authority of Abū Ṣāliḥ[283] (may Allāh bestow His mercy upon him), from Abū Huraira (may Allāh be well pleased with him), the latter stated that Allāh's Messenger (Allāh bless him and give him peace) once said:

> The prayer leader *[imām]* has been appointed for no other purpose than to set an example for the congregation to follow *[li-yuʾtamma bi-hi]*. So, when he pronounces the declaration of Allāh's Supreme Greatness, you must then pronounce the declaration of Allāh's Supreme Greatness *[idhā kabbara fa-kabbirū]*.[284] When he bows down, you must then bow down *[idhā rakaʿa fa-'rkaʿū]*. When he raises his head, you must then raise your heads. When he says:
>
> May Allāh hear and accept — *samiʿa 'llāhu*
> the praise of one who praises Him! — *li-man ḥamidah.*
>
> —you must then say, all of you together:
>
> Our Lord, to You be the praise! — *Rabba-nā la-ka 'l-ḥamd.*
>
> When he prostrates himself, you must then prostrate yourselves *[idhā sajada fa-'sjudū]*, but you must not prostrate yourselves before he prostrates himself.
>
> When he raises his head, you must then raise your heads, but you must not raise your heads before he raises his. And if he performs the entire prayer in a sitting position, you must all remain seated throughout the prayer *[idhā ṣallā jālisan fa-ṣallū jamīʿan julūsā]*.[285]

[282] ʿAbdu'llāh ibn ʿUmar, the son of the Caliph ʿUmar ibn al-Khaṭṭāb (may Allāh be well pleased with them both), was a revered Companion in his own right. He died in A.H. 73 or 74.

[283] Abū Ṣāliḥ as-Sammān al-Madanī (may Allāh bestow His mercy upon him) was a famous *muḥaddith* [narrator of Prophetic tradition], from whom al-Aʿmash (may Allāh bestow His mercy upon him) is said to have transmitted a thousand traditions *[aḥādīth]*. He died in A.H. 101.

[284] In other words: "When he says: '*Allāhu Akbar* [Allāh is Supremely Great!],' you must say: '*Allāhu Akbar* [Allāh is Supremely Great!].'"

[285] This last sentence refers to a situation where the prayer leader *[imām]* is physically incapable of assuming an upright posture. According to a manual of Ḥanbalī jurisprudence *[fiqh]*:

"In the exceptional case of a long-bearded [i.e., very old] prayer leader *[imām alḥā]*, who performs the entire prayer in a sitting posture, on account of a sickness from which he can be expected to recover, the members of the congregation must remain seated behind him throughout the performance of the ritual prayer." (See: Imām Muwaffaq ad-Dīn ʿAbdu'llāh ibn Aḥmad ibn Qadāma al-Maqdisī. *Al-ʿUmda: fī fiqh Imām as-Sunna Aḥmad ibn Ḥanbal ash-Shaibānī [raḍiya 'llāhu ʿan-hu]*. Cairo, Egypt: *Al-Maktabat as-Salafiyya*, n.d.: p. 36.)

In a scholarly treatise *[risāla]* of his, our own Imām, Abū ʿAbdu'llāh Aḥmad [ibn Ḥanbal] (may Allāh bestow His mercy upon him), has informed us that Abū Mūsā al-Ashʿarī (may Allāh be well pleased with him), the Companion *[Ṣāḥib]* of Allāh's Messenger (Allāh bless him and give him peace), is reported as having said:[286]

"It was Allāh's Messenger (Allāh bless him and give him peace) who taught us how to perform our ritual prayer *[ṣalāt]*, and it was he who taught us what we had to say in the course of performing it.

"Allāh's Messenger (Allāh bless him and give him peace) gave us these instructions:

> "'When the prayer leader pronounces the declaration of Allāh's Supreme Greatness, you must then pronounce the declaration of Allāh's Supreme Greatness *[idhā kabbara 'l-imām fa-kabbirū]*.[287]
>
> "'When he recites from the Qur'ān, you must listen in silence *[idhā qaraʾa fa-anṣitū]*.
>
> "'Then, when he [reaches the end of *al-Fātiḥa* and] pronounces the words:
>
> not of those who earn Your wrath, — *ghairi 'l-maghḍūbi ʿalai-him*
> nor of those who go astray. (1:7) — *wa la 'ḍ-ḍāllīn*.
>
> —you must say: "*Āmīn* [Amen]," so that Allāh (Exalted is He) may grant you a favorable response.
>
> "'When he pronounces the declaration of Allāh's Supreme Greatness, and bows down, you must then pronounce the declaration of Allāh's Supreme Greatness, and bow down *[idhā kabbara wa rakaʿa fa-kabbirū wa 'rakaʿū]*.[288]
>
> "'When he raises his head [from the bowing posture], and says:
>
> May Allāh hear and accept — *samiʿa 'llāhu*
> the praise of one who praises Him! — *li-man ḥamidah*.
>
> —you must then raise your heads, and say:
>
> O Allāh, — *Allāhumma*
> our Lord, to You be the praise! — *Rabba-nā la-ka 'l-ḥamd*.[289]
>
> —so that Allāh may hear you.
>
> "'When he says "*Allāhu Akbar* [Allāh is Supremely Great!]," and prostrates himself, you must then say "*Allāhu Akbar* [Allāh is Supremely Great!]," and prostrate yourselves *[idhā kabbara wa sajada fa-kabbirū wa 'sjudū]*.

[286] ***Author's note***: Imām Aḥmad ibn Ḥanbal (may Allāh bestow His mercy upon him) has provided a chain of transmitting authorities *[isnād]* to establish the authenticity of this report.

[287] This refers to the consecratory declaration of Allāh's Supreme Greatness *[takbīrat al-iḥrām]*.

[288] This refers to the declaration of Allāh's Supreme Greatness at the stage of bowing *[takbīrat ar-rukūʿ]*.

[289] Note the addition of *Allāhumma* [O Allāh!] in this instance.

> "'When he raises his head and says "*Allāhu Akbar* [Allāh is Supremely Great!]," you must then raise your heads and say "*Allāhu Akbar* [Allāh is Supremely Great!]" *[idhā...kabbara...fa-...kabbirū].*'"

"At this point, Allāh's Messenger (Allāh bless him and give him peace) remarked:

> "'And so on, and so forth *[fa-tilka bi-tilka].*
>
> "'When he is in the sitting posture *[qa'da]*, each of you must repeat the words:

Greetings, prayers and good deeds are due to Allāh...	*at-taḥiyyātu li'llāhi wa 's-ṣalawātu wa 'ṭ-ṭayyibāt...*

> —until you come to the end of the testimony *[tashahhud].*'"[290]

The following explanations have been provided by Imām Abū 'Abdu'llāh Aḥmad ibn Muḥammad ibn Ḥanbal ash-Shaibānī (may Allāh bestow His mercy upon him; may He allow us to die faithful, root and branch, to the doctrine of his school *[madhhab]*, and may He assemble us at the Resurrection as members of his company!):

"Let us first consider the statement of the Prophet (Allāh bless him and give him peace):

> When he pronounces the declaration of Allāh's Supreme Greatness, you must then pronounce the declaration of Allāh's Supreme Greatness *[idhā kabbara fa-kabbirū].*

"This means that the members of the congregation must wait for the prayer leader *[imām]* to say: '*Allāhu Akbar* [Allāh is Supremely Great!]' *[ḥattā yukabbira]*. They must wait and listen until he has completed his declaration of Allāh's Supreme Greatness *[takbīr]*, and until the sound of his voice can no longer be heard. Then, and only then, should they repeat after him: '*Allāhu Akbar* [Allāh is Supremely Great!]' *[yukabbirūna ba'dah]*.

"People grossly misinterpret these Prophetic sayings *[aḥādīth]*, and even ignore them altogether, not to mention the fact that most of them regard the ritual prayer *[ṣalāt]* as a trivial matter, which hardly deserves their serious attention. So it sometimes happens that, as soon as the prayer leader *[imām]* starts to pronounce the declaration of Allāh's Supreme Greatness *[takbīr]*, they all launch into the *takbīr* simultaneously with him, thereby committing a grave mistake. It is not correct for them to start pronouncing the *takbīr* until the prayer leader *[imām]*

[290] For the complete wording of the testimony *[tashahhud]*, see pp. 84 and 85 above.

has finished saying: '*Allāhu Akbar* [Allāh is Supremely Great!],' and the sound of his voice can no longer be heard. This is what the Prophet (Allāh bless him and give him peace) meant, when he said:

> When the prayer leader pronounces the declaration of Allāh's Supreme Greatness, you must then pronounce the declaration of Allāh's Supreme Greatness *[idhā kabbara 'l-imām fa-kabbirū]*.

"The prayer leader *[imām]* does not become a proclaimer of Allāh's Supreme Greatness *[mukabbir]* until he says: '*Allāhu Akbar* [Allāh is Supremely Great!]' If he were to say: '*Allāhu*...,' and then fall silent, the prayer leader *[imām]* would not yet be a proclaimer of Allāh's Supreme Greatness *[mukabbir]*—not before having said: '*Allāhu Akbar* [Allāh is Supremely Great!]'

"The people [in the congregation] should therefore pronounce the declaration of Allāh's Supreme Greatness *[yukabbiru 'n-nās]* after he has said: '*Allāhu Akbar* [Allāh is Supremely Great!]' By launching into the *takbīr* simultaneously with the prayer leader *[imām]*, they are committing a grave mistake. They are also guilty of disregarding the word of the Prophet (Allāh bless him and give him peace), for the following reason:

"Suppose you were to say: 'When so-and-so performs his ritual prayer *[idhā ṣallā fulān]*, I shall speak to him.' The meaning you intended to convey would be: 'I shall wait for him to perform his ritual prayer, and then, when he has finished praying, I shall speak to him.' You would not mean to suggest that you were going to speak to him while he was still performing his prayer! Well then, the same principle applies to the meaning intended by the Prophet (Allāh bless him and give him peace), when he used the expression:

> When the prayer leader pronounces the declaration of Allāh's Supreme Greatness, you must then pronounce the declaration of Allāh's Supreme Greatness *[idhā kabbara 'l-imām fa-kabbirū]*.

"If the prayer leader *[imām]* lacks training in religious jurisprudence *[fiqh]*, he is all too likely to prolong the declaration of Allāh's Supreme Greatness *[takbīr]*, while someone who utters it simultaneously with him *[yukabbiru ma'a-hu]* is all too likely to pronounce it abruptly, so that he finishes the *takbīr* before the leader has finished. The person concerned will thus become a proclaimer of Allāh's Supreme Greatness *[mukabbir]* in advance of the prayer leader *[imām]*.

"If a member of the congregation pronounces the declaration of Allāh's Supreme Greatness in advance of the prayer leader *[imām]*, he will not be credited with the performance of a ritual prayer *[ṣalāt]*. Since he has embarked upon the prayer in advance of the leader *[qabla 'l-imām]*, and has said: '*Allāhu Akbar* [Allāh is Supremely Great!]' before [the leader completed] the sentence *[qabla 'l-kalām]*, he does not have a ritual prayer *[ṣalāt]* to his credit.

"Let us now move on to consider the statement of the Prophet (Allāh bless him and give him peace):

> "'When he pronounces the declaration of Allāh's Supreme Greatness, and bows down, you must then pronounce the declaration of Allāh's Supreme Greatness, and bow down *[idhā kabbara wa rakaʿa fa-kabbirū wa 'rakaʿū]*.

"This means that the members of the congregation must remain standing upright, as they wait for the prayer leader *[imām]* to say: '*Allāhu Akbar* [Allāh is Supremely Great!]' and adopt the bowing posture *[ḥattā yukabbira wa yarkaʿa]*, and that they must maintain their upright posture until the sound of his voice can no longer be heard. Then, and only then, should they follow him.

"Next comes the statement of the Prophet (Allāh bless him and give him peace):

> "'When he raises his head [from the bowing posture], and says:
>
> May Allāh hear and accept — *samiʿa 'llāhu*
> the praise of one who praises Him! — *li-man ḥamidah.*
>
> —you must then raise your heads, and say:
>
> O Allāh, — *Allāhumma*
> our Lord, to You be the praise! — *Rabba-nā la-ka 'l-ḥamd.*

"This means that the members of the congregation must remain quite still in the bowing posture *[rukūʿ]*, until the prayer leader *[imām]* raises his head, and says:

> May Allāh hear and accept — *samiʿa 'llāhu*
> the praise of one who praises Him! — *li-man ḥamidah.*

"They must maintain the bowing posture *[rukūʿ]* until the sound of his voice can no longer be heard. Then, and only then, should they follow him, raising their heads and saying:

> O Allāh, — *Allāhumma*
> our Lord, to You be the praise! — *Rabba-nā la-ka 'l-ḥamd.*

"Next comes the statement of the Prophet (Allāh bless him and give him peace):

> "'When he says "*Allāhu Akbar* [Allāh is Supremely Great!]," and prostrates himself, you must then say "*Allāhu Akbar* [Allāh is Supremely Great!]," and prostrate yourselves *[idhā kabbara wa sajada fa-kabbirū wa 'sjudū]*.

"This means that the members of the congregation must remain standing upright, while the prayer leader *[imām]* says: '*Allāhu Akbar* [Allāh is Supremely Great!],' and sinks down into the posture of prostration *[sujūd]*. They must maintain their upright posture until he places his forehead on the ground. Then, and only then, should they follow him.

"This interpretation is confirmed by the traditional report, according to which it was al-Barā' ibn 'Āzib (may Allāh be well pleased with him and with his father) who said:

"'We used to pray behind the Prophet (Allāh bless him and give him peace), and whenever he sank down from his upright posture [to perform the act of prostration], not one of us would bend his back until Allāh's Messenger (Allāh bless him and give him peace) had placed his forehead on the ground.'

"Besides, all of this is fully in accordance with statement of the Prophet (Allāh bless him and give him peace):

> "'The prayer leader *[imām]* bows down *[yarka'u]* before you do, prostrates himself *[yasjudu]* before you do, and raises his head before you do.'

"Let us now go on to consider the statement of the Prophet (Allāh bless him and give him peace):

> "'When he raises his head [from the posture of prostration] and says "*Allāhu Akbar* [Allāh is Supremely Great!]," you must then raise your heads and say "*Allāhu Akbar* [Allāh is Supremely Great!]" *[idhā...kabbara...fa-...kabbirū]*.'

"This means that the members of the congregation must remain quite still in the posture of prostration *[sujūd]*, until the prayer leader *[imām]* raises his head, and says: "*Allāhu Akbar* [Allāh is Supremely Great!]" They must maintain the posture of prostration *[sujūd]* until the sound of his voice can no longer be heard. Then, and only then, should they follow him, for at that point they must raise their heads.

"Finally, we must consider the terse statement of the Prophet (Allāh bless him and give him peace):

"'And so on, and so forth *[fa-tilka bi-tilka]*.'

"This is a way of saying that, as you now proceed to perform the second cycle *[rak'a]* of the ritual prayer *[ṣalāt]*, you must observe each of these instructions at the appropriate stage. For instance:

"You must remain standing upright, as you wait for the prayer leader *[imām]* to say: '*Allāhu Akbar* [Allāh is Supremely Great!]' and adopt the bowing posture *[ḥattā yukabbira wa yarka'a]*, and you must maintain your upright posture until the sound of his voice can no longer be heard. Then, and only then, should you follow him.

"You must remain quite still in the bowing posture *[rukū']*, until the prayer leader *[imām]* raises his head, and says:

May Allāh hear and accept	*sami'a 'llāhu*
the praise of one who praises Him!	*li-man ḥamidah.*

"You must maintain the bowing posture *[rukū']* until the sound of his voice can no longer be heard. Then, and only then, should you follow him, raising your heads and saying:

Our Lord, to You be the praise!	*Rabba-nā la-ka 'l-ḥamd.*

"In other words, the statement of the Prophet (Allāh bless him and give him peace):

"'And so on, and so forth *[fa-tilka bi-tilka]*.'

—is a succinct reference to every raising and lowering [of the head].

"This is all about perfecting the valid performance of the ritual prayer *[itmām aṣ-ṣalāt]*, so you must grasp it with your understanding, study it in depth, and master it thoroughly. You must realize that there will be many people, on the Day of Resurrection *[Yawm al-Qiyāma]*, who have no ritual prayer *[ṣalāt]* to their credit, due to their habit of anticipating the prayer leader *[imām]* in adopting the postures of bowing *[rukū']* and prostration *[sujūd]*, and in the raising and lowering [of the head]. In the words of the Prophetic tradition *[ḥadīth]*:

There will come a time when people pray, yet do not perform the prayer *[yuṣallūna wa lā yuṣallūn]*.

"That time could well be this present age of ours, since people nowadays are generally in the habit of anticipating the prayer leader *[imām]*, and of failing to perform the basic essentials *[arkān]* of the ritual prayer *[ṣalāt]*, not to mention their neglect of its necessary elements *[wājibāt]*, its recommended practices *[masnūnāt]*, and [other elements that contribute to] its complete refinement *[tamām]*."[291]

[291] For lists of the basic essentials *[arkān]* of the ritual prayer *[ṣalāt]*, its necessary practices *[wājibāt]*, recommended practices *[masnūnāt]*, and formal refinements *[hai'āt]*, see Vol. 1, pp. 13–16.

28.
Concerning what is required of someone who notices that another person is performing his ritual prayer *[ṣalāt]* incorrectly.

If someone happens to notice that another person is not performing his ritual prayer *[ṣalāt]* correctly, especially if he sees him omitting some of its basic essentials *[arkān]*[292] and necessary elements *[wājibāt]*,[293] as well as its customary refinements *[ādāb]*,[294] it is incumbent upon the observer to admonish him, to make him aware of his shortcomings, and to offer him sound advice, so that he may correct his mistakes from that time on, and seek forgiveness for those he has made in the past. If the observer fails to do this, he will be counted as a partner *[sharīk]* in the culprit's misconduct, and will thus be charged with the burden of the latter's guilt and sin.

As we are informed in the tradition *[ḥadīth]*, the Prophet (Allāh bless him and give him peace) once said:

> Woe betide the learned *[ʿālim]* on account of the ignorant *[jāhil]*, inasmuch as the former fails to teach the latter.

If it had not been the case that teaching the ignorant *[jāhil]* is incumbent upon the man of learning *[ʿālim]*, as a strict obligation and a prescribed religious duty, the Prophet (Allāh bless him and give him peace) would not have threatened him with woe, as the dire consequence of his failure to provide instruction. In order to deserve such a threat *[waʿīd]*, a person must be guilty of failing to carry out a duty that is strictly incumbent *[wājib]* and obligatory *[farḍ]*, as opposed to one that is merely voluntary and supererogatory *[nafl]*.

[292] See note 291 on p. 216 above.

[293] See note 291 on p. 216 above.

[294] In this context, the term *ādāb* [good manners; proprieties] is obviously meant to cover those elements in the performance of the ritual prayer *[ṣalāt]* that are customary and highly recommended, though not absolutely essential to its validity.

Bilāl ibn Sa'd[295] (may Allāh bestow His mercy upon him) is traditionally reported as having said:

"As long as the sinful error remains concealed from public view, it causes harm to no one except the person who commits it. But once it becomes openly apparent, and if it does not get to be corrected, it causes harm to members of the community in general."

That is because of their failure to do their duty, which requires them to change the situation for the better, and to express their disapproval to the person whose sinful error has become so conspicuous, instead of saying nothing about it. As a result of their failure to speak out, the situation is bound to deteriorate still further, and the entire community becomes responsible for the unfortunate consequences. The virtuous individual *[muḥsin]* is actually participating with the wrongdoer in his wrongdoing, as long as he fails to admonish him and offer him good advice."

As we learn from traditional sources, it was Ibn Mas'ūd (may Allāh be well pleased with him) who said:

"When someone happens to notice that another person is doing something wrong in the way he performs his ritual prayer *[ṣalāt]*, but fails to warn him of the consequences, the observer is associating himself with the culprit as his partner in sin and shame, and he is serving as an accomplice of Satan the accursed *[ash-Shaiṭān al-la'īn]*."

That is because the Devil wants him to keep quiet and say nothing about the problem, and to refrain from engaging in mutual assistance toward piety *[birr]* and true devotion *[taqwā]*, the two virtues enjoined by Allāh (Exalted is He) in His words (Almighty and Glorious is He):

And help one another to practice	*wa ta'āwunū 'ala 'l-birri*
piety and true devotion.	*wa 't-taqwā.*
And do not help one another	*wa lā ta'āwanū*
to practice sin and enmity,	*'ala 'l-ithmi*
and be careful	*wa 'l-'udwān:*
to observe your duty to Allāh;	*wa 'ttaqu 'llāh:*
surely Allāh is terrible	*Inna 'llāha*
in retribution. (5:2)	*Shadīdu'l-'iqāb.*

[295] Bilāl ibn Sa'd Tamīm as-Sakūrī (may Allāh bestow His mercy upon him) was the regular prayer leader *[imām]* at the Great Mosque of Damascus. He was renowned for his pious devotion, which is said to have been comparable to that of al-Ḥasan al-Baṣrī (may Allāh bestow His mercy upon him). He died in A.H. 122.

The Devil wants him to refrain from offering the good advice which they [as fellow servants of Allāh] are duty-bound to give to one another. He wishes to see the religion *[dīn]* fade away, to see Islām disappear, and to see all creatures engaged in sinful conduct. For an intelligent person, therefore, it makes no sense to obey the Devil *[ash-Shaiṭān]*. Allāh (Almighty and Glorious is He) has told us:

O Children of Adam,	*yā Banī Ādama*
let not Satan	*lā yaftinanna-kumu 'sh-shaiṭānu*
tempt you as he brought your parents	*ka-mā akhraja abawai-kum*
out of the Garden [of Paradise],	*mina 'l-jannati*
stripping them of their garments.	*yanziʿu ʿan-humā sawʾāti-himā.*
(7:27)	

He has also told us (Glorious and Exalted is He):

[The Devil] summons his party only	*innamā yadʿū*
that they may be among	*ḥizba-hu*
the inhabitants	*li-yakūnū*
of the blazing inferno. (35:6)	*min aṣḥābi 's-saʿīr.*

As you ought to be aware, everything that is currently found wanting in the performance of the ritual prayer *[ṣalāt]*, in the payment of the alms-due *[ṣalāt]*, and in the observance of all the other forms of worshipful service *[ʿibādāt]*, is due to the silence and reticence of the experts in religious knowledge and Islāmic jurisprudence *[ahl al-ʿilm wa 'l-fiqh]*, and to their failure to provide sound advice, instruction and education. This tendency may originate in the first place among the ignorant, but then it spreads to include the people of knowledge, and comes to represent their typical attitude.

What a strange state of affairs! If one of these people happened to see a man stealing a single grain of wheat, let alone a whole loaf of bread, from a Jewish person or a Muslim, he would not restrain himself for a moment from yelling at the thief, scolding him, and rebuking him for his bad behavior. Yet when he notices that someone, while praying, is stealing the basic essentials of the ritual prayer *[arkān aṣ-ṣalāt]*, omitting them along with necessary elements, and moving in advance of the prayer leader, that same observer remains silent and says nothing to the culprit. What he ought to do, of course, is let him know that he is doing something wrong, provide him with instruction, and make him aware of the need for improvement.

Allāh's Messenger (Allāh bless him and give him peace) is reported as having said:

> The worst kind of thief is a person who steals from his own ritual prayer *[ṣalāt]*.

His listeners asked: "O Messenger of Allāh, how can a person steal from his own ritual prayer *[ṣalāt]*?" So he explained (Allāh bless him and give him peace):

> [He steals from it when] he does not perform its bowing *[rukū']* and its prostration *[sujūd]* correctly and completely.

According to a traditional report transmitted on the authority of al-Ḥasan al-Baṣrī (may Allāh bestow His mercy upon him), the Prophet (Allāh bless him and give him peace) once said:

> Shall I tell you who is the worst kind of thief?

His listeners said: "Yes, of course, O Messenger of Allāh, do tell us who he is!" So he explained (Allāh bless him and give him peace):

> He is someone who performs neither the bowing posture *[rukū']* of the ritual prayer *[ṣalāt]*, nor its prostration *[sujūd]*, correctly and completely.

It was Salmān al-Fārisī (may Allāh be well pleased with him) who said: "The ritual prayer is a measure *[aṣ-ṣalātu mikyāl]*, so to one who performs it in full, the recompense will be paid in full. As for anyone who gives short measure, you know what Allāh (Exalted is He) has said about those who give short measure *[al-muṭaffifīn]*!"[296]

According to a traditional report transmitted on the authority of 'Abdu'llāh ibn 'Alī, or 'Alī ibn Shaibān (may Allāh be well pleased with him), who was a member of one of the deputations *[wafd]* that came to visit Allāh's Messenger (Allāh bless him and give him peace) [after the conquest of Mecca],[297] the Prophet (Allāh bless him and give him peace) once said:

> Allāh takes no notice of the ritual prayer *[ṣalāt]* performed by a servant [of His] who does not straighten his spine in his act of bowing *[rukū']* and his act of prostration *[sujūd]*.

[296] Salmān al-Fārisī (may Allāh be well pleased with him) was alluding to Q. 83:1–9.

[297] In A.H. 9, after the Prophet (Allāh bless him and give him peace) had gained possession of Mecca, Arab tribal deputations came to him from all directions.

Abū Huraira[386] (may Allāh be well pleased with him) is reported as having said:

"A man once came into the mosque *[masjid]*, while Allāh's Messenger (Allāh bless him and give him peace) was sitting to one side of the place of worship, and proceeded to perform the ritual prayer *[fa-ṣallā]*. Then he came over to Allāh's Messenger (Allāh bless him and give him peace) and saluted him with the greeting of peace *[sallama ʿalai-hi]*. The Messenger returned his greeting *[radda ʿalai-hi 's-salām]*, and said: 'Now go back and pray *[ṣalli]*, for you have not yet performed the ritual prayer *[lam tuṣalli]*.' So the man performed the prayer as he had performed it the first time *[fa-ṣallā ka-mā ṣallā]*, then he came over and offered the greeting of peace *[sallama]*. Once again, Allāh's Messenger (Allāh bless him and give him peace) said to him: 'Now go back and pray *[ṣalli]*, for you have not yet performed the ritual prayer *[lam tuṣalli]*.' When he had done this three times, the man said: 'By Him who sent you to convey the Truth as a Prophet *[bi'l-Ḥaqqi Nabiyyan]*, if there is a better way [of performing the prayer] than this, please tell me what it is!'

"Allāh's Messenger (Allāh bless him and give him peace) responded to this by telling him:

> "'When you are ready to perform your ritual prayer *[ṣalāt]*, you must start by making a thorough job of the ritual ablution *[wuḍūʾ]*. Then you must stand facing the *Qibla* [direction of the Kaʿba in Mecca], and proclaim the Supreme Greatness of Allāh *[kabbir]*.[298] Then you must recite as much of the Qurʾān as you can manage with ease. Then you must bow down, so that you are calmly composed in the bowing posture *[ḥattā taṭmaʾinna rākiʿan]*. Then you must straighten up, so that you assume a steady upright posture *[ḥattā taʿtadila qāʾiman]*. Then you must prostrate yourself, so that you are calmly composed in the posture of prostration *[ḥattā taṭmaʾinna sājidan]*. Then you must sit up, so that you are are calmly composed in the sitting posture *[ḥattā taṭmaʾinna jālisan]*. Then you must prostrate yourself [a second time], so that you are calmly composed in the posture of prostration *[ḥattā taṭmaʾinna sājidan]*. Then you must sit up [again], so that you are are calmly composed in the sitting posture *[ḥattā taṭmaʾinna jālisan]*. Then you must do likewise at every stage in your performance of the ritual prayer *[ṣalāt]*.'"

According to another traditional account *[ḥadīth]*, Rifāʿa ibn Rāfiʿ[299]

[298] The word *kabbir* is the imperative form of the verb *kabbara* (see note 248 on p. 181 above).

[299] Abū Muʿādh Rifāʿa ibn Rāfiʿ ibn Mālik az-Zarqī (may Allāh be well pleased with him) was a Companion of the Prophet (Allāh bless him and give him peace), from whom he related many traditions *[aḥādīth]*. He died in A.H. 41.

(may Allāh be well pleased with him) is reported as having said:

"While we were sitting in a circle around Allāh's Messenger (Allāh bless him and give him peace), a man came in [to the mosque], stood facing the *Qibla,* and proceeded to perform the ritual prayer *[fa-ṣallā].* As soon as he had finished his ritual prayer *[ṣalāt]*, he came over and offered the greeting of peace *[sallama]* to Allāh's Messenger (Allāh bless him and give him peace) and to the people in his company. Then Allāh's Messenger (Allāh bless him and give him peace) told him: 'Now go back and pray *[ṣalli]*, for you have not yet performed the ritual prayer *[lam tuṣalli].*' He gave him this same instruction two or three times, so the man said: 'I am simply incapable of doing what you require of me, since I do not know what it is that you find lacking in my performance of the ritual prayer *[ṣalāt]*!'

"Allāh's Messenger (Allāh bless him and give him peace) responded to this by saying:

> "'The ritual prayer *[ṣalāt]* is not performed correctly and completely by any one of you, unless he starts by by making a thorough job of the ritual ablution *[wuḍū']*, as commanded by Allāh (Exalted is He). This means that he must wash his face, and his hands [and lower arms] up to the elbows, that he must rub his head [with his wet hands],[300] and that he must wash his feet up to the ankles.
>
> "'He must then proclaim the Supreme Greatness of Allāh (Exalted is He) and extol Him *[yukabbiru 'llāha—ta'āla—wa yaḥmadu-hu].*
>
> "'Then he must recite as much of the Qur'ān as his knowledge of it permits.
>
> "'Then he must proclaim the Supreme Greatness of Allāh *[yukabbiru]* and place the palms of his hands on his knees, so that his joints are comfortable and relaxed.
>
> "'Then he must say:
>
> May Allāh hear and accept — *sami'a 'llāhu*
> the praise of one who praises Him! — *li-man ḥamidah.*
>
> —and assume an upright posture, so that his spine is straight and erect, and so that every member of his body is in its proper position.
>
> "'Then he must proclaim the Supreme Greatness of Allāh *[yukabbiru]* and prostrate himself *[yasjudu]*, placing his forehead firmly on the ground, so that all his joints are comfortable and relaxed.
>
> "'Then he must proclaim the Supreme Greatness of Allāh *[yukabbiru]*, sit evenly on his buttocks, and straighten his spine.'

[300] As Shaikh 'Abd al-Qādir al-Jīlānī (may Allāh be well pleased with him) has explained in Vol. 1, pp. 8–9, when listing the obligatory elements *[farā'iḍ]* of ritual purification:

> Rubbing the head *[masḥ ar-ra's].* The way to do this is by dipping the hands in water, then raising them [wet but] empty, placing them on the front part of the head, drawing them to the back of the head, then returning them to their original position.

"The Prophet (Allāh bless him and give him peace) continued in this vein, until he had described every stage of a ritual prayer *[ṣalāt]* consisting of four cycles *[raka'āt]*. When he had finished, he added:

> "'The ritual prayer *[ṣalāt]* is not performed correctly and completely by any one of you, unless and until he does it in the manner I have just described.'"

From this we learn that the Prophet (Allāh bless him and give him peace) insisted on the correct and complete performance of the ritual prayer *[ṣalāt]*, including the act of bowing *[rukū']* and the act of prostration *[sujūd]*. He has let it be known, in fact, that the the ritual prayer *[ṣalāt]* will not be accepted unless it is duly performed in this manner. We also learn that it was out of the question for him (Allāh bless him and give him peace) to remain silent, when he noticed that the man was performing a defective version of the ritual prayer *[yuṣallī ṣalāt nāqiṣa]*.

If it had been permissible to postpone the explanation beyond the moment of need, and to refrain from rebuking the ignorant person and offering him instruction, the Prophet (Allāh bless him and give him peace) would surely have kept silent. He would have entrusted the handling of the situation to the discretion of the Companions *[Ṣaḥāba]* (may Allāh be well pleased with them all), and would have been content to let it pass without comment. Since he actually went to such great lengths in order to rebuke the man, and to provide him with instruction, he clearly meant to indicate the necessity of active intervention.

To those of his Companions (may Allāh be well pleased with them) who were present with him on that occasion, it must have been obvious that the Prophet (Allāh bless him and give him peace) was exhorting them to take the same action he was taking, whenever they noticed someone doing the kind of thing that man was doing in the performance of his ritual prayer *[ṣalāt]*. They must have realized that he expected them to instruct their own companions, and their companions' companions, concerning the nature and application of the rules of the Sacred Law *[kaifiyya aḥkām ash-Shar']*, from then until the arrival of the final Hour *[as-Sā'a]*.

29.
Concerning the qualifications of the muezzin *[mu'adhdhin]*, and how he should act when giving the call to prayer *[adhān]* and the announcement that the prayer is about to begin *[iqāma]*.

It is incumbent upon the muezzin *[mu'adhdhin]* to improve his elocution, to make sure that he does not commit any mispronunciation in the two declarations of faith *[shahādatain]*.[301]

He must be thoroughly familiar with the times prescribed for the performance of the five obligatory daily prayers.

He must not give the call to prayer *[lā yu'adhdhina]* until after the commencement of the period of time prescribed for a particular prayer, except in the case of the [prayer of] daybreak *[al-fajr]*.[302]

In giving his call to prayer *[adhān]*, he must count on obtaining the favor of Allāh (Exalted is He), and he must not accept any worldly remuneration for giving the call.

He must face the *Qibla* [direction of the Ka'ba in Mecca] while

[301] The first declaration of faith *[shahāda]* is:

I bear witness that there is no god but Allāh.	*ashhadu an lā ilāha illa 'llāh.**

The second declaration of faith *[shahāda]* is:

I bear witness that Muḥammad is the Messenger of Allāh.	*ashhadu anna Muḥammadan Rasūlu 'llāh.***

(* The final *n*-sound in *an* assimilates to the following *l*-sound, so that the actual pronunciation is "*al lā ilāha*...." ** The final *n*-sound in *Muḥammadan* assimilates to the following *r*-sound, so that the actual pronunciation is "...*Muḥammadar rasūlu 'llāh*.")

[302] In the case of the dawn or daybreak prayer *[ṣalāt aṣ-ṣubḥ / ṣalāt al-fajr]*, the call to prayer *[adhān]* may be given earlier, to allow people time to wake up and prepare themselves. As their authority for this solitary exception to the general rule, the religious scholars cite the saying of Allāh's Messenger (Allāh bless him and give him peace):

> Bilāl will give the call to prayer *[yu'adhdhinu]* while it is still nighttime, so you may eat and drink until Ibn Umm Maktūm gives the call [at daybreak].

(See: Imām Muwaffaq ad-Dīn 'Abdu'llāh ibn Aḥmad ibn Qadāma al-Maqdisī. *Al-'Umda: fī fiqh Imām as-Sunna Aḥmad ibn Ḥanbal ash-Shaibānī [raḍiya 'llāhu 'an-hu]*. Cairo, Egypt: Al-Maktabat as-Salafiyya, n.d.: p. 27.)

uttering the proclamation of Allāh's Supreme Greatness *[takbīr]* and the two declarations of faith *[shahādatain]*.

While uttering the actual summons to prayer *[ad-du'ā' ila 'ṣ-ṣalāt]*, he must turn his face to the right and to the left.

When he has given the call to the sunset prayer *[adhdhana li-ṣalāt al-maghrib]*, he must sit down for a little while, allowing a brief interval to elapse between the *adhān* [the summoning call][303] and the *iqāma* [the announcement that the actual performance of the ritual prayer is about to begin].[304]

303 The call to prayer *[adhān]* is uttered in the following words:

Allāh is Supremely Great! Allāh is Supremely Great! Allāh is Supremely Great! Allāh is Supremely Great!	*Allāhu Akbar: Allāhu Akbar.* *Allāhu Akbar: Allāhu Akbar.*
I bear witness that there is no god but Allāh. I bear witness that there is no god but Allāh.	*ashhadu an lā ilāha illa 'llāh.** *ashhadu an lā ilāha illa 'llāh.**
I bear witness that Muḥammad is the Messenger of Allāh. I bear witness that Muḥammad is the Messenger of Allāh.	*ashhadu anna Muḥammadan Rasūlu 'llāh.** *ashhadu anna Muḥammadan Rasūlu 'llāh.**
Come to prayer! Come to prayer!	*ḥayya 'ala 'ṣ-ṣalāh: ḥayya 'ala 'ṣ-ṣalāh.*
Come to salvation! Come to salvation!	*ḥayya 'ala 'l-falāḥ: ḥayya 'ala 'l-falāḥ.*
Allāh is Supremely Great! Allāh is Supremely Great!	*Allāhu Akbar: Allāhu Akbar.*
There is no god but Allāh!	*lā ilāha illa 'llāh.*

(* See note 301 on p. 224.)

In the call *[adhān]* to the dawn prayer *[ṣalāt al-fajr]*, the words:

Prayer is better than sleep! Prayer is better than sleep!	*aṣ-ṣalātu khairun mina 'n-nawm,* *aṣ-ṣalātu khairun mina 'n-nawm.*

—are added after:

Come to salvation! Come to salvation!	*ḥayya 'ala 'l-falāḥ: ḥayya 'ala 'l-falāḥ.*

304 The *iqāma*, the announcement that the ritual prayer is about to begin, is an abbreviated version of the *adhān* [call to prayer], with the addition of the words (repeated twice): *qad qāmati' ṣ-ṣalāh* [The prayer is about to begin!] Thus:

Allāh is Supremely Great! Allāh is Supremely Great!	*Allāhu Akbar: Allāhu Akbar.*
I bear witness that there is no god but Allāh.	*ashhadu an lā ilāha illa 'llāh.**
I bear witness that Muḥammad is the Messenger of Allāh.	*Muḥammadan ashhadu anna Rasūlu 'llāh.**
Come to prayer!	*ḥayya 'ala 'ṣ-ṣalāh.*
Come to salvation!	*ḥayya 'ala 'l-falāḥ.*
The prayer is about to begin! The prayer is about to begin!	*qad qāmati 'ṣ-ṣalāh.* *qad qāmati 'ṣ-ṣalāh.*
Allāh is Supremely Great! Allāh is Supremely Great!	*Allāhu Akbar: Allāhu Akbar.*
There is no god but Allāh!	*lā ilāha illa 'llāh.*

(* See note 301 on p. 224.)

It is reprehensible on his part, that he should give the call to prayer *[an yu'adhdhina]* while he is in a state of major or minor ritual impurity *[junub aw muḥdith]*.[305]

When he has finished pronouncing the *iqāma*, it is not appropriate for him to split the ranks [formed by the members of the congregation], in order to station himself in the first row.

Once he has delivered the call to prayer *[adhān]* from a particular spot, it is not appropriate for him to move to a different spot in order to pronounce the *iqāma*. This does not apply, however, if it would be difficult for him to do both in the same place. If he has given the call *[qad adhdhana]* from a minaret *[manāra]*,[306] for instance, he should pronounce the *iqāma* in a spot that is suitable for performing the prayer *[ṣalāt]*, or wherever is most convenient for him.

[305] The term *junub* is applied to a man who is in a state of major ritual impurity, by reason of sexual intercourse and discharge of the semen, and who is therefore disqualified from performing a valid ritual prayer *[ṣalāt]* until he has completed a total ablution *[ghusl]*.

The term *muḥdith* is applied to a man who is in a state of minor ritual impurity, and who is therefore disqualified from performing a valid ritual prayer *[ṣalāt]* until he has completed a lesser ablution *[wuḍū']*. Causes of minor ritual impurity include the discharge of urine, fecal excrement, or wind, and the loss of consciousness (through normal sleep, as well as insanity and other abnormal states).

[306] The words *ma'dhana* and *mi'dhana*—derived from the same root, *'–dh–n*, as *adhān* [the call to prayer] and *mu'adhdhin* [muezzin, one who gives the call to prayer]—are also used in Arabic as synonyms for *manāra* [minaret].

30.
On the importance of approaching the ritual prayer *[ṣalāt]* with an attitude of true humility and complete dedication.

Allāh will surely bestow His mercy upon the worshipper who approaches his ritual prayer *[ṣalāt]* with an attitude of humility, meekness, and submissiveness toward Allāh (Almighty and Glorious is He), fearfully and attentively, eagerly and apprehensively, anxiously and hopefully. He feels that nothing is more important to him than performing his prayer *[ṣalāt]* for the sake of his Lord (Exalted is He), engaging in intimate converse *[munājāt]* with Him, and establishing himself in His presence, in the postures of standing *[qā'im]* and sitting *[qā'id]*, and in the acts of bowing *[rāki']* and prostration *[sājid]*. In order to commit himself to this completely, he empties his heart and mind of their concerns. He makes a dedicated effort to fulfill his obligatory duties *[farā'iḍ]*, for he does not know whether he will be able to perform another ritual prayer *[hal yuṣallī ṣalāt]*, after the one in which he is currently engaged, or whether his demise *[wafāt]* will suddenly overtake him, before that opportunity can arise. So he stands in the presence of his Lord (Almighty and Glorious is He), melancholy and apprehensive, hoping that his performance will be accepted, and fearing its rejection. If He accepts it, he will experience blissful happiness, and if He rejects it, he will suffer painful distress.

How much is therefore at stake where you are concerned, O believer *[mu'min]* endowed with the radiant lights of Islām, in this ritual prayer *[ṣalāt]* and in the other components of your religious practice *['amal]*! All the more reason why you should approach it, as well as all those other duties, with an attitude of anxiety, despondency, timidity and apprehension.

As part of what He has prescribed for you, Allāh (Exalted is He) has decreed that you may never know whether or not a ritual prayer *[ṣalāt]*, or any good deed, has been accepted of you, and that you may never know whether or not you have been forgiven for committing a bad deed. Yet there you go, laughing and making merry, heedlessly immersed in the pleasures of worldly life! I wonder how you can be so free of care, in light of the certain knowledge *[yaqīn]*, which has come from an Informant who is Truthful and Trustworthy *[Mukhbir Ṣādiq Amīn]*, that you are heading toward the Fire of Hell. For He has said (Glorious and Exalted is He):

And there is not one of you but shall go down to it [the Fire of Hell];	*wa in min-kum* *illā wāridu-hā:*
that, for your Lord, is a thing decreed, determined. (19:71)	*kāna ʿalā Rabbi-ka* *ḥatman maqḍiyyā.*

What you have not received is the certain knowledge *[yaqīn]* that you will also emerge from it! For whom, therefore, is a prolonged state of lamentation and sorrow more suitable than for you, until Allāh sees fit to accept your offering?

Even then, you will not know exactly what lies in store for you. When evening falls, will you live to see the break of day? You may see the dawn, but will you still be alive when the evening comes around? Will you be greeted with tidings of the Garden of Paradise, or with tidings of the Fire of Hell? You have very good reason, therefore, to be less than completely happy with a wife, a child, or a piece of property.

Nothing could be more utterly astounding than the extent of your heedlessness, and the extent of your indifference to this enormously important matter. You are being driven toward your destination at a rapid pace, every day and every night, with every hour and with every twinkling of an eye, so you must prepare yourself for imminent arrival at your appointed term *[ajal]*. You must not continue to be heedless of this mighty peril that hangs over you like a shadow, for you are bound to experience death, and your encounter with it is inevitable; it may alight in your personal space tomorrow morning or tomorrow night. You must dispose of your worldly interests, for you will soon be extracted from all of that, and dispossessed of it completely. Whether you are bound for the Garden of Paradise or for the Fire of Hell, those interests will cease to be of any relevance whatsoever.

Especially in the case of the Fire of Hell, verbal explanations and stories fall far short of describing the reality of its nature, of imparting a true understanding of its size and scope and the variety of its torments, and of communicating the full extent of what it represents.

Al-ʿAbd aṣ-Ṣāliḥ [the Righteous Servant] (may Allāh bestow His mercy upon him) once said:

"Where the Fire of Hell is concerned, I find it astonishing that someone who is supposed to be fleeing from it can fall asleep, and as for the Garden of Paradise, I find it astonishing that someone who is supposed to be seeking it can fall asleep."

By Allāh, if you ever withdraw from the flight from the one, and the quest for the other, you will surely be doomed to manifest disaster. Great will be your agony, and prolonged will be your grief and lamentation, tomorrow [at the Resurrection] in the company of those miserable wretches who are condemned to suffer painful torment.

If, on the other hand, you are determined to be a refugee [from the Fire of Hell] and a seeker [of the Garden of Paradise], you must on no account allow yourself to be misled by entertaining fanciful desires, or by taking pride in the signs of grace with which you are endowed. You must make a truly earnest commitment and a truly dedicated effort. You must be on your guard against the lower self *[nafs]* and the Devil *[Shaiṭān]*, for each of them exerts a subtle influence, each of them poses a serious threat, and each of them is capable of wicked tricks and ruses. You must also be on your guard against this world, so that it does not captivate you with its charm, and so that it does not deceive you with vanities, its falsehood, its opulence and its glamorous appeal.

In the words of the tradition *[ḥadīth]* that has come down to us from the Chief of Mankind *[Sayyid al-Bashar]*:[307]

> This world is ever deceiving, fickle, and harmful.[308]

Allāh (Almighty and Glorious is He) has told us:

O mankind, be careful to observe	*yā ayyuha 'n-nāsu 'ttaqū*
your duty to your Lord,	*Rabba-kum*
and dread a day	*wa 'khshaw yawman*
when no parent shall give	*lā yajzī wālidun*
satisfaction on his child's behalf,	*ʿan waladi-hi*
and no child shall	*wa lā mawlūdun*
give any satisfaction whatsoever	*huwa jāzin ʿan wālidi-hi shaiʾā:*

[307] That is to say, from Allāh's Messenger, the Prophet Muḥammad (Allāh bless him and give him peace).

[308] *inna 'd-dunyā taghurru tamurru wa taḍurru.*

for his parent. Allāh's promise is true
indeed, so do not let
the life of this world delude you,
and do not let the Deceiver
deceive you in regard to Allāh.
(31:33)

inna wa'da 'llāhi ḥaqqun fa-lā
taghurranna-kumu 'l-
ḥayātu 'd-dunyā:
wa lā yaghurranna-kum
bi-'llāhi 'l-gharūr.

The Deceiver *[al-Gharūr]*[309] is none other than Satan the accursed *[ash-Shaiṭān ar-rajīm]*. [From him we take refuge with] Allāh, Allāh, and then again Allāh!

You must be on your guard against the pitfalls that lead to perdition and ruination. You must faithfully observe the ritual prayer *[ṣalāt]*, as well as all the other commandments, and you must beware of infringing any of the prohibitions [imposed by the Sacred Law]. You must refrain from sinful behavior, in private as well as in public. You must surrender to your Lord, by accepting with resignation whatever has been destined for you and for other people. You must submit to your Lord, through obedience to Him in whatever He commands or forbids you to do. You must not distance yourself from Him, by committing that which he has forbidden you to perpetrate. You must not incur His displeasure, by remonstrating with Him against the course He has prepared for you, and by refusing to be satisfied with what He has allotted to you in the form of worldly goods and means of livelihood, and with the actions He has taken for your sake. He has hidden from you some of the benefits that will eventually accrue from those actions, and He has concealed from you their ultimate consequences, but some of their finest fruits and beneficial results will soon become apparent to you.

He has said (More Glorious is He than any other sayer):

But it may happen that you hate
a thing that is good for you,
and it may happen that you love
a thing which is bad for you.
Allāh knows,
and you know not. (2:216)

wa 'asā an takrahū shai'ān
wa huwa khairun la-kum:
wa 'asā an tu'ibbū shai'an
wa huwa sharrun la-kum:
wa 'llāhu ya'lamu
wa antum lā ta'lamūn.

You must always be obedient to your Master *[Mawlā]*, content with His verdict, patient in the face of His trials and tribulations, grateful for

[309] Allāh (Almighty and Glorious is He) has also mentioned the Deceiver *[al-Gharūr]* in the following verse *[āya]* of the Qur'ān:

And wishful expectations beguiled you
until the ordinance of Allāh came to pass,
and the Deceiver deceived you
concerning Allāh. (57:14)

wa gharratkumu 'l-amāniyyu
ḥattā jā'a amru 'llāhi
wa gharrakum
bi'llāhi 'l-Gharūr.

His blessings, invoking His Names, remembering His gracious favors and His revelations *[āyāt]*, harmonizing with His work *[fiʿl]* and His will *[murād]*, and harboring no doubts concerning the wisdom of His management *[tadbīr]*, as it applies to you, and as it applies to His entire creation. You must make this your constant practice, until death comes to claim you, for then you will be taken from this world in the company of the good *[aṭ-ṭayyibīn]*, you will be resurrected in the company of the Prophets *[al-Anbiyāʾ]*, and you will enter the Gardens of Bliss, by the Mercy of the Lord of All the Worlds *[Rabb al-ʿĀlamīn]*, and by the Will of the God of the First and the Last *[Ilāh al-Awwalīn wa 'l-Ākhirīn]*.

31.
Concerning the ritual prayer of the spiritual élite *[ṣalāt al-khāṣṣa]*.

As for the ritual prayer of the spiritual élite *[ṣalāt al-khāṣṣa]*, it serves to alert the wakeful, the humbly submissive, the vigilant, the guardians of hearts, the welcome guests of the All-Merciful *[ar-Raḥmān]* (may they enjoy the good pleasure of Allāh, and may His peace be upon them all). A good description of it is related in the following report:

Yūsuf ibn ʿIṣām was passing through one of the large congregational mosques *[jāmiʿ min jawāmiʿ]* of Khurāsān, when he came across an enormous circle *[ḥalqa]* of people. He stopped to ask someone about it, and he was told: "That is the circle of Ḥātim. He is speaking on the subjects of abstinence *[zuhd]* and pious caution *[waraʿ]*, and about fear and hope."

Yūsuf then turned to his companions and said: "Come on, let us ask him a question on the subject of the ritual prayer *[ṣalāt]*! Then, if he gives us a satisfying answer, we shall sit with him and join his circle." He thereupon went up to Ḥātim, saluted him with the greeting of peace *[sallama ʿalai-hi]*, and said: "May Allāh bestow His mercy upon you *[raḥima-ka 'llāh]*! I have a question I wish to put to you." "Go ahead and ask it," said Ḥātim, and the following conversation then took place between the two of them:

Yūsuf said: "I wish to ask you about the ritual prayer *[ṣalāt]*."

Ḥātim said: "Do you wish to ask me about its significance as a spiritual experience *[maʿrifa]*, or about the discipline *[adab]* to be observed in its performance? There are two distinct questions here, requiring two separate answers."

Yūsuf said: "In that case, let me ask you about the discipline *[adab]* to be observed in its performance."

Ḥātim said: "It means that you rise to the occasion, and walk [to the place of worship] with an attitude of total dedication *[iḥtisāb]*. It means that you begin the actual prayer with the appropriate intention *[niyya]*, and pronounce the declaration of Allāh's Supreme Greatness [by saying '*Allāhu Akbar*'] in a spirit of glorification *[tukabbiru bi't-taʿẓīm]*. It means that you recite [from the Qur'ān] with a clear and distinct enunciation *[tartīl]*.[310] It means that you perform the act of bowing with humility *[tarkaʿu bi'l-khushūʿ]*, the act of prostration with submissiveness *[tasjudu bi't-tawāḍuʿ]*, the testimony with sincerity *[tatashahhadu bi'l-ikhlāṣ]*, and the salutation with a feeling of compassion *[tusallimu bi'r-raḥma]*."

Yūsuf's companions then prompted him to ask about its significance as a spiritual experience *[maʿrifa]*, so he went ahead and asked this second question, to which Ḥātim responded by explaining:

"It means that you set the Garden of Paradise to your right, the Fire of Hell to your left, the Bridge *[aṣ-Ṣirāṭ]* beneath your feet, and the Balance *[al-Mīzān]* beneath your eyes, and [that you worship] the Lord as if you could see Him, for, even if you do not see Him, He does see you."

"O young man *[yā shābb]*," said Yūsuf, "how long have you been performing this kind of ritual prayer *[ṣalāt]*?"

"For twenty years," said Ḥātim.

Yūsuf said to his companions: "Come now, let us commit ourselves to peforming such a prayer *[ṣalāt]* for the next fifty years!"

Then he turned to Ḥātim and asked him: "Where did you find out about this?"

Ḥātim replied: "From those books of yours, which you used to dictate to us!"

The traditional report *[ḥadīth]* of Abū Ḥāzim al-Aʿraj ["the Lame"] (may Allāh bestow His mercy upon him) is highly relevant to this whole topic, so we shall now proceed to recount it.

To quote the actual words of Abū Ḥāzim al-Aʿraj (may Allāh bestow His mercy upon him):

"One day, while I was at the seashore, one of the Companions of Allāh's Messenger (Allāh bless him and give him peace) came up to me and said: 'O Abū Ḥāzim, do you know how to perform the ritual prayer *[a-tuḥsinu an tuṣalliya]*?'

"'How could I not know how to perform the ritual prayer,' said I, 'since I am thoroughly familiar with its strictly obligatory elements *[farā'iḍ]*,

[310] In the technical vocabulary of *tajwīd* [the art of reciting the Qur'ān], the term *tartīl* is applied to the slowest and most deliberate of the three rates of recitation.

as well as with the customary observances *[ma 'stanna]* established by Allāh's Messenger (Allāh bless him and give him peace)?'

"'O Abū Ḥāzim,' he then said to me, 'what is required of you, as an obligatory duty *[farḍ]*, before you stand ready to perform the ritual prayer *[ṣalāt]*?'

"'There are six requirements,' I replied.

"'What are they?' he asked.

"I said: 'They are (1) a state of ritual purity *[ṭahāra]*, (2) covering oneself [to conceal the private parts] *[istitār]*, (3) choosing a suitable spot on which to perform the prayer *[ikhtiyār mawḍiʿ aṣ-ṣalāt]*, (4) standing ready to perform the prayer *[al-qiyām ila 'ṣ-ṣalāt]*, (5) formulating the intention *[niyya]*, and (6) facing toward the *Qibla* [direction of the Kaʿba in Mecca].'

"'O Abū Ḥāzim,' he asked me next, 'with what intention *[niyya]* do you set out from your house toward the mosque *[masjid]*?'

"I said: 'With the intention to visit [the place of worship] *[bi-niyyat az-ziyāra]*.'

"He said: 'With what intention *[niyya]* do you enter the mosque *[masjid]*?'

"I said: 'With the intention to perform an act of worship *[bi-niyyat al-ʿibāda]*.'

"He said: 'With what intention *[niyya]* do you stand ready to perform the ritual prayer *[ṣalāt]*?'

"I said: 'With the intention of servitude *[bi-niyyat al-ʿubūdiyya]*, acknowledging the state of servitude to Him.'"

Abū Ḥāzim (may Allāh bestow His mercy upon him) then continued his account of his conversation with the Companion of the Prophet (Allāh bless him and give him peace):

"He came closer to me, and said: 'O Abū Ḥāzim, with what do you confront the *Qibla*?'

"I said: 'With three obligatory observances *[farāʾiḍ]* and one customary practice *[sunna]*.'

"He said: 'And what are they?'

"I said: 'Facing toward the *Qibla* is an obligatory observance *[farḍ]*. Formulating the intention *[niyya]* is an obligatory observance *[farḍ]*. The initial declaration of Allāh's Supreme Greatness *[at-takbīrat al-ūlā]*[311]

[311] This initial declaration—"*Allāhu Akbar* [Allāh is Supremely Great!]"—is often called the consecratory declaration of Allāh's Supreme Greatness *[takbīrat al-iḥrām]*.

is also an obligatory observance *[farḍ]*. The act of raising the hands[312] is a customary practice *[sunna]*.'

"He said: 'In how many instances is pronouncing the declaration of Allāh's Supreme Greatness *[takbīr]* required of you as an obligatory observance *[farḍ]*, and how often as a customary practice *[sunna]*?'

"I said: 'The basic principle of *takbīr* [the affirmation of the Supreme Greatness of Allāh] is expressed through ninety-four *takbīra's* [utterances of the declaration: "*Allāhu Akbar* (Allāh is Supremely Great!)"]. Five of these are strictly obligatory *[farḍ]*, while all the rest of them are customary *[sunna]*.'

"He said: 'With what do you mark the opening of the ritual prayer *[bi-mā tastaftiḥu 'ṣ-ṣalāt]*?'

"I said: 'With the affirmation of Allāh's Supreme Greatness *[bi't-takbīr]*.'

"He said: 'And what [element of the prayer] is its manifest proof *[burhān]*?'

"I said: 'Its Qur'ānic recitation *[qirā'a]*.'

"He said: 'And what is its jewel, its very essence *[jawhar]*?'

"I said: 'Its glorification [of the Lord] *[tasbīḥ]*.'

"He said: 'And what is its animation *[iḥyā']*?'

"I said: 'Its humble submission *[khushū']*.'

"He said: 'And what is its humble submission *[khushū']*?'

"I said: 'Fixing one's gaze on the spot where the act of prostration *[sujūd]* is to be performed.'

"He said: 'And what is its solemn dignity *[waqār]*?'

"I said: 'Its state of calm tranquillity *[sukūn]*.'

"He said: 'And what is its consecration *[taḥrīm]*?'

"I said: 'The [initial] declaration of Allāh's Supreme Greatness *[takbīr]*.'

"He said: 'And what is its deconsecration *[taḥlīl]*?'

"I said: 'The [concluding] salutation *[taslīm]*.'

"He said: 'And what is its emblem *[shi'ār]*?'

"I said: 'The glorification [of the Lord] *[tasbīḥ]* when its performance has been duly completed.'

[312] See Vol. 1, p. 15, where Shaikh 'Abd al-Qādir al-Jīlānī (may Allāh be well pleased with him) has explained:

> This means that one's hands are brought up close to the shoulders, the thumbs are held beside the lobes of the ears, and the tips of the fingers next to upper parts of the ears. Then the hands are lowered again.

"He said: 'And what is the key to all of that, O Abū Ḥāzim?'

"I said: 'The ritual ablution *[wuḍū']*.'

"He said: 'And what is the key to the ritual ablution *[miftāḥ al-wuḍū']*?'

"I said: 'The invocation of Allāh's Name *[tasmiya]*.'[313]

"He said: 'And what is the key to the invocation of Allāh's Name *[miftāḥ at-tasmiya]*?'

"I said: 'The intention *[niyya]*.'

"He said: 'And what is the key to the intention *[miftāḥ an-niyya]*?'

"I said: 'Certitude *[yaqīn]*.'

"He said: 'And what is the key to certitude *[miftāḥ al-yaqīn]*?'

"I said: 'Absolute trust [in the Lord] *[tawakkul]*.'

"He said: 'And what is the key to absolute trust *[miftāḥ at-tawakkul]*?'

"I said: 'Fear *[khawf]*.'

"He said: 'And what is the key to fear *[miftāḥ al-khawf]*?'

"I said: 'Hope *[rajā']*.'

"He said: 'And what is the key to hope *[miftāḥ ar-rajā']*?'

"I said: 'Patience *[ṣabr]*.'

"He said: 'And what is the key to patience *[miftāḥ aṣ-ṣabr]*?'

"I said: 'Contentment *[riḍā]*.'

"He said: 'And what is the key to contentment *[miftāḥ ar-riḍā]*?'

"I said: 'Worshipful obedience *[ṭā'a]*.'

"He said: 'And what is the key to worshipful obedience *[miftāḥ aṭ-ṭā'a]*?'

"I said: 'Acknowledgment [of truth and reality] *[i'tirāf]*.'

"He said: 'And what is the key to acknowledgment [of truth and reality] *[miftāḥ al-i'tirāf]*?'

"I said: 'Acknowledgment of the Divine Oneness and Lordship *[al-i'tirāf bi'l-waḥdāniyya wa 'r-rubūbiyya]*.'

"He said: 'And by what means did you become acquainted with all of that?'

"I said: 'Through knowledge *['ilm]*.'

"He said: 'And by what means did you acquire knowledge *['ilm]*?'

"I said: 'Through the process of learning *[ta'allum]*.'

"He said: 'And by what means did you pursue the process of learning *[ta'allum]*?'

"I said: 'Through intelligence *['aql]*.'

313 The *tasmiya* [invocation of Allāh's Name] is pronounced by saying: "*Bismi'llāh* [In the Name of Allāh]."

"He said: 'And by what means did you acquire intelligence *[ʿaql]*?'

"I said: 'There are two kinds of intelligence *[al-ʿaql ʿaqlān]*. For the making of one kind of intelligence, Allāh is solely responsible, to the exclusion of His creatures. The other kind of intelligence is one that human beings can develop, through the discipline of training and education. When the two kinds are combined together as a team, each of them assists and supports the other.'

"He said: 'And by what means did you accomplish all of that?'

"I said: 'Through the enabling grace [of Allāh] *[tawfīq]*. May Allāh enable us, and you, to succeed in achieving that which is worthy of love and approval.'

"Then he said: 'By Allāh, you have already perfected the keys to the Garden of Paradise! So let me hear your answers to the following questions: (1) What is the obligatory duty *[farḍ]* that you must perform? (2) What is the obligatory duty of the obligatory duty *[farḍ al-farḍ]*? (3) What is an obligatory duty that leads to an obligatory duty *[farḍ yuʾaddī ilā farḍ]*? (4) What is the customary practice *[sunna]* that is included within the obligatory duty *[farḍ]*? (5) What is a customary practice *[sunna]* by which the obligatory duty *[farḍ]* is completed?

"I answered his questions as follows: '(1) As for the obligatory duty *[farḍ]*, that is the ritual prayer *[ṣalāt]*. (2) As for the obligatory duty of the obligatory duty *[farḍ al-farḍ]*, that is the state of ritual purity *[ṭahāra]*. (3) As for an obligatory duty that leads to an obligatory duty *[farḍ yuʾaddī ilā farḍ]*, that refers to your taking water in your right hand, and using it to wash your left hand. (4) As for the customary practice *[sunna]* that is included within the obligatory duty *[farḍ]*, that refers to your making water flow between your fingers and toes [when performing the ritual ablution]. (5) As for a customary practice *[sunna]* by which the obligatory duty *[farḍ]* is completed, that is circumcision *[khitān]*.'

"He said: 'You have not left yourself vulnerable to any charge that might be brought against you, O Abū Ḥāzim! Now let me ask you this: 'How many duties, obligatory *[farḍ]* and customary *[sunna]*, are you required to observe in connection with the consumption of food?'

"I said: 'Are there obligatory and customary observances *[farḍ wa sunna]* connected with the consumption of food?'

"He said: 'Yes, there are. Four of them are obligatory *[farḍ]*, four are customary *[sunna]*, and four are acts of courtesy *[makruma]*.

"'1. As for the four that are obligatory *[farḍ]*, they are: (a) the invocation of Allāh's Name *[tasmiya]*; (b) giving praise [to Allāh] *[ḥamd]*; (c) giving thanks [to Allāh] *[shukr]*; and (d) the conscious recognition *[ma'rifa]* of that which Allāh has provided for you to eat.

"'2. As for the four that are customary *[sunna]*, they are: (a) sitting so that your weight is supported on your left thigh; (b) eating with three fingers; (c) thoroughly chewing your food; and (d) licking your fingers.

"'3. As for the four that are acts of courtesy *[makruma]* they are: (a) washing your hands; (b) taking small mouthfuls; (c) eating from the part of the dish that is close to you; and (d) seldom looking at the person who is sitting and eating beside you. Such was the practice of Allāh's Messenger (Allāh bless him and give him peace).'"

* * * * * * *

This brings us to the end of the Chapter concerning
the five daily ritual prayers *[aṣ-ṣalawāt al-khams]*,
the times times prescribed for their performance,
their customary elements *[sunan]*,
and their special qualities.

Praise be to Allāh, the Lord of All the Worlds!
[al-ḥamdu li'llāhi Rabbi 'l-'ālamīn].

CHAPTER NINE

In this Chapter we provide a concise treatment of certain special ritual prayers *[ṣalawāt]*, namely:

1. The ritual prayer of the Friday congregation *[ṣalāt al-jumʿa]*.
2. The ritual prayer of each of the Two Festivals *[ṣalāt al-ʿĪdain]*.
3. The ritual prayer for relief from drought *[ṣalāt al-istisqāʾ]*.
4. The ritual prayer at the eclipse of the sun *[ṣalāt al-kusūf]*, and at the eclipse of the moon *[ṣalāt al-khusūf]*.
5. The ritual prayer in time of danger *[ṣalāt al-khawf]*.
6. The shortened version of the ritual prayer *[qaṣr aṣ-ṣalāt]*.
7. The combination of two ritual prayers *[al-jamʿ baina 'ṣ-ṣalātain]*.
8. The ritual prayer at the funeral service *[aṣ-ṣalāt ʿala 'l-jināza]*.

1.
Concerning the ritual prayer of the Friday congregation *[ṣalāt al-jumʿa]*.

As for the ritual prayer of the Friday congregation *[ṣalāt al-jumʿa]*, the necessity *[wujūb]*[314] of its performance is based on the words of Allāh (Exalted is He):

O you who believe! When the call	*yā ayyuha 'lladhīna āmanū*
is proclaimed for the prayer	*idhā nūdiya li'ṣ-ṣalāti*
on the Day of Congregation,	*min yawmi 'l-jumuʿati*
hasten to the remembrance of Allāh	*fa-'sʿaw ilā dhikri 'llāhi*
and leave trading aside.	*wa dharu 'l-baiʿ:*
That is better for you,	*dhālikum khairun la-kum*
if you did but know. (62:9)	*in kuntum taʿlamūn.*

It is also based on the saying of the Prophet (Allāh bless him and give him peace):

> If someone fails to attend the Friday congregation *[jumʿa]* on three [consecutive] occasions, without having a valid excuse to offer, Allāh will stamp a seal on his heart.

The duty to attend the Friday congregational prayer *[farḍ al-jumʿa]* is incumbent, therefore, upon every individual for whom the five daily prayers *[aṣ-ṣalawāt al-khams]*[315] are obligatory—provided that he is a permanent local resident *[mustawṭin]*, settled in a town or in a rural community *[qarya jāmiʿa]*, in which there is a population of at least forty legally mature males, all of whom must be of sound mind, and all of whom must be free men.

[314] The noun *wujūb* corresponds to the adjectival form *wājib*, which is applied—as a technical term of Islāmic jurisprudence *[fiqh]*—to a religious duty that is "necessary," but which cannot be classed as "absolutely obligatory" *[farḍ]*.

[315] Shaikh ʿAbd al-Qādir al-Jīlānī (may Allāh be well pleased with him) has devoted an earlier Chapter to the subject of the five daily prayers *[aṣ-ṣalawāt al-khams]*. (See pp. 110–238.)

If he resides in a village or settlement in which there are fewer than forty men, and his situation is such that he can hear the call *[nidā᾽]* from another village, or a town or city, from which he is separated by the distance of a league *[farsakh]*,[316] it is incumbent upon him to go there.

It is not permissible for him to absent himself from it [the Friday congregational prayer], unless he has a valid excuse. Under certain circumstances, he will be excused for failing to attend, not only this, but also the congregational performance of all other [prescribed] prayers *[ṣalawāt]*. This exemption will apply in cases like the following:

1. He is sick.
2. He has reason to fear the loss or destruction of some property of his.
3. He has reason to fear the death or disappearance of a close relative.
4. His freedom of movement is restricted by a serious problem connected with the bladder and the bowel, or one of the two.
5. A meal has been prepared for him, and he is urgently in need of it.
6. He has reason to fear being arrested by a worldly authority, or being grabbed by a creditor who is constantly harassing him, when he has nothing on him to give the man.
7. He is getting ready to travel, and is afraid of missing his caravan.
8. He is afraid of damage to his property, or hopes to locate its whereabouts by staying away from the Friday congregation *[jum῾a]*, as well as other congregational attendance *[jamā῾a]*.
9. Sleepiness *[nu῾ās]* overwhelms him, so that he misses the prescribed time.
10. He is afraid of being badly affected by the rain, the mud, and the strong wind.

The Friday congregational prayer *[ṣalāt al-jum῾a]* consists of two cycles *[rak῾atān]*, performed after the sermon *[khuṭba]*[317] and together with the prayer leader *[imām]*. If someone misses it, he must perform a noon prayer *[ẓuhr]* of four cycles.[318] He may do this either by himself, if he so wishes, or as a member of a congregational group.

[316] The *farsakh* [parasang, or league] is three miles of the Hāshimī measure, i.e. thirty bow-shots reckoning the bow-shot as four hundred cubits, or sixty bow-shots reckoning the bow shot as two hundred cubits. (See E.W. Lane, *Arabic-English Lexicon*, art. *F-R-S-KH*.)

[317] Since this sermon is delivered in two parts, it is sometimes referred to as "the two sermons *[al-khuṭbatān]*." (See, for instance, p. 242 below.)

[318] The regular noon prayer *[ṣalāt aẓ-ẓuhr]*, which is one of the five prescribed prayers *[aṣ-ṣalāt al-khams]* on the other days of the week, is replaced on a Friday by the congregational prayer *[ṣalāt al-jum῾a]*—except, as noted here, for those who fail to attend the latter.

The appropriate time for it is before the sun's decline from the meridian, coinciding with the time when the ritual prayer of the Festival *[ṣalāt al-ʿĪd]* is performed. According to some of our fellow [Ḥanbalī] scholars, [it should be performed] in the fifth hour [of daylight].

One prerequisite, without which it cannot be convened, is the presence of forty men, from among those on whom it is incumbent to perform the Friday congregational prayer *[al-jumʿa]*.[319] (According to one reported version [of the Ḥanbalī doctrine], the required number is fifty, and according to another it is only thirty.)

In the course of its performance, it is customary[320] to pronounce the Qurʾānic recitation in an audible voice *[jahr]*. It is also customary for that recitation to consist of the Sūra of the Congregation *[Sūrat al-Jumuʿa]*[321] —after the Opening Sūra *[al-Fātiḥa]*—in the first cycle, and the Sūra of the Hypocrites *[Sūrat al-Munāfiqīn]*[322] in the second cycle.

Is it necessary to obtain official authorization *[idhn al-imām]*? On this point, there are two [conflicting] accounts of the [Ḥanbalī] doctrine.

One of the preconditions for the valid performance of the Friday congregational prayer *[ṣalāt al-jumʿa]* is that it must be preceded by the two sermons *[al-khuṭbatān]*.

It has no customary ritual prayer *[sunna]* to precede it. As for the one that may be performed afterwards, it should consist of at least two cycles *[rakʿatān]*, and of six cycles at the very most. There is a tradition *[ḥadīth]* to this effect, reported by some of the Companions (may Allāh be well pleased with them all), who attribute it to the Prophet (Allāh bless him and give him peace). According to a certain scholar, however, one of those well versed in the knowledge of Allāh (Almighty and Glorious is He), the recommended practice is to perform twelve cycles of [voluntary] ritual prayer in advance of the Friday congregational prayer *[ṣalāt al-jumʿa]*, and six cycles after it.

[319] That is to say, they must be legally mature, of sound mind, and free men.

[320] By "customary" we mean following the exemplary custom [*Sunna* in Arabic] of the Prophet (Allāh bless him and give him peace).

[321] The Sūra of the Congregation *[Sūrat al-Jumuʿa]* takes its title from the verse *[āya]* quoted at the beginning of this Chapter (p. 240 above).

[322] The Sūra entitled "The Hypocrites" *[Sūrat al-Munāfiqūn]* is the 63rd Sūra of the Qurʾan.

As soon as the call to prayer *[adhān]* has been delivered beside the pulpit *[minbar]*, everyone must desist from buying and selling, in accordance with the words of Allāh (Exalted is He):

O you who believe! When the call	*yā ayyuha 'lladhīna āmanū*
is proclaimed for the prayer	*idhā nūdiya li'ṣ-ṣalāti*
on the Day of Congregation,	*min yawmi 'l-jumu'ati*
hasten to the remembrance of Allāh	*fa-'s'aw ilā dhikri 'llāhi*
and leave trading aside. (62:9)	*wa dharu 'l-bai':*

This is a reference to the call to prayer *[adhān]* as it was delivered [beside the pulpit] in the lifetime of Allāh's Messenger (Allāh bless him and give him peace). It is necessary *[wājib]*[323] according to our understanding of the [Ḥanbalī] doctrine, while others maintain that it is a collective duty *[farḍ 'ala 'l-kifāya]*.[324] He [Imām Aḥmad ibn Ḥanbal] is also reported as having declared it a customary practice *[sunna]*.

As for the call to prayer delivered from the minaret *[adhān al-manāra]*,[325] it was ordained by 'Uthmān ibn 'Affān (may Allāh be well pleased with him) during his time [as Caliph],[326] as a measure to promote the public interest *[li-maṣlaḥa 'āmma]*, its purpose being to

[323] In the technical vocabulary of Islāmic jurisprudence *[fiqh]*, the term *wājib* is applied to a religious duty that is "necessary," but which cannot be classed as "absolutely obligatory" *[farḍ]*.

[324] In Islāmic jurisprudence *[fiqh]*, a distinction is drawn between *farḍ 'ain*, i.e., a religious duty that is incumbent on every individual Muslim, and *farḍ 'ala 'l-kifāya*, meaning a collective duty, incumbent on the Islāmic community as a whole, though not on every individual Muslim. As Shaikh 'Abd al-Qādir al-Jīlānī (may Allāh be well pleased with him) has pointed out in an earlier Chapter of the present work, duties classed as *farḍ 'ain* include the obligation to acquire knowledge of the rules governing the five fundamentals or "pillars," namely, the profession of faith *[shahāda]*; the ritual prayer *[ṣalāt]*; the alms-due *[zakāt]*; fasting *[ṣawm]* during the month of Ramaḍān; and the pilgrimage *[ḥajj]*. There is also an obligation to study subjects that go beyond these fundamentals, but the pursuit of "higher learning" is an example of a collective duty *[farḍ 'ala 'l-kifāya]*, which can be discharged by qualified experts on behalf of the community as a whole. (See Vol. 1, n. 63, p. 87.)

[325] The words *ma'dhana* and *mi'dhana*—derived from the same root, *'–dh–n*, as *adhān* [the call to prayer] and *mu'adhdhin* [muezzin, one who gives the call to prayer]—are also used in Arabic as synonyms for *manāra* [minaret].

[326] The Caliphate *[Khilāfa]* of 'Uthmān ibn 'Affān (may Allāh be well pleased with him) began in A.H. 23/643 C.E., when he succeeded 'Umar ibn al-Khaṭṭāb (may Allāh be well pleased with him) as Commander of the Believers [Amīr al-Mu'minīn], and ended when he was assassinated in A.H. 35/656 C.E., at the age of eighty-two. He is often referred to as Dhu 'n-Nūrain [He of the Two Lights], in honor of the fact that he married two daughters of the Prophet (Allāh bless him and give him peace): first Ruqayya, then, after her death, which occurred during the Battle of Badr, her sister Umm Kulthūm (may Allāh be well pleased with them).

Shaikh 'Abd al-Qādir al-Jīlānī (may Allāh be well pleased with him) has described his succession to the Caliphate in an earlier Chapter of the present work. (See Vol. 1, pp. 261-62.)

broadcast to people outside the main urban centers *[amṣār]*[327] and the smaller towns, thereby preventing invalid commercial transactions.

As soon as the worshipper enters the congregational mosque *[jāmiʿ]*, he is recommended—provided there is time to spare—to perform four cycles of [voluntary] ritual prayer *[rakaʿāt]*, in the course of which he should recite "*Qul Huwa'llāhu Aḥad* [Say: 'He is Allāh, One!']"[328] two hundred times (that is to say, fifty times in each cycle). This practice is recommended on good authority, because the Prophet (Allāh bless him and give him peace) is reported as having said:

> If someone does this, he will not die without having seen his place of abode in the Garden of Paradise, or having been absolved [of all sin].

This saying was reported by Ibn ʿUmar (may Allāh be well pleased with him and with his father).

[It is also recommended that] whenever he enters the congregational mosque *[jāmiʿ]*, the worshipper should not sit down until he has performed two cycles of [voluntary] ritual prayer *[rakʿatain]*; only then may he sit down.

We have already mentioned the special qualities of the Friday, the Day of the Congregation *[al-Jumʿa]*, described how one should behave when setting out for the congregational mosque *[jāmiʿ]*, and discussed all other relevant topics, in earlier sections of the present work.[329]

[327] The *amṣār* were the regional capitals established in places like Kūfa and Baṣra, in the wake of the rapid expansion of Islām beyond the confines of Arabia.

[328] Sūra 112.

[329] For the passages alluded to here by Shaikh ʿAbd al-Qādir al-Jīlānī (may Allāh be well pleased with him), see Vol. 1, pp. 83–84, and Vol. 3 pp. 295–325).

2.
Concerning the ritual prayer of the Two Festivals *[ṣalāt al-ʿĪdain]*.[330]

As for the ritual prayer of the Two Festivals *[ṣalāt al-ʿĪdain]*, it is a collective duty *[farḍ ʿala 'l-kifāya]*.[331] Provided that it is performed by a congregation *[jamāʿa]* attended by some of the inhabitants of a given locality, the duty is thereby discharged as far as the rest of them are concerned. If the inhabitants unanimously agree to omit its performance, however, the Leader of the Islamic Community *[al-Imām]* must take forceful action to combat them, until they repent.

The time prescribed for its performance begins when the sun has risen, and ends when the sun has declined from the meridian. Its performance on the early side is recommended, in the case of the Festival of Sacrifices *[ʿĪd al-Aḍḥā]*, for the sake of the animal to be sacrificed *[uḍḥiya]*. In the case of the Festival of Fastbreaking *[ʿĪd al-Fiṭr]*, on the other hand, it is preferable to delay, since this is not a factor to be considered.

Its preconditions of validity include permanent local residence *[istīṭān]*, a sufficient number [of qualified males], and official authorization *[idhn al-imām]*, as in the case of the Friday congregational prayer *[al-jumʿa]*. According to another account of his doctrine, however, our Imām Aḥmad [ibn Ḥanbal][332] (may Allāh bestow His mercy upon him) maintained that none of that is stipulated. This latter view is also held

[330] The Two Festivals *[al-ʿĪdān/-ain]* are the Festival of Fastbreaking *[ʿĪdu 'l-Fiṭr]* at the end of the month of Ramaḍān, and the Festival of Sacrifices *[ʿĪdu 'l-Aḍḥā]* in Dhu' l-Ḥijja, the month of Pilgrimage.

[331] See note 324 on p. 243 above.

[332] Imām Abū ʿAbdi'llāh Aḥmad ibn Muḥammad ibn Ḥanbal ash-Shaibānī (may Allāh bestow His mercy upon him) was the founder of one of the four schools *[madhāhib]* of Islamic jurisprudence. He died in the year A.H. 241/855 C.E. The legal doctrines of the Ḥanbalī school were those studied most intensively by the author, Shaikh ʿAbd al-Qādir al-Jīlānī (may Allāh be well pleased with him) as a young man.

by the school *[madhhab]* of Imām ash-Shāfiʿī (may Allāh bestow His mercy upon him).

Those who attend are recommended to arrive early, to wear elegant clothes, and to perfume themselves, as we have mentioned previously, in connection with the special qualities of Friday, the Day of Congregational Prayer *[al-Jumʿa]*.[333]

The most appropriate setting for its performance is a large space in the open air,[334] and it is considered improper to convene it inside the congregational mosque *[jāmiʿ]*, unless there is a valid pretext for doing so.

There is no objection to the attendance of women.

The most appropriate course is to make one's way to the site on foot, and then to return home by a different route. We have mentioned the reason *[ʿilla]* for this in our discussion of the special qualities of the Two Festivals *[al-ʿĪdain]*.[335]

The summons to it is the cry:

The ritual prayer is being convened!	*aṣ-ṣalātu jāmiʿa.*[336]

[The ritual prayer of the Two Festivals] consists of two cycles *[rakʿatān]*. In the first cycle, seven affirmations of Allāh's Supreme Greatness *[takbīrāt]* are proclaimed,[337] after the introductory invocation *[duʿāʾ al-istiftāḥ]*,[338] but before the plea for refuge with Allāh *[taʿawwudh]*.[339] In the second cycle, five affirmations of Allāh's Supreme

[333] See Vol. 3, pp. 295–325, where Shaikh ʿAbd al-Qādir al-Jīlānī (may Allāh be well pleased with him) has devoted a lengthy Discourse to the special qualities of Friday, the Day of Congregational Prayer *[al-Jumʿa]*.

[334] Literally, "in the desert *[ṣaḥrāʾ]*."

[335] See Vol. 3, pp. 146–49, 162–65 and 276–77.

[336] This brief announcement takes the place of the usual call to prayer *[adhān]*.

[337] The affirmation of Allāh's Supreme Greatness is expressed by declaring: "*Allāhu Akbar* [Allāh is Supremely Great!]" The general term for this affirmation is *takbīr*. A specific utterance thereof is called a *takbīra*, and the form *takbīrāt* is the plural of *takbīra*.

[338] The introductory invocation *[duʿāʾ al-istiftāḥ]*, is often referred to simply as *al-istiftāḥ* or *al-iftitāḥ* [the introduction]. It is uttered quietly, in the following words:

Allāh is Supremely Great, immensely so!	*Allāhu Akbar kabīrā:*
And praise be to Allāh, abundantly!	*wa 'l-ḥamdu li'llāhi kathīrā:*
And glory be to Allāh, both early and late.	*wa subḥāna 'llāhi bukratan wa aṣīlā:*

[339] The plea for refuge with Allāh *[taʿawwudh]* is made by uttering the words:

I take refuge with Allāh	*aʿūdhu bi-'llāhi*
from Satan the accursed.	*mina 'sh-shaiṭāni 'r-rajīm.*

Greatness *[takbīrāt]* are proclaimed, before the Qur'ānic recitation. With each affirmation *[takbīra]*, the worshipper raises his hands [to the lobes of his ears] and says:

Allāh is Supremely Great,	*Allāhu Akbar*
immensely so!	*kabīrā:*
And praise be to Allāh, abundantly!	*wa 'l-ḥamdu li'llāhi kathīrā:*
And glory be to Allāh,	*wa subḥāna 'llāhi*
both early and late.	*bukratan wa aṣīlā:*
And Allāh's blessings	*wa ṣalawātu 'llāhi*
upon our Master	*'alā Sayyidi-nā*
Muḥammad the Prophet,	*Muḥammadini 'n-Nabiyyi*
and his family,	*wa āli-hi*
and may He grant [him] peace.	*wa sallama taslīmā.*

When he has finished affirming Allāh's Supreme Greatness *[takbīr]*, he must seek refuge with Him *[ista'ādha]*, and recite the Opening Sūra *[al-Fātiḥa]*. Then [in the first cycle] he should recite [the Sūra that begins with the words]: "*Sabbiḥi 'sma Rabbi-ka 'l-A'lā*... [Glorify the Name of your Lord the Most High...]."[340] In the second cycle, he should recite [the Sūra that begins with the words]: "*Hal atā-ka ḥadīthu 'l-ghāshiya* [Have you received the story of the Calamity?]"[341]

As an acceptable alternative, he may recite, in the first cycle, [the Sūra that begins with the words]: "*Qāf: wa 'l-Qur'āni 'l-majīd* [*Qāf*: By the glorious Qur'ān!],"[342] and in the second cycle, [the Sūra that begins with the words]: "*Iqtarabati 's-sā'atu wa 'nshaqqa 'l-qamar* [The Hour has drawn near and the moon has been split in two]."[343] A statement to this effect has been attributed to our Imām Aḥmad [ibn Ḥanbal] (may Allāh bestow His mercy upon him).

The recitation of yet other Sūras [instead of those mentioned above] is also permissible.

Concerning the postponement of the introductory invocation *[al-istiftāḥ]* until the moment of the Qur'ānic recitation, there are likewise two [conflicting] reports. According to one of them, it should be pronounced immediately after the consecratory affirmation of Allāh's Supreme Greatness *[takbīrat al-iḥrām]*. According to the other,

[340] That is to say, the Sūra of the Most High *[Sūrat al-A'lā]*. (Q. 87.)

[341] That is to say, the Sūra of the Calamity *[Sūrat al-Ghāshiya]*. (Q. 88.)

[342] That is to say, the Sūra entitled "Qāf" *[Sūra Qāf]*. (Q. 50.)

[343] That is to say, the Sūra of the Moon *[Sūrat al-Qamar]*. (Q. 54.)

it should be deferred, together with the plea for refuge *[ta'awwudh]*, until the moment of the Qur'ānic recitation.

When a worshipper takes part in the Festival prayer *[ṣalla 'l-'Īd]*, he should not concern himself with supererogatory ritual practices *[nawāfil mina 'ṣ-ṣalāt]*, nor should he perform any [voluntary] prayer in advance of it. He should rather go home to his family, so that all of its members may rally together in his presence. He should be on his very best behavior with his family, and should make every effort to provide for them with extra generosity, because, as the Prophet (Allāh bless him and give him peace) has told us:

> The days of the Festival *['Īd]* are the days of eating, drinking, and cultivating family ties.

This applies to the two days of the Two Festivals *['Īd]*, and also to the Days of Drying Meat *[Ayyām at-Tashrīq.]*[344]

If they [the members of a local community] choose to perform it [the Festival prayer] in the mosque *[masjid]* [rather than in an open space], it is permissible for them to do so. When the worshipper enters the mosque, he should not sit down until he has performed the two cycles of ritual prayer *[rak'atain]* known as "the greeting of the mosque *[taḥiyyat al-masjid]*," in accordance with the saying of the Prophet (Allāh bless him and give him peace):

> Whenever one of you enters the mosque, he should not sit down until he has performed two cycles of ritual prayer *[rak'atain]*.

This applies to the two days of the Two Festivals *['Īd]*, as well as to all other occasions.

When our Imām Aḥmad [ibn Ḥanbal] propounded the ban on supererogatory observance *[tanafful]*, he obviously assumed that the site of the prayer *[al-muṣallā]* would be in an open space, because it is traditionally reported, through several lines of transmission, that the Prophet (Allāh bless him and give him peace) performed no ritual prayer beforehand, and none afterward. This was stated explicitly by [the Caliph] 'Umar [ibn al-Khaṭṭāb], by 'Abdu'llāh ibn 'Abbās, and by Ibn 'Umar (may Allāh be well pleased with them all). [On the days of the Two Festivals], the Prophet's own prayer *[ṣalāt an-Nabī]* (Allāh bless him and give him peace) was always performed at the [open-air] site of

[344] The term *tashrīq* denotes the drying up of the blood from the animals sacrificed. The Days of Drying Meat *[Ayyām at-Tashrīq]* are the three days immediately following the Day of Sacrifice *[Yawm an-Naḥr]*.

prayer in the area of the burial ground *[al-muṣallā fi 'l-jabbāna]*.[345] Had it been in the mosque *[masjid]*, he would certainly not (Allāh bless him and give him peace) have omitted [the two cycles of ritual prayer known as] the greeting of the mosque *[taḥiyyat al-masjid]*.

If a worshipper misses the whole of the ritual prayer of the Festival *[ṣalāt al-ʿĪd]*, it is considered commendable for him to make it up. In order to do so, he may adopt either of two options: He may perform four cycles, as in the forenoon prayer *[ṣalāt aḍ-ḍuḥā]*,[346] without the [multiple] affirmation of Allāh's Supreme Greatness *[takbīr]*, or he may copy the format [of the Festival prayer], by including the [multiple] affirmation of Allāh's Supreme Greatness *[takbīr]*.

All of this should rally his family and friends around him, and he will thereby earn considerable grace and favor.

[345] As Shaikh ʿAbd al-Qādir al-Jīlānī (may Allāh be well pleased with him) has informed us in Vol. 3, p. 147:

The Prophet (Allāh bless him and give him peace) is reported as having said:

When the Day of Breaking the Fast *[Yawm al-Fiṭr]* comes around, and the people emerge from their homes to pray in the open space near the burial ground *[jabbāna]*, Allāh (Exalted is He) will take notice of them, and He will say: "My servants, for My sake you have kept the fast, and for My sake you have performed the prayers. Now take your leave, knowing that you have been granted forgiveness!"

[346] See note 98 on p. 83, also pp. 90–92 above.

3.
Concerning the ritual prayer for relief from drought [*ṣalāt al-istisqā'*].

As for the ritual prayer for relief from drought [*ṣalāt al-istisqā'*], it is performed as a customary observance [*sunna*].

The prayer leader [*imām*] goes out [of town] to conduct it in the forenoon [*ḍaḥwa*], as he does in the case of the Two Festivals [*'Īdain*]. It closely resembles the ritual prayer of the Two Festivals [*ṣalāt al-'Īdain*] in all of its characteristic features, the site of its performance, and its rules [*aḥkām*].

It is appropriate for those who attend it to be neatly dressed, and scrupulously purified of all forms of defilement and dirt. It is not appropriate for them to perfume themselves, however, because the situation calls for begging, self-abasement, and petitioning for relief that is sorely needed. What is recommended, therefore, is that they should set out to attend it in their everyday work-clothes [*thiyāb al-bidhla*], with an attitude of submissiveness, earnest entreaty, abject humility, contrition and sorrow. They should be accompanied by the old men and old women, the youths, and the handicapped members of their community.

They should also extricate themselves from acts of injustice, from liabilities incurred through misappropriation and other forms of misconduct, and from obligations owed to Allāh (Almighty and Glorious is He), such as alms-dues [*zakawāt*], vows [*nudhūr*], and expiations [*kaffārāt*]. They should do a great deal of charitable giving [*ṣadaqa*], and a great deal of fasting [*ṣiyām*]. They should renew their repentance [*tawba*], and commit themselves to steadfast perseverance in it until death. They should not affront the Lord (Glory be to Him) with sins, whether they be major [*kabīra*] or minor [*ṣaghīra*]. They should be modestly aware of Him (Almighty and Glorious is He) in their private quarters, since there is no place so private as to be secluded from Him. No secret can be kept hidden from Him, neither on earth nor in heaven, for He is Aware of the secret and of all hidden things *[Huwa ʿĀlimun bi-'s-sirri wa 'l-khafiyyāt]*.[347]

It is likewise recommended that they should invoke the good offices of the pious abstainers *[zuhhād]*, the righteous *[ṣāliḥīn]*, and people devoted to learning, virtue and religion. This recommendation is based on the precedent set by [the Caliph] ʿUmar ibn al-Khaṭṭāb (may Allāh be well pleased with him), when he once went out to pray for relief from drought *[kharaja yastasqī]*. As we learn from a traditional report, he took al-ʿAbbās (may Allāh be well pleased with him) by the hand, then turned his face toward the *Qibla* [the direction of the Kaʿba in Mecca], and said: "O Allāh, this is the paternal uncle of our Prophet. We have come to appeal to You, invoking his good offices, so grant us water *[fa-'sqi-nā]* for his sake!" The reporter added: "And before they got back home, they were blessed with rain."

In order to grasp the point of this, one must understand that the withholding of rain is a chastisement, a requital for the sinful acts of disobedience committed by human beings *[maʿāṣī banī Ādam]*. This explains why [according to the traditional account]:

> When the unbeliever *[kāfir]* dies and is buried in his grave, and when [the interrogating angels called] Munkir and Nakīr come and ask him about his Lord *[Rabb]*, his Prophet *[Nabī]* and his religion *[dīn]*, and when he cannot answer their questions, the pair of them will beat him with an iron hammer *[mirzabba]*. This will cause him to yell so loud that his screams will be heard by all created beings, apart from the jinn and humankind. Every single thing will curse him, even the sheep held by the butcher, with the knife at its throat, for it will say: "May Allāh curse him! It was because of him that we were deprived of the rainfall!"

This is in keeping with the words of Allāh (Almighty and Glorious is He):

They will be cursed by Allāh,	*ulāʾika yalʿanu-humu 'llāhu*
and all who can curse will curse them. (2:159)	*wa yalʿanu-humu 'l-lāʿinūn.*

[347] As Allāh (Exalted is He) has told us in His own words:

Say: "The death from which you flee	*qul inna 'l-mawta 'lladhī tafirūna*
is bound to meet up with you;	*min-hu fa-inna-hu mulāqī-kum*
then you will be returned	*thumma turaddūna*
to the Knower of the unseen	*ilā ʿĀlimi 'l-ghaibi*
and the visible,	*wa 'sh-shahādati*
and He will tell you	*fa-yunabbiʾu-kum*
what you have been doing." (62:8)	*bi-mā kuntum taʿmalūn:*

For, when the human being *[ādamī]* becomes corrupt, his corruption infects every other living creature, and when he behaves righteously, his righteousness extends its influence to everything. His corruption is the result of his sinful disobedience to his Lord, while his righteousness is the result of his worshipful obedience to Him (Almighty and Glorious is He).

[This is how the prayer must be performed]:

The Leader of the Community *[al-Imām]*, or his deputy, must lead the people in a ritual prayer of two cycles *[rakʿatain]*, without a call to prayer *[adhān]*, and without a last-minute announcement *[iqāma]*.[348]

In the first cycle, he must pronounce the affirmation of Allāh's Supreme Greatness six times, in addition to the consecratory affirmation *[takbīrat al-iḥrām]*, and then five times in the second cycle, in addition to the affirmation uttered when rising from the posture of prostration *[takbīrat al-qiyām mina 's-sujūd]*. This should all be done in the manner we have described above, in connection with the Festival prayer *[ṣalāt al-ʿĪd]*.[349] He must likewise extol Allāh (Almighty and Glorious is He) between every two affirmations of His Supreme Greatness *[takbīratain]*.

As soon as he has finished leading the people in the ritual prayer *[idhā ṣallā bi-him]*, he should deliver a sermon *[khuṭba]* to the assembled congregation. It is also permissible for him to deliver the sermon before the performance of the prayer *[ṣalāt]*. According to one account of the [Ḥanbalī] doctrine, he is free to choose either option. It is also reported that he [Imām Aḥmad ibn Ḥanbal] (may Allāh bestow His mercy upon him) maintained that he [the prayer leader] is not required to deliver any sermon at all on this occasion, and that he should simply offer a prayer of supplication *[yadʿū fa-ḥasb]*.

The prayer leader *[imām]* should therefore do whatever is easiest and most convenient for him in this regard. If he does deliver a sermon, he should open it with the affirmation of Allāh's Supreme Greatness *[takbīr]*, as he would in the case of the Festival sermon *[khuṭbat al-ʿĪd]*, and he should repeat the invocation of blessings upon Allāh's Messenger (Allāh bless him and give him peace) many times over. In the course of his sermon, he should recite the Qurʾānic verses *[āyāt]*:

And I have said: "Seek forgiveness from your Lord;	*fa-qultu 'staghfirū Rabba-kum:*

[348] The *iqāma*, the announcement that the ritual prayer is about to begin, is an abbreviated version of the *adhān* [call to prayer], with the addition of the words (repeated twice): *qad qāmati' ṣ-ṣalāh* [The prayer is about to begin!]

[349] See pp. 246–47 above.

He is ever All-Forgiving, and He	*inna-hu kāna Ghaffārā*
will let loose the sky for you,	*yursilu 's-samā'a*
in plenteous rain	*'alai-kum midrārā.*
and He will succor you	*wa yumdid-kum*
with wealth and sons,	*bi-amwālin wa banīna*
and He will assign unto you gardens,	*wa yaj'al la-kum jannātin*
and He will assign unto you rivers."	*wa yaj'al la-kum anhārā.*
(71:10–12)	

When he has finished delivering his sermon, he should stand with his face toward the *Qibla*, then turn his cloak around, moving the part that was on his right shoulder over to the left, and the part that was on his left shoulder over to the right, without turning it upside down. All the people present should do likewise, and they should leave their cloaks reversed until they get back home to their families, at which point they may remove them, when they change their other clothes. They should do this as a gesture of optimism, betokening the transformation of the drought, and because the Tradition *[Sunna]* provides a precedent for it, as we know from the report of 'Abbād ibn Tamīm, whose paternal uncle (may Allāh be well pleased with him) told him:

"Allāh's Messenger (Allāh bless him and give him peace) led the people out [into the desert] to pray for rain *[yastasqī]*. He then led them in the performance of two cycles of ritual prayer *[ṣallā bi-him rak'atain]*, pronouncing the Qur'ānic recitation in an audible voice in each cycle. He reversed his cloak, offered a supplication *[da'ā]*, prayed for rain *[istasqā]*, and stood facing the *Qibla*."

Then, having reversed his cloak, the prayer leader *[imām]* should raise his hands, facing the *Qibla* as he does so, and offer the prayer of supplication *[du'ā']* offered by the Prophet (Allāh bless him and give him peace):

O Allāh, grant us a rainfall	*Allāhumma 'sqi-nā*
that is helpful,	*ghaithan*
wholesome, healthful, productive,	*mughīthan marī'an hanī'an*
copious and widespread.[350]	*marī'an ghadaqan mujallilā.*
O Allāh, grant us the gift of rain,	*Allāhumma 'sqi-na 'l-ghaitha*
and do not include us	*wa lā taj'al-nā*
among the hopeless.	*mina 'l-qāniṭīn:*
O Allāh, let it be a downpour of mercy,	*Allāhumma suqyā raḥmatin*
not a downpour of torment,	*lā suqyā 'adhābin*
nor of obliteration, nor of tribulation,	*wa lā maḥqin wa lā balā'in*
nor of destruction, nor of flooding.	*wa lā hadmin wa lā gharaq.*

[350] ***Author's note***: According to one traditional report, the wording at this point should rather be:

widespread, general, layer-upon-layer,	*mujallilan 'āmman*
streaming, continuous.	*ṭabaqan saḥḥan dā'imā*

O Allāh, in these lands,	*Allāhumma inna bi'l-bilādi*
and among [Your] servants	*wa 'l-ʿibādi*
and creatures,	*wa 'l-khalqi*
there is such great hardship	*mina 'l-laʾwāʾi*
and affliction,	*wa 'l-balāʾi*
and so much trouble and distress,	*wa 'l-jahdi wa 'ḍ-ḍanki*
that no complaint [is meaningful],	*mā lā shakwā*
unless it be addressed to You.	*illā ilai-k.*
O Allāh, irrigate the crops for us,	*Allāhumma anbit la-na 'z-zarʿa*
and cause the udders to yield	*wa adirra*
milk for us.	*la-na 'ḍ-ḍarʿa*
Let us drink from the bounty	*wa 'sqi-nā min barakati 's-*
of the sky,	*samāʾi*
and let the bounties of the earth	*wa anbit la-nā min*
grow for us.	*barakāti 'l-arḍ.*
O Allāh, relieve us of the agony,	*Allāhumma 'rfaʿ ʿan-na 'l-juhda*
the hunger and the destitution,	*wa 'l-jūʿa wa 'l-ʿurya*
and remove from us the suffering	*wa 'kshif ʿan-nā mina 'l-balāʾi*
that none but You can take away.	*mā lā yakshifu-hu ghairu-k.*
O Allāh,	*Allāhumma*
we seek forgiveness from You.	*innā nastaghfiru-ka*
Surely You are ever All-Forgiving,	*inna-ka kunta Ghaffārā:*
so let loose the sky for us	*fa-arsili 's-samāʾa*
in plenteous rain.[351]	*ʿalai-nā midrārā.*

—He should likewise plead *[yadʿū]:*

O Allāh, You have	*Allāhumma inna-ka amarta-nā*
commanded us to appeal to You,	*amarta-nā bi-duʿāʾi-ka*
and You have promised us	*wa waʿadta-nā*
Your response.	*ijābati-ka*
Now we have appealed	*fa-qad daʿawnā*
as You commanded us,	*ka-mā amarta-nā*
so respond to us as You promised us!	*fa-'stajib la-nā ka-mā waʿadta-nā.*

It has also been maintained that he should turn his face toward the *Qibla* while delivering the sermon, and that he should be facing the *Qibla* when he brings it to its conclusion, at which point he should follow it immediately with the prayer of supplication *[duʿāʾ]*. The most appropriate procedure, however, is the one we have already mentioned,

351 This is the very plea invited by (Almighty and Glorious is He), in the words of the Qurʾānic recitation included in the sermon *[khuṭba]* referred to above, namely:

And I have said: "Seek forgiveness from	*fa-qultu 'staghfirū Rabba-kum:*
your Lord; He is ever All-Forgiving,	*inna-hu kāna Ghaffārā*
and He will let loose the sky for you	*yursilu 's-samāʾa*
in plenteous rain." (71:10,11)	*ʿalai-kum midrārā.*

namely, that he should finish delivering the sermon, and only then turn his face toward the *Qibla*. This is because the purpose of the sermon is to exhort, to admonish and to intimidate, and this can only be achieved if the preacher faces the people and addresses them directly, so that he can reach both their ears and their hearts. If he stands facing the *Qibla*, he will be turning his back on them again, as he had to do when he stood out in front and led them in the ritual prayer *[ṣallā bi-him]*.

4.
The ritual prayer at the eclipse of the sun *[ṣalāt al-kusūf]* and at the eclipse of the moon *[ṣalāt al-khusūf]*.

As for the ritual prayer at the eclipse of the sun *[ṣalāt al-kusūf]*, it is a firmly established custom *[sunna mu'akkada]*.

The time for its performance lasts from the moment of the eclipse *[kusūf]* until the point of clarity, when the light is fully restored to the sun or the moon. That is to say, the period begins when the sun is eclipsed *[kasafat as-shams]*, or when the moon is eclipsed *[khasafa 'l-qamar]*.

In other words, the time of the ritual prayer *[ṣalāt]* extends from the first appearance of blackness, opaqueness and diminished radiance, until the disappearance thereof, at which point the time of the ritual prayer *[ṣalāt]* expires.

According to customary practice *[sunna]*, this prayer should be performed in the congregational mosque *[jāmi']*, the site of the Friday prayer *[ṣalāt al-jum'a]*.

The summons to it is the cry:

The ritual prayer is being convened!	*aṣ-ṣalātu jāmi'a.*[352]

The prayer leader *[imām]* must lead the congregation in the performance of two cycles of ritual prayer *[rak'atain]*. In the first cycle, he should proceed as follows:

1. Pronounce the consecratory affirmation of Allāh's Supreme Greatness.[353]
2. Pronounce the introductory invocation.[354]
3. Pronounce the the plea for refuge with Allāh.[355]

[352] As in the case of the prayer of the Two Festivals *[ṣalāt al-'Īdain]*, this brief announcement takes the place of the usual call to prayer *[adhān]*. (See p. 246 above.)

[353] See note 236 on p. 174 above.

[354] See note 338 on p. 246 above.

[355] The plea for refuge with Allāh *[ta'awwudh]* is made by uttering the words:

I take refuge with Allāh	*a'ūdhu bi-'llāhi*
from Satan the accursed.	*mina 'sh-shaiṭāni 'r-rajīm.*

4. Recite the Opening Sūra of the Qur'ān *[al-Fātiḥa]*.

5. Recite the Sūra of the Cow *[Sūrat al-Baqara]*.[356]

6. Perform the act of bowing, and maintain the posture of bowing *[rukū']* for a considerable period of time, while repeating the glorification of Allāh *[tasbīḥ]* for as long as it would take to recite one hundred verses *[āyāt]* of the Qur'ān.

7. Raise his head, saying as he does so:

May Allāh hear and accept	*sami'a 'llāhu*
the praise of one who praises Him!	*li-man ḥamidah.*

8. Recite the Opening Sūra *[al-Fātiḥa]* and the Sūra of the Family of 'Imrān *[Āl 'Imrān]*.[357]

9. Perform a second act of bowing *[rukū']*, distinct from the first.

10. Raise his head, in the same way as before.

11. Perform two prolonged acts of prostration *[sajdatain]*, repeating the glorification of Allāh *[tasbīḥ]*, in each of the two, for as long as it would take to recite one hundred verses *[āyāt]* of the Qur'ān.

12. Stand erect, in readiness to perform the second cycle.

In the second cycle, he should recite the Opening Sūra *[al-Fātiḥa]*, followed by the Sūra of Women *[an-Nisā']*.[358] Then he should perform the act of bowing, and maintain the posture of bowing *[rukū']* for a considerable period of time. He should then straighten up, and recite the Opening Sūra *[al-Fātiḥa]* and the Sūra of the Table *[al-Mā'ida]*.[359]

If he is not proficient in the recitation of these long Sūras, he may recite other Sūras of the Qur'ān instead, so long as the verses *[āyāt]* add up to the same total number. If he only knows the Sūra that begins with "*Qul Huwa'llāhu Aḥad* [Say: 'He is Allāh, One!']," [360] he should therefore recite it in precisely that manner.

[356] The Sūra of the Cow *[Sūrat al-Baqara]* is the second Sūra of the Qur'ān. It consists of 286 verses *[āyāt]*.

[357] The Sūra of the Family of 'Imrān *[Sūrat Āl 'Imrān]* is the third Sūra of the Qur'ān. It consists of 200 verses *[āyāt]*.

[358] The Sūra of Women *[Sūrat an-Nisā']* is the fourth Sūra of the Qur'ān. It consists of 177 verses *[āyāt]*.

[359] The Sūra of the Table *[Sūrat al-Mā'ida]* is the fifth Sūra of the Qur'ān. It consists of 120 verses *[āyāt]*.

[360] Sūra 112.

In the second upright posture, the length of his Qur'ānic recitation should be two thirds of his recitation in the first upright posture. In the third upright posture, the one he assumes on rising from the posture of prostration *[sujūd]*, the length of his recitation should be half of his recitation in the first upright posture. In the final upright posture, i.e., the fourth, it should be two thirds the length of the recitation in the third upright posture, i.e., the one before it.

As for the glorification of Allāh *[tasbīḥ]*, it should be the equivalent of two thirds of his recitation, in each upright posture. Once he has completed it, he should immediately adopt the bowing posture *[rukūʿ]*; there is no disagreement on this point.

Then [after the two final prostrations] he should conclude the prayer by pronouncing the salutation. Thus [in the complete prayer] there are four acts of bowing *[rakaʿāt]* and four acts of prostration *[sajadāt]*, since the bowing posture *[rukūʿ]* is adopted twice in each cycle *[rakʿa]*.[361]

If the eclipse departs while the people are still engaged in the ritual prayer *[ṣalāt]*, the recommended practice is to complete a simplified version its performance, rather than discontinue it abruptly.

If a person wishes to perform this prayer at home, either by himself or with his family, it is permissible for him to do so. The preferable course, however, is the one we have described.

Our basic authority concerning the ritual prayer at the eclipse of the sun *[ṣalāt al-kusūf]*, as we have explained its performance, is the traditional account provided by ʿĀʾisha (may Allāh be well pleased with her), who is reported as having said:

"An eclipse of the sun occurred in the time of Allāh's Messenger (Allāh bless him and give him peace), so the Prophet (Allāh bless him and give him peace) came to the place of prayer *[muṣallā]*. He proclaimed the Supreme Greatness of Allāh *[kabbara]*, and the people did likewise. Then he recited from the Qurʾān, pronouncing his recitation in an audible voice. He remained standing erect for a considerable length of time, then he bowed down *[rakaʿa]* and maintained the bowing posture *[rukūʿ]* for a long time. Then he raised his head, and declared:

May Allāh hear and accept the praise of one who praises Him!	*samiʿa 'llāhu* *li-man ḥamidah.*

[361] The term *rakʿa* [an act of bowing] has acquired an extended meaning, since it is generally used to denote the whole series of movements and postures—including the bowing posture *[rukūʿ]*—that constitute one cycle of the ritual prayer *[ṣalāt]*. (The dual and plural forms, corresponding to the singular form *rakʿa*, are *rakʿatān/-ain* and *rakaʿāt*, respectively.)

"Then he recited again from the Qur᾽ān, and continued his recitation for a long time. Then he bowed down *[raka῾a]* and maintained the bowing posture *[rukū῾]* for a long time. Then he raised his head. Then he prostrated himself *[sajada]*. Then he stood up straight, and went on to perform the second [cycle of prayer] in similar fashion. Then he said (Allāh bless him and give him peace):

> "'The sun and the moon are two of the signs of Allāh's *[āyatān min āyāti'llāh]*. They do not become eclipsed on account of someone's death, nor on account of someone's birth. So, if you see that [eclipse] occurring, take refuge at once in the ritual prayer *[ṣalāt]*.'"

5.
Concerning the ritual prayer in time of danger *[ṣalāt al-khawf]*.

As for the ritual prayer in time of danger *[ṣalāt al-khawf]*, its performance is permissible, provided that four preconditions are fulfilled, namely:

1. The enemy [who poses the danger] must be one against whom it is permissible to wage war.
2. The enemy must not be positioned directly in front of the *Qibla*[472] [direction of the Kaʿba in Mecca].
3. There must be no security from attack by the enemy.
4. The numerical strength of the people [threatened by the enemy] must be sufficient to enable them to split into two contingents, with a mininum of three members to each contingent, so that one of the two contingents can be stationed in the face of the enemy, while the other lines up behind the prayer leader *[imām]*.

The prayer leader *[imām]* should lead one contingent in one cycle of ritual prayer *[rakʿa]*. Then, when he stands up [after the prostration], in readiness to perform the second cycle, that contingent should move away from him, and perform the second cycle by themselves. They must formulate the intention to move away, because it is never permissible for the follower *[maʾmūm]* to move away from his prayer leader *[imām]* without a specifically formulated intention *[niyya]*. Then, having pronounced the salutation [at the conclusion of the second cycle of prayer], they must station themselves in the direction of the enemy.

The second contingent should then line up behind the prayer leader *[imām]*, pronounce the consecratory affirmation of Allāh's Supreme Greatness, and perform the [second] cycle of ritual prayer *[rakʿa]* together with him. Then, while the prayer leader *[imām]* remains in the sitting posture [at the end of the second cycle], the second contingent must stand up and perform the first cycle [which they have missed].

Once they have adopted the sitting posture [after the two prostrations], and have pronounced the testimony *[tashahhud]*, the prayer leader *[imām]* will lead them in the final salutation *[yusallimu bi-him]*.

The prayer leader *[imām]* should prolong his Qur'ānic recitation in the second cycle, thereby allowing sufficient time for the first contingent to complete the second cycle [by themselves], before changing places with their comrades. The second contingent can then come and consecrate themselves to prayer in his company. He should also prolong the testimony *[tashahhud]* for the benefit of the second contingent, thereby giving them time to complete the cycle they have missed, until they catch up with him in the testimony, at which point he should lead them in the final salutation.

The second contingent will thus obtain the merit of pronouncing the salutation *[salām]* together with the prayer leader *[imām]*, while the first contingent will obtain the merit of pronouncing the initial consecration *[taḥrīm]* together with the prayer leader *[imām]*.

This was how Allāh's Messenger (Allāh bless him and give him peace) led the Muslims in the performance of this ritual prayer *[ṣallā-hā bi'l-Muslimīn]* during the military campaign *[ghazwa]* of Dhāt ar-Riqā'.[362]

According to the traditional report *[ḥadīth]* of Sahl ibn Abī Khuzaima (may Allāh be well pleased with him), the Prophet (Allāh bless him and give him peace) explained:

> The prayer leader *[imām]* should stand with one row behind him, and one row in front of the enemy. He should lead those behind him in one act of bowing *[rak'a]* and two acts of prostration *[sajdatain]*, then stand up and maintain an upright posture, until they have performed a cycle of prayer *[rak'a]* by themselves. Then they should change places with the contingent at the front, and he should then lead the second contingent in turn in one act of bowing *[rak'a]* and two acts of prostration *[sajdatain]*. Then he should remain in the sitting posture, until they have completed another cycle *[rak'a]* to make up for the one they missed. Then he should lead them in pronouncing the final salutation.

According to a statement attributed to our Imām [Aḥmad ibn Ḥanbal] (may Allāh bestow His mercy upon him), there is evidence to support the permissibility of postponing the ritual prayer *[ṣalāt]*, in wartime situations of close combat and hot pursuit, until such conditions no longer prevail, and war has laid down its burdens.

In our treatment of it up to this point, we have described the ritual prayer in time of danger *[ṣalāt al-khawf]* as a two-cycle prayer, corresponding

[362] In the campaign of Dhāt ar-Riqā', the Muslim troops were four hundred strong.

to the prayer of daybreak *[ṣalāt al-fajr]* and to the four-cycle prayers[363] that are shortened to two cycles during a journey.[364]

As for the [three-cycle] sunset prayer *[ṣalāt al-maghrib]*, its performance in time of danger should be conducted as follows: The prayer leader *[imām]* should lead the first contingent in two cycles *[rakʿatain]*, and the second contingent in one cycle *[rakʿa]*. There must be no subtraction from it, because it is not a prayer that can be curtailed.

When should the first contingent move away from the prayer leader *[imām]*? Should they do so when he adopts the sitting posture to pronounce the first testimony *[tashahhud]*, or when he stands up in readiness to perform the third cycle? There are two conflicting opinions with regard to this question.

If danger threatens troops in their home base [where four-cycle prayers may not be curtailed], the prayer leader *[imām]* should lead each contingent in the performance of two cycles [of a four-cycle prayer],[476] and they should then complete the other two cycles by themselves. If he divides them into four sections, his own prayer *[ṣalāt]* will not be valid, nor will the prayer *[ṣalāt]* of the third and fourth sections. As for whether the prayer *[ṣalāt]* of the first and second sections will also be rendered null and void, there are two conflicting opinions on the subject.

In the account we have given thus far, we have assumed that the enemy's position is either to the rear of the *Qibla*, or to the right and left of it. If the enemy is stationed directly in front of the *Qibla*, so that the opposing forces can see each other, and there is no reason to suspect a lurking ambush, it is still permissible for the prayer leader *[imām]* to conduct the ritual prayer of danger *[ṣalāt al-khawf]*. In this case, however, he should arrange the troops in two or three rows, depending on how many or how few they happen to be, and then lead them all together in the consecratory affirmation. Then he should lead them all together in the performance of the first cycle *[rakʿa]*. When he reaches the act of prostration *[sujūd]*, they should all prostrate themselves, with the exception of those in the first row, the row immediately behind him.

They must remain standing to keep watch over the others, until the latter stand up in readiness to perform the second cycle, at which point they should also prostrate themselves, and then rejoin the rest in the

[363] Under normal conditions, the noon prayer *[ṣalāt aẓ-ẓuhr]*, the afternoon prayer *[ṣalāt al-ʿaṣr]* and the late evening prayer *[ṣalāt al-ʿishāʾ]* are all prayers of four cycles *[rakaʿāt]*.

[364] See pp. 264–67 below.

upright posture. When the prayer leader *[imām]* prostrates himself in the second cycle, the row to remain standing should be the first of the rows that performed the prostration with him in the first cycle. This row must now keep watch over the others, until the prayer leader *[imām]* adopts the sitting posture to pronounce the testimony *[tashahhud]*, at which point they must join him in the testimony. They should follow him, therefore, so that he can lead all of them together in the final salutation.

According to traditional report, this is how the Prophet (Allāh bless him and give him peace) conducted the prayer, when danger threatened at ʿUsfān [a place near Mecca].

As a permissible alternative, in the second cycle, the first row can move to the rear, while the second row moves forward and takes its place, in order to stand guard in front.

If the danger is extremely intense, and the combat is being waged at very close quarters, the troops may pray in congregation, or as separate individuals, in whatever manner they find possible under the circumstances: walking or riding, facing the *Qibla* or with their backs to it, by making gestures or without making gestures. As to whether or not they are required to face the *Qibla* at the very beginning of the prayer *[ṣalāt]*, there are two conflicting traditional reports.

Then, if safety is assured, and the enemy is routed, they should bring their prayer *[ṣalāt]* to completion. They should dismount from their riding beasts, turning to face the *Qibla* as they do so.

If they embark on the ritual prayer *[ṣalāt]* with a sense of security, but then grave danger suddenly threatens, they should mount up and complete the prayer of danger *[ṣalāt al-khawf]*, even if they need to strike and thrust, as they charge to and fro in battle.

This form of the ritual prayer *[ṣalāt]* is permissible for anyone who is in danger of being attacked by any kind of enemy, including savage beasts, torrential floods, highway robbers, and other such menacing threats. According to one of two conflicting reports, it is likewise permissible if he is in pursuit of the enemy, and in danger of letting him escape, just when his defeat is imminent.

6.
Concerning the shortened version of the ritual prayer *[qaṣr aṣ-ṣalāt]*.

As for the shortened version of the ritual prayer *[qaṣr aṣ-ṣalāt]*, it is permissible for the long-distance traveler to perform it, once he has passed beyond the houses of his own town or village, or beyond the tents of his nomadic tribe.

In the case of a four-cycle prayer *[rubāʿiyya]*,[365] the traveler may shorten it to two cycles *[rakʿatain]*, provided that his journey is a long one. In this context, a long journey means one that covers a distance of sixteen leagues, i.e., four courier-stages, or forty-eight miles according to the Hāshimī measure, one courier-stage *[barīd]* being equal to four leagues *[farāsikh*, pl. of *farsakh]*.

The traveler may shorten his prayer while he is on the road, whether he is outward bound or making the homeward journey.

If he enters a town or village along the way, and intends to perform twenty-two prescribed prayers during his stay there, he must perform them in full, since his status will then be the same as that of a local resident. If he intends to perform twenty-one prescribed prayers, there are two conflicting accounts of the doctrine regarding his status. If the number is less than that, he may unquestionably shorten his prayers.

If he breaks his journey in a town, without knowing when he is going to move on—if he has no specific intention, but says: "I may leave today, or I may leave tomorrow"—he may shorten his prayers. This is based on a traditional report, according to which the Prophet (Allāh bless him and give him peace) once stopped in Mecca for eighteen days—some say fifteen days—and he shortened his prayers throughout his stay.

[365] Under normal conditions, the noon prayer *[ṣalāt aẓ-ẓuhr]*, the afternoon prayer *[ṣalāt al-ʿaṣr]* and the late evening prayer *[ṣalāt al-ʿishāʾ]* are all prayers of four cycles *[rakaʿāt]*. There is no shortened version of the dawn/daybreak prayer *[ṣalāt aṣ-ṣubḥ/al-fajr]*, which always consists of two cycles, nor of the sunset prayer *[ṣalāt al-maghrib]*, which invariably consists of three cycles.

To quote the traditional report *[ḥadīth]* of ʿImrān ibn al-Ḥuṣain (may Allāh be well pleased with him and with his father):

"During the conquest *[fatḥ]* of Mecca, at which I was present in the company of Allāh's Messenger (Allāh bless him and give him peace), the ritual prayers he performed were all of two cycles *[rakʿatain]* only. But then he said to the inhabitants of the city: 'Unlike us, you must perform four cycles of ritual prayer, for we are people on a journey *[qawm safar]*.'"

On another occasion, when the Prophet (Allāh bless him and give him peace) spent twenty days at Tabūk, he likewise shortened his ritual prayers, as did his Companions *[Ṣaḥāba]* (may Allāh be well pleased with them all).

It was Anas ibn Mālik (may Allāh be well pleased with him) who said:

"The Companions of Allāh's Messenger (Allāh bless him and give him peace) spent seven months in Rāmhurmuz, and they shortened the ritual prayer *[ṣalāt]* throughout that period."

According to another traditional report, Ibn ʿUmar (may Allāh be well pleased with him and with his father) once stayed for six months in Azerbaijān, and the ritual prayers he performed there were all of two cycles *[rakʿatain]* only.

It may sometimes happen that a person is a local resident, at the moment when he enters the consecrated state of ritual prayer *[aḥrama bi-'ṣ-ṣalāt]*, but then he becomes a traveler. Take the case of a passenger aboard a ship. When he starts to perform his ritual prayer, the ship is still moored within the limits of his own town, in a dock inside the walls of its port. But then the ship's captain sets sail, and the vessel leaves the confines of the town. In a case like this, the worshipper is obliged to perform the ritual prayer in full.

A similar rule would apply, if a person entered the state of consecration *[aḥrama]* while still traveling, but then arrived in a town. If he was himself a resident of that town, or if he was following the lead *[iʾtamma]* of a local resident—or of someone who might be either a resident or a traveler, for all he knew—and he had not begun the prayer with the express intention of shortening it, he would be obliged to perform the prayer in full, in any such case.

When someone is performing the ritual prayer to make up for having missed it at the prescribed time *[qāḍiyan li'ṣ-ṣalāt]*, it is not permissible for him to shorten it, because it rests on his conscience in the complete form. The fact that he is on a journey is irrelevant, except from the purely practical standpoint.

If someone enters the state of consecration *[aḥrama]* with the intention *[niyya]* of shortening the ritual prayer, but then decides to regard himself as a resident, he must perform the prayer in full. By the same token, if he enters the state of consecration *[aḥrama]* as a local resident, but then decides to set out on a journey, he must perform the prayer in full.

Furthermore, if a person's journey constitutes a sinful act of disobedience, or a trip undertaken for idle sport and entertainment, he is not entitled to take advantage of the traveler's dispensation. No one can legitimately avail himself of that dispensation, unless his journey is undertaken for some obligatory purpose, such as the Pilgrimage *[Ḥajj]* or the Sacred Struggle *[Jihād]*, or for one that is permissible, such as trade, or the settlement of a debt, and any comparable endeavor.

If we allow the sinner to enjoy it on his travels, we shall actually be helping him to disobey his Lord, encouraging him to persist in his sinful disobedience, and giving him no incentive to reform himself through worshipful obedience to Him. Far from offering him positive support and assistance in the right direction, we shall be holding him back and discouraging him from taking a better course.

According to the doctrine of our Imām Aḥmad [ibn Ḥanbal] (may Allāh bestow His mercy upon him), it is more meritorious to shorten the ritual prayer than to perform it in full. The traveler may choose to perform either the complete or the shortened version of the prayer, just has he may choose to keep the fast or to break it. In all such cases, however, it is better to refrain from trying to impress Allāh (Almighty and Glorious is He) with a show of hardy endurance, and to accept His dispensation and His kindness instead.

If, in choosing to perform the complete version of the ritual prayer *[ṣalāt]* and keep the fast *[ṣiyām]*, the traveler had no motive other than personal pride, vanity, conceit and self-aggrandizement—and if, in choosing to shorten the prayer and break the fast, he had no motive other than to make the lower self *[nafs]* humble, contrite, and submissively resigned to forsaking complete worship and strict observance—it could certainly be said, with total credibility: "It is better to shorten the prayer and break the fast."

Indeed, how could it be otherwise, in view of the Prophet's response (Allāh bless him and give him peace), when someone remarked to him concerning the shortened version of the ritual prayer *[qaṣr aṣ-ṣalāt]*: "Why should we continue to perform the shortened version, now that we are safe from danger [on this journey]?" To this he replied (Allāh bless him and give him peace):

> That is a charitable gift *[ṣadaqa]*. Allāh has graciously bestowed it on His servants, so accept His charitable gift!

The Prophet (Allāh bless him and give him peace) also said:

> Allāh loves to have His dispensations accepted, just as He loves to have His strict injunctions accepted.

What astounding arrogance, therefore, on the part of someone who performs the complete prayer on a journey, and keeps the fast, thereby refusing to accept the dispensation, even though he is guilty of such major sins *[kabā'ir]* as eating unlawful food, drinking intoxicating liquor, wearing silk, committing adultery *[zinā]*[366] and sodomy *[liwāṭa]*,[367] holding false beliefs concerning fundamental principles *[uṣūl]*, and other atrocious offenses.

[366] In the vocabulary of Islāmic jurisprudence *[fiqh]*, the Arabic word *zinā* covers both adultery and fornication. For a precise technical definition, see J. Schacht, *An Introduction to Islamic Law* (Oxford University Press, 1979), p. 178.

[367] The noun *liwāṭa* is derived from the triliteral root *l-w-ṭ*, which indicates that it refers to the homosexual vices of the people of Lot *[Lūṭ]*, whose name is spelled *l-w-ṭ* in the Arabic script.

7.
Concerning the combination of two ritual prayers *[al-jam' baina 'ṣ-ṣalātain]*.

As for the combination of two ritual prayers *[al-jam' baina 'ṣ-ṣalātain]*, it is permissible for the traveler to combine the prayers of noon *[ẓuhr]* and afternoon *['aṣr]*, and those of sunset *[maghrib]* and late evening *['ishā']*, with the proviso that the journey must be a long one. In this context, a long journey is one that covers a distance of sixteen leagues *[farsakh]*, as we have already explained.[368] This practice is not permissible on a short journey, i.e., one that covers less than the distance mentioned.

The traveler is free to choose either of two options, namely:

1. He may postpone the first [of the two prayers concerned] until the earliest time prescribed for the second.

2. He may bring the second prayer forward to the time prescribed for the first.

The recommended choice is postponement, meaning that he should delay his performance of the first prayer, and perform the second early [in its prescribed period]. In other words, he should perform them both at the beginning of the period of time prescribed for the second.

If he chooses to perform both prayers in the period of time prescribed for the first, he must begin with the first, and then perform the second immediately after it.

He must formulate the intention to combine [the two prayers] at the point of consecration *[iḥrām]* for the first. He should not leave any interval between the two, except to allow for the *iqāma*,[369] and for the ritual ablution *[wuḍū']*, if his ablution needs to be renewed.

[368] In connection with the shortened version of the ritual prayer *[qaṣr aṣ-ṣalāt]*, on p. 264 above.

[369] The *iqāma*, the announcement that the ritual prayer is about to begin, is an abbreviated version of the *adhān* [call to prayer], with the addition of the words (repeated twice): *qad qāmati' ṣ-ṣalāh* [The prayer is about to begin!]

If he performs a customary ritual *[sunnat aṣ-ṣalāt]* between the two [obligatory prayers], the combination *[jam']* is rendered null and void, according to one of the two accounts of the relevant doctrine. According to the other, it is not rendered null and void. In any event, the best course is for him to postpone the customary practice *[sunna]*, until after he has duly completed the obligatory observance *[farḍ]*, and to refrain from anything else that would separate the combined prayers.

If he performs the combination during the time prescribed for the second prayer, having formulated his intention *[niyya]* during the time prescribed for the first, that intention will be sufficient. He does not need to renew the intention, at the time when he actually performs the two prayers, because his only reason for postponing the first was to combine it with the second. It makes no difference, whether he formulates the relevant intention at the beginning of the time prescribed for the first prayer, or whether he does so with only a fraction of that time remaining. But if the time prescribed for the first prayer expires completely, before the intention to combine *[niyyat al-jam']* has been formulated, it is not permissible to perform the two prayers in combination.

If he chooses to perform the combination during the time prescribed for the second prayer, he must begin with the first, and then perform the second immediately after it, as if he were performing them in the time prescribed for the first.

Is it strictly stipulated that he must not separate the two [obligatory] prayers, by interposing a customary practice *[sunna]*, or any other [supererogatory observance]? There are two conflicting opinions regarding this matter.

Among our fellow [Ḥanbalī] scholars, there is one who maintains that combining *[jam']* and shortening *[qaṣr]* do not require a specific intention *[niyya]*. The scholar in question is Abū Bakr[370] (may Allāh bestow His mercy upon him).

As for the combining of prayers *[jam']* on account of rain, this is permissible when the prayers concerned are those of sunset *[maghrib]*

[370] Abū Bakr al-Khallāl (may Allāh bestow His mercy upon him) was responsible for compiling and systematizing the legal teachings of Imām Aḥmad ibn Ḥanbal (may Allāh bestow His mercy upon him). He died in A.H. 311/923-4 C.E.

and late evening *[ʿishāʾ]*. Is it also permissible to combine the prayers of noon *[ẓuhr]* and afternoon *[ʿaṣr]*? On this point there are two conflicting opinions.

What if people are sheltering indoors, on account of bad weather? Is that sufficient reason to permit the combining of prayers *[jamʿ]*, even if no rain is actually falling, and no bitterly cold wind is actually blowing? Here again, there are two conflicting opinions. We must therefore examine the particular situation in detail, if someone does in fact combine two prayers under such conditions. If he does so during the time prescribed for the first prayer, because rain is then falling, he is justified in assuming that rain will be present at the beginning of the first prayer, at the conclusion thereof, and at the beginning of the second. If he performs the combination during the time prescribed for the second prayer, it will likewise be permissible, regardless of whether the rain is still falling, or whether it has stopped by then, because he had a valid excuse for postponing the first prayer. The fact that the excuse has disappeared is irrelevant, because the first period has now elapsed and expired, so there is no possibility of restoring and recapturing it.

If we advise such a person that the combining of prayers *[jamʿ]* is permissible, we do so in recognition of the hardship that people suffer in wet weather. Since their clothes, their shoes and their pouches get soaked and damp, it is extremely inconvenient for them to move in and out of doors [between their homes and the mosques]. The Prophet himself (Allāh bless him and give him peace) has told us:

> When the hard and rugged tracts of ground are wet and slippery, the ritual prayer should be performed in the shelter of people's homes *[idha 'btallati 'n-niʿāl—fa-'ṣ-ṣalātu fi 'r-riḥāl]*.[371]

This saying is reported in the *Ṣaḥīḥain* [the two most famous collections of authentic traditions].

According to our [Ḥanbalī] doctrine, the status of the sick person is the same as that of the traveler, as far as the combining of ritual prayers *[jamʿ]* is concerned, because Allāh (Exalted is He) has linked them

[371] In the context of this saying of the Prophet (Allāh bless him and give him peace), the word *niʿāl*—which usually means 'shoes; sandals'—is interpreted by traditional authorities as synonymous with *ḥirār* [hard and rugged tracts of ground]. (See: E.W. Lane, *Arabic-English Lexicon*, art. *R–Ḥ–L*.)

together. He has mentioned them both in a single sentence, for He has said (Almighty and Glorious is He):

And whoever of you is sick,	*fa-man kāna min-kum marīḍan*
or on a journey, [let him fast the same]	*aw ʿalā safarin*
number of other days. (2:184)	*fa-ʿiddatun min ayyāmin ukhar.*

The reason for the alleviation is the incidence of disability and hardship, and this is more unequivocally and obviously applicable to the person who is sick, because the traveler may be a comfortable and pampered passenger, pleasantly relaxed, perfectly fit and sprightly. While he is on a journey, the traveler may enjoy even greater ease and luxury than at home, through the influence of his wealth, authority and power, yet he is nonetheless entitled to avail himself of the relevant dispensations *[rukhaṣ]*. The sick person is at the opposite extreme, so he is even more entitled to the dispensations than is the traveler.

8.
The ritual prayer at the funeral service *[aṣ-ṣalāt ʿala 'l-jināza]*.

As for the ritual prayer at the funeral service *[aṣ-ṣalāt ʿala 'l-jināza]*,[372] it is a collective duty *[farḍ ʿala 'l-kifāya]*.[373] According to our [Ḥanbalī] doctrine, the person best qualified to lead this prayer is the executor *[waṣī]* of the deceased, followed by the head of state *[sulṭān]*, then by the male relatives of the deceased, in order of closeness.

The prayer leader *[imām]* should stand opposite the chest of a male corpse, and opposite the waist of a female.

If there are several corpses, they should be arranged so that their heads are in line with one another.[374] If they are of various classes, they should be arranged in order of priority, with the most distinguished lying closest to the prayer leader *[imām]*. Suppose, for instance, that the corpses are those of men, women, slaves, hermaphrodites *[khanāthā]*, and boys. The men should take precedence, then the slaves, then the boys, then the hermaphrodites, and then the women.[375] Each class should then be inspected in detail, and rearranged if necessary, so that, within each class, those lying closest to the prayer leader *[imām]* are the most distinguished in terms of learning *[ʿilm]*, knowledge of the Qurʾān, religious devotion *[dīn]* and piety *[waraʿ]*.

When the prayer leader *[imām]* stands in his place at the head of the congregation, he must turn and look to right and left, making sure that the rows are straight, as he does in all other ritual prayers *[ṣalawāt]*. He must beg forgiveness of Allāh (Exalted is He), repent his sins, and remember his own mortality, as well as the abode of the Hereafter. He

[372] The form *janāza* is also used, as an acceptable alternative to *jināza*.

[373] See note 324 on p. 243 above.

[374] ***Author's note:*** If a male corpse and a female corpse are lying next to each other, some authorities maintain that the waist of the woman should be placed opposite the chest of the man.

[375] ***Author's note:*** According to one account of his doctrine, he [Imām Aḥmad ibn Ḥanbal] maintained that boys should take precedence over slaves.

must be thoroughly convinced that death is a cup from which he is bound to drink, and that it will inevitably be passed to him. He must therefore ensure that his inner feeling is fully conscious, and that his limbs and organs are in a state of humble submissiveness, so that he can respond to his summons with alacrity. Only then should he perform the ritual prayer for the deceased *[yuṣallī ʿala 'l-mayyit]*, in the manner now to be described:

He will begin by saying:

I am performing the ritual prayer	*uṣallī*
for this person deceased,	*ʿalā hādha 'l-mayyiti*
in fulfillment of a collective duty.	*farḍan ʿala 'l-kifāya.*

(There is no need for him to specify whether the person concerned is male or female.)

He will then pronounce four affirmations of the Supreme Greatness of Allāh *[yukabbiru arbaʿa takbīrāt]*.[376] Immediately after pronouncing the first of these, he should recite the Opening Sūra *[al-Fātiḥa]*, because Ibn ʿAbbās (may Allāh be well pleased with him and with his father) is reported as having said:

"Allāh's Messenger (Allāh bless him and give him peace) instructed us to recite the Opening Sūra of the Book *[Fātiḥat al-Kitāb]* at the funeral service *[ʿala 'l-jināza]*."

After the second affirmation of Allāh's Supreme Greatness *[takbīra]*, he should invoke His blessings on the Prophet (Allāh bless him and give him peace), just as he invokes them in the testimony *[tashahhud]*,[377] because Mujāhid (may Allāh bestow His mercy upon him) is reported as having said:

"I asked eighteen men, from among the Companions of Allāh's Messenger (Allāh bless him and give him peace), about how to conduct the ritual prayer at the funeral service *[aṣ-ṣalāt ʿala 'l-jināza]*, and all of them told me:

"'Pronounce the affirmation of Allāh's Supreme Greatness *[kabbir]*. Then recite the Opening Sūra of the Book *[Fātiḥat al-Kitāb]*. Then pronounce the [second] affirmation of Allāh's Supreme Greatness

[376] The affirmation of Allāh's Supreme Greatness is expressed by declaring: "*Allāhu Akbar* [Allāh is Supremely Great!]" The general term for this affirmation is *takbīr*. A specific utterance thereof is called a *takbīra*, and the form *takbīrāt* is the plural of *takbīra*.

[377] See pp. 84 and 85 above.

[kabbir]. Then invoke Allāh's blessings on the Prophet (Allāh bless him and give him peace). Then pronounce the [third] affirmation of Allāh's Supreme Greatness *[kabbir]*.

"'Immediately after the third affirmation, you should offer prayers of supplication for the deceased, and also for yourself, for your parents, and for the Muslims in general. Various kinds of supplication *[duʿāʾ]* are permissible, so you may choose whichever you know best, and whichever you find easiest.'"

The recommended practice, however, is for the prayer leader *[imām]* to say:

O Allāh, forgive	*Allāhumma 'ghfir li-ḥayyi-nā*
our living and our dead,	*li-ḥayyi-nā wa mayyiti-nā*
and those of us who are present	*wa shāhidi-nā*
and those of us who are absent,	*wa ghāʾibi-nā*
and our young and our old,	*wa ṣaghīri-nā wa kabīri-nā*
and those of us who are male	*wa dhakari-nā*
and those of us who are female.	*wa unthā-nā.*
O Allāh,	*Allāhumma*
those of us whom You keep alive,	*man aḥyaita-hu*
let them live in accordance	*min-nā fa-aḥyi-hi*
with Islām and the Sunna,	*ʿala 'l-Islāmi wa 's-Sunna:*
and those of us whom	*wa man*
You cause to die,	*tawaffaita-hu*
let them die in	*min-nā fa-tawaffa-hu*
accordance with the same.	*ʿalai-himā.*
You surely know	*inna-ka taʿlamu*
our destination	*munqalaba-nā*
and our final resting place,	*wa mathwā-nā*
and You are Powerful over all things.	*wa Anta ʿalā kulli shaiʾin Qadīr.*
O Allāh, he is Your servant,	*Allāhumma inna-hu ʿabdu-ka*
and the son of Your servant.	*wa 'bnu ʿabdi-ka*
He has now lodged with You,	*nazala bi-ka*
and You are the Best to lodge with,	*wa Anta khairu manzūlin bi-hi*
and we know nothing but good	*wa lā naʿlamu illā khairā.*
[about him].	
O Allāh, if he has been beneficent,	*Allāhumma in kāna muḥsinan*
reward him for his beneficence,	*fa-jāzi-hi bi-iḥsāni-hi*
and if he has been maleficent,	*wa in kāna musīʾan*
grant him an amnesty.	*fa-tajāwaz ʿan-h.*
O Allāh, we have come to You	*Allāhumma innā jiʾnā-ka*
as intercessors on his behalf,	*shufaʿāʾa la-hu*
so accept our intercession	*fa-shaffiʿ-nā*

for his sake.	*fī-hi*
Protect him from the	*wa qi-hi min*
torture of the grave,	*fitnati 'l-qabri*
and from the torment of the Fire [of Hell].	*wa ʿadhābi 'n-nāri*
Pardon him,	*wa 'ʿfu ʿan-hu*
and honor his resting place.	*wa akrim mathwā-hu*
Grant him a home	*wa abdil-hu dāran*
that is better than his [earthly] home,	*khairan min dāri-hi*
and an environment that is better	*wa jiwāran*
than his [earthly] environment.	*khairan min jiwāri-hi*
And do the same for us	*wa 'fʿal dhālika bi-nā*
and for all the Muslims.	*wa bi-jamīʿi 'l-muslimīn.*
O Allāh, do not deprive us	*Allāhumma lā taḥrim-nā*
of his recompense,	*ajra-hu*
and do not desert us after him.	*wa lā tafut-nā baʿda-h.*

Immediately after the fourth affirmation of Allāh's Supreme Greatness *[takbīra]*, the prayer leader *[imām]* should say:

O Allāh, our Lord, give us	*Allāhumma Rabba-nā āti-nā*
in this world that which is good,	*fi 'd-dunyā ḥasanatan*
and in the Hereafter	*wa fi 'l-ākhirati*
that which is good,	*ḥasanatan*
and guard us against	*wa qi-nā*
the torment of the Fire [of Hell]. (2:201)[378]	*ʿadhāba 'n-nār.*

(Among our fellow [Ḥanbalī] scholars, however, there are some who maintain that the prayer leader *[imām]* should stand still for a little while [after the fourth affirmation], without saying anything at all [before the salutation].)

He should then pronounce a single salutation *[taslīma]*,[379] while turning his face to his right. If he pronounces two salutations [one to the right and then one to the left], this is also permissible. The twofold salutation is preferred by the school *[madhhab]* of Imām ash-Shāfiʿī (may Allāh bestow His mercy upon him), while the single salutation *[taslīma]* represents the preference of our Imām Aḥmad [ibn Ḥanbal] (may Allāh bestow His mercy upon him).

[378] The word *Allāhumma* [O Allāh] is not part of the Qur'ānic quotation.

[379] In other words, the prayer leader *[imām]* should say:

Peace be upon you, and the mercy of Allāh.	*as-salāmu ʿalaikum wa raḥmatu'llāh.*

According to traditional reports, at least six of the Companions *[Ṣaḥāba]* are known to have pronounced only one salutation *[taslīma]* at the funeral service, namely: ʿAlī ibn Abī Ṭālib, ʿAbdu'llāh ibn ʿAbbās, Ibn ʿUmar, Ibn Abī Awfā, Abū Huraira, and Wāthila ibn al-Asqaʿ (may Allāh be well pleased with them all).

There is also a traditional report concerning the Prophet himself (Allāh bless him and give him peace), in which it is stated: "He performed the ritual prayer at a funeral service *[ṣallā ʿalā jināza]*, so he pronounced the salutation to his right."

If the prayer leader *[imām]* wishes to offer a different supplication *[duʿāʾ]*, instead of the one suggested above, he may do so. He may also say:

Praise be to Allāh,	*al-ḥamdu li'llāhi*
who has caused some to die	*'lladhī amāta*
and some to live,	*wa aḥyā*
and praise be to Allāh,	*wa 'l-ḥamdu li'llāhi 'lladhī*
who restores the dead to life.	*yuḥyi 'l-mawtā*
To Him belongs the Majesty	*la-hu 'l-ʿaẓamatu*
and the Grandeur and the Kingdom	*wa 'l-kibriyāʾu wa 'l-mulku*
and the Power and the Glory,	*wa 'l-qudratu wa 'th-thanāʾu*
and He is Powerful over all things.	*wa Huwa ʿalā kulli shaiʾin Qadīr.*
O Allāh, bless Muḥammad,	*Allāhumma ṣalli ʿalā Muḥammadin*
and the family of Muḥammad,	*wa ʿalā āli Muḥammadin*
as You have bestowed Your blessings	*ka-mā ṣallaita wa raḥimta*
and Your mercy and Your grace	*wa bārakta*
upon Abraham	*ʿalā Ibrāhīma*
and the family of Abraham.	*wa ʿalā āli Ibrāhīma*
Surely You deserve	*inna-ka*
to be praised and extolled!	*Ḥamīdun Majīd.*
O Allāh, he is Your servant,	*Allāhumma inna-hu ʿabdu-ka*
and the son of Your servant,	*wa 'bnu ʿabdi-ka*
and the son of Your maidservant.	*wa 'bnu amati-ka*
You created him and nourished him.	*Anta khalaqta-hu wa razaqta-hu*
You caused him to die,	*wa Anta amatta-hu*
and You will restore him to life.	*wa Anta tuḥyī-hi*
You know his innermost secret.	*Anta taʿlamu bi-sirri-h.*
We have come to You	*jiʾnā-ka*
as intercessors on his behalf,	*shufaʿāʾa la-hu*
so accept our intercession for his sake.	*fa-shaffiʿ-nā fī-h.*
O Allāh, we invoke the bond	*Allāhumma innā nastajīru*
of Your compact to afford him refuge.	*bi-ḥabli juwāri-ka la-hu*
You are indeed Reliable	*inna-ka Dhū wafāʾin*
and Faithful to Your covenant.	*wa dhimma.*

O Allāh, protect him	*Allāhumma qi-hi*
from the torture of the grave,	*min fitnati 'l-qabri*
and from the torment of Hell.	*wa min ʿadhābi Jahannam.*
O Allāh, forgive him,	*Allāhumma 'ghfir la-hu*
and have mercy on him,	*wa 'rḥam-hu*
and excuse him, and pardon him.	*wa ʿāfi-hi wa 'ʿfu ʿan-hu*
Honor his resting place,	*wa akrim mathwā-hu*
and make its entrance wide.	*wa wassiʿ madkhla-hu*
Wash him with the water	*wa 'ghsil-hu*
of snow and ice,	*bi-māʾi 'th-thalji wa 'l-baradi*
and cleanse him of sinful mistakes,	*wa naqqi-hi mina 'l-khaṭāyā*
as white cloth is cleansed	*ka-mā yunaqqa 'th-thawbu 'l-abyaḍu*
of the stain of dirt.	*mina 'd-danas.*
Grant him a home to live in,	*wa anzil-hu dāran*
that is better than his [earthly] home,	*khairan min dāri-hi*
with a spouse who is better	*wa zawjan khairan*
than his [earthly] spouse,	*min zawji-hi*
and a family that is better	*wa ahlan khairan*
than his [earthly] family.	*min ahl-hi*
Cause him to enter the Garden	*wa adkhil-hu 'l-jannata*
and save him from the Fire.	*wa najji-hi mina 'n-nār.*
O Allāh, if he has been beneficent,	*Allāhumma in kāna muḥsinan*
add to his beneficence,	*fa-zid fī iḥsāni-hi*
and reward him for his beneficence;	*fa-jāzi-hi bi-iḥsāni-hi*
and if he has been maleficent,	*wa in kāna musīʾan*
grant him an amnesty.	*fa-tajāwaz ʿan-h.*
O Allāh,	*Allāhumma*
he has now lodged with You,	*inna-hu qad nazala bi-ka*
and You are the Best to lodge with.	*wa Anta khairu manzūlin bi-hi*
He is poor, in need of Your mercy,	*wa huwa faqīrun ilā raḥmati-ka*
whereas You are Rich,	*wa Anta Ghaniyyun*
in no need of his punishment.	*ʿan ʿadhābi-h.*
O Allāh, confirm his speech	*Allāhumma thabbit*
at his interrogation.	*ʿinda masʾalati-hi manṭiqa-hu*
and do not try him in his grave	*wa lā tabtali-hi fī qabri-hi*
with more than he	*bi-mā lā*
is capable of bearing.	*ṭāqata la-hu bi-h.*
O Allāh, do not deprive us	*Allāhumma lā taḥrim-nā*
of his recompense,	*ajra-hu*
and do not desert us after him.	*wa lā tafut-nā baʿda-h.*

If the deceased person is a woman, the prayer leader *[imām]* should say [at the appropriate point]:

O Allāh, she is Your maidservant,	*Allāhumma inna-hā amatu-ka*
and the daughter of Your servant	*wa 'bnatu ʿabdi-ka*
and Your maidservant.	*wa amati-ka.*

He should then complete the supplication *[du'ā']*, [using the feminine form of the pronoun, etc., wherever necessary].

The person best entitled to conduct the funeral service—according to the doctrine of our Imām Aḥmad [ibn Ḥanbal] (may Allāh bestow His mercy upon him)—is the person appointed to the task by the deceased, in his last will and testament. Second in line is the ruler or governor *[wālī]*. After that, the order of precedence is as follows:

1. The closest male relative in the direct line of ascent, viz., the father, the father's father, and so on, by however many generations.
2. The closest male relative in the direct line of descent, viz., the son, the son's son, and so on, by however many generations.
3. The closest male collateral, viz., the brother, the brother's son, the paternal uncle, the son of the paternal uncle.

Should the husband take precedence over the son? On this point there are two conflicting opinions.

The Companions *[Ṣaḥāba]* (may Allāh be well pleased with them all) usually bequeathed the task of conducting their funeral prayer *[aṣ-ṣalāt 'alai-him]* to a person named in their last will and testament. For instance, as we know from traditional reports:

Abū Bakr (may Allāh be well pleased with him) bequeathed the task of conducting his funeral prayer *[waṣṣā an yuṣaliyya 'alai-hi]* to 'Umar (may Allāh be well pleased with him).

'Umar (may Allāh be well pleased with him) bequeathed the task of conducting his funeral prayer to Ṣuhaib (may Allāh be well pleased with him), even though his own son, 'Abdu'llāh (may Allāh be well pleased with him), was alive and available.

Shuraiḥ bequeathed the task of conducting his funeral prayer to Zaid ibn al-Arqam.

Maisara bequeathed the task of conducting his funeral prayer to Shuraiḥ.

[The Prophet's wife] 'Ā'isha (may Allāh be well pleased with her) appointed Abū Huraira (may Allāh be well pleased with him) as her executor.

[The Prophet's wife] Umm Salama (may Allāh be well pleased with her) bequeathed the task of conducting her funeral prayer *[waṣṣat an yuṣaliyya 'alai-hā]* to Sa'īd ibn Jubair.

When the supplication *[du'ā']* is offered on behalf of an infant, the prayer leader *[imām]* should say:

O Allāh, he is Your servant,
and the son of Your servant,
and the son of Your maidservant.
You created him and nourished him.
You caused him to die,
and You will restore him to life.

Allāhumma inna-hu ʿabdu-ka
wa 'bnu ʿabdi-ka
wa 'bnu amati-ka
Anta khalaqta-hu wa razaqta-hu
wa Anta amatta-hu
wa Anta tuḥyī-h.

O Allāh, let him be for his parents
a predecessor and a treasure,
a precursor and a recompense.
Let him weigh heavy in their scales,
and enhance their rewards
on his account.

Allāhumma 'jʿal-hu li-wālidai-hi
salafan wa dhukhran
wa faraṭan wa ajran
wa thaqqil bi-hi mawāzīna-humā
wa ʿaẓẓim bi-hi
ujūra-humā.

Deprive neither us
nor the two of them
of his recompense,
and desert neither us
nor them, after him.

wa lā taḥrim-nā
wa iyyā-humā
ajra-hu
wa lā tafut-nā
wa iyyā-humā baʿda-h.

O Allāh, join him together with
the righteous believers of the past,
in the custody of Abraham.
Grant him a home
that is better than his [earthly] home,
and a family that is better
than his [earthly] family,
and save him from
the torment of Hell.

Allāhumma alḥiq-hu
bi-ṣāliḥi salafi 'l-muʾminīna
fī kafālati Ibrāhīma
wa abdil-hu dāran
khairan min dāri-hi
wa ahlan khairan
min ahl-hi
wa ʿāfi-hi min
ʿadhābi Jahannam.

O Allāh, forgive
our children who die before us,
and our ancestors,
and those who have
preceded us in faith.

Allāhumma 'ghfir
li-afrāṭi-nā
wa aslāfi-nā
wa man sabaqa-nā
bi-'l-īmān.

O Allāh,
those of us whom You keep alive,
let them live
in accordance with Islām,
and those of us
whom You cause to die,
let them die in faith.

Allāhumma
man aḥyaita-hu min-nā
fa-aḥyi-hi
ʿala 'l-Islām:
wa man
tawaffaita-hu min-nā
fa-tawaffa-hu ʿala 'l-īmān.

Forgive the believing men
and the believing women:
those of them who are still alive,
as well as those who are dead.

wa 'ghfir li'l-muʾminīna
wa 'l-muʾmināti 'l-aḥyāʾi
min-hum
wa 'l-amwāt.

In the case of a miscarried fetus *[siqṭ]*, the funeral prayer and ritual washing may also be required, but only if it has developed to the point where the shape of a human being is already apparent. If it is merely a piece of flesh, in which no embryonic form can be discerned, it should simply be buried, with neither ritual washing nor funeral prayer. When ritual washing is legally required *[yushra'u fī-hi 'l-ghusl]*, in a case of this sort, it does not matter whether the washing is performed by a man or by a woman, because it is traditionally reported that Ibrāhīm, the son of the Prophet (Allāh bless him and give him peace), died at the age of eighteen months, and the women washed his corpse.

Concerning the proper treatment of someone whose moment of death has arrived, and the procedures to be followed in the ritual washing *[ghusl]*, enshrouding *[takfīn]*, embalming *[taḥnīṭ]* and burial *[dafn]* of his corpse.

a.
Concerning the preparations a true believer *[mu'min]* should make, in order to be ready for his own inevitable death.

For every intelligent believer *[mu'min]*, convinced of the certainty of death, it is commendable to remember death frequently, and to prepare for it. He should maintain a state of readiness and vigilant anticipation, through the hourly renewal of repentance, through self-examination, through disengagement from wrongs and debts, and by writing a definitive testamentary disposition. He should not be heedless of this sure and certain fact, general and universal in its significance for all humanity, for there is no escape from its arrival, its onslaught and its advent, and it is a cup from which all are bound to drink.

When we say that it is commendable for him to practice this advice, we do so for the simple reason that the Prophet (Allāh bless him and give him peace) is reported as having said:

> Remember often the wrecker of delights *[hāzim al-ladhdhāt]*.[380]

—and, in another wording:

> Remember death often, for if you remember it in affluence, it will shake your confidence in wealth, and if you remember it in straitened circumstances, it will make your hardship easier to bear.

[380] As the German scholar Bauer has pointed out, "the wrecker of delights *[hāzim / hādim / hādhim al-ladhdhāt]*." became the standard epithet of Death in the stories of *A Thousand and One Nights [Alf laila wa laila]*.

The Prophet (Allāh bless him and give him peace) also said:

> Do you know which is the cleverest of all people, and which is the most prudent? The cleverest of them is the one who most frequently remembers death, and the most prudent of them is the one who prepares for it most frequently.

"O Messenger of Allāh," his listeners asked, "what symptom is indicative of that?" So he replied:

> Utter indifference to the abode of delusion *[dār al-ghurūr]*, and keen interest in the abode of eternity *[dār al-khulūd]*.

Luqmān[381] (peace be upon him) said to his son:

"O my dear son, do not put off repentance till tomorrow, for death may come and take you by surprise."

The Prophet (Allāh bless him and give him peace) also said:

> By what right does a man of property spend two whole nights, without having his will and testament written in his presence?

—and:

> Call yourselves to account before you are called to account, and weigh your own selves before they are weighed.

ʿAbdu'llāh ibn ʿUmar (may Allāh be well pleased with him and with his father) once said: "I heard Allāh's Messenger (Allāh bless him and give him peace) say:

> "'For the sake of your worldly interests, work as if you are going to live forever, and for your interest in the Hereafter, work as if you are going to die tomorrow.'"

The intelligent believer *[muʾmin]* must therefore strive to acquit himself, before death comes, of all his outstanding obligations, whether they be sins and wrongs committed, or debts incurred. If he fails to do so, he must recognize and acknowledge the fact that he will be taken in pledge for those obligations. He must realize that, before very long, he will be chastised and punished in his grave. All his energies will then be cut off, and his faculties and senses will be out of action. His relatives and his neighbors will dissociate themselves from him, and his enemies and friends—men, women and children alike—will conspire to gain control of his property.

[381] Luqmān is commonly known as Luqmān the Wise *[Luqmān al-Ḥakīm]*, because Allāh (Exalted is He) has told us in the Qurʾān:

> And We did indeed give Luqmān wisdom. (31:12) — *wa la-qad ātainā Luqmāna 'l-ḥikmata*

To save himself from the consequences of leaving obligations unfulfilled, he must therefore do whatever he can to discharge them while he is still in this world, by making payment *[adhā']*, appealing for absolution *[istiḥlāl]*,[382] expressing repentance *[tawba]*, and demonstrating his willingness to make concessions *[idh'ān]*. Nothing else can save him from those consequences, apart from the covering provided by the All-Compassionate *[ar-Raḥīm]*, through His Kindness *[Ra'fa]* and His Mercy *[Raḥma]*. Since He is the Most Merciful of the merciful *[Arḥam ar-Rāḥimīn]*, He may compensate the claimants with whatever He wills in the Abode of Eternity and the Gardens of Paradise.

Samura ibn Jundab (may Allāh be well pleased with him) is reported as having said:

"We were in the company of Allāh's Messenger (Allāh bless him and give him peace) when he conducted the ritual prayer at a funeral service *[ṣallā 'alā jināza]*. When he was leaving, he said: 'Is there anyone here who belongs to the family of So-and-so?' A man said: 'I do,' so he (blessing and peace be upon him) said to him: 'So-and-so is held as a prisoner because of his debt.'

"As I then observed, his family, and others who were mourning over him, got up and took to settling debts on his behalf, until there was no one left who had any claim against him."

In another version of this traditional report, the wording is: "So-and-so is held in confinement at the gate of the Garden of Paradise, because of an unpaid debt of his."

[382] In Vol. 2, p. 159, Shaikh 'Abd al-Qādir al-Jīlānī (may Allāh be well pleased with him) has explained:

> It is strictly necessary for the penitent to acquaint his victim with the full extent of each offense he has committed against him, and he must not give him an ambiguous description of any of the wrongs to which he is confessing. A vaguely worded plea for absolution *[istiḥlāl]* is not sufficient in such cases, because it is always possible that the injured party *[maẓlūm]*, if he came to know all the facts concerning the extent of his injury, would not feel disposed to waive his right to exact retribution. He might prefer to postpone that retribution to the Day of Resurrection *[Yawm al-Qiyāma]*, in order to receive his compensation by having good deeds transferred to his account from that of his malefactor, or by having some of his own bad deeds transferred to the debit scale of the latter.
>
> This rule does not apply, however, if the victim would suffer further injury from the knowledge of every specific item in the whole catalog of offenses against him. For instance, the offender would only add to the harm he had already caused, if he told his victim that he was guilty of sexual misconduct *[zinā]* with his maidservant or his wife, or that he had spread rumors about some hidden defect in his character. In cases like this, the penitent has no alternative but to couch his plea for absolution in rather vague terms. Even if he succeeds in obtaining the pardon he seeks, he will still be in debt to his victim because of a certain element of unrequited wrong, so he must repair that wrong by performing good deeds, just as he would have to repair the wrong if his victim happened to be dead or otherwise absent beyond his reach.

ʿAlī [ibn Abī Ṭālib] (may Allāh be well pleased with him) is reported as having said:

"A man died—he was one of the People of the Bench *[Ahl aṣ-Ṣuffa]*[383] —and someone said: 'O Messenger of Allāh, he has left a dīnār [gold coin] and a dirham [silver coin] behind.' So the Prophet (Allāh bless him and give him peace) replied: 'Two purses of fire! Perform the funeral prayer for your companion, for there may be a debt outstanding against him.'"

According to another traditional report *[ḥadīth]*:

"Allāh's Messenger (Allāh bless him and give him peace) was present at the funeral service *[jināza]* of a man who was one of the Helpers *[Anṣār]*,[384] so he said: 'Has he left any unpaid debt?' 'Yes,' someone said, so he turned to leave, but ʿAlī (may Allāh be well pleased with him) said: 'I accept responsibility for what he owes.' The Prophet (Allāh bless him and give him peace) thereupon came back and performed the funeral prayer for him *[ṣallā ʿalai-hi]*, then said: 'O ʿAlī, may Allāh redeem your pledge, as you have ransomed your Muslim brother! Whenever a man redeems another man of his debt, Allāh will redeem him on the Day of Resurrection *[Yawm al-Qiyāma]*.'"

The Prophet (Allāh bless him and give him peace) also said:

> All rightful claims will surely be awarded to their claimants on the Day of Resurrection *[Yawm al-Qiyāma]*, so that even the hornless sheep will receive compensation from the sheep with horns.

He also said (Allāh bless him and give him peace):

> Beware of injustice *[ẓulm]*, for it will result in murky shades of darkness *[ẓulumāt]* on the Day of Resurrection *[Yawm al-Qiyāma]*. Beware of obscenity *[fuḥsh]*, for Allāh does not like obscenity. And beware of greed *[shuḥḥ]*, for greed was the downfall of your kinsfolk who preceded you. It incited them to sever the bonds of kinship, so they severed those bonds, then it incited them to perpetrate injustice *[ẓulm]*, so they took to acting unjustly.

[383] A special group of materially impoverished Muslims were known as the People of the Bench *[Ahl aṣ-Ṣuffa]*, or the Companions of the Bench *[Aṣḥāb aṣ-Ṣuffa]*, because they used to shelter on a bench in the porch outside the mosque of the Prophet (Allāh bless him and give him peace) in Medina.

[384] See note 267 on p. 200 above.

b.
Concerning the treatment of a fellow believer *[mu'min]* who is sick, and who seems unlikely to recover.

If a fellow believer *[mu'min]* has fallen sick, it is commendable to pay him a visit.

When his Muslim brother visits the sick person, he should examine his condition carefully, and if he finds evidence to suggest that he is likely to recover from his illness, the visitor should offer a prayer of supplication on his behalf *[da'ā la-hu]*, then take his leave.

If, on the other hand, the visitor has reason to fear that the sick person's death may be imminent, he should encourage him to repent his sins, and to make a testamentary disposition *[waṣiyya]*, bequeathing one third of his property to the poor among those of his relatives who will not inherit from him automatically.[385] If all those relatives are rich, the bequest should be made in favor of the poor and the needy [in the community at large], and the people of learning *['ilm]* and virtue *[faḍl]* and religion *[dīn]*. It should be made in favor of those whom destiny *[qadar]* has deprived of material means *[asbāb]*, and whom pious restraint *[wara']* has inhibited from taking an active interest in their acquisition.

From the viewpoint of such pious paupers, the material means *[asbāb]* have turned into lords *[arbāb]*, so they have abandoned them, insistently declaring that the Lord *[ar-Rabb]* (Glory be to Him) can have no partner *[sharīk]*, and resorting directly to Him for sustenance. Their property has thus become reliance on the Lord of Truth (Almighty and Glorious is He), and renunciation of what is in the hands of people. Their affirmation of Oneness *[tawḥīd]* is thus preserved intact, and they yearn for Him with all parts of their being, purely and spontaneously,

[385] In accordance with the Islāmic law of inheritance, the estate of a deceased Muslim is distributed automatically to the prescribed heirs. The power of testamentary disposition *[waṣiyya]* is restricted to a maximum of one third of a Muslim's property. (For details of the Islāmic rules of inheritance, see *Shorter Encyclopedia of Islam*, arts. FARĀ'IḌ, MĪRĀTH and WAṢĪYA.)

without penalty in this world or punishment in the Hereafter. So congratulations to anyone who grants them a gift, or makes them a present, or treats them with gracious favor, or spends a day in their service, or devotes an hour to saying "*āmīn*" to their prayer of supplication *[ammana ʿalā duʿāʾi-him]*, or seizes an opportunity to speak well of them. Congratulations to him, and congratulations to him yet again!

He deserves to be congratulated because they are the people of Allāh, because they are His favored élite *[khāṣṣa]*. Who can gain access to the presence of the king, without the assistance of his favored élite? How can one receive recompense from the ruler *[sulṭān]*, except by way of his attendants and his servants? If someone establishes friendly relations with the attendants and servants, treats them well and serves their interests, they will soon introduce him to the King Almighty *[al-Malik al-Aʿẓam]*, at which point every one of them will mention his good qualities and refer to his noble deeds. The King will then bestow gracious favors upon him, in recompense for the beneficial services and meritorious acts he has performed.

So, if the symptom of death is clearly apparent, it is recommended that a member of the sick person's family should remain constantly by his side. The relative who undertakes this task should be the one who is most kindly disposed toward him, the one who is most familiar with his traits of character and the factors that govern his behavior, and the one who is most conscious of his duty to his Lord, so that he can make him aware of Allāh (Almighty and Glorious is He), and encourage him to obey Him by attending to the matters we have discussed above. He should take care to maintain the moisture of the dying person's throat, by keeping it supplied with drops of water or some other suitable liquid, and he should use a piece of damp cotton to wet his lips. He should also prompt him to say, one time at least: "There is no god but Allāh *[lā ilāha illa 'llāh]*." He should not urge him to say it more than three times, however, in case the effort makes him irritated and disturbed, with the result that his spirit departs while he is feeling an aversion to that. If he prompts him to say these words, but then the dying person utters something else, he should repeat his prompting, to ensure that his final utterance will be: "There is no god but Allāh *[lā ilāha illa 'llāh]*." For, as the Prophet (Allāh bless him and give him peace) has told us:

> If someone's last words are: "There is no god but Allāh *[lā ilāha illa 'llāh]*," that person will enter the Garden of Paradise.

The attendant relative should do his prompting in a gentle and coaxing manner. It is also appropriate for him to recite in his presence the Sūra entitled *Yā Sīn*, so that it can be an aid to the departure of his spirit, and so that it can make the experience easier for him to bear.[386]

As soon as his spirit has departed, his attendant should arrange the body of the deceased so that he is stretched out on his back, with his face toward the *Qibla* [direction of the Kaʿba in Mecca], in other words, in such a manner that his face will be toward it when he is caused to sit up. Then he should waste no time in closing the eyes of the deceased, because, as we know from the traditional report of Shaddād ibn Aws (may Allāh be well pleased with him), the Prophet (Allāh bless him and give him peace) once said:

> When you approach your dead, you must be sure to close their eyes, for the eyesight follows the spirit. And say something good, for he will say "*āmīn*" to what is said by the members of the family, then he will clamp his jawbones tight.

As for the manner in which the eyes of the dead should be closed, we have a description of it in the following traditional report: When [the Caliph] ʿUmar ibn al-Khaṭṭāb (may Allāh be well pleased with him) realized that he was at the point of death, he said to his son ʿAbdu'llāh (may Allāh be well pleased with him): "Stand close beside me. Then, when you see that my spirit has reached my uvula, place the palm of your right hand upon my forehead, [draw it down] beneath my chin, and close my eyes."

Next, the attendant should loosen the joints of the deceased, by moving his forearms back until they come in contact with his upper arms, then putting them straight again. He should bend his legs to meet his thighs, and move his thighs up to his stomach, then return them to their normal positions.

He should remove the clothes of the deceased, and shroud him in a garment that covers his entire body, because the whole of him becomes a private part *[ʿawra]* by reason of death. This is why it is necessary to conceal the whole of his body in the shroud.

A heavy object, such as a mirror or a sword, should also be placed upon his stomach, because the corpse of the deceased becomes puffed up and inflated when his spirit has departed.

Then he should be laid out on the bench for his ritual washing *[ghusl]*, arranged so that his body is sloping down toward his feet.

[386] The Sūra entitled *Yā Sīn* is the 36th Sūra of the Qur'an.

Prompt measures should then be taken to discharge his obligations, and to relieve him of all responsibility for debts and legacies, so that he can meet his Lord in a state of innocence, free of any liability for acts of injustice, exempt from unpaid dues and unfulfilled commitments.

c.
Concerning the ritual washing *[ghusl]*, grooming *[tajhīz]*, shrouding *[takfīn]* and burial *[dafn]* of the deceased.

As soon as the abovementioned matters have been duly attended to, no time should be wasted in performing the ritual washing *[ghusl]* of the deceased, followed by his grooming *[tajhīz]*, his shrouding *[takfīn]* and his burial *[dafn]*. There should be no delay, unless the person's death has occurred suddenly and unexpectedly, in which case these actions must be postponed until his death has been established with absolute certainty. His palms must be unclenched, his legs unbent, his nose running, and his temples sunk into his head; only then can the process be expedited.

As for the ritual washing *[ghusl]*, it may be described as follows:

The ritual washer *[ghāsil]* must lay the corpse bare, though keeping it veiled from the navel to the knees, because this is most convenient for him, and most conducive to a really thorough washing. He must avert his gaze as much as possible, especially from the area of the private parts *[ʿawra]*. (Some authorities maintain that it is most appropriate for him to wash the corpse inside a loosely fitting gown, made from a light material. If it proves to be too tight, he can always split the stitching at the top of the panels.)

Then he must gently loosen its joints, if it is easy for him to do so. If not, he should leave them alone, because the use of force might result in their being broken, and the Prophet (Allāh bless him and give him peace) has told us:

> Breaking the bone of the corpse is like breaking it when the person is alive.

Then he should bend the dead body slightly, enough to bring it close to the sitting position. He should then squeeze its belly, applying only gentle pressure.

Next, he should wrap a rag around his hand, as a precaution against touching the private region *[ʿawra]* of the corpse with his hand, and also because the rag is a more effective means of removing the dirt, on account of its rough surface. He is likewise recommended to avoid touching the rest of the body, except with the rag. He should keep pouring water over his hand, then throw the rag away and replace it with one that is clean. Then, after repeating this process three times, he should discard the rag completely, and give his hand a thorough wash.

He should then proceed to give the corpse the ritual ablution *[wuḍūʾ]* that is normally performed in preparation for the ritual prayer *[ṣalāt]*, following the prescribed sequence. This means that he must begin by formulating the intention, and then invoke the Name of Allāh. He must insert his two fingers, wet with water, between the lips of the corpse, and rub its teeth. He must do the same with its nostrils, in order to clean them out. He must pour water over its mouth and its nose, as if for the actions called *maḍmaḍa* [moving water all around inside the mouth, then spitting it out and ejecting it] and *istinshāq* [snuffing water up the nostrils, then blowing it out]—except that the water will not actually enter the mouth and nose of the corpse.

He must proceed in this fashion, until he has performed the ritual ablution *[wuḍūʾ]* on the last member of the body [for which it is prescribed]. Next, when he has finished that part of his task, he must wash the head of the corpse with water and the ground leaves of the lotus tree *[sidr]*. Then he must wash its beard. He should not comb the hair, however.

Then he must pour fresh water over the entire body, from its head to its feet, and thoroughly wash its right side. Then he must turn it over to the left, and give its left side a thorough wash. He must wash the rest of the body in similar fashion, using water and lotus leaves in each act of washing, but he should also wipe it dry immediately after each washing with lotus leaves and fresh water. If he needs waterskins for washing dirt away, and a spike for cleaning out what lies beneath the nails of fingers and toes, he may use such implements. He may also wrap cotton around the spike, in order to remove unpleasant substances from the nose and the ear canals, and to make them properly clean.

Then [having completed the first washing of the corpse] he should begin the process all over again. He should bend the body, then repeat its ritual ablution *[wuḍū']* a second time, in the manner we have described.

Then [having completed the second washing of the corpse] he should wash it for the last time, using water containing camphor. Then he must wipe it dry with a piece of cloth.

(The corpse must be washed at least three times, and seven times at most. If three washings are not sufficient to make it properly clean, it should therefore be given extra washings, up to a maximum of seven. Whatever the final total, however, it must always be an odd number, in other words, three or five or seven.)

If something is excreted from the corpse after that [third washing], the washing should be repeated up to seven times. If that is still not enough to put a stop to the excretion, the orifice should be plugged with cotton, and covered with a patch and hot perfume. According to some of our fellow [Ḥanbalī] scholars, however, the corpse should not be plugged, because Imām Aḥmad [ibn Ḥanbal] (may Allāh bestow His mercy upon him) disapproved of the practice.

According to certain authorities, if something is excreted from the corpse after the washing has been completed, the entire process of washing should not be repeated. Further washing should rather be confined to the place of the impurity.

Then the corpse should be given the ritual ablution *[wuḍū']* that is normally performed in preparation for the ritual prayer *[ṣalāt]*, wrapped in its shroud, and carried to the place of burial.

The best practice is to perform the first washing of the corpse with water and ground lotus leaves *[sidr]*, and the rest of the washings with pure water, as in the ritual ablution normally performed to remove a state of major impurity *[ghusl al-janāba]*. Camphor should be added in the final washing, then the corpse should be wiped dry and wrapped in its shroud.

The shrouding *[takfīn]* of the corpse.

As for the shrouding *[takfīn]* of the corpse, three pieces of cloth are used for the purpose of wrapping it completely. They must be plain white sheets *[lafā'if]*. They must not include any kind of shirt or gown *[qamīṣ]*, waist wrapper *[mi'zar]*, baggy trouser pants *[sarāwīl]*, or anything stitched or sewn. The sheets themselves may be stitched, however, if the available cloth would otherwise be too narrow and too small.

The sheets must be spread out, one on top of the other, after they have been fumigated with aloeswood *['ūd]*, incense *[nadd]*[387] and camphor *[kāfūr]*. Perfume should also be placed between each pair of sheets.

According to certain authorities, however, the corpse must be shrouded in a gown *[qamīṣ]*, a waist wrapper *[mi'zar]* and a sheet *[lafīfa]*. The waist wrapper should be next to the skin of the corpse, and the gown should not be buttoned up over it.

Three pieces of plain cloth are more appropriate, in view of the fact that [the Prophet's wife] 'Ā'isha (may Allāh be well pleased with her) is reported as having said:

"Allāh's Messenger (Allāh bless him and give him peace) was shrouded in three pieces of white cotton cloth, none of them being a gown *[qamīṣ]* or a turban *['imāma]*."

Imām Aḥmad [ibn Ḥanbal] (may Allāh bestow His mercy upon him) confirmed the authenticity of the tradition *[ḥadīth]* of 'Ā'isha (may Allāh be well pleased with her), and he based his doctrine *[madhhab]* upon it.

The perfume, consisting of an embalming mixture *[ḥanūṭ]*[388] and camphor, should then be placed in a piece of cotton. Some of this

[387] According to some of the classical Arabic lexicographers, the term *nadd* or *nidd* is applied to a compound of aloeswood aromatized with musk, ambergris and frankincense. (See E.W. Lane, *Arabic-English Lexicon*, art. *N–D–D*.)

[388] According to the classical Arabic lexicographers, the term *ḥanūṭ* is applied to "odiferous substances of any kind that are mixed for a corpse, in particular, or for grave-clothes and for the bodies of the dead, consisting of musk, or ambergris, or camphor, or Indian cane, or sandalwood, bruised..., and other things that are sprinkled upon it for the purpose of perfuming it and drying up its moisture." (See E.W. Lane, *Arabic-English Lexicon*, art. *Ḥ–N–Ṭ*.)

should be inserted between the buttocks of the corpse, and kept there by fixing a rag on top of it. The rest of it should be applied to the parts of the body that touch the ground in the act of prostration *[sujūd]*,[389] and to places where the skin is creased, like the thighs, under the armpits, the facial apertures, the ear holes, the brow, the knees, the palms of the hands, and the area outside the eyes. The embalmer must not insert the mixture into the eyes themselves. If he is afraid that the state of purity may be annulled, and that what is inside the body may be excreted to the outside, he should plug the inside of the nose and the ear holes with cotton and camphor. If he perfumes the whole of the corpse with camphor and sandalwood, that is even better. As we learn from the traditional report of Nāfi', Ibn 'Umar (may Allāh be well pleased with him and with his father) used to apply musk to the creases and elbows of the corpse.

Next, he should fetch the corpse and set it down on the sheets. He should fold one edge of the uppermost sheet over the right side of the corpse, then pull the other edge over its left side, thereby wrapping it completely in the sheet. Then he should do the same with the second and third sheets in turn, placing the one beside his head away from the one beside his feet. Then, having tucked the top edges together as they are tucked in a turban, he should repeat the process over the face and the feet, unless he has reason to fear that the tucked edges could come apart, in which case he should knot them together. Then, when the corpse is laid in the grave, he should untie the knots, without creating any gap in the shroud *[kafan]*.

[389] The act of prostration *[sujūd]* is performed during the ritual prayer *[ṣalāt]*. The Prophet (Allāh bless him and give him peace) once said:

> I have been commanded to perform the act of prostration *[sujūd]* by resting on seven bones.

That is to say: (1) the skull bone in the forehead, (2,3) the bones in the two hands, (4,5) the two kneecaps, and (6,7) the bones in the two big toes.

The shrouding *[takfīn]* of a female corpse.

As for the corpse of a woman, it must be shrouded in five pieces of cloth, namely, a shawl *[izār]*, a smock or chemise *[dirʿ]*, a head-and-face veil *[khimār]*, and two plain sheets *[lifāfatain]*. Her corpse must be wrapped in these completely, and the shawl alone must be big enough to envelop her entire body.

According to some of our fellow [Ḥanbalī] scholars, it is recommended that a fifth piece of cloth should be used in her case, for the purpose of binding her thighs together. [The pieces are still five in number] so this will take the place of one of the two sheets.

The hair of the female corpse should be braided in three plaits, and should be arranged so that it hangs down behind her. Both the male and the female should be treated to the kind of preparation given to a bride or bridegroom.

If the circumstances are such that it is not feasible to provide the female corpse with all that we have mentioned, even one single piece of cloth can serve the necessary purpose.

The washing, shrouding and burial of a ritually consecrated pilgrim *[muḥrim]*.

As for the ritually consecrated pilgrim *[muḥrim]*, his corpse should be washed with water and ground lotus leaves *[sidr]*. It should not have perfume applied to it. Neither the head nor the feet should be veiled, and the corpse should not be clothed in anything that has been stitched or sewn. It must be shrouded only in the two pieces of cloth [worn by the pilgrim in a state of consecration], because Ibn ʿAbbās (may Allāh be well pleased with him and with his father) is reported as having said:

"Suddenly, while Allāh's Messenger (Allāh bless him and give him peace) was waiting at ʿArafa, a man who was also waiting there [as a pilgrim] fell down from his riding camel, and the animal broke his neck. So Allāh's Messenger (Allāh bless him and give him peace) said:

> "'Wash him with water and ground lotus leaves *[sidr]*, and shroud him in the two pieces of cloth he is wearing [as a ritually consecrated pilgrim]. Do not veil his head, for, when Allāh brings him forth on the Day of Resurrection *[Yawm al-Qiyāma]*, he will be uttering the pilgrim's cry of readiness to serve his Lord *[mulabbiyan]*.'"[390]

[390] That is to say, he will be pronouncing the *talbiyya* [expression of willing compliance]. In the context of the Pilgrimage *[Ḥajj]*, the term *talbiyya* refers to the declaration, repeatedly uttered by the pilgrim:

Doubly at Your service, O Allāh!	*labbaika Allāhumma*
Doubly at Your service!	*labbaik*
No partner have You!	*lā sharīka laka*
Doubly at Your service!	*labbaik*
Yours is the praise and the gracious favor,	*inna 'l-ḥamda wa 'n-niʿmata laka*
and Yours is the kingdom!	*wa 'l-mulku lak*
No partner have You!	*lā sharīka lak.*

The ritual washing of the miscarried fetus *[ghusl as-siqṭ]*.

As for the miscarried fetus *[siqṭ]*, if it is delivered after more than four months in the womb, it should be given a ritual washing and a funeral prayer.[391] If it is not clear whether it is a male or a female, it should be given a name that is equally suitable for a person of either sex.

In a case of this sort, it does not matter whether the washing is performed by a man or by a woman, because the women washed the corpse of Ibrāhīm, the son of the Prophet (Allāh bless him and give him peace), when he died at the age of eighteen months. This fact is mentioned in the tradition *[ḥadīth]* of Umm ʿAṭiyya (may Allāh be well pleased with her).

[391] As Shaikh ʿAbd al-Qādir al-Jīlānī (may Allāh be well pleased with him) has explained on pp. 279–80:

In the case of a miscarried fetus *[siqṭ]*, the funeral prayer and ritual washing may also be required, but only if it has developed to the point where the shape of a human being is already apparent. If it is merely a piece of flesh, in which no embryonic form can be discerned, it should simply be buried, with neither ritual washing nor funeral prayer.

With certain exceptions, the ritual washing should be performed by a person of the same sex as the deceased.

The ritual washing of a male corpse should normally be performed by a man, and of a female corpse by a woman. If the wife washes the corpse of her husband, however, this is permissible; on this point there is no disagreement in the [Ḥanbalī] school *[madhhab]*. The same rule applies to the mother of the male child. As to whether the husband may wash the corpse of his wife, there are two conflicting reports [of the Ḥanbalī doctrine], although it is known for a fact that ʿAlī performed the funeral washing of [his wife] Fāṭima the Radiant *[az-Zahrā']* (may Allāh be well pleased with them both).[392]

[392] Fāṭima the Radiant *[az-Zahrā']*, daughter of the Prophet (Allāh bless him and give him piece), became the wife of the latter's cousin, ʿAlī ibn Abī Ṭālib, and bore him two sons, al-Ḥasan and al-Ḥusain. May Allah be well pleased with them all.

Defraying the cost of the shroud *[kafan]*.

As a charge on a man's estate, the cost of his shroud *[kafan]* takes precedence over the settlement of his debts and the distribution of his testamentary disposition *[waṣiyya]*. If he has no property, the cost must be defrayed by the person responsible for his maintenance. If there is no such person, the expense must be met from the public treasury *[bait al-māl]*. The same applies to the cost of a woman's shroud, which is not incumbent upon her husband.

The burial *[dafn]*.

The best practice is for the burial *[dafn]* of the corpse to be carried out by the same person who took charge of its ritual washing *[ghusl]*. The grave *[qabr]* should be dug to the depth of one fathom *[qāma]*[393] and an arm's length *[busṭa]*. Its length should be three cubits and a span, and in width it should measure one cubit *[dhirā']*[394] and a span *[shibr]*.[395] This is in accordance with the words addressed by the Prophet (Allāh bless him and give him peace) to 'Umar ibn al-Khaṭṭāb (may Allāh be well pleased with him):

> How will it be for you, when a hole in the ground is made ready to receive you, three cubits and a span [in length] by one cubit and a span in width? Then your family will approach you, to wash you and shroud you and embalm you. Then they will carry you [to your grave], in order to bury you in it. Then they will pile the earth on top of you. Then they will go away and leave you....[396]

Following the recommended practice, the corpse should be drawn headforemost from the bier. If this is too difficult, however, it may be taken from the side of the grave, or from whichever direction happens to be easiest. This is in accordance with one report of the doctrine of Imām Aḥmad [ibn Ḥanbal] (may Allāh bestow His mercy upon him).

As for the corpse of a women, its burial *[dafn]* should be carried out by women, just as they take charge of its ritual washing *[ghusl]*. If this is impracticable in a particular instance, the task should be performed by men who are closely related to her. If this is also unfeasible, it should be carried out by old men who are unrelated to her.

[393] The *qāma* [fathom] is equal to six feet.

[394] As a unit of length, the Arabic term *dhirā'*—like the medieval English cubit—is based on the length of the forearm from the elbow to the tip of the middle finger. While it is usually equal to about 18 inches, it sometimes signifies a length of 21 inches or even more. (See E.W. Lane, *Arabic-English Lexicon*, art. *DH–R–'*.)

[395] A span *[shibr]* is defined by the Arabic lexicographers as "the space between the extremity of the thumb and the little finger, when extended apart in the usual manner." (See E.W. Lane, *Arabic-English Lexicon*, art. *SH–B–R*.)

[396] **Author's note:** This is only a partial quotation of the tradition *[ḥadīth]*, which continues beyond this point.

It is recommended that her grave should be veiled, as opposed to that of a man, because she is subject to concealment *[ʿawra]*. ʿAlī (may Allāh be well pleased with him) once passed by a group of people, just when they had spread a cloth over [the grave of] of man, so he pulled it away and said: "This treatment is appropriate only for women."

As soon as the corpse has been laid to rest in the grave, facing toward the *Qibla* [direction of the Kaʿba in Mecca], three handfuls of dust should be scattered over it. That is in accordance with the Sunna [the exemplary practice of the Prophet (Allāh bless him and give him peace)]. Then the earth should be heaped on top of the corpse.

The grave should be raised above the ground to the extent of one span *[shibr]*.[397] Water should be sprinkled over it, and pebbles should be placed upon it. If it is coated with clay, this is permissible, but the application of whitewash is subject to disapproval.

It is customary to give a humped shape to the surface of the grave, rather than to make it flat, because al-Ḥasan [al-Baṣrī] (may Allāh bestow His mercy upon him) is reported as having said:

"I noticed that the grave of the Prophet (Allāh bless him and give him peace) was humped in shape, as were those of his Companions."

When the person in charge has finished the interment *[taqbīr]* of the corpse, it is customary for him to address the deceased, prompting him to respond. This practice is based on the traditional report of Abū Umāma (may Allāh be well pleased with him), who stated that the Prophet (Allāh bless him and give him peace) once said:

> When one of you has died, and you have spread the dust upon him, one of you should stand at the head of his grave, and then say: "O So-and-so, son of the lady So-and-so!" For he will hear, although he will not answer. Then the prompter should say a second time: "O So-and-so, son of the lady So-and-so!" For he will then sit up straight. Then the prompter should say again: "O So-and-so, son of the lady So-and-so!" For then he will say, although you will not hear him: "Guide us aright! May Allāh bestow His mercy upon you!"
>
> So then the prompter should say: "Remember that with which you left the abode of this world, namely, the testimony *[shahāda]* that there is no god but Allāh *[an lā ilāha illa 'llāh]*, and that Muḥammad is His servant and His Messenger *[wa anna Muḥammadan ʿabdu-hu wa Rasūlu-hu]*. Remember that you are well pleased with Allāh as a Lord *[Rabban]*, and with Islām as a religion *[dīnan]*, and with Muḥammad as a Prophet *[Nabiyyan]*, and with the Qurʾān as a leader *[imāman]*." For [the interrogating angels] Munkar and Nakīr[531] will then say: "We shall not sit beside this one, for he has already stated his case."

[397] See note 395 on p. 299 above.

"O Messenger of Allāh," a man asked, "what if the prompter does not know the name of the mother of the deceased?" So he told him: "In that case, he may simply address him as the son of Eve *[Ḥawwā']*."

If he wishes to do so, it is quite permissible for the prompter to add: "And [that you are well content] with the believers *[mu'minīn]* as brothers *[ikhwānan]*, and with the Ka'ba as a direction in which to turn in prayer *[qiblatan]*," and other such distinctive features of Islām.

* * * * * * *

This brings us to the end of the Chapter in which we have provided a concise treatment of certain special ritual prayers *[ṣalawāt]*, namely:

1. The ritual prayer of the Friday congregation *[ṣalāt al-jum'a]*.
2. The ritual prayer of each of the Two Festivals *[ṣalāt al-'Īdain]*.
3. The ritual prayer for relief from drought *[ṣalāt al-istisqā']*.
4. The ritual prayer at the eclipse of the sun *[ṣalāt al-kusūf]* and at the eclipse of the moon *[ṣalāt al-khusūf]*.
5. The ritual prayer in time of danger *[ṣalāt al-khawf]*.
6. The shortened version of the ritual prayer *[qaṣr aṣ-ṣalāt]*.
7. The combination of two ritual prayers *[al-jam' baina 'ṣ-ṣalātain]*.
8. The ritual prayer at the funeral service *[aṣ-ṣalāt 'ala 'l-jināza]*.

Praise be to Allāh, the Lord of All the Worlds!
[al-ḥamdu li'llāhi Rabbi 'l-'ālamīn].

CHAPTER TEN

Concerning the special qualities of the [voluntary] ritual prayers *[ṣalawāt]* performed in the daytime on each of the days of the week.[398]

1. Traditional reports concerning [voluntary] ritual prayers performed during the daytime *[ṣalawāt an-nahār]*.

As for what has come down to us on the subject of the daytime ritual prayers *[ṣalawāt an-nahār]*, one item is the traditional report, transmitted on the authority of Abū Salama, according to which Abū Huraira (may Allāh be well pleased with him) said:

"Allāh's Messenger (Allāh bless him and give him peace) once said to me:

> "'Whenever you are about to go out of your place of residence, you should perform two cycles of ritual prayer *[fa-ṣalli rak'atain]*, for they will prevent you from making a bad exit, and whenever you enter your place of residence, you should likewise perform two cycles of ritual prayer, for they will prevent you from making a bad entrance.'"

According to another traditional report, this one transmitted on the authority of Anas ibn Malik (may Allāh be well pleased with him), Allāh's Messenger (Allāh bless him and give him peace) once said, with reference to the prayer of daybreak *[ṣalāt aṣ-ṣubḥ]*:

> Whenever someone performs the ritual ablution *[tawaḍḍa']*, then sets out for the mosque *[masjid]*, and then performs the ritual prayer *[ṣalāt]* inside it, for every

[398] While some of the ritual prayers *[ṣalāwāt]* discussed in this Chapter are obligatory in themselves, the emphasis here is on their performance in congregation *[jamā'a]*, which, while strongly recommended, is not strictly compulsory.

step he takes, he will be credited with a good deed, and a bad deed will be erased from his record. Moreover, the good deed will carry the value of ten of its kind. If he performs the ritual prayer *[ṣallā]*, then takes his leave [from the mosque] at the rising of the sun, Allāh (Exalted is He) will record a good deed in his favor for every hair on his body, and he will return home with an accepted Pilgrimage *[Ḥijja mabrūra]*[537] to his credit.

If he sits until he is ready to perform a cycle of prayer *[ḥattā yarkaʿa]*, for every act of sitting *[jalsa]* Allāh (Exalted is He) will record a million good deeds in his credit column.

Whenever someone performs the late evening prayer *[ṣalāt al-ʿatama]*,[399] he is entitled to receive a similar reward, and he will return home with an accepted Visitation *[ʿUmra mabrūra]*[400] to his credit.

[The Caliph] ʿUthmān ibn ʿAffān (may Allāh be well pleased with him) is reported as having said: "I once heard Allāh's Messenger (Allāh bless him and give him peace) say:

"'When someone performs the late evening prayer *[ṣalāt al-ʿishāʾ]* in a congregation *[jamāʿa]*, it is as if he has devoted half the night to worship. And when someone performs the dawn prayer *[ṣalāt al-fajr]* in a congregation *[jamāʿa]*, it is as if he has spent the entire night in prayer.'"

According to another traditional report, this one transmitted on the authority of Abū Ṣāliḥ, Abū Huraira (may Allāh be well pleased with him) stated that Allāh's Messenger (Allāh bless him and give him peace) once said:

No ritual prayer *[ṣalāt]* is more burdensome for the hypocrites *[munāfiqīn]* than the prayer of late evening and that of the dawn *[ṣalāt al-ʿishāʾ wa 'l-fajr]*. If they did but know what [blessings] these two contain, they would surely come to perform them, even if they had to come crawling on their hands and knees! I once considered the idea of ordering my servants to gather firewood, so I could make it too hot for men who do not attend [the congregation] with us to stay in their houses!

According to ʿAṭāʾ ibn Yasār, Abū Huraira (may Allāh be well pleased with him) reported that the Prophet (Allāh bless him and give him peace) once said:

If someone performs four cycles of ritual prayer *[ṣallā arbaʿa rakaʿāt]* after the sun has declined from the meridian, paying proper attention to their Qurʾānic recitation *[qirāʾa]* and to their acts of bowing *[rukūʿ]* and prostration *[sujūd]*, seventy thousand angels will pray together with him, begging forgiveness on his behalf until the night sets in.

[399] The term *Ḥijja* is applied to a specific performance of the *Ḥajj* [Pilgrimage]. For a full account of the rites of *Ḥājj* [Pilgrimage] and *ʿUmra* [Visitation; Lesser Pilgrimage], see Vol. 1, pp. 26–52.

[400] See Vol. 1, pp. 44 and 47.

According to this same report, Abū Huraira (may Allāh be well pleased with him) went on to say:

"Allāh's Messenger (Allāh bless him and give him peace) would never fail to perform four [voluntary cycles of prayer] after the sun's decline from the meridian. He would prolong them, and he used to say:

> "'The gates of heaven are opened at this hour, so I would like to have a good deed of mine rise up into it.'

"Someone asked: 'O Messenger of Allāh, is there a [ritual salutation of] "Peace!" in them, marking a division [of the four cycles into two segments]?' 'No,' said he (Allāh bless him and give him peace)."

The Prophet (Allāh bless him and give him peace) is also reported as having said:

> May Allāh bestow His mercy upon any servant [of His] who performs four [voluntary cycles of prayer] before [the obligatory ritual prayer of] the afternoon *[al-ʿaṣr]*.

2.
Concerning [voluntary] ritual prayer performed on a Sunday *[ṣalāt yawm al-aḥad]*.

According to a traditional report transmitted on the authority of Abū Huraira (may Allāh be well pleased with him), the Prophet (Allāh bless him and give him peace) once said:

> If someone performs four cycles of ritual prayer *[ṣallā arbaʿa rakaʿāt]* on a Sunday—reciting the Opening Sūra of the Book *[Fātiḥat al-Kitāb]* in each cycle, and [the passage that begins with] "*Āmana 'r-Rasūlu*... [The Messenger believes...]" (2:285) one time —Allāh (Exalted is He) will record in his favor a number of good deeds, a number corresponding to the total figure arrived at by counting every Christian man and Christian woman *[Naṣrānī wa Naṣrāniyya]*. He will grant him the spiritual reward of a Prophet *[Nabī]*. He will record a Pilgrimage *[Ḥijja]* and a Visitation *[ʿUmra]* in his credit column. For each cycle *[rakʿa]*, He will credit him with a thousand ritual prayers *[alf ṣalāt]*. Then, for every letter [in the words of his Qur'ānic recitation], Allāh (Exalted is He) will grant him, in the Garden of Paradise, a city constructed from the most fragrantly aromatic musk.

According to another traditional report, this one transmitted on the authority of [the Caliph] ʿAlī ibn Abī Ṭālib (may Allāh be well pleased with him), the Prophet (Allāh bless him and give him peace) once said:

> Affirm the Oneness of Allāh (Exalted is He) by performing the ritual prayer *[ṣalāt]* frequently on Sunday, for He is Single *[Wāḥid]*, without any partner *[lā sharīka la-h]*. If someone performs four [voluntary] cycles of ritual prayer *[ṣallā arbaʿa rakaʿāt]* on a Sunday, after the noon prayer *[ṣalāt aẓ-ẓuhr]* that is strictly obligatory *[farīḍa]* and that which is customary *[sunna]*—reciting, in the first cycle, the Opening Sūra of the Book *[Fātiḥat al-Kitāb]* and the Sūra of Prostration *[as-Sajda]*, which begins with "*Alif–Lām–Mīm*...," (Q. 32) and, in the second cycle, the Opening Sūra of the Book *[Fātiḥat al-Kitāb]* and the Sūra of Sovereignty *[al-Mulk]*, which begins with "*Tabāraka*... [Blessed is He...];" (Q. 67) then pronouncing the testimony and the salutation *[yatashahhad wa yusallim]*; then standing up and proceeding to perform the last two cycles, reciting in both of them the Opening Sūra of the Book *[Fātiḥat al-Kitāb]* and the Sūra of the Congregation *[Sūrat al-Jumuʿa]*; (Q. 62) and asking [in his supplication] for his need to be satisfied—it will be an obligation *[ḥaqq]* incumbent upon Allāh (Exalted is He) to satisfy his need, and to declare him innocent of the errors committed by the Christians *[Naṣārā]*.

3.
Concerning [voluntary] ritual prayer performed on a Monday *[ṣalāt yawm al-ithnain]*.

According to a traditional report transmitted by Abu 'z-Zubair, on the authority of Jābir ibn ʿAbdi 'llāh [al-Anṣārī] (may Allāh be well pleased with him and with his father), Allāh's Messenger (Allāh bless him and give him peace) once said:

> If someone performs two [voluntary] cycles of ritual prayer *[rakʿatain]* at daybreak on a Monday—reciting the Opening Sūra of the Book *[Fātiḥat al-Kitāb]* once in each cycle, the Verse of the Throne *[Āyat al-Kursī]*[401] one time, "*Qul Huwa'llāhu Aḥad* [Say: 'He is Allāh, One!']"[402] one time, and the Two Pleas for Divine Refuge *[al-Muʿawwidhatain]*[403] one time each—and if, when he pronounces the salutation *[idhā sallama]*, he appeals ten times to Allāh for forgiveness, and invokes His blessing upon the Prophet (Allāh bless him and give him peace) ten times—Allāh will forgive him all his sins.

According to another traditional report, this one transmitted by Thābit al-Bunānī, on the authority of Anas ibn Mālik (may Allāh be well pleased with him), Allāh's Messenger (Allāh bless him and give him peace) once said:

> If someone performs twelve [voluntary] cycles of ritual prayer *[ṣallā ithnatai ʿashrata rakʿa]* on a Monday, reciting the Opening Sūra of the Book *[Fātiḥat al-Kitāb]* in each cycle, and the Verse of the Throne *[Āyat al-Kursī]* one time—and if, when he has concluded his performance of the prayer *[ṣalāt]*, he recites "*Qul Huwa'llāhu Aḥad* [Say: 'He is Allāh, One!']" twelve times, and seeks forgiveness twelve times—an angelic voice will call for him on the Day of Resurrection *[Yawm al-Qiyāma]*, saying: "Where is So-and-so, the son of So-and-so? Let him step forward to receive his reward from Allāh (Exalted is He)!" He will then be given, as the first part of his reward, a thousand fine articles of clothing. A crown will be placed upon his head, and he will be told: "Enter the Garden of Paradise!" A thousand angels will bid him welcome, each angel bearing a gift, and they will escort him on a tour of a thousand palaces constructed from glittering light.

[401] Q. 2:255.

[402] Sūra 112.

[403] Sūra 113 and Sūra 114.

4.
Concerning [voluntary] ritual prayer performed on a Tuesday *[ṣalāt yawm ath-thalāthā']*.

According to a traditional report transmitted by Yazīd ar-Raqāshī, on the authority of Mālik ibn Anas (may Allāh be well pleased with him), Allāh's Messenger (Allāh bless him and give him peace) once said:

> If someone performs ten [voluntary] cycles of ritual prayer *[raka'āt]* on a Tuesday, in the middle of the day—reciting the Opening Sūra of the Book *[Fātiḥat al-Kitāb]* once in each cycle, the Verse of the Throne *[Āyat al-Kursī]*[404] one time, and "*Qul Huwa'llāhu Aḥad* [Say: 'He is Allāh, One!']"[405] three times—no sinful error will be recorded in his debit column for seventy days. Then, if he dies before the seventy days are up, he will die as a martyr *[shahīd]*, and he will be forgiven the sins of seventy years.

[404] Q. 2:255

[405] Sūra 112.

5.
Concerning [voluntary] ritual prayer performed on a Wednesday *[ṣalāt yawm al-arbaʿāʾ]*.

According to a traditional report transmitted by Abū Idrīs al-Khawlānī, on the authority of Muʿādh ibn Jabal (may Allāh be well pleased with him), Allāh's Messenger (Allāh bless him and give him peace) once said:

> If someone performs twelve [voluntary] cycles of ritual prayer *[ithnatai ʿasharata rakʿa]* on a Wednesday, at the high point of the day—reciting the Opening Sūra of the Book *[Fātiḥat al-Kitāb]* in each cycle, the Verse of the Throne *[Āyat al-Kursī]*[406] one time, "*Qul Huwa'llāhu Aḥad* [Say: 'He is Allāh, One!']"[407] three times, and the Two Pleas for Divine Refuge *[al-Muʿawwidhatain]*[408] three times—an angel will call out to him from beside the Heavenly Throne *[ʿArsh]*: "O servant of Allāh, you may now set to work with a clean slate, for all your previous sins have been forgiven!" Allāh will exempt him from the torment of the tomb, and from its narrowness and gloom. He will also exempt him from the terrible hardships of the Resurrection, and He will accept his day's work with the honor conferred on the work of a Prophet *[Nabī]*.

[406] Q. 2:255.

[407] Sūra 112.

[408] Sūras 113 and 114.

6.
Concerning [voluntary] ritual prayer performed on a Thursday *[ṣalāt yawm al-khamīs]*.

According to a traditional report transmitted by ʿIkrima, on the authority of Ibn ʿAbbās (may Allāh be well pleased with him and with his father), Allāh's Messenger (Allāh bless him and give him peace) once said:

> If someone performs two [voluntary] cycles of ritual prayer *[rakʿatain]* on a Thursday, at some point between the [obligatory prayers of] noon *[aẓ-ẓuhr]* and afternoon *[al-ʿaṣr]*—reciting in the first cycle the Opening Sūra of the Book *[Fātiḥat al-Kitāb]* one time, and the Verse of the Throne *[Āyat al-Kursī]*[409] one hundred times, and in the second cycle the Opening Sūra of the Book *[Fātiḥat al-Kitāb]* [one time], and "*Qul Huwa'llāhu Aḥad* [Say: 'He is Allāh, One!']"[410] one hundred times—and if, when he has finished [performing the ritual prayer], he invokes Allāh's blessing upon me one hundred times—Allāh (Exalted is He) will grant him the spiritual reward of someone who fasts in the months of Rajab, Shaʿbān and Ramaḍān. The amount of his spiritual reward will be comparable to that of a Pilgrim of the House [of Allāh] *[Ḥājj al-Bait]*. As for the good deeds to be recorded in his credit column, their number will be equal to the total figure arrived at by adding up all the people who believe in Allāh (Exalted is He) and put their trust in Him.

[409] Q. 2:255.

[410] Sūra 112.

7.
Concerning [voluntary] ritual prayer performed on a Friday *[ṣalāt yawm al-jumʿa]*.

According to a traditional report, ʿAlī ibn al-Ḥusain heard from his father that his grandfather[411] (may Allāh's good pleasure be upon them all) had told him: "I once heard the Prophet (Allāh bless him and give him peace) say:

> "'The whole of Friday, the Day of the Congregation, is [a time devoted to] ritual prayer *[Yawm al-Jumʿa kullu-hu ṣalāt]*. If any truly believing servant of the Lord *[ʿabd muʾmin]* gets up—when the sun has emerged and risen by the length of a spear, or more than that—and performs the ablution and does so thoroughly *[tawaḍḍaʾa fa-asbagha ʾl-wuḍūʾ]*, and performs two cycles *[rakʿatain]* of the supererogatory forenoon prayer *[subḥat aḍ-ḍuḥā]*,[412] as an act of faith and with an attitude of total dedication *[iḥtisāb]*, Allāh (Exalted is He) will record two hundred good deeds in his credit column, and He will also erase two hundred bad deeds from his debit column.
>
> "'If someone performs four cycles *[rakaʿāt]*, Allāh (Exalted is He) will upgrade his status in the Garden of Paradise by four hundred degrees.
>
> "'If someone performs eight cycles *[rakaʿāt]*, Allāh (Exalted is He) will upgrade his status in the Gardens of Paradise by eight hundred degrees, and He will forgive him all his sins.
>
> "'If someone performs twelve cycles *[ithnatai ʿasharata rakʿa]*, Allāh (Exalted is He) will record one thousand two hundred good deeds in his credit column, and He will also erase one thousand two hundred bad deeds from his debit column. He will also upgrade his status in the Garden of Paradise by one thousand two hundred degrees.'"

According to another traditional report, this one transmitted on the authority of Abū Ṣāliḥ, Abū Huraira (may Allāh be well pleased with him) stated that Allāh's Messenger (Allāh bless him and give him peace) once said:

> If someone performs the [obligatory] daybreak prayer *[ṣalla ʾṣ-ṣubḥ]* on a Friday, as a member of a congregation *[jamāʿa]*, then sits in the mosque *[masjid]*,

[411] That is to say, the Caliph ʿAlī ibn Abī Ṭālib (may Allāh ennoble his countenance).

[412] See note 98 on p. 83, also pp. 90–921 above.

> practicing the remembrance of Allāh (Exalted is He), until the sun has risen into view, he will be entitled to seventy degrees in Paradise *[Firdaws]*. Moreover, in the space between two degrees, he will have trained horses at his disposal for seventy years.
>
> If someone performs the Friday [Congregational] prayer *[ṣalla 'l-jum'a]*, as a member of a congregation *[jamā'a]*, he will be entitled to fifty degrees in Paradise *[Firdaws]*, and he will have thoroughbred horses at his disposal for fifty years.
>
> If someone performs the [obligatory] afternoon prayer *[ṣalla 'l-'aṣr]* on a Friday, as a member of a congregation *[jamā'a]*, it will be to his credit as if he had emancipated eighty of the offspring of Ishmael *[Ismā'īl]*, delivering each of them from slavery.
>
> If someone performs the [obligatory] sunset prayer *[ṣalla 'l-maghrib]* on a Friday, as a member of a congregation *[jamā'a]*, it will be to his credit as if he had performed a Pilgrimage *[Ḥijja]* blessed with acceptance and a Visitation *['Umra]* worthy of approval.

According to yet another traditional report, this one transmitted on the authority of Mujāhid, Ibn 'Abbās (may Allāh be well pleased with him and with his father) stated that Allāh's Messenger (Allāh bless him and give him peace) once said:

> If someone performs two [voluntary] cycles of ritual prayer *[rak'atain]* on a Friday, at some point between the [obligatory prayers of] noon *[aẓ-ẓuhr]* and afternoon *[al-'aṣr]*—reciting in the first cycle the Opening Sūra of the Book *[Fātiḥat al-Kitāb]* one time, the Verse of the Throne *[Āyat al-Kursī]*[413] one time, and "*Qul a'ūdhu bi-Rabbi 'l-Falaq* [Say: I take refuge with the Lord of the Daybreak']"[414] twenty-five times; and reciting in the second cycle the Opening Sūra of the Book *[Fātiḥat al-Kitāb]* one time, "*Qul Huwa'llāhu Aḥad* [Say: 'He is Allāh, One!']"[415] one time, and "*Qul a'ūdhu bi-Rabbi 'l-Falaq* [Say: I take refuge with the Lord of the Daybreak']" twenty times—and if, when he has pronounced the salutation *[sallama]*, he says, fifty times:
>
> | | |
> |---|---|
> | There is no power, | *lā ḥawla* |
> | nor is there any strength, | *wa lā quwwata* |
> | except through Allāh, | *illā bi'llāhi 'l-* |
> | the All-High, the Almighty! | *'Aliyyi 'l-'Aẓīm!* |
>
> —he will not depart from this world until he has seen his Lord (Almighty and Glorious is He) in a dream, and has seen his situation in the Garden of Paradise, or had it shown to him.

It is related that an Arab of the desert *[A'rābī]* once came to town to visit the Prophet (Allāh bless him and give him peace). "O Messenger

413 Q. 2:255.

414 Sūra 113.

415 Sūra 112.

of Allāh," he said, "we are out in the desert, far from the city, and we cannot come to join you every Friday. So advise me of some practice that can appropriately be observed on the Day of Congregation, and I shall tell my people about it when I return to them." To this Prophet (Allāh bless him and give him peace) responded by saying:

> O Arab of the desert, when Friday [the Day of Congregation] comes around, perform two cycles of ritual prayer *[ṣalli rakʿatain]* when the day is near its height. In the first cycle, recite the Opening Sūra of the Book *[Fātiḥat al-Kitāb]* and "*Qul aʿūdhu bi-Rabbi 'l-Falaq* [Say: I take refuge with the Lord of the Daybreak']. In the second cycle, recite the Opening Sūra of the Book *[Fātiḥat al-Kitāb]* and "*Qul aʿūdhu bi-Rabbi 'n-Nās* [Say: I take refuge with the Lord of Mankind']."[416] Then pronounce the testimony and the salutation *[tashahhad wa sallim]*, and recite the Verse of the Throne *[Āyat al-Kursī]*[417] seven times, remaining in a sitting posture while you do so.
>
> Then perform eight cycles of ritual prayer *[rakaʿāt]*, as two sets of four. In the each cycle, recite the Opening Sūra of the Book *[Fātiḥat al-Kitāb]* and "*Idhā jāʾa naṣru 'llāhi wa 'l-fatḥ*... [When the help of Allāh comes, and victory...']" [418] one time, and "*Qul Huwa'llāhu Aḥad* [Say: 'He is Allāh, One!']"[419] twenty-five times. Then, when you have finished performing your prayer *[ṣalāt]*, say, seventy times:
>
> | | |
> |---|---|
> | There is no power, | *lā ḥawla* |
> | nor is there any strength, | *wa lā quwwata* |
> | except through Allāh, | *illā bi'llāhi 'l-* |
> | the All-High, the Almighty! | *ʿAliyyi 'l-ʿAẓīm!* |
>
> By the One who holds the soul of Muḥammad in His hand, no truly believing man *[muʾmin]*, and no truly believing woman *[muʾmina]*, will perform this particular ritual prayer *[ṣalāt]* on a Friday, exactly as I have just described it, without my being his [or her] guarantor of the Garden of Paradise. Nor will any such person leave his place [of prayer] until Allāh has granted forgiveness to him and to his parents, if they are Muslims. And an angelic herald will cry out from beneath the Heavenly Throne *[ʿArsh]*: "O servant of Allāh, you may now set to work with a clean slate, for all your previous and more recent sins have been forgiven!"

Many more special qualities have been attributed to it [i.e., to voluntary ritual prayer performed on a Friday], but it would take too long to mention them all here. As we have in fact mentioned previously, in connection with other special qualities, there is another [voluntary] ritual prayer *[ṣalāt]*, appropriately performed on a Friday, in which "*Qul Huwa'llāhu Aḥad* [Say: 'He is Allāh, One!']" is recited eighteen times. So, if anyone wishes to perform such a prayer, let him perform it!

[416] Sūra 114.

[417] Q. 2:255.

[418] That is to say, the Sūra of [Divine] Help *[Sūrat an-Naṣr]* (Q. 110).

[419] Sūra 112.

8.
Concerning [voluntary] ritual prayer performed on a Saturday *[ṣalāt yawm as-sabt]*.

According to a traditional report transmitted by Saʿīd, Abū Huraira (may Allāh be well pleased with him) stated that Allāh's Messenger (Allāh bless him and give him peace) once said:

> If someone performs four [voluntary] cycles of ritual prayer *[rakaʿāt]* on a Saturday—reciting in each cycle the Opening Sūra of the Book *[Fātiḥat al-Kitāb]* one time, and "*Qul yā ayyuha 'l-kāfirūn*... [Say: 'O unbelievers...']"[420] three times—and if, when he has finished performing his ritual prayer *[ṣalāt]* and has pronounced the salutation *[sallama]*, he recites the Verse of the Throne *[Āyat al-Kursī]*[421]—for every letter [in the words of his Qur'ānic recitation] Allāh (Exalted is He) will record a Pilgrimage *[Ḥijja]* and a Visitation *[ʿUmra]* in his credit column. For every letter, He will confer upon him the merit of a whole year devoted to fasting by day and keeping vigil by night. For every letter *[ḥarf]*,[422] Allāh will grant him the spiritual reward of a martyr *[shahīd]*, and [in the Hereafter] he will be in the company of the Prophets *[Anbiyā']* and the martyrs *[shuhadā']* beneath the Heavenly Throne *[ʿArsh]*.

* * * * * * *

This brings us to the end of the Chapter concerning the special qualities of the [voluntary] ritual prayers *[ṣalawāt]* performed in the daytime on each of the days of the week.

Praise be to Allāh, the Lord of All the Worlds!
[al-ḥamdu li'llāhi Rabbi 'l-ʿālamīn].

[420] Sūra 109.

[421] Q. 2:255.

[422] The basic meaning of the term *ḥarf* (of which *ḥurūf* and *aḥruf* are plural forms) is "a letter of the Arabic alphabet." In some contexts, however, it may also signify "a connected group of Arabic letters, representing either a separate word, or, in some cases, a grammatical combination of two or more elements, only one of which can normally be written separately."

CHAPTER ELEVEN

Concerning the special qualities of [voluntary] ritual prayers *[ṣalawāt]* performed in the nighttime on each of the days of the week.[423]

1. Concerning the special quality of [voluntary] ritual prayer performed during the night of Sunday *[ṣalāt lailat al-aḥad]*.[424]

Anas ibn Mālik (may Allāh be well pleased with him) is reported as having said: "I once heard Allāh's Messenger (Allāh bless him and give him peace) say:

> "'If someone performs twenty [voluntary] cycles of ritual prayer *[ʿishrīn rakʿa]* on a Sunday night—reciting in each cycle "*Al-ḥamdu li'llāhi...* [Praise be to Allāh...']"[425] one time, "*Qul Huwa'llāhu Aḥad* [Say: 'He is Allāh, One!']"[426] fifty times, and the Two Pleas for Divine Refuge *[al-Muʿawwidhatain]*[427] three times—and if he begs forgiveness of Allāh (Glory be to Him) one hundred times, and begs forgiveness of Allāh for himself and his parents one hundred times, and invokes Allāh's blessing on the Prophet (Allāh bless him and give him peace) one hundred times, and renounces all personal claim to power and strength *[tabarra'a min al-ḥawli wa 'l-quwwa]*, and takes refuge in the power and strength of Allāh[428]—and if he then says:

[423] While some of the ritual prayers *[ṣalāwāt]* discussed in this Chapter are obligatory in themselves, the emphasis here is on their performance in congregation *[jamāʿa]*, which, while strongly recommended, is not strictly compulsory.

[424] It is important to remember that the Islāmic day (in the sense of a 24-hour period) begins at sunset. This means that the night of Sunday *[lailat al-aḥad]* begins when the sun sets on Saturday.

[425] Sura 1.

[426] Sūra 112.

[427] Sūras 113 and 114.

[428] In other words, if he declares:

There is no power,	*lā ḥawla*
nor is there any strength,	*wa lā quwwata*
except through Allāh,	*illā*
the All-High, the Almighty!	*bi'llāhi 'l-ʿAliyyi 'l-ʿAẓīm.*

I bear witness	*ashhadu an*
that there is no god but Allāh,	*lā ilāha illa 'llāh:*
and I bear witness that Adam	*wa ashhadu anna Ādama*
is the Choice of Allāh,	*Ṣafwatu 'llāhi*
and His Creation,	*wa Fiṭratu-h:*
and Abraham is the Bosom Friend	*wa Ibrāhīma*
of Allāh	*Khalīlu 'llāhi*
(Almighty and Glorious is He),	*('azza wa jall):*
and Moses is the Interlocutor	*wa Mūsā Kalīmu 'llāhi*
of Allāh (Exalted is He),	*(ta'ālā):*
and Jesus is the Spirit of Allāh	*wa 'Īsā Rūḥu 'llāhi*
(Glory be to Him),	*(subḥāna-h):*
and Muḥammad is the Beloved	*wa Muḥammadan*
of Allāh	*Ḥabību 'llāhi*
(Almighty and Glorious is He).	*('azza wa jall).*

—he will be entitled to as many grants of recompense and reward as the total figure arrived at by counting all those who call Allāh (Almighty and Glorious is He) a "Son," as well as all those who do not call Him a "Son." On the Day of Resurrection *[Yawm al-Qiyāma]*, Allāh (Exalted is He) will bring him back to life in the company of those who have nothing to fear *[al-āminīn]*, and it will be an obligation *[ḥaqq]* incumbent upon Allāh to admit him to the Garden of Paradise in the company of the Prophets *[an-Nabiyyīn]*.

2.
Concerning the special quality of [voluntary] ritual prayer performed during the night of Monday *[ṣalāt lailat al-ithnain]*.[429]

According to a traditional report, transmitted on the authority of al-A'mash, Anas ibn Malik (may Allāh be well pleased with him) stated that Allāh's Messenger (Allāh bless him and give him peace) once said:

> If someone performs four [voluntary] cycles of ritual prayer *[raka'āt]* on a Monday night—reciting in the first cycle "*Al-ḥamdu li'llāhi*... [Praise be to Allāh...']"[430] one time, and "*Qul Huwa'llāhu Aḥad* [Say: 'He is Allāh, One!']"[431] ten times, and in the second cycle "*Al-ḥamdu li'llāhi*... [Praise be to Allāh...']" one time, and "*Qul Huwa'llāhu Aḥad* [Say: 'He is Allāh, One!']" twenty times, and in the third cycle "*Al-ḥamdu li'llāhi*... [Praise be to Allāh...']" one time, and "*Qul Huwa'llāhu Aḥad* [Say: 'He is Allāh, One!']" thirty times, and in the fourth cycle "*Al-ḥamdu li'llāhi*... [Praise be to Allāh...']" one time, and "*Qul Huwa'llāhu Aḥad* [Say: 'He is Allāh, One!']" forty times—and if he then pronounces the testimony and the salutation *[tashahhada wa sallama]*, and recites "*Qul Huwa'llāhu Aḥad* [Say: 'He is Allāh, One!']" seventy-five times, and begs forgiveness of Allāh for himself and his parents seventy-five times, and invokes Allāh's blessing on the Prophet (Allāh bless him and give him peace) seventy-five times, and then asks [in his supplication] for his need to be satisfied—it will be an obligation *[ḥaqq]* incumbent upon Allāh (Exalted is He) to satisfy his need.

This is actually called the Ritual Prayer of Need *[ṣalāt al-ḥāja]*.

According to another traditional report, this transmitted on the authority of Abū Umāma (may Allāh be well pleased with him), Allāh's Messenger (Allāh bless him and give him peace) once said:

> If someone performs two [voluntary] cycles of ritual prayer *[rak'atain]* on a Monday night—reciting in the each cycle the Opening Sūra of the Book *[Fātiḥat al-Kitāb]* one time, and "*Qul Huwa'llāhu Aḥad* [Say: 'He is Allāh, One!']" fifteen times—and if he recites the Verse of the Throne *[Āyat al-Kursī]*[432] fifteen

[429] The night of Monday *[lailat al-ithnain]* begins when the sun sets on Sunday.

[430] Sūra 1.

[431] Sūra 112.

[432] Q. 2:255.

times after the salutation *[taslīm]*, and begs forgiveness of Allāh (Glorified and Exalted is He) fifteen times—Allāh (Exalted is He) will include his name among the names of those who belong to the Garden of Paradise, even if he is one of those who [would otherwise] belong to the Fire of Hell, and He will forgive him his sins of flagrant wrongdoing. For every Qur'ānic verse *[āya]* he recites, He will credit him with a Pilgrimage *[Ḥijja]* and a Visitation *['Umra]*, and if he dies between that Monday and the next Monday, he will die as a martyr *[shahīd]*.

3.
Concerning the special quality of [voluntary] ritual prayer performed during the night of Tuesday *[ṣalāt lailat ath-thalāthāʾ]*.[433]

The Prophet (Allāh bless him and give him peace) is reported as having said:

> If someone performs twelve [voluntary] cycles of ritual prayer *[ithnatai ʿasharata rakʿa]* on a Tuesday night—reciting in each cycle the Opening Sūra of the Book *[Fātiḥat al-Kitāb]* one time, and "*Idhā jāʾa naṣru 'llāhi*... [When the help of Allāh comes...']"[434] five times—Allāh (Exalted is He) will build him a house in the Garden of Paradise, and each of the dimensions of that house will be ten times the size of this lower world.

[433] The night of Tuesday *[lailat al-thalāthāʾ]* begins when the sun sets on Monday.

[434] Sūra 110.

4.
Concerning the special quality of [voluntary] ritual prayer performed during the night of Wednesday *[ṣalāt lailat al-arbaʿāʾ]*.[435]

The Prophet (Allāh bless him and give him peace) is reported as having said:

> If someone performs two [voluntary] cycles of ritual prayer *[rakʿatain]* on a Wednesday night—reciting in the first cycle the Opening Sūra of the Book *[Fātiḥat al-Kitāb]* one time, and "*Qul aʿūdhu bi-Rabbi 'l-Falaq* [Say: I take refuge with the Lord of the Daybreak']"[436] ten times, and in the second cycle the Opening Sūra of the Book *[Fātiḥat al-Kitāb]* one time, and "*Qul aʿūdhu bi-Rabbi 'n-Nās* [Say: I take refuge with the Lord of Mankind']"[437] ten times—seventy thousand angels will come down from every heaven, recording the reward in his credit column until the Day of Resurrection *[Yawm al-Qiyāma]*.

[435] The night of Wednesday *[lailat al-arbaʿāʾ]* begins when the sun sets on Tuesday.

[436] Sūra 113.

[437] Sūra 114.

5.
Concerning the special quality of [voluntary] ritual prayer performed during the night of Thursday *[ṣalāt lailat al-khamīs]*.[438]

According to another traditional report, this one transmitted on the authority of Abū Ṣāliḥ, Abū Huraira (may Allāh be well pleased with him) stated that Allāh's Messenger (Allāh bless him and give him peace) once said:

> If someone performs two [voluntary] cycles of ritual prayer *[rakʿatain]* on a Thursday night, at some point between the [obligatory prayers of] sunset *[al-maghrib]* and late evening *[al-ʿishāʾ]*—reciting in each cycle the Opening Sūra of the Book *[Fātiḥat al-Kitāb]* one time, "*Qul Huwa'llāhu Aḥad* [Say: 'He is Allāh, One!']" five times, and the Two Pleas for Divine Refuge *[al-Muʿawwidhatain]*[439] five times—and if, when he has finished performing his ritual prayer *[ṣalāt]*, he begs forgiveness of Allāh (Exalted is He) fifteen times, and donates the spiritual reward for it [his prayer] to his parents—he will have discharged his obligation to them both, even if he has been undutiful *[ʿāqq]* in his treatment of them,[440] and Allāh (Glorified and Exalted is He) will grant him the gracious favor that He bestows upon the champions of truth *[ṣiddīqīn]* and the martyrs *[shuhadāʾ]*.[441]

[438] The night of Thursday *[lailat al-khamīs]* begins when the sun sets on Wednesday.

[439] Sūras 113 and 114.

[440] As Shaikh ʿAbd al-Qādir al-Jīlānī (may Allāh be well pleased with him) has explained in Vol. 2, p. 110:

The undutiful treatment of one's parents *[ʿuqūq al-wālidain]*...may mean any or all of the following: failing to respect their solemn warnings, striking them when they speak to you reproachfully, refusing to give them something when they ask you for it, or refusing to feed them when they are hungry and begging you to feed them.

Nevertheless, as the Shaikh (may Allāh be well pleased with him) also points out in Vol. 1, p. 97:

Obedience to parents cannot go so far as to include the abandonment of obligatory religious duties *[farā'iḍ]*, such as the testimony of Islām *[ḥujjat al-islām]*, the five ritual prayers *[aṣ-ṣalāwāt al-khams]*, payment of the alms-due *[zakāt]*, an act of atonement *[kaffāra]* or the fulfillment of a solemn vow *[nadhr]*.

[441] This is an allusion to Q. 4:69.

6.
Concerning the special quality of [voluntary] ritual prayer performed during the night of Friday *[ṣalāt lailat al-jumʿa]*.[442]

According to another traditional report, this one transmitted on the authority of Jābir ibn ʿAbdi 'llāh [al-Anṣārī] (may Allāh be well pleased with him and with his father) the Prophet (Allāh bless him and give him peace) once said:

> If someone performs twelve [voluntary] cycles of ritual prayer *[ithnatai ʿasharata rakʿa]* on a Friday night, at some point between the [obligatory prayers of] sunset *[al-maghrib]* and late evening *[al-ʿishāʾ]*—reciting in each cycle the Opening Sūra of the Book *[Fātiḥat al-Kitāb]*, and "*Qul Huwa'llāhu Aḥad* [Say: 'He is Allāh, One!']" ten times—it will be as if he had devoted himself to the worshipful service of Allāh (Exalted is He) for twelve whole years, by fasting every day and keeping vigil every night throughout that time.

According to yet another traditional report, this one transmitted on the authority of Kathīr ibn Salama, Anas ibn Mālik (may Allāh be well pleased with him) stated that Allāh's Messenger (Allāh bless him and give him peace) once said:

> If, on a Friday night, someone performs the [obligatory] late evening ritual prayer *[ṣalāt al-ʿishāʾ al-ākhira]* in a congregation *[jamāʿa]*, and follows it with the performance of the two cycles of customary prayer *[rakʿatayi 's-sunna]*, then goes on to perform ten cycles [of additional, voluntary] prayer—reciting in each cycle "*Al-ḥamdu li'llāhi...* [Praise be to Allāh...']"[443] one time, "*Qul Huwa'llāhu Aḥad* [Say: 'He is Allāh, One!']"[444] one time, and the Two Pleas for Divine Refuge *[al-Muʿawwidhatain]*[445] one time each—and if he then performs a *witr*[446] prayer of three cycles, and sleeps on his right side, with his face turned toward the *Qibla* [the direction of the Kaʿba in Mecca]—it will be as if he had kept vigil throughout the Night of Power *[Lailat al-Qadr]*.

[442] The night of Friday *[lailat al-jumʿa]* begins when the sun sets on Thursday.

[443] Sūra 1.

[444] Sūra 112.

[445] Sūras 113 and 114.

[446] See note 50 on p. 42 above.

The Prophet (Allāh bless him and give him peace) also said:

> Invoke Allāh's blessing upon me, many times over, in the course of the illustrious night *[al-lailat al-gharrā']*, and during the brightly shining day *[al-yawm al-azhar]*—on the night of Friday, the Day of Congregational Prayer *[Lailat al-Jum'a]*, and then on the Day itself.

7.
Concerning the special quality of [voluntary] ritual prayer performed during the night of Saturday *[ṣalāt lailat as-sabt]*.[447]

According to a traditional report transmitted on the authority of Anas ibn Mālik (may Allāh be well pleased with him), the Prophet (Allāh bless him and give him peace) once said:

> If someone performs twelve [voluntary] cycles of ritual prayer *[ithnatai ʿasharata rakʿa]* on a Saturday night, at some point between the [obligatory prayers of] sunset *[al-maghrib]* and late evening *[al-ʿishāʾ]*, Allāh (Exalted is He) will build a palatial mansion for him in the Garden of Paradise. It will be as if he had made a charitable donation *[taṣaddaqa]* to every believing man and woman *[muʾmin wa muʾmina]*. He will be uncontaminated by the errors of Judaism *[al-Yahūdiyya]*, and it will be an obligation *[ḥaqq]* incumbent upon Allāh to grant him forgiveness.

[447] The night of Saturday *[lailat as-sabt]* begins when the sun sets on Friday.

A reminder concerning the importance of fulfilling one's obligatory religious duties *[farā'iḍ]* before engaging in the performance of supererogatory devotions *[nawāfil]*; and before performing supererogatory devotions *[nawāfil]* with the intention of making up for previous omissions in the performance of obligatory religious duties *[farā'iḍ]*.

We have already discussed this topic in the Discourse on Repentance *[Majlis at-Tawba]*,[448] as well as elsewhere in the course of this book, but the following points deserve to be reiterated here:

The worshipper's first priority must be the complete and proper performance of all obligatory religious duties *[farā'iḍ]* and customary observances *[sunan]*. After these have been discharged, and only then, he may engage in supererogatory devotions *[nawāfil]*, whether these be connected with ritual prayer *[ṣalāt]*, fasting *[ṣiyām]*, charitable donation *[ṣadaqa]*, or any of the various forms of worshipful service *['ibādāt]*.

In all his acts of worshipful service *['ibādāt]*, of whatever type they may be, his conscious intention should be to fulfill the strict obligations *[farā'iḍ]* that are incumbent upon him. Thus, with respect to all these [voluntary] ritual prayers *[ṣalāwāt]* we have mentioned, as being appropriate to the various nights and days of the week, the worshipper should perform them with the intention of making up *[qaḍā']* for previous omissions. He will thereby acquit himself of outstanding duty *[farḍ]*, and he will also obtain additional merit *[faḍl]*. Allāh (Exalted is He) will combine the two, through His grace, His mercy, and His noble generosity.

[448] Shaikh 'Abd al-Qādir al-Jīlānī (may Allāh be well pleased with him) is referring to the Third Discourse of the present work. (See Vol. 2, pp. 105–208.)

Finally, once he has really and truly acquitted himself of strictly obligatory duties *[farā'iḍ]*, the worshipper may legitimately intend *[yanwī]* his performance of all that [additional worship] to be a purely supererogatory devotion *[nāfila]*.

* * * * * * *

This brings us to the end of the Chapter concerning the special qualities of the [voluntary] ritual prayers *[ṣalawāt]* performed in the nighttime on each of the days of the week.

Praise be to Allāh, the Lord of All the Worlds!
[al-ḥamdu li'llāhi Rabbi 'l-'ālamīn].

CHAPTER TWELVE

Concerning certain special ritual prayers *[ṣalawāt]*, namely:

1. The ritual prayer of glorification *[ṣalāt at tasbīḥ]*.
2. The ritual prayer for guidance in choosing the best option *[ṣalāt al-istikhāra]*.
3. The ritual prayer for sufficient protection *[ṣalāt al-kifāya]*.
4. The ritual prayer for one's adversaries in litigation *[ṣalāt al-khuṣamāʾ]*.
5. The ritual prayer of those who are emancipated [from the Fire of Hell] in the month of Shawwāl *[ṣalāt al-ʿutaqāʾ fī Shawwāl]*.
6. The ritual prayer for the removal of the torment of the tomb *[aṣ-ṣalāt li-rafʿ ʿadhāb al-qabr]*.
7. The ritual prayer for help in time of need *[ṣalāt al-ḥāja]*.

1.
Concerning the special merit of the ritual prayer of glorification *[ṣalāt at-tasbīḥ]*.[449]

As for the special quality of the ritual prayer of glorification *[ṣalāt at-tasbīḥ]*, we learn from a traditional report, transmitted [by a chain of reliable authorities][450] from Ibn ʿAbbās (may Allāh be well pleased with him and with his father), that Allāh's Messenger (Allāh bless him and give him peace) once said to al-ʿAbbās ibn ʿAbdi'l-Muṭṭālib (may Allāh be well pleased with him):

> O ʿAbbās, my dear uncle! I really must give you a gift! I really must make you a present! I really must do you a favor! I really must let you know about ten special practices *[khiṣāl]*, for, if you carry them out, Allāh will forgive you your sin, the first and the last of it, the old and the new, the unintentional and the deliberate, the small and the great, the private and the public.
>
> You must perform four cycles of ritual prayer *[rakaʿāt]*, reciting in each cycle the Opening Sūra of the Book *[Fātiḥat al-Kitāb]* and one other Sūra.
>
> When you have finished the Qurʾānic recitation in the first cycle *[rakʿa]*, and while you are still standing erect, you must say—fifteen times:
>
> | | |
> |---|---|
> | Glory be to Allāh, | *subḥāna 'llāhi* |
> | and praise be to Allāh, | *wa 'l-ḥamdu li'llāhi* |
> | and there is no god but Allāh, | *wa lā ilāha illa 'llāhu* |
> | and Allāh is Supremely Great! | *wa 'llāhu Akbar.* |
>
> Then you must perform the act of bowing, pronouncing it [the same affirmation] ten times while you are in the posture of bowing *[rākiʿ]*.

[449] The verbal noun *tasbīḥ* is derived from the three-consonant root *s–b–ḥ*, which occurs in the expression "*subḥāna 'llāh* [Glory be to Allāh]!"

[450] ***Author's note:*** This report was conveyed to us by Shaikh Abū Naṣr Muḥammad ibn al-Bannāʾ, on the authority of his father, Shaikh Abū ʿAlī ibn Aḥmad ibn ʿAbdi 'llāh ibn al-Bannāʾ, who cited the following chain of transmission *[isnād]*: **Abu'l-Fatḥ Muḥammad ibn Aḥmad ibn Abi 'l-Fawāris and Abū Muḥammad al-Ḥasan ibn Muḥammad al-Khallāl** [the Vinegar Merchant]—**Abū Ḥafṣ ʿUmar ibn Aḥmad al-Wāʿiẓ** [the Preacher]—**ʿAbdu'llāh ibn Muḥammad al-Baghawī—Isḥāq ibn Abī Isrāʾīl—Mūsā ibn ʿAbdi'l-ʿAzīz—al-Ḥakam ibn Abbān—ʿIkrima—Ibn ʿAbbās** (may Allāh be well pleased with him and with his father—**al-ʿAbbās ibn ʿAbdi 'l-Muṭṭālib** (may Allāh be well pleased with him)—**the Prophet** (Allāh bless him and give him peace).

> Then you must raise your head from the act of bowing *[rak'a]*,[451] and pronounce it ten times.
>
> Then you must perform the act of prostration, and pronounce it ten times.
>
> Then you must raise your head from the posture of prostration *[sujūd]*, and pronounce it ten times.
>
> Then you must perform the [second] act of prostration, and pronounce it ten times.
>
> Then you must raise your head from the posture of prostration *[sujūd]*, and pronounce it ten times.
>
> That all adds up to a total of seventy-five in each cycle *[rak'a]*. You must do the same in all four cycles *[raka'āt]*.
>
> If you are able to perform this special prayer once every day, then do so. If you cannot do it that often, then once every Friday [the Day of Congregation]. If you cannot do it that often, then once every month. If you cannot do it that often, then once every year. If you cannot do it that often, then at least once in your lifetime.

According to another version of this report, the Qur'ānic recitation should be:

> In the first cycle: the Opening Sūra of the Book *[Fātiḥat al-Kitāb]* and "*Sabbiḥi 'sma Rabbi-ka 'l-A'lā*... [Glorify the Name of your Lord the Most High...]."[452]
>
> In the second cycle: the Opening Sūra of the Book *[Fātiḥat al-Kitāb]* and "*Idhā zulzilat*... [When (the earth) is shaken...]."[453]
>
> In the third cycle: the Opening Sūra of the Book *[Fātiḥat al-Kitāb]* and "*Qul yā ayyuha 'l-kāfirūn*... [Say: 'O you unbelievers...']."[456]
>
> In the fourth cycle: the Opening Sūra of the Book *[Fātiḥat al-Kitāb]* and "*Qul Huwa 'llāhu Aḥad* [Say: 'He is Allāh, One!']"[457]

According to yet another traditional report,[458] the Prophet (Allāh bless him and give him peace) once said to Ja'far ibn Abī Ṭālib (may Allāh be well pleased with him):

> I really must make you a present! I really must do you a favor! I really must give you a gift!

(Our informant went on to quote the rest of the report *[ḥadīth]*.)

[451] In this instance, the term *rak'a* is applied specifically to the act of bowing, rather than to the whole "cycle" of which it constitutes a major element. (See note 246 on p. 180 above.)

[452] Sūra 87.

[453] Sūra 99.

[454] Sūra 109.

[455] Sūra 112.

[456] ***Author's note:*** This report was conveyed to us by Shaikh Abū Naṣr Muḥammad ibn al-Bannā', on the authority of his father, Shaikh Abū 'Alī ibn Aḥmad ibn 'Abdi 'llāh ibn al-Bannā', complete with its chain of transmission *[isnād]*.

2.
Concerning the ritual prayer for guidance in choosing the best option *[ṣalāt al-istikhāra]*, and the prayer of supplication *[duʿāʾ]* appropriate to it.

According to a traditional report transmitted on the authority of Muḥammad ibn al-Munkadir, it was Jābir ibn ʿAbdi'llāh (may Allāh be well pleased with him and with his father) who said:

"Allāh's Messenger (Allāh bless him and give him peace) used to teach us how to seek guidance in choosing the best option available in a practical enterprise *[al-istikhāra fi 'l-amr]*, just as he would sometimes teach us a Chapter *[Sūra]* from the Qurʾān:

> "'If one of you is concerned about some practical undertaking, or about making plans for a journey, he should perform two cycles of ritual prayer *[rakʿatain]*, not as an obligatory observance *[farīḍa]*, but voluntarily. Then he should say:

"'O Allāh, I ask You to show me	*Allāhumma innī*
what is best, through Your knowledge,	*astakhīru-ka bi-ʿilmi-ka*
and I ask You to empower me,	*wa astaqdiru-ka*
through Your power,	*bi-qudrati-ka*
and I beg You to grant me	*wa asʾalu-ka*
Your tremendous favor,	*min faḍli-ka 'l-ʿaẓīm:*
for You have power,	*fa-inna-ka taqdiru*
while I am without power,	*wa lā aqdiru*
and You have knowledge,	*wa taʿlamu*
while I am without knowledge,	*wa lā aʿlamu*
and You are the One who knows	*wa Anta*
all things invisible.	*ʿAllāmu 'l-ghuyūb:*
O Allāh, if You know that this	*Allāhumma in kunta taʿlamu*
undertaking[457] is in the best interests	*anna hādha 'l-amra khairun lī*
of my religion, my life in this world,	*fī dīnī wa dunyāya*
and my life in the Hereafter,	*wa ākhiratī*
and can yield successful results in both	*wa ʿāqibati amrī*
the short term and the long term,	*wa ʿājili-hi wa ājili-h:*

[457] An instruction is inserted at this point in the Arabic text, to the effect that the supplicant should state the exact nature of the proposed undertaking.

then make it possible for me
and make it easy for me,
and then bless me in it.

fa-'qdir-hu lī
wa yassir-hu lī
thumma bārik lī fī-h:

If not, then turn it away from me,
and make it easy for me to do well,
wherever I may happen to be, and
make me content with Your verdict,
O Most Merciful of the merciful.'"

wa illā fa-'ṣrif-hu ʿan-nī
wa yassir liya 'l-khaira
ḥaithu kāna mā kuntu
wa raḍḍi-nī bi-qaḍāʾi-ka
yā Arḥama 'r-rāḥimīn:

2a.
Prayers of supplication *[ad'iya]* to be offered at the start of a journey and during the course of one's travels.[458]

As soon as someone has made a definite decision to embark on a journey away from home, whether it be a business expedition, a Pilgrimage *[Ḥajj]*, or a visit, he should say, immediately after performing the two cycles of ritual prayer *[rak'atain]*:

O Allāh, I intend to set set out	*Allāhumma innī urīdu 'l-khurūja*
on this expedition of mine	*fī wajhī hādha*
with no reliance on anyone	*bi-lā thiqati min-nī*
other than You,	*bi-ghairi-k:*
and no expectation	*wa lā rajā'i*
of anyone but You.	*illā bi-k:*
In no power do I place my trust,	*wa lā quwwati atawakkalu 'alai-hā:*
and to no stratagem do I resort,	*wa lā ḥīlati alja'u ilai-hā*
apart from seeking	*illā ṭalabi*
Your gracious favor,	*faḍli-k:*
and applying for Your kindness	*wa 't-ta'arruḍi li-ma'rūfi-ka*
and Your mercy,	*wa raḥmati-k:*
and relying on the value	*wa 's-sukūni ilā ḥusni*
of serving You well.	*'ibādati-k:*
You know best,	*wa Anta*
through Your foreknowledge,	*A'lamu bi-mā*
what has been predestined for me	*qad sabaqa lī fī 'ilmi-k:*
in this expedition of mine—	*fī wajhī hādha*
both what I like and what I dislike.	*mim-mā uḥibbu wa akrah:*
O Allāh, avert from me therefore,	*Allāhumma fa-'ṣrif 'an-nī*
through Your power,	*bi-qudrati-ka*
all possibilities of disaster,	*maqādīra kulli balā':*
and dispel from me	*wa naffis 'an-nī*
all trouble and sickness,	*kulla karbin wa dā':*

[653] In an earlier Chapter of the present work, where he has devoted a lengthy subsection to the good manners to be observed when traveling *[ādāb as-safar]*, Shaikh 'Abd al-Qādir al-Jīlānī (may Allāh be well pleased with him) has also recommended certain traditional prayers of supplication *[ad'iya]*, which differ in some respects from those provided here. (See Vol. 1, pp. 85–90.)

and spread over me	*wa 'bsuṭ ʿalayya*
a wing of Your mercy,	*kanafan min raḥmati-ka*
a gracious gift of Your help,	*wa luṭfan min ʿawni-ka*
a shield of Your safekeeping,	*wa ḥirzan min ḥifẓi-ka*
and every form of Your protection.	*wa jamīʿa muʿāfāti-k.*

Then he should load up his luggage and start out on his journey, saying as he does so:

O my Lord, Your verdict on me	*yā Rabbi qaḍāʾu-ka ʿalayya*
is sure to be realized.	*ḥaqīqa:*
Let my expectation turn out well,	*aḥsin amalī*
and protect me	*wa 'dfaʿ*
from that of which I am wary,	*ʿan-nī mā aḥdhiru*
of which You are More Aware	*mim-mā Anta Aʿlamu*
than I,	*bi-hi min-nī:*
and cause that to be good for me,	*wa 'jʿal dhālika khairan lī*
for the sake of my religion	*fī dīnī*
and my life hereafter.	*wa ākhiratī:*
I beseech You, O my Lord,	*asʾalu-ka yā Rabbi*
to deputize for me	*an takhlufa-nī*
by taking care	*fī mā khalaftu*
of those I have left behind—	*warāʾī*
my wife,	*min ahlī*
my children and my close relatives—	*wa wuldī wa qarābatī*
with the best caretaking	*bi-aḥsani mā*
You ever performed	*khalafta bi-hi*
for any believer away from home,	*ghāʾiban*
in order to ensure the chastity	*mina 'l-muʾminīna*
of every genital organ.	*fī taḥṣīni kulli ʿawra:*
[I beg You] to provide protection	*wa ḥifẓan*
from every cause of harm,	*min kulli maḍarra:*
to satisfy every serious concern,	*wa kifāyata kulli muhimm:*
to ward off everything	*wa ṣarfa kulli*
that is repugnant,	*makrūh:*
and to grant me	*wa kamāla mā*
a perfect combination	*tajmaʿu lī bi-hi*
of all that contributes	*mina 'r-riḍā*
to my contentment	*wa 's-surūri*
and happiness in this world	*fi 'd-dunyā*
and the Hereafter.	*wa 'l-ākhira.*
Then grant that	*thumma 'rzuq-nī*
I may acknowledge all of that	*fī dhālika kulli-hi*
by showing gratitude to You,	*shukra-ka*
by remembering You,	*wa dhikra-ka*
and by serving You well,	*wa ḥusna ʿibādati-k:*
so that You will approve of me	*ḥattā tarḍā ʿan-nī*
and cause me to enter	*wa tudkhila-nī*

Your Garden of Paradise,	*jannata-k:*
through Your mercy	*bi-raḥmati-ka*
after that approval	*ba'da 'r-riḍā:*
O Most Merciful of the merciful.	*yā Arḥama 'r-rāḥimīn:*

He should repeat the following prayer of supplication *[du'ā']* frequently in the course of his travels, for the Prophet (Allāh bless him and give him peace) used to utter it frequently:

Praise be to Allāh, who created me,	*al-ḥamdu li'llāhi 'lladhī khalqa-nī:*
though I was a thing	*wa lam aku shai'an*
of no importance.	*madhkūrā:*
O Allāh,	*Allāhumma*
help me to face the terrors	*a'in-nī 'alā*
of this world,	*ahāwīli 'd-dunyā*
and the calamities of the ages,	*wa bawā'iqi 'd-duhūri*
and the misfortunes	*wa maṣā'ibi 'l-*
of the nights and the days,	*layālī wa 'l-ayyām:*
and guard me from the wickedness	*wa 'kfi-nī sharra*
of what the tyrants do.	*mā ya'malu 'ẓ-ẓālimūn:*
O Allāh, accompany me therefore	*Allāhumma fī safarī*
in my journey, and deputize for me	*fa-'ṣḥab-nī*
in looking after my family,	*wa fī ahlī fa-'khluf-nī:*
and bless me	*wa fī-mā razaqta-nī*
in what You have provided for me,	*fa-bārik lī:*
and make me humble in myself,	*wa fī nafsī fa-dhallil-nī:*
and exalt me in the eyes	*wa fī a'yuni 'n-nāsi*
of other people,	*fa-'aẓẓim-nī:*
and reform me in my character	*wa fī khulqī fa-qawwim-nī:*
and make me dear, O my Lord, to You.	*wa ilai-ka yā Rabbi fa-ḥabbib-nī:*
I take refuge	*a'ūdhu*
with Your Noble Countenance,	*bi-Wajhi-ka 'l-karīmi 'lladhī*
by which the heavens	*ushriqat*
have been made to shine,	*bi-hi 's-samāwāt:*
and the darknesses	*wa kushifat*
have been dispelled,	*bi-hi 'ẓ-ẓulumāt:*
and the welfare of the ancients	*wa ṣaluḥa 'alai-hi*
and the moderns has been assured,	*amru 'l-awwalīna wa 'l-ākhirīn:*
so that You will not cause Your anger	*an lā tuḥilla 'alayya*
to alight upon me,	*ghaḍaba-k:*
and so that You will not	*wa lā*
make me suffer	*tunzila bī*
Your displeasure.	*sukhṭa-k:*
To You belongs the credit	*la-ka 'l-'utbā*
for whatever I have been able to do,	*fī-ma 'staṭa't:*
and there is no power,	*wa lā ḥawla*

nor any strength,	*wa lā quwwata*
except through You.	*illā bi-k:*
O Allāh, I take refuge with You	*Allāhumma innī aʿūdhu bi-ka*
from hardship on the journey,	*min waʿthāʾi 's-safar:*
and from trouble on the way home,	*wa kaʾābati 'l-munqalab:*
and from depletion after plenty,	*wa mina 'l-ḥawri baʿda 'l-kawr:*
and the claim of one	*wa daʿwati 'l-*
who has been wronged.	*maẓlūm:*
O Allāh, make the distance	*Allāhumma 'ṭwi*
seem short to us,	*la-na 'l-arḍa*
and make the journey	*wa hawwin*
a smooth one for us	*ʿalai-na 's-safar.*
I beg You to convey	*asʾalu-ka*
a communication	*balāghan*
that conveys a blessing from You,	*yuballighu khairan*
and forgiveness	*wa maghfiratan*
and a sign of approval.	*wa riḍwānā.*
I beg You to grant me	*asʾalu-ka 'l-khaira*
all that is good,	*kulla-h:*
You are indeed Powerful	*inna-ka ʿalā*
over all things.	*kulli shaiʾin Qadīr.*

At the moment of departure from the place where he has made a halt, the traveler should say:

In the Name of Allāh,	*Bismi'llāhi*
I put my trust in Allāh,	*tawakkaltu ʿala 'llāh:*
and there is no power,	*wa lā ḥawla*
nor any strength,	*wa lā quwwata*
except through Allāh.	*illā bi'llāhi.*

—for, according to the traditional report *[khabar]*, he will then be told:

You are protected,	*wuqīta*
guarded and shielded.	*wa kufīta wa ḥumīt.*

On mounting his riding camel *[rāḥila]*, he should say:

Allāh is Supremely Great!	*Allāhu Akbar.*

—three times, and:

Praise be to Allāh!	*al-ḥamdu li'llāh.*

—also three times. Then he should say:

Glory to the One who has made	*subḥāna 'lladhī sakhkhara*
this subservient for us (to use),	*la-nā hādha*

for we would not have been equal to the task. (43:13)	*wa mā kunnā* *la-hu muqrinīn.*
Glory be to You! There is no god but You. I have wronged myself, so forgive me. No one can forgive sins except You.	*subḥāna-ka* *lā ilāha illā Ant:* *ẓalamtu nafsī* *fa-'ghfir lī: inna-hu* *lā yaghfiru 'dh-dhunūba* *illā Ant.*

—because this practice is traditionally attributed to the Prophet (Allāh bless him and give him peace).

According to the tradition *[ḥadīth]* of Ibn ʿUmar (may Allāh be well pleased with him and with his father), whenever the Prophet (Allāh bless him and give him peace) went traveling, he used to say, when he mounted his means of transport:

O Allāh, I beg You to let me practice true devotion in the course of this journey, and behavior that is pleasing to You.	*Allāhumma* *innī as'alu-ka* *fī safarī* *hādha 't-tuqā:*[459] *wa mina 'l-ʿamali* *mā tarḍā:*
O Allāh, make the journey a smooth one for us, and make the distance seem short to us.	*Allāhumma* *hawwin* *ʿalai-na 's-safar:* *wa 'ṭwi la-na* *buʿda 'l-arḍ:*
O Allāh, You are the Companion on the journey, and the Deputy in charge of the family [left at home].	*Allāhumma Anta 'ṣ-Ṣāḥibu* *fi 's-safar:* *wa 'l-Khalīfatu* *fi 'l-ahl:*
O Allāh, keep us company on our journey, and deputize for us in the interest of our family.	*Allāhumma 'ṣḥab-nā* *fī safari-nā:* *wa 'khluf-nā* *fī ahli-nā:*

Ibn Juraij added the words:

I take refuge with You from hardship on the journey, and from trouble on the way home,	*innī aʿūdhu bi-ka* *min waʿthā'i 's-safar:* *wa sū'i 'l-munqalab:*

[459] The Arabic noun *tuqan* (pronounced *at-tuqā* when the definite article *al-* is prefixed to it) is virtually synonymous with *taqwā* [true devotion], the subject to which Shaikh ʿAbd al-Qādir al-Jīlānī (may Allāh be well pleased with him) has devoted the Fourth Discourse of the present work. (See Vol. 2, pp. 209–303.)

and from finding	*wa ka'ābati 'l-*
that things look bad	*manẓari*
where my family	*fi 'l-ahli*
and property are concerned.	*wa 'l-māl:*

Whenever the traveler proposes to enter a village or a town, it is appropriate for him to say what the Prophet (Allāh bless him and give him peace) is reported as having said, namely:

O Allāh,	*Allāhumma*
Lord of the seven heavens	*Rabba 's-samāwāti 's-sab'i*
and all that they overshadow,	*wa mā aẓlalna:*
Lord of the devils	*wa Rabba 'sh-shayāṭīna*
and all that they lead astray,	*wa mā aḍlalna:*
I beg You to grant me the goodness	*as'alu-ka min khairi*
of this village,	*hādhihi 'l-qaryati*
and the goodness of its people,	*wa khairi ahli-hā*
and the best of what it contains.	*wa khairi mā fī-hā:*
I take refuge with You from its evil,	*wa a'ūdhu bi-ka min sharri-hā*
and the evil of its people,	*wa sharri ahli-hā*
and the worst of what it contains.	*wa sharri mā fī-hā:*
I beg You to grant me	*as'alu-ka*
the loving friendship	*mawaddata*
of the very best of them.	*khiyāri-him:*
and to keep me from having to deal	*wa an tajnuba-nī*
with the worst of the worst of them.	*min sharri ashrāri-him.*

2b.
More traditional reports concerning prayers of supplication *[adʿiya]* for the protection of the traveler.

For safe refuge from every thief, predatory animal, and harmful nuisance, the traveler should offer the following prayer of supplication *[duʿāʾ]*:

O Allāh, keep watch over us	*Allāhumma 'ḥrus-nā*
with Your eye that never sleeps,[460]	*bi-ʿain-ka 'llatī lā tanām:*
and protect us with Your support	*wa 'kfi-nā bi-rukn-ka 'lladhī*
that cannot be dislodged,	*lā yurām:*
and mercifully shield us	*wa 'rḥam-nā*
with Your power.	*bi-qudrati-ka ʿalai-nā*
that we may not perish,	*lā nahlik*
for You are our hope.	*wa Anta rajāʾu-nā.*

[The Caliph] ʿUthmān ibn ʿAffān (may Allāh be well pleased with him) is reported as having said: "I once heard Allāh's Messenger (Allāh bless him and give him peace) say:

"'If someone says, three times, in the first part of the night:

In the Name of Allāh,	*bismi 'llāhi*
in the presence of whose Name	*'lladhī lā yaḍurru*
there is nothing on earth or in	*maʿa 'smi-hi shaiʾun fi 'l-arḍi*
heaven that can cause any harm,	*wa lā fi 's-samāʾ:*
for He is the All-Hearing,	*wa Huwa 's-Samīʿu 'l-*
the All-Knowing.	*ʿAlīm.*

—no sudden calamity will afflict that person before he wakes up in the morning.'"

According to Abū Yūsuf al-Khurāsānī, it was Abū Saʿīd ibn Abi 'r-Rawḥāʾ who recounted the following experience:

"I had lost my way one night on the road to Mecca, when I heard the sound of a voice behind me. I was terrified, so I listened to it—and it was reciting the Qurʾān! Then it caught up with me and said: 'Do you

[460] This is an allusion to Q. 2:255.

consider yourself lost?' 'Yes,' said I, so it went on to ask: 'Shall I teach you something to say when you are lost, so that you will be guided aright, or when you are lonely, so that you will find yourself in good company, or when you are suffering from insomnia, so that you will be able to get off to sleep?' 'Oh yes,' I replied, so the voice told me to say:

In the Name of Allāh,	*bismi'llāhi*
the All-Competent,	*Dhi 'sh-sha'n:*
Sublime in the demonstration	*'Aẓīmi 'l-*
of theTruth,	*burhān:*
Stern in the wielding of authority.	*Shadīdi 's-sulṭān.*
Every day He is about	*kulla yawmin Huwa*
some awesome business.[461]	*fī sha'n.*
I take refuge with Allāh	*a'ūdhu bi'llāhi*
from Satan.	*mina 'sh-shaiṭān.*
Whatever Allāh wills,	*mā shā'a*
comes into being.[462]	*'llāhu kān.*
There is no power,	*lā ḥawla*
nor is there any strength,	*wa lā quwwata*
except through Allāh.	*illā bi'llāh.*

"So I said it, and lo and behold, my companions turned out to be close by! Then I looked for the man, but I could not find him anywhere."

Abū Bilāl, who is one of the respected narrators of tradition *[ruwāt al-ḥadīth]*, remarked:

"I once lost contact with my family at Minā,[463] so I said this, then turned to look in a certain direction—and there I was, reunited with my family!"

According to Abu 'd-Dardā' (may Allāh be well pleased with him), Allāh's Messenger (Allāh bless him and give him peace) once said:

If someone says, seven times each day:

My Protecting Friend is Allāh,	*inna Waliyyiya 'llāhu 'lladhī*
who has sent down the Book,	*nazzala 'l-Kitāba*
and He befriends	*wa Huwa*
and protects the righteous.[464]	*yatawalla 'ṣ-ṣāliḥīn.*
Allāh is enough for me;	*ḥasbiya 'llāhu*
there is no god but He.	*lā ilāha illā Hū:*
In Him I have put my trust,	*'alai-hi tawakkaltu*
for He is the Lord	*wa Huwa Rabbu 'l-*
of the Mighty Throne.[465]	*'arshi 'l-'aẓīm.*

461 This sentence is a direct quotation from the Qur'ān (55:29).

462 This sentence is an allusion to several verses *[āyāt]* of the Qur'ān, including Q. 2:117.

463 Minā is a valley near Mecca, where some of the rites of the Pilgrimage *[Ḥajj]* are conducted.

464 This is a direct quotation from the Qur'ān (7:196).

465 This is a also direct quotation from the Qur'ān (9:129).

—Allāh (Exalted is He) will provide that person with a satisfactory solution to whatever happens to be troubling him, regardless of whether he is honest or deceitful, if Allāh (Exalted is He) so wills.

The following saying *[ḥadīth]* is also attributed to the Prophet (Allāh bless him and give him peace):

If someone says, while in distress:

There is no god but Allāh,	*lā ilāha illa 'llāhu 'l-*
the All-Forbearing, the All-Generous,	*Ḥalīmu 'l-Karīm:*
Glory be to Allāh,	*subḥāna 'llāhi*
the Lord of the Mighty Throne.	*Rabbi 'l-ʿArshi 'l-ʿAẓīm:*
Praise be to Allāh,	*al-ḥamdu li'llāhi*
the Lord of All the Worlds.	*Rabbi 'l-ʿĀlamīn.*

—he will be relieved of his distress, with the permission of Allāh (Exalted is He).

3.
Concerning the ritual prayer for sufficient protection *[ṣalāt al-kifāya]*.[466]

The ritual prayer for sufficient protection *[ṣalāt al-kifāya]* consists of two cycles *[rakʿatān]*, which may be performed at any time whatsoever. In each cycle *[rakʿa]*, the worshipper must recite the Opening Sūra of the Book *[Fātiḥa]* one time, "*Qul Huwa'llāhu Aḥad* [Say: 'He is Allāh, One!']" [467] ten times, and:

Allāh will give you	*fa-sa-yakfī-*
sufficient protection against them;	*ka-humu 'llāh:*
He is the All-Hearing,	*wa Huwa 's-Samīʿu 'l-*
the All-Knowing. (2:137)	*ʿAlīm.*

—fifty times. Then, having pronounced the salutation, he should offer the following prayer of supplication *[duʿāʾ]*:

O Allāh! O All-Merciful One!	*yā Allāh: yā Raḥmān:*
O Most Beneficent One!	*yā Mannān:*
O Most Compassionate One!	*yā Ḥannān:*
O You who are glorified	*yā Musabbaḥan*
in every tongue!	*bi-kulli lisān:*
O You whose hands are extended,	*yā Man yadā-hu*
offering all that is good!	*bi'l-khairi mabsūṭatān:*
O Protector of Muḥammad	*yā Kāfiya Muḥammadan*
(Allāh bless him and give him peace)	*(ṣalla 'llāhu'alai-hi wa sallam)*
from the confederates![468]	*al-aḥzāb:*

[466] The word *kifāya* is one of many Arabic terms for which it is hard, if not impossible, to find a satisfactory one-word equivalent in English. The basic idea conveyed by the root *k–f–y* is "enough; sufficient," and "sufficiency" is sometimes an adequate translation of *kifāya*. In certain contexts, however, the meaning is "sufficient protection," or even "spiritual protection" (which is ultimately sufficient for the believer, whatever suffering he or she may be exposed to in the outer life).

[467] Sūra 112.

[468] As explained by Yūsuf ʿAlī in his commentary on his translation of the Qur'ān (33:1): "The fifth year A.H. was a critical year in the external history of early Islam.... The Grand Confederacy against Islam came and invested Medina and failed utterly. It consisted of the Meccan Unbelievers, the desert Arabs of Central Arabia, the Jews previously expelled for treachery from Medina, the Jews remaining in Medina, and the Hypocrites led by ʿAbdullāh ibn Ubai."

The Day of [the Battle with] the Confederates *[Yawm al-Aḥzāb]* is also known as *Yawm al-Khandaq* [the Day, or Battle, of the Trench or Moat].

O Protector of Abraham (peace be upon him) from the fires!	*wa yā Kāfiya Ibrāhīma* *(ʿalai-hi 's-salām) an-nīrān:*
O Protector of Moses (peace be upon him) from Pharaoh!	*yā Kāfiya Mūsā* *(ʿalai-hi 's-salām)* *Firʿawn:*
O Protector of Jesus (peace be upon him) from the cruel tyrants!	*yā Kāfiya ʿĪsā* *(ʿalai-hi 's-salām)* *al-jabābira:*
O Protector of Noah (peace be upon him) from drowning [in the Flood]!	*wa yā Kāfiya Nūḥan* *(ʿalai-hi 's-salām)* *al-gharaq:*
O Protector of Lot (peace be upon him) from the lewdness of his people!	*wa yā Kāfiya Lūṭan* *(ʿalai-hi 's-salām)* *fuḥsha qawmi-h:*
O Protector from everything, but from Whom nothing can be protected!	*yā Kāfiya min kulli shaiʾin* *wa lā* *yukfā min-hu shaiʾ:*
O Protector of ʿĀʾisha[670] (may Allāh be well pleased with her) and of Āsiya![671]	*yā Kāfiya ʿĀʾishata* *(raḍiya 'llāhu ʿan-hā)* *wa Āsiya:*
Protect me from mighty affliction due to anything at all, so that, with Your Mighty Name "the Almighty," I may have nothing whatsoever to fear and dread.	*ikfi-nī ʿaẓīma 'l-balāʾi* *min kulli shaiʾin* *ḥattā lā akhāfa wa lā akhshā* *maʿa 'smi-ka 'l-ʿaẓīmi 'l-aʿẓami* *shaiʾā.*

469 As Shaikh ʿAbd al-Qādir al-Jīlānī (may Allāh be well pleased with him) has explained in Vol. 1, p. 267:

> We hold a good opinion of all the wives of the Prophet (Allāh bless him and give him peace). We firmly believe that they are the Mothers of the Believers *[Ummahāt al-Muʾminīn]*, and that ʿĀʾisha (may Allāh be well pleased with her) is one of the most excellent women in the entire universe. Allāh (Exalted is He) has declared her completely innocent of the charges [of marital infidelity] brought against her by the renegades, as we read [in the Qurʾān] and as people will go on reading until the Day of Judgment *[Yawm ad-Dīn]*. *

* This is a reference to the words of Allāh (Exalted is He):

Those who spread the slander are a gang among you. (24:11) They are liars in the sight of Allāh. (24:13)	*inna 'lladhīna jāʾū bi'l-ifki* *ʿuṣbatun min-kum:* *fa-ulāʾika ʿinda 'llāhi humu 'l-kādhibūn.*

470 The lady Āsiya (may Allāh bestow His mercy upon her) maintained her faith in the One Almighty God in the face of cruel torment, inflicted by her husband, Pharaoh. She is mentioned, though not by name, in Q. 66:11.

4.
Concerning the ritual prayer for one's adversaries in litigation *[ṣalāt al-khuṣamā᾿]*.

The ritual prayer for one's adversaries in litigation *[ṣalāt al-khuṣamā᾿]* consists of four cycles *[raka῾āt]*, with only one salutation *[taslīma]*.

In the first cycle, the worshipper must recite the Opening Sūra of the Book *[Fātiḥat al-Kitāb]* [one time] and "*Qul Huwa'llāhu Aḥad* [Say: 'He is Allāh, One!']"[471] eleven times. In the second cycle, he must recite the Opening Sūra *[al-Fātiḥa]* [one time], "*Qul Huwa'llāhu Aḥad* [Say: 'He is Allāh, One!']" ten times, and "*Qul yā ayyuha 'l-kāfirūn*... [Say: 'O unbelievers...']"[472] three times. In the third cycle, he must recite the Opening Sūra *[al-Fātiḥa]* [one time], "*Qul Huwa'llāhu Aḥad* [Say: 'He is Allāh, One!']" ten times, and "*Alhā-kumu 't-takāthuru*... [Gross rivalry distracts you...]"[473] one time. In the fourth cycle, he must recite the Opening Sūra *[al-Fātiḥa]* [one time], "*Qul Huwa'llāhu Aḥad* [Say: 'He is Allāh, One!']" fifteen times, and the Verse of the Throne *[Āyat al-Kursī]*[474] one time.

Then he must donate the spiritual reward [earned by his performance of this prayer] to his adversaries in litigation *[khuṣamā᾿]*, so that Allāh may satisfy their claim on the Day of Resurrection *[Yawm al-Qiyāma]*, if Allāh (Exalted is He) so wills.

He must perform this ritual prayer *[ṣalāt]* on seven specific occasions, namely: (1) on the first night of [the month of] Rajab; (2) on the night of the middle of [the month of] Sha῾bān; (3) on the last Friday of [the month of] Ramaḍān; (4,5) on each of the two Days of Festival *[al-῾Īdain]*; (6) on the Day of ῾Arafa; and (7) on the Day of ῾Āshūrā᾿.

471 Sūra 112.

472 Sūra 109.

473 That is to say, the Sūra of Rivalry in Worldly Increase *[Sūrat at-Takāthur]* (Q. 102).

474 Q. 2:255.

5.
Concerning the ritual prayer of those who are emancipated [from the Fire of Hell] in the month of Shawwāl [*ṣalāt al-ʿutaqāʾ fī Shawwāl*].[475]

As for the ritual prayer of those who are emancipated [from the Fire of Hell] in [the month of] Shawwāl [*ṣalāt al-ʿutaqāʾ fī Shawwāl*], we learn from a traditional report, transmitted [by a chain of reliable authorities][476] from Anas [ibn Mālik] (may Allāh be well pleased with him), that Allāh's Messenger (Allāh bless him and give him peace) once said:

> If someone performs eight cycles of ritual prayer [*rakaʿāt*] in the month of Shawwāl, either during the night or during the day—reciting in each cycle the Opening Sūra of the Book [*Fātiḥat al-Kitāb*] [one time] and "*Qul Huwa'llāhu Aḥad* [Say: 'He is Allāh, One!']"[686] fifteen times—and if, when he has finished performing his ritual prayer [*ṣalāt*], he glorifies Allāh [*sabbaḥa*] seventy times, and invokes Allāh's blessing upon the Prophet (Allāh bless him and give him peace) seventy times—by Him who sent me as a Prophet bearing the Truth [*bi'l-Ḥaqqi Nabiyyan*], no servant [of the Lord] will perform this ritual prayer [*ṣalāt*], without Allāh causing the fountains of wisdom [*yanābīʿ al-ḥikma*] to well up in his heart, and causing his tongue to speak with wisdom, and showing him both the sickness of this world and the cure for that sickness.
>
> By Him who sent me as a Prophet bearing the Truth [*bi'l-Ḥaqqi Nabiyyan*], if someone performs this ritual prayer [*ṣalāt*], exactly as I have just described it, that person will not raise his head from his final prostration [*sujūd*] until Allāh has granted him forgiveness, and if he dies, he will die as a martyr [*shahīd*] to whom forgiveness has been granted.

[475] In the Islāmic calendar, Shawwāl is the month that follows the month of Ramaḍān.

[476] ***Author's note:*** This report was conveyed to us by Shaikh Abū Naṣr Muḥammad ibn al-Bannāʾ, on the authority of his father, Shaikh Abū ʿAlī ibn Aḥmad ibn ʿAbdi'llāh ibn al-Bannāʾ, who cited the following chain of transmission [*isnād*]: **Abū ʿAbdi'llāh al-Ḥusain ibn ʿUmar al-ʿAllāf—Abu 'l-Qāsim al-Qāḍī [the Judge]—Muḥammad ibn Aḥmād ibn Ṣiddīq—Yaʿqūb ibn ʿAbd ar-Raḥmān—Abū Bakr Aḥmād ibn Jaʿfar al-Marwazī—ʿAlī ibn Maʿrūf—Muḥammad ibn Maḥmūd—Yaḥyā ibn Shubaib—Ḥamīd—Anas [ibn Mālik]** (may Allāh be well pleased with him)—**the Prophet** (Allāh bless him and give him peace).

[686] Sūra 112.

> Nor will any servant [of the Lord] perform this ritual prayer *[ṣalāt]*, in the course of a journey, without Allāh making it smooth and easy for him to travel and arrive at his intended destination. If he is burdened with debt, Allāh will settle his debt. If he is needy, Allāh will satisfy his needs.
>
> By Him who sent me as a Prophet bearing the Truth *[bi'l-Ḥaqqi Nabiyyan]*, no servant [of the Lord] will perform this ritual prayer *[ṣalāt]*, without Allāh (Exalted is He) granting him—for every letter *[ḥarf]* and every verse *[āya]* [of his Qur'ānic recitation]—a *makhrafa* in the Garden of Paradise.[477]

Someone asked: "And what is this *makhrafa*, O Messenger of Allāh?" So he went on to explain (Allāh bless him and give him peace):

> [The term *makhrafa* is applied to] orchards in the Garden of Paradise, through which the rider may travel for a hundred years without passing beyond the shade of just one of the trees that grow there.

[477] According to the classical Arabic lexicographers, the term *makhrafa*, or *makhraf*, denotes "a garden of palm trees," or "an avenue between two rows of palm trees, such that one may gather, or pluck, the fruit from whichever of them he will." (See: E.W. Lane, *Arabic-English Lexicon*, art. *KH–R–F*.)

6.
Concerning the ritual prayer for the removal of the torment of the tomb *[aṣ-ṣalāt li-raf' 'adhāb al-qabr]*.

According to a traditional report, transmitted on the authority of 'Abdu'llāh ibn al-Ḥasan, 'Alī (may Allāh be well pleased with him) stated that Allāh's Messenger (Allāh bless him and give him peace) once said:

> If someone performs two cycles of ritual prayer *[rak'atain]*—reciting in one of the two cycles the last part of [the Sūra of] the Criterion *[al-Furqān]*, from "*Tabāraka 'lladhī ja'ala fi 's-samā'i burūjan* [Blessed is He who has placed in the heaven mansions of the stars]" until he reaches the end of the Sūra[478]—then starting into the second cycle, and reciting in it, after the Opening Sūra *[al-Fātiḥa]*, from the beginning of the Sūra of the Believers *[Sūrat al-Muminīn]* until he reaches "*Fa-tabāraka 'llāhu Aḥsanu 'l-khāliqīn* [So Blessed be Allāh, the Fairest of creators]"[479]—he will be safe from the double-dealing of the jinn and of humankind. He will receive his record sheet with his right hand on the Day of Resurrection *[Yawm al-Qiyāma]*.
>
> He will be safe from the torment of the tomb, and safe from the greatest terrror *[al-faza' al-akbar]*.[480] The Book will teach him, even if he is not an eager student. He will be relieved of poverty. Allāh will bring him [into compliance with] the law *[ḥukm]*. He will give him insight into His Book, which He has sent down to His Prophet (Allāh bless him and give him peace). He will instill in him the evidence he will need [in order to make his case] on the Day of Resurrection *[Yawm al-Qiyāma]*. He will install a light in his heart.
>
> Thus he will not grieve when other people grieve, and he will not be afraid when they are afraid. Light will be installed in his faculty of vision, the love of this world will be extracted from his heart, and he will be recorded in the presence of Allāh as one of the champions of truth *[aṣ-ṣiddīqīn]*.

[478] That is to say, Q. 25:61–77 (from the Sūra of the Criterion *[Sūrat al-Furqān]*) must be recited.

[479] That is to say, Q. 23:1–14 (from the Sūra of the Believers *[Sūrat al-Muminīn]*) must be recited.

[480] This is an allusion to Q. 21:103.

7.
Concerning the ritual prayer for help in time of need *[ṣalāt al-ḥāja]*.

According to a traditional report, transmitted by Abū Hāshim al-Ayyilī on the authority of Anas ibn Mālik (may Allāh be well pleased with him), the Prophet (Allāh bless him and give him peace) once said:

> If someone has a seriously pressing need, requiring Allāh's help, he should perform the ritual ablution *[wuḍū']* with proper care. He should then perform two cycles of ritual prayer *[rak'atain]*. In the first cycle he should recite the Opening Sūra of the Book *[Fātiḥat al-Kitāb]* and the Verse of the Throne *[Āyat al-Kursī]*,[481] and in the second cycle, the Opening Sūra of the Book *[Fātiḥat al-Kitāb]* and "*Āmana 'r-Rasūlu*... [The Messenger believes...]" to the end of that passage.[482] Then, having pronounced the testimony *[tashahhud]* and the salutation *[taslīma]*, he should make his plea by offering this prayer of supplication *[du'ā']*, for his need will then be satisfied. The words of the prayer of supplication *[du'ā']* are as follows:

O Allāh! O Intimate Friend	*Allāhumma: yā Mu'nisa*
of every lonely individual!	*kulli waḥīd:*
O Companion of	*wa yā Ṣāḥiba*
every solitary individual!	*kulli farīd:*
O You who are Near, not distant!	*wa yā Qarīban ghaira ba'īd:*
O You who are Present, not absent!	*wa yā Shāhidan ghaira ghā'ib:*
O You who are Invisible,	*wa yā Ghā'iban*
but not vanquished!	*ghaira maghlūb:*
I beseech you	*as'alu-ka*
by invoking Your Name:	*bi'smi-ka*
In the Name of Allāh,	*bi'smi'llāhi 'r-*
the All-Merciful,	*Raḥmāni 'r-*
the All-Compassionate,	*Raḥīm:*
the Ever-Living,	*al-Ḥayyi 'l-*
the Eternally Self-Sustaining,	*Qayyūm:*
the One whom neither slumber	*alladhī lā ta'khudhu-hu*
nor sleep can overtake.[483]	*sinatun wa lā nawm.*

[481] Q. 2:255.

[482] That is to say, the concluding passage of the Sūra of the Cow *[Sūrat al-Baqara]* (Q. 2:285–86).

[483] This invocation echoes the beginning of the Verse of the Throne *[Āyat al-Kursī]* Q. 2:255.

Again I beseech you	*wa as'alu-ka*
by invoking Your Name:	*bi'smi-ka*
In the Name of Allāh	*bi'smi'llāhi 'r-*
the All-Merciful,	*Raḥmāni 'r-*
the All-Compassionate,	*Raḥīm:*
the Ever-Living,	*al-Ḥayyi 'l-*
the Eternally Self-Sustaining,	*Qayyūm:*
the One before whom	*alladhī ʿanat*
faces are humbled,	*la-hu 'l-wujūh:*
and voices are subdued	*wa khashaʿat la-hu 'l-aṣwāt:*
and hearts quake and tremble.	*wa wajilat min-hu 'l-qulūb:*
[I beseech You] to bless Muḥammad	*an yuṣalliya ʿalā Muḥammadin*
and the family of Muḥammad	*wa ʿalā āli Muḥammad*
and to grant me a happy solution	*wa an tajʿala lī min amrī*
and a way out of my problem,	*farajan wa makhrajan*
and to satisfy my need.	*wa taqḍiya ḥājatī.*

* * * * * * *

This brings us to the end of the Chapter concerning:

The ritual prayer of glorification *[ṣalāt at-tasbīḥ]*.
The ritual prayer for guidance in choosing the best option *[ṣalāt al-istikhāra]*.
The ritual prayer for sufficient protection *[ṣalāt al-kifāya]*.
The ritual prayer for one's adversaries in litigation *[ṣalāt al-khuṣamāʾ]*.
The ritual prayer of those who are emancipated [from the Fire of Hell] in the month of Shawwāl *[ṣalāt al-ʿutaqāʾ fī Shawwāl]*.
The ritual prayer for the removal of the torment of the tomb *[aṣ-ṣalāt li-rafʿ ʿadhāb al-qabr]*.
The ritual prayer for help in time of need *[ṣalāt al-ḥāja]*.

Praise be to Allāh, the Lord of All the Worlds!
[al-ḥamdu li'llāhi Rabbi 'l-ʿālamīn].

CHAPTER THIRTEEN

Concerning prayers of supplication *[ad'iya]* to be offered in certain special circumstances.

1.
The prayer of supplication *[du'ā']* for the removal of oppression *[ẓulm]* and precaution against it.

According to a traditional report narrated by Jābir ibn 'Abdi'llāh (may Allāh be well pleased with him and with his father), Allāh's Messenger (Allāh bless him and give him peace) taught this prayer of supplication *[du'ā']* to [his son-in-law] 'Alī and [his daughter] Fāṭima[484] (may Allāh be well pleased with them both). He said to the pair of them:

"If an affliction ever befalls you, if you are afraid of the tyrannical oppression of a worldly ruler *[jawr sulṭān]*, or if the attainment of a long-cherished goal eludes you, perform the ritual ablution *[wuḍū']* with proper care, perform two cycles of ritual prayer *[ṣalliyā rak'atain]*, then raise your hands toward heaven and say:

'O Knower of the unseen and of all secret things; O You who must be Obeyed! O Omnipotent One! O All-Knowing One! O Allāh! O Allāh! O Allāh!	*yā 'Ālima 'l-ghaibi wa 's-sarā'ir: yā Muṭā': yā 'Azīz: yā 'Alīm: yā Allāh: yā Allāh: yā Allāh:*
O Vanquisher of the confederates for the sake of Muḥammad (Allāh bless him and give him peace);	*yā Hāzima 'l-aḥzābi li-Muḥammad (ṣalla 'llāhu 'alai-hi wa sallam):*
O Deceiver of Pharaoh for the sake of Moses (peace be upon him);	*yā Kā'ida Fir'awna li-Mūsā ('alai-hi 's-salām):*

[484] The Lady Fāṭima, daughter of the Prophet (Allāh bless him and give him peace), became the wife of the latter's cousin, 'Alī ibn Abī Ṭālib, and bore him two sons, al-Ḥasan and al-Ḥusain. May Allah be well pleased with them all.

O Savior of Jesus (peace be upon him) from the hands of his oppressors;	*yā Munjiya ʿĪsā* *(ʿalai-hi 's-salām)* *min yadi ẓalamati-h:*
O Rescuer of the people of Noah (peace be upon him) from drowning [in the Flood];	*yā Mukhalliṣa qawmi Nūḥin* *(ʿalai-hi 's-salām)* *mina 'l-gharaq:*
O You who took pity on the tears of Jacob (peace be upon him);	*yā Rāḥima ʿabrati Yaʿqūb* *(ʿalai-hi 's-salām):*
O Reliever of the suffering of Job (peace be upon him);	*yā Kāshifa ḍurri Ayyūb* *(ʿalai-hi 's-salām):*
O Rescuer of Jonah (peace be upon him) from the threefold gloom;	*yā Munjiya Dhi 'n-Nūn* *(ʿalai-hi 's-salām)* *mina 'ẓ-ẓulumāti 'th-thalāth:*
O Doer of all that is good; O Guide to all that is good; O Director to all that is good; O Proprietor of all that is good; O Creator of all that is good; O Proprietor of all good things;	*yā Fāʿila kulli khair:* *yā Hādiyan ilā kulli khair:* *yā Dāllan ʿalā kulli khair:* *yā Ahla 'l-khair:* *yā Khāliqa 'l-khair:* *yā Ahla 'l-khairāt:*
You are Allāh. I have requested of You that which You already know, for You are the One who knows all things invisible. I beseech You to bless Muḥammad and the family of Muḥammad.'	*Anta 'llāh:* *aghibtu ilai-ka* *fī-mā qad ʿalimt:* *wa Anta* *ʿAllāmu 'l-ghuyūb:* *as'alu-ka an* *tuṣalliya ʿalā Muḥammadin* *wa ʿalā āli Muḥammad.*

"Then ask for your need to be satisfied, and you will receive a positive response, if Allāh (Exalted is He) so wills."

2.
Another prayer of supplication *[du'ā']*.

This is the prayer of supplication offered *[du'ā']* by the Prophet (Allāh bless him and give him peace) on the Day of the Confederates *[Yawm al-Aḥzāb]*,[485] as reported by Ibn 'Umar (may Allāh be well pleased with him and with his father):

O Allāh, I take refuge You,	*Allāhumma innī a'ūdhu bi-ka:*
and with the light of Your Holiness,	*wa bi-nūri Qudsi-k:*
and the splendor of Your Purity,	*wa 'aẓamati Ṭahārati-k:*
and the blessed grace	*wa barakāti*
of Your Majesty,	*Jalāli-k:*
from every plague and blight,	*min kulli āfatin wa 'āhatin*
and from every nocturnal visitor,	*wa ṭāriqi 'l-jinni*
of the jinn or of humankind,	*wa 'l-ins:*
unless it be a visitor who comes	*illā ṭāriqan*
at night with something	*yaṭruqu*
good from You.	*min-ka bi-khair:*
You are indeed my refuge,	*inna-ka Anta 'iyādhī*
so with You do I take refuge,	*fa-bi-ka a'ūdh:*
and You are my shelter,	*wa Anta malādhī*
so with You do I take shelter.	*fa-bi-ka alūdh:*
O You before whom the necks	*yā man dhallat la-hu*
of cruel tyrants bow,	*riqābu 'l-jabābira:*
and by whom all the keys	*wa jumi'at la-hu*
of guardianship are held!	*maqālīdu 'r-ri'āya:*
I take refuge with the majesty	*a'ūdhu*
of Your Countenance,	*bi-jalāli Wajhi-k:*
and the nobility of Your Majesty,	*wa karami Jalāli-k:*
from Your scorn and	*min khizyi-ka:*
the removal of Your protection,	*wa kashfi sitri-k:*
and the forgetful neglect	*wa nisyāni*
of Your remembrance.	*dhikri-k:*
and failure to persist	*wa 'l-inṣirāfi*
in giving thanks to You.	*'an shukri-k:*
I am under Your wing	*ana fī kanafi-ka*
by day and by night, and in	*fī lailī wa nahārī:*

[485] See note 468 on p. 340 above.

my sleep, in the time I spend at home,	*wa nawmī wa qarārī:*
and in my travels and my journeys.	*wa ẓaʿnī wa asfārī:*
Your remembrance is	*dhikru-ka*
my undergarment,	*shiʿārī*
and Your praise	*wa thanāʾu-ka*
is my outer garment.[486]	*dithārī:*
There is no god but You,	*lā ilāha illā Anta*
so hallowed be Your Name,	*tanzīhan li'smi-k:*
and honored be	*wa takrīman*
the glories of Your Countenance.	*li-subuḥāti Wajhi-k:*
Grant me asylum from Your scorn,	*ajir-nī min khizyi-k:*
and from the agony of Your torment	*wa min sharri ʿadhābi-k:*
and the wickedness of Your servants,	*wa ʿibādi-k:*
and pitch over me the canopies	*wa 'ḍrib ʿalayya*
of Your safekeeping,	*surādiqāti ḥifẓi-k:*
and admit me into the safekeeping	*wa adhkhil-nī fī ḥifẓi*
of Your providential care,	*ʿināyati-k:*
and guard me against the trials	*wa qi-nī sayyiʾāti*
of Your punishment,	*ʿadhābi-k:*
and enrich me with goodness	*wa aghni-nī bi-khairin*
from You, and with Your Mercy,	*min-ka wa bi-Raḥmati-k:*
O Most Merciful of the merciful!	*yā Arḥama 'r-rāḥimīn.*

486 The term *shiʿār* is applied to the garment that is worn next to the body, while the *dithār* is defined as "a garment which one wears for warmth, above the *shiʿār*." According to a traditional report, the Prophet (Allāh bless him and give him peace) once said to the *Anṣār* [Helpers]: "You are the *shiʿār*, while the people in general are the *dithār*."

3.
Concerning the prayer of supplication *[du'ā']* for the dispelling of worries and the settlement of debts.

According to a traditional report transmitted on the authority of Abū Mūsā (may Allāh be well pleased with him), the Prophet (Allāh bless him and give him peace) once said:

> Whenever a person is beset with worry or grief, he should offer a prayer of supplication *[fa-'l-yad'u]* in these words:

O Allāh, I am Your servant	*Allāhumma ana 'abdu-ka*
and the son of Your servant.	*wa 'bnu 'abdi-k:*
My forelock is in Your hand.	*nāṣiyatī bi-yadi-k:*
Your verdict upon me is already cast.	*māḍin fiyya ḥukmu-k:*
Your judgment concerning me is just.	*'adlun fiyya qaḍā'u-k:*
O Allāh, I beseech You,	*Allāhumma innī as'alu-ka*
by every Name of Your Power,	*bi-kulli 'smi hawli-k:*
by which You have called Yourself,	*sammaita bi-hi nafsa-k:*
or which You have revealed	*aw anzalta-hu*
in Your Book,	*fī Kitābi-k:*
or which You have taught	*aw 'allamta-hu*
to anyone among Your creatures,	*aḥadan min khalqi-k:*
or which You have kept to Yourself	*awi 'sta'tharta bi-hi*
in the knowledge of the unseen.	*fī 'ilmi 'l-ghaibi 'inda-k:*
[I beg You] to make the Noble Qur'ān	*an taj'ala 'l-Qur'āna 'l-karīma*
the springtime of my heart,	*rabī'a qalbī:*
and the light of my breast,	*wa nūra ṣadrī:*
and the dispersal of my sorrow,	*wa jalā'a ḥuznī:*
and the removal of my grief	*wa dhahāba ghammī*
and my worry.	*wa hammī:*

Someone said: "O Messenger of Allāh, anyone who misses the opportunity to memorize these words will surely be the loser!" "Yes, indeed!" he replied (Allāh bless him and give him peace). "So you must repeat them and learn them, for if someone repeats them, as a request for what they contain, Allāh (Almighty and Glorious is He) will remove his sorrow and prolong his happiness."

ʿĀʾisha (may Allāh be well pleased with her) is reported as having said that [her father] Abū Bakr, the Champion of Truth *[aṣ-Ṣiddīq]* (may Allāh be well pleased with him), once entered her presence and said: "Did you hear from Allāh's Messenger (Allāh bless him and give him peace) the prayer of supplication *[duʿāʾ]* that he used to teach us? He mentioned that Jesus the son of Mary *[ʿĪsa 'bnu Maryam]* (peace be upon him) used to teach it to his disciples, and that he used to say: 'Even if one of you happened to be burdened with a debt the size of a whole mountain, Allāh (Almighty and Glorious is He) would settle it for him.'"

To this she replied: "He used to say:

'O Allāh, the Dispeller of care,	*Allāhumma Fārija 'l-hamm:*
the Remover of grief,	*Kāshifa 'l-ghamm:*
Ever-Responsive to the plea	*Mujība*
of those in dire need,	*daʿwati 'l-muḍṭarrīn:*
the All-Merciful Lord of this world,	*Raḥmāna 'd-dunyā*
the All-Compassionate Lord	*Raḥīma 'l-*
of the Hereafter,	*ākhira:*
I beseech You to bestow upon me	*asʾalu-ka an tarḥama-nī*
a mercy from You,	*raḥmatan min ʿinda-k:*
by which You will leave me	*tughnī-nī*
in no need of mercy	*bi-hā*
from anyone other than You.'"	*ʿan raḥmatin min siwā-k.*

4.
Another prayer of supplication [*du'ā'*] for the same purpose [the settlement of debt].

According to a traditional report, [Abū Sa'īd] al-Ḥasan al-Baṣrī (may Allāh bestow His mercy upon him) once received a visit from a friend of his, a man who held him in very high esteem. "O Abū Sa'īd," said the friend, "I am burdened with a debt, and I would like you to teach me the Mightiest Name of Allāh (Exalted is He) [*Ismu 'llāhi—ta'ālā—al-A'ẓam*]." So he told him: "If that is what you wish, get up and perform the ritual ablution [*tawaḍḍā'*]." The friend got up at once and performed the ritual ablution, whereupon al-Ḥasan told him to say:

O Allāh! O Allāh! You are Allāh!	*yā Allāh: yā Allāh: Anta 'llāh:*
Yes indeed, by Allāh, You are Allāh!	*balā wa 'llāhi Anta 'llāh:*
There is no god but You!	*lā ilāha illā Ant:*
Allāh! Allāh! Allāh!	*Allāh: Allāh: Allāh:*
By Allāh, there is no god but Allāh!	*wa 'llāhi lā ilāha illa 'llāh:*
Settle my debt for me, and	*aqḍi 'an-niya 'd-dain:*
provide for me after the debt [is settled].	*wa 'rzuq-nī ba'da 'd-dain.*

When the next morning came around, the man discovered a hundred thousand genuine dirhams [silver coins] in the room where he performed his private prayers. These assorted silver coins were stored inside a traveling case, the top of which bore the inscription:

Even if you had asked	*law sa'alta*
for more than this,	*akthara min hādhā*
We would have granted	*la-a'ṭainā-k.*
your request, so why	*fa-kaifa*
did you not ask for	*lam tas'ali 'l-*
the Garden of Paradise?	*Janna.*

The man came to al-Ḥasan (may Allāh bestow His mercy upon him) and told him about this, so he accompanied his friend back to his house, where he saw the silver coins with his own eyes. Then the man said: "I feel a sense of remorse, inasmuch as I did not ask Allāh to grant me the

Garden of Paradise." So al-Ḥasan said: "He who taught you [the invocation of] this Name *[Ism]*[487] had no intention, in teaching it to you, other than to do you a good turn, for I would normally treat this Name as my personal secret. [The cruel governor] al-Ḥajjāj [488] must not get to hear it, for no one at all would then be able to escape from him!"

[487] The Arabic word *ism*, for which "name" is in most instances a perfectly satisfactory translation, can sometimes mean "the act of calling by a name." The term "appellation" conveyed this latter meaning in archaic English usage, but in the modern language it almost always means "an identifying name or title."

[488] As governor of the province of ʿIrāq, in the time of al-Ḥasan al-Baṣrī (may Allāh bestow His mercy upon him), al-Ḥajjāj ibn Yūsuf was notorious for his cruelty and brutality. He killed many righteous men who incurred his displeasure, including Abū ʿAbdi'llāh [or Abū Muḥammad] Saʿīd ibn Jubair ibn Hishām al-Asadī (may Allāh bestow His mercy upon him), a pious Tabi'ī [member of the generation following that of the Companions], who was renowned for his learning in Qur'ānic exegesis *[tafsīr]*, Prophetic tradition *[ḥadīth]* and Islāmic jurisprudence *[fiqh]*.

5.
Another prayer of supplication *[du'ā']*, taught by Gabriel (peace be upon him) to our Prophet Muḥammad (Allāh bless him and give him peace).

This prayer of supplication *[du'ā']* was taught by Gabriel (peace be upon him) to our Prophet Muḥammad (Allāh bless him and give him peace), at the time when he set out from Mecca, the Ennobled City *[al-Musharrafa]*, and headed for Mount Ḥirā', in fear of Quraish[489] and in pursuit of his purpose and provision.

According to the account narrated by Abū Bakr Abū Bakr, the Champion of Truth *[aṣ-Ṣiddīq]* (may Allāh be well pleased with him), Gabriel (peace be upon him) said:

"O Muḥammad, Allāh (Exalted is He) extends to you the greeting of peace *[yuqri'u-ka 's-salām]*. He has taught me a prayer of supplication *[du'ā']* for you to offer, so that Allāh may establish a protective screen between you and them. Shall I teach it to you now?" "Yes, O Gabriel," said the Prophet (Allāh bless him and give him peace), so he told him to say:

O Supremely Great One!	*yā Kabīru kullu kabīr:*
O All-Hearing One!	*yā Samī':*
O All-Seeing One!	*yā Baṣīr:*
O You who have no partner	*yā man lā sharīka la-hu*
and no minister!	*wa lā wazīr:*
O Creator of the sun	*yā Khāliqa 'sh-shamsi*
and the shining moon!	*wa 'l-qamari 'l-munīr:*
O Safeguard of the fearful wretch	*yā 'Iṣmata 'l-bā'isi 'l-*
who seeks protection!	*khā'ifi 'l-mustajīr:*
O Nourisher of the little child!	*yā Rāziqa 'ṭ-ṭifli 'ṣ-ṣaghīr:*
O Mender of the broken bone!	*yā Jābira 'l-'aẓmi 'l-kasīr:*
O Crusher of every stubborn tyrant!	*yā Qāṣima kulli jabbārin 'anīd:*

[489] Quraish is the name of the Arab tribe into which the Prophet Muḥammad (Allāh bless him and give him peace) was born.

I beseech You	*as'alu-ka*
and entreat You with	*wa ad'ū-ka*
the supplication,	*du'ā'a 'l-*
of the wretched pauper	*bā'isi 'l-faqīr:*
the supplication	*du'ā'a 'l-*
of the destitute cripple,	*muḍṭarri 'ḍ-ḍarīr:*
and I beg You	*as'alu-ka*
by the nodes of glory[490]	*bi-ma'āqidi 'l-'izzi*
concentrated in Your Throne,	*min 'arshi-k:*
and the keys of mercy	*wa mafātīḥi 'r-raḥmati*
contained within Your Book,	*min kitābi-k:*
and by the eight Names inscribed	*wa bi'l-asmā'i 'th-thamāniyati 'l-*
on the horn of the sun,	*maktūbati 'alā qarni 'sh-shams:*
to do such-and-such	*an taf'ala bī*
and such-and-such with me.	*kadhā wa kadhā.*

* * * * * * *

This brings us to the end of the Chapter concerning prayers of supplication *[ad'iya]* to be offered in certain special circumstances.

Praise be to Allāh, the Lord of All the Worlds!
[al-ḥamdu li'llāhi Rabbi 'l-'ālamīn].

[490] The word *ma'qid* (of which *ma'āqid* is the plural form) signifies "the place where a cord or rope is tied, knit, or tied in a knot or knots; a joint, an articulation." According to the classical Arabic lexicographers, the somewhat unusual supplication *as'alu-ka bi-ma'āqidi 'l-'izzi min 'arshi-k* is understood to mean: "I beg You by the properties wherein consists the title of Your Throne to glory," or "by the places wherein those properties are [as it were] knit together," or simply "by the glory of Your Throne." The use of this particular supplication is said to be viewed with disapproval by the school *[madhhab]* of Imām Abū Ḥanīfa (may Allāh bestow his mercy upon him). (See: E.W. Lane, *Arabic–English Lexicon*, art. *'–Q–D.*)

CHAPTER FOURTEEN

Concerning the prayers of supplication *[adʿiya]* offered after the obligatory ritual prayers *[aṣ-ṣalawāt al-farḍ]*; the supplication following the recital of the entire Qurʾān *[duʿāʾ al-khatma]*; etc.

1.
Concerning the prayers of supplication *[adʿiya]* that may be offered immediately after the obligatory ritual prayers *[aṣ-ṣalawāt al-farḍ]*.

a.
The prayer of supplication *[duʿāʾ]* that is most appropriately offered immediately after the ritual prayer of the early morning *[ṣalāt al-ghadāh]*, and also immediately after the ritual prayer of the late afternoon *[ṣalāt al-ʿaṣr]*.

As for the prayer of supplication *[duʿāʾ]* that is most appropriately offered immediately after the ritual prayer of the early morning *[ṣalāt al-ghadāh]*, and also immediately after the ritual prayer of the late afternoon *[ṣalāt al-ʿaṣr]*, it is expressed in the following words:

O Allāh, to You be praise in thankfulness, and to You be gratitude in abundance. By Your grace may good works be accomplished!	*Allāhumma la-ka ʾl-ḥamdu shukran wa la-ka ʾl-mannu faḍlā: bi-niʿmati-ka tamma ʾṣ-ṣāliḥāt.*
We beg You, O Allāh, to grant a prompt relief—	*nasʾalu-ka ʾllāhumma farajan qarībā:*

for You have always
been Responsive—[491]
and a seemly patience,[492]
and an immunity
from all afflictions,
and a security
from the path of disasters,
through Your Mercy,
O Most Merciful of the merciful!

fa-inna-ka lam
tazal Mujībā:
wa ṣabran jamīlā:
wa ʿāfiyatan
min jamīʿi 'l-balāyā
wa salāmatan
min ṭarīqi 'r-razāyā:
bi-raḥmati-ka
yā Arḥama 'r-rāḥimīn.

O Allāh,
let our gathering together
be mercifully blessed,
and may we be safely protected
when we go our separate ways.

Allāhumma
'jʿali 'jtimāʿa-na 'jtimāʿan
marḥūman
wa tafarruqa-nā
tafarruqan maʿṣūmā:

Let no one amongst us
be unprosperous,
and let no one be deprived.
Do not make us turn in poverty
to others apart from You.

wa lā tajʿal
fī-nā shaqiyyan
wa lā maḥrūmā:
wa lā tarudda-nā bi'l-fāqati
ilā ghairi-k:

Do not deprive us
of the wealth of Your goodness,
and the real experience
of total trust in You,
and the genuine desire
for that which is in Your presence.

wa lā taḥrim-nā
siʿata khairi-ka
wa ḥaqīqata 't-tawakkuli
ʿalai-ka
wa khāliṣa 'r-raghbati
fī-mā ladai-k:

Fill our hearts with enrichment
provided by You,
and clothe our faces with modesty
in deference to You.

wa 'mlaʾ qulūba-nā
min-ka 'l-ghinā:
wa 'ksu wujūha-nā
min-ka 'l-ḥayāʾ:

And grant us the goodness
of the Hereafter,
as well as of this world,
through Your Mercy,
O Most Merciful of the merciful!

wa 'rzuq-nā
khaira 'l-ākhirati
wa 'd-dunyā:
bi-raḥmati-ka
yā Arḥama 'r-rāḥimīn.

O Lord!
O Allāh, grant that we may enjoy
the goodness of the morning
and the goodness of the evening,
and the goodness
of the verdict of fate
and the goodness
of the decree of destiny.

yā Rabb:
Allāhumma 'rzuq-nā
khaira 'ṣ-ṣabāḥi
wa khaira 'l-masāʾi
wa khaira 'l-
qaḍāʾi
wa khaira 'l-
qadar:

[491] This is an allusion to Q. 11:61.

[492] This is an allusion to Q. 70:5.

And keep away from us
the evil of the morning
and the evil of the evening,
and the evil of the verdict of fate
and the evil of the decree of destiny.

wa 'ṣrif ʿan-nā
sharra 'ṣ-ṣabāḥi
wa sharra 'l-masāʾi
wa sharra 'l-qaḍāʾi
wa sharra 'l-qadar.

O Allāh,
whatever You have sent down
on this day—in the way of goodness,
welfare, security, profit,
and plentiful sustenance—
grant us the most abundant
portion and share therein!

Allāhumma
wa mā anzalta
fī hādha 'l-yawmi min khairin
wa ʿāfiyatin wa salāmatin
wa ghanīmatin wa siʿati rizq:
fa-'jʿal la-nā fī-hi
awfara 'l-ḥazzi wa 'n-naṣīb.

O Allāh,
and whatever You have sent down
—in the way of wickedness,
affliction, evil,
sickness, and mischief—
keep it away from us,
and from all the Muslim men
and Muslim women,
O Most Merciful of the merciful!

Allāhumma
wa mā anzalta
min sūʾin
wa balāʾin wa sharrin
wa dāʾin wa fitna:
fa-'ṣrif-hu ʿan-nā
wa ʿan jamīʿi 'l-muslimīna
wa 'l-muslimāt
yā Arḥama 'r-rāhimīn.

b.
Another prayer of supplication *[du‘ā’]*.[493]

Praise be to Allāh,	*al-ḥamdu li'llāhi 'lladhī*
Who has encompassed	*aḥāṭa*
every single thing	*bi-kulli shai'in*
in knowledge,[494]	*‘ilmā:*
and Who has computed	*wa aḥṣā*
every single thing	*kulla shai'in*
in number.[495]	*‘adadā:*
There is no god but He,	*lā ilāha illā Hū:*
the Possessor of Grandeur	*Ahlu 'l-kibriyā'i*
and Might,	*wa 'l-‘aẓama :*
the Protective Provider	*wa Waliyyu 'l-*
of saving grace	*ghaithi*
and mercy,[496]	*wa 'r-raḥma:*
the Ruler of this world	*Māliku 'd-dunyā*
and the Hereafter,	*wa 'l-ākhira:*
Almighty in sovereign sway,	*‘Aẓīmu 'l-malakūt:*
Stern in the wielding of power,	*Shadīdu 'l-jabarūt:*
Gentle and Kind	*Laṭīfun*
to whatever He will,[497]	*li-mā yashā':*
Effective in doing	*Fa‘‘ālun*
whatever He wishes,[498]	*li-mā yurīd:*
the First of everything,	*Awwalu kulli shai'in*
and the Creator of everything,	*wa Khāliqu kulli shai'in*
and the Sustainer thereof.	*wa Rāziqu-h.*
O Allāh, let our morning be	*Allāhumma 'j‘al ṣabāḥa-nā*
a good and righteous morning,	*ṣabāḥan ṣāliḥā:*
not one that is shameful	*lā mukhziyan*
or disgraceful.	*wa lā fāḍiḥā.*

[493] Although Shaikh ‘Abd al-Qādir al-Jīlānī (may Allāh be well pleased with him) has presented this supplication *[du‘ā']* without introductory comment, we may conclude from the wording of it that it is appropriately offered after the ritual prayer of dawn/daybreak *[ṣalāt al-fajr/aṣ-ṣubḥ]*, presumably as an alternative to the one presented above.

[494] This is an allusion to Q. 65:12.

[495] This is an allusion to Q. 18:47.

[496] The literal meaning of the word *ghaith* (translated as "saving grace") is "abundant rain." This is an allusion to Q. 42:28.

[497] Q. 12:100.

[498] Q 11:107 and 85:16.

O Allāh, protect us from the worst of Time's vicissitudes, and its adversity, and from the arenas of iniquity, and the snares of the Devil, and the despotic impositions of the government.	*Allāhumma 'kfi-nā sharra nawā'iba 'z-zamāni wa makrūha-hu wa maṣāriʿa 's-sū'i wa maṣāyida 'sh-Shaiṭāni wa mawārida ṣawlati 's-sulṭāni.*
Enable us, during this day of ours, and during all other days, to make the most of opportunities for good, and to avoid committing evil deeds.	*wa waffiq-nā fī yawmi-nā hādhā wa fī sā'iri 'l-ayyām: li'stiʿmāli 'l- khairāti wa hijrāni 's-sayyi'āt.*
O Allāh, improve our hearts, and improve our characters, and improve our behavior, and improve our fathers and our sons, and our grandfathers and our grandmothers, and our condition in this world and the Other.	*Allāhumma aṣliḥ qulūba-nā wa aṣliḥ akhlāqa-nā wa aṣliḥ afʿala-nā wa aṣliḥ ābā'a-nā wa abnā'a-nā wa ajdāda-nā wa jaddāti-nā wa dunyā-nā wa ukhrā-nā.*
O Allāh, as You have let us spend the night in peace and well-being, let us spend the time of day in safety and well-being, through Your mercy, O Most Merciful of the merciful!	*Allāhumma ka-mā amḍaita 'l-laila ta bi-'s-salāmati wa 'l-ʿāfiya: fa-amḍi ʿalai-na 'n-nahāra bi-'s-salāmati wa 'l-ʿāfiya: bi-raḥmati-ka yā Arḥama 'r-rāhimīn.*
O Allāh! Our Lord, give us in this world that which is good, and in the Hereafter that which is good, and guard us against the torment of the Fire [of Hell],[499] through Your mercy, O Most Merciful of the merciful!	Allāhumma Rabba-nā āti-nā fi 'd-dunyā ḥasanatan *wa fi 'l-ākhirati ḥasanatan wa qi-nā ʿadhāba 'n-nār: bi-raḥmati-ka yā Arḥama 'r-rāhimīn.*
Āmīn, O Allāh! Āmīn, O Allāh, O Lord of All the Worlds!	*Āmīn Allāhumma Āmīn yā Allāh yā Rabba 'l-ʿĀlamīn.*

[499] Q. 2:201.

c.
Another prayer of supplication *[du'ā']*.[500]

Praise be to Allāh, Who created the heavens and the earth.[501]	*al-ḥamdu li'llāhi 'lladhī* *khalaqa 's-samāwāti* *wa 'l-arḍ:*
There is no god but He. In Him I have put my trust, and He is the Lord of the Mighty Throne.[502]	*lā ilāha illā Hū:* *'alai-hi tawakkalt u* *wa Huwa Rabbu 'l-* *'arshi 'l-'aẓīm.*
Glory be to Him, and Exalted is He, far above and beyond whatever they associate [with Him].[503]	*ṣubḥana-hu* *wa ta'ālā* *'ammā* *yushrikūn.*
O Allāh, forgive us our sins: those we have committed openly, as well as those we have kept secret, those we have concealed, as well as those we have made public, and those of which You are More Aware than we ourselves.	*Allāhumma 'ghfir* *la-nā dhunūba-nā* *mā ẓaharnā* *wa mā asrarnā* *wa mā akhfainā* *wa mā a'lannā* *wa mā* *Anta A'lamu bi-hi* *min-nā.*
O Allāh, grant us Your approval in this world and the Hereafter, and let our final outcome be a state of bliss, of witnessing and forgiveness.	*Allāhumma a'ṭi-nā riḍā-ka* *fi 'd-dunyā wa 'l-ākhira:* *wa 'khtim la-nā* *bi's-sa'ādati* *wa 'sh-shahādati wa 'l-maghfira.*
O Allāh, let the last part of our lives be good, and let our endings be good, and let the best of all our days be the day when we shall meet You.	*Allāhumma 'j'al* *ākhira a'māri-nā* *khairan wa khawātima-nā khairan* *wa khaira ayyāmi-nā* *yawma nalqā-k.*

[500] As in the preceding instance, Shaikh 'Abd al-Qādir al-Jīlānī (may Allāh be well pleased with him) has presented this supplication *[du'ā']* without introductory comment. In this case, however, we may conclude from the wording of it that it may appropriately be offered after any of the ritual prayers *[ṣalawāt]*. (Allāh knows best!)

[501] This declaration of praise occurs in Q. 6:1.

[502] This affirmation occurs in Q. 9:129.

[503] Q. 10:18, 16:1 and 30:40.

O Allāh, we take refuge with You	*Allāhumma innā naʿūdhu bi-ka*
from the disappearance	*min zawāli*
of Your blessing,	*niʿmati-ka*
from the surprise attack	*wa min fajʾati*
of Your affliction,	*niqmati-ka*
and from the alteration	*wa min taḥwīli*
of Your gracious favor.	*ʿāfiyati-k.*
O Allāh, we take refuge with You	*Allāhumma innā naʿūdhu bi-ka*
from the onslaught of misery,	*min daraki 'sh-shaqāʾi*
from the trouble of adversity,	*wa jahdi 'l-bālāʾi*
from the transformation of prosperity,	*wa taghyīri 'n-naʿmāʾi*
and from unfortunate calamity.	*wa sūʾi 'l-qaʿḍāʾ.*
We take refuge with You	*wa naʿūdhu bi-ka*
from all things loathsome and bad,	*min jamīʿi 'l-makārihi wa 'l-aswāʾ.*
and we beg You, O Allāh,	*wa nasʾalu-ka 'llāhumma*
to grant us the very best.	*khaira 'l-ʿaṭāʾi.*
O Allāh, we beg You	*Allāhumma innā nasʾalu-ka*
to remove our sickness,	*an takshifa saqama-nā*
to heal our illness,	*wa tubriʾa maraḍa-nā*
to bestow Your mercy on our dead,	*wa tarḥama mawtā–nā*
to make our bodies healthy,	*wa tuṣiḥḥa abdāna-nā*
and to make them	*wa tukhliṣa-hā*
sincerely devoted to You.	*la-k:*
O Allāh,	*Allāhumma*
let our religious convictions	*akhliṣ*
be sincere!	*adyāna-nā.*
[We beg You]	
to preserve our safekeeping,	*wa an taḥfaẓa ʿiyādha-nā*
to expand	*wa tashraḥa*
[the feeling in] our breasts,[504]	*ṣudūra-nā*
to direct the management	*wa tudabbira*
of our affairs,	*umūra-nā*
to put our children	*wa tujabbira*
through useful training,	*awlāda-nā*
to overlook our misbehavior,	*wa tastura jurma-nā*
to reinstate us	*wa tarudda*
though we have been absent,	*ghiyāba-nā*
and to confirm our commitment	*wa an tuthbita-nā*
to our religion.	*ʿalā dīni-nā*
We beg You for goodness	*wa nasʾalu-ka khairan*
and right guidance.	*wa rushdā.*
O Allāh! Our Lord, we beg You	*Allāhumma Rabba-nā*
to give us that which is good	*innā nasʾalu-ka an*
in this world,	*tuʾtiya-nā ḥasanatan fi 'd-dunyā*
and that which is good	*wa ḥasanatan*

[504] This is an allusion to Q 20:25–28.

in the Hereafter,	*fi 'l-ākhira:*
and to let us die as Muslims,	*wa an tatawaffa-nā muslimīn:*
through Your mercy.	*bi-raḥmati-k:*
Guard us against	*wa qi-nā*
the torment of the Fire,	*ʿadhāba 'n-nāri*
and the torment of the tomb,	*wa ʿadhāba 'l-qabr:*
O Most Merciful of the merciful!	*yā Arḥama 'r-rāḥimīn:*
O Lord of All the Worlds!	*yā Rabba 'l-ʿālamīn.*

d.
Concerning the very great importance of the prayer of supplication *[du'ā']*.

The offering of the prayer of supplication *[du'ā']* has been commanded, and it is of great importance *[bi-makān]* in the sight of Allāh, as we have explained many times in the course of this book. It is therefore quite improper for the prayer leader *[imām]*, and for anyone who follows his lead *[ma'mūm]*, to leave the mosque *[masjid]* without having offered the prayer of supplication *[du'ā']*.

Allāh (Exalted is He) has told us:

> So, as soon as you have finished, — *fa-idhā faraghta*
> set to work, — *fa-'nṣab*
> and present your request — *wa ilā Rabbi-ka*
> to your Lord. (94:7,8) — *fa-'rghab.*

That is to say: "As soon as you have finished performing the ritual act of worship *['ibāda]*, you must set to work on the prayer of supplication *[du'ā']*. You must wish for that which Allāh has at His disposal, and beseech Him to grant it."

According to the tradition *[ḥadīth]* that has come down to us on the authority of Anas ibn Malik (may Allāh be well pleased with him), the Prophet (Allāh bless him and give him peace) is reported as having said:

> As soon as the prayer leader *[imām]* is standing at the ready in his niche *[miḥrāb]*, and the ranks [of the congregation] are properly aligned, the merciful blessing [of Allāh] will descend [upon the assembled worshippers]. The first to receive it will be the prayer leader *[imām]*, then the person next to him on his right, then the person next to him on his left. The merciful blessing *[raḥma]* will then distribute itself throughout the congregation.
>
> An angel will then call out: "So-and-so has gained a benefit, and So-and-so has suffered a loss!" The beneficiary will be anyone who lifts up his hands in offering the supplication *[du'ā']* to Allāh (Exalted is He), as soon he has finished performing his prescribed ritual prayer *[ṣalāt maktūba]*. The loser will be anyone who leaves the mosque *[masjid]* without having offered a supplication *[du'ā']*. If someone does leave without having offered a prayer of supplication *[du'ā']*, the angels will say: "O So-and-so, how can you manage without Allāh (Exalted is He)? Do you have no need of anything that Allāh has at His disposal?"

2.
The prayer of supplication that should be offered after the recital of the entire Qur'ān *[du'ā' khatmat al-Qur'ān].*

As for the special prayer of supplication *[du'ā']* that should be offered when the recital of the entire Qur'ān *[khatmat al-Qur'ān]* has been completed, the wording of it is as follows:

Allāh the Almighty has told the truth,	*ṣadaqa 'llāhu 'l-'Aẓīmu'lladhī*
He who created the Creation,	*khalaqa 'l-khalqa*
and so originated it;	*fa-'btada'a-h:*
He who established the [true] religion,	*wa sanna 'd-dīna*
and laid down its laws;[505]	*wa shara'a-h:*
He who caused the light to shine,	*wa nawwara 'n-nūra*
and made it radiate;	*wa sha'sha'a-h:*
He who appointed sustenance,	*wa qaddara 'r-rizqa*
and rendered it amply sufficient;	*wa wassa'a-h:*
He who inflicted injury	*wa ḍarra*
on His Creation,	*khalqa-hu*
and provided it with benefit;	*wa nafa'a-h:*
He who made the water flow,	*wa ajra 'l-mā'a*
and caused it to gush forth;	*wa anba'a-h:*
He who made the heaven	*wa ja'ala 's-samā'a*
a roof well-kept[506]	*saqfan maḥfūẓan*
and held aloft,	*marfū'an*
which He raised up.[507]	*rafa'a-h:*
and the earth a carpet ,	*wa 'l-arḍa bisāṭan*
which He laid down[508]	*waḍa'a-h:*
He who set the moon in motion,	*wa sayyara 'l-qamara*
and caused it to rise and shine.	*wa aṭla'a-h.*
Glory be to Him!	*subḥāna-hu*
How exalted is His status,	*mā a'lā makāna-hu*
and how elevated!	*wa arfa'a-h:*

[505] This is an allusion to Q. 42:13.

[506] This is an allusion to Q. 21:32

[507] This is an allusion to Q. 52:5

[508] This is a paraphrase of Q. 71:19.

How splendid is His sovereignty,	*wa aʿazza sulṭāna-hu*
and how unique!	*wa abdaʿa-h:*
None can undo what He has made,	*lā rādda li-mā ṣanaʿa-h:*
and none can alter	*wa lā mughayyira*
what He has created.	*li-ma 'khtaraʿa-h:*
None can humiliate those	*wa lā mudhilla*
whom He has raised in dignity,	*li-man rafaʿa-h:*
and none can dignify those	*wa lā muʿizza*
whom He has reduced to degradation.	*li-man waḍaʿa-h:*
None can separate that	*wa lā mufarriqa*
which He has joined together.	*li-mā jamaʿa-h:*
No partner has He,	*wa lā sharīka la-h:*
and there is no god besides Him.	*wa lā ilāha maʿa-h.*
Allāh has told the truth, He who	*ṣadaqa 'llāhu 'lladhī*
has prearranged the pattern	*dabbara 'd-*
of the ages,	*duhūr:*
and predetermined	*wa qaddara 'l-*
the course of destiny,	*maqdūr:*
and settled the conduct of all affairs;	*wa ṣarrafa 'l-umūr:*
and the alternation of	*wa taʿāquba 'd-*
[daylight and] the dark;	*daijūr:*
He who facilitates	*wa sahhala 'l-*
that which is difficult,	*maʿsūr:*
and makes even easier	*wa yassara 'l-*
that which is easy;	*maisūr:*
He who has tamed the raging sea;[509]	*wa sakhkhara 'l-baḥra 'l-masjūr:*
He who sent down the Criterion	*wa anzala 'l-Furqāna*
and the Light,[510]	*wa 'n-Nūr:*
and the Torah and the Gospel[511]	*wa 't-Tawrāta wa 'l-Injīla*
and the Psalms;[512]	*wa 'z-Zabūr:*
He who has sworn	*wa aqsama*
by the Criterion[513]	*bi'l-Furqāni*
and the Mount,	*wa 'ṭ-Ṭūr:*
and the Book inscribed	*wa 'l-Kitābi 'l-masṭūr:*
on the parchment unrolled,	*fi 'r-raqqi 'l-manshūr:*
and the House frequented,[514]	*wa 'l-Baiti 'l-maʿmūr:*

[509] This is an allusion to Q. 52:6.

[510] The Qurʾānic verses *[āyāt]* alluded to here include Q. 5:15, 21:48, 25:1 and 64:8.

[511] Allāh (Almighty and Glorious is He) has mentioned His sending down of the Torah *[at-Tawrāh]* and the Gospel *[al-Injīl]* in several verses *[āyāt]* of the Qurʾān, including 3:1–4, in which He also mentions the Criterion *[al-Furqān]*.

[512] Allāh (Almighty and Glorious is He) has mentioned the Psalms *[Zabūr]* in three verses *[āyāt]* of the Qurʾān: 4:163, 17:55 and 21:105.

[513] In uttering the words:

Qāf. By the glorious Qurʾān. (50:1) — *Qāf: wa 'l-Qurʾāni 'l-majīd.*

—Allāh (Exalted is He) is implicitly swearing by the Criterion *[Furqān]*, which He uses as another name for the Qurʾān in several verses *[āyāt]* of His Book, notably 2:185 and 25:1.

[514] These four lines constitute a slightly paraphrased version of the first four verses *[āyāt]* of the Sūra of the Mount *[Sūrat aṭ-Ṭūr]* (Q. 52:1–4).

and the Raising and the Resurrection;	*wa 'l-baʿthi wa 'n-nushūr:*
He who is the Creator of darkness	*wa Jāʿilu 'z-ẓulumāti*
and light,	*wa 'n-nūr:*
and of children,	*wa 'l-wuldāni*
and of the heavenly brides,[515]	*wa 'l-ḥūr:*
and of the Gardens and palaces	*wa 'l-jināni wa 'l-quṣūr.*
[of Paradise].	
Allāh causes whom He will to hear.	*inna 'llāha yusmiʿu man yashāʾ:*
You cannot make yourself heard	*wa mā anta bi-musmʿin*
by those who are in the graves.	*man fi 'l-qubūr.*
(35:22)	
Allāh the Almighty has told the truth,	*ṣadaqa 'llāhu 'l-ʿAẓīmu*
He who is Omnipotent,	*'lladhī*
and therefore reigns Supreme,	*ʿazza fa-'rtafaʿ:*
and is so Exalted	*wa ʿalā*
that He cannot be surmounted;	*fa-'mtanaʿ:*
He before whose Might and Majesty	*wa dhalla kullu shaiʾin*
all things are humbly submissive	*li-ʿaẓamati-hi*
and subdued;	*wa khaḍaʿ:*
He who lifted up the sky	*wa samaka 's-samāʾa*
and raised it aloft,[516]	*wa rafaʿ:*
and laid out the earth	*wa farasha 'l-arḍa*
and spread it wide;[517]	*wa awsaʿ:*
He who made the rivers gush forth,	*wa fajjara 'l-anhāra*
and so caused them to flow;[518]	*fa-anbaʿ:*
He who partitioned	*wa maraja*
the seas and oceans,[519]	*'l-biḥāra*
and so made them become full;	*fa-atraʿ:*
He who tamed the stars,	*wa sakhkhara 'n-nujūma*
and so caused them to rise and shine;	*fa-aṭlaʿ:*
He who sent forth the clouds,	*wa arsala 's-saḥāba*
so that they rose high in the sky;	*fa-'rtafaʿ:*
He who brightened the light,	*wa nawwara 'n-nūra*
so that it shone;	*fa-lamaʿ:*
He who sent down the rain,	*wa anzala 'l-ghaitha*
so that it fell;	*fa-hamaʿ:*
He who spoke to Moses,	*wa kallama Mūsā*
and so let him hear;	*fa-asmaʿ:*
He who revealed Himself	*wa tajallā*
to the mountain,	*li'l-jabala*
so that it was shattered to pieces;[520]	*fa-taqaṭṭaʿ:*

[515] See note 9 on p. 9 above.

[516] This is an allusion to Q. 79:27,28.

[517] This is an allusion to Q. 51:48.

[518] This is an allusion to Q. 18:33.

[519] This is an allusion to Q. 25:53 and 55:20,21.

[520] The story of Moses (peace be upon him) and the mountain is told by Allāh (Exalted is He) in Q. 7:143.

He who has given and taken away;	*wa wahaba wa-nazaʿ:*
He who has inflicted injury	*wa ḍarra*
and provided benefit;	*wa-nafaʿ:*
He who has bestowed and withheld;	*wa aʿṭā wa manaʿ:*
He who has established the practices	*wa sanna*
and laid down the laws	*wa sharaʿ:*
[of religion];	
He who has set apart	*wa farraqa*
and joined together;	*wa jamaʿ:*
He who has brought you all into being	*wa anshaʾa-kum*
from a single soul,	*min nafsin wāḥida:*
so that [here you have] a lodging-place	*fa-mustaqarrun*
and a repository.[521]	*wa mustawdaʿ.*
Allāh has told the truth,	*ṣadaqa 'llāhu 'l-*
the Almighty, the Ever-Relenting,	*ʿAẓīmu 't-Tawwāb:*
the All-Forgiving, the Ever-Giving;	*al-Ghafūru 'l-Wahhāb:*
He before whose Might and Majesty	*alladhī khaḍaʿat*
all necks are humbly bowed;	*li-ʿaẓamati-hi 'r-riqāb:*
He to whose All-Compelling Power	*wa dhallat*
the obstinate meekly submit;	*li-jabarūti-hi 'ṣ-ṣiʿāb:*
He toward whom	*wa lānat*
the stubbornly unyielding	*la-hu 'sh-shidādu 'ṣ-*
soften and relax;	*ṣilāb:*
He in whose work	*wa 'stadallat*
intelligent minds find	*bi-ṣanʿati-hi 'l-*
evidence that leads to understanding;	*albāb:*
He whose praise	*wa yusabbiḥu*
is extolled by the thunder	*bi-ḥamdi-hi 'r-raʿdu*
and the clouds,	*wa 's-saḥāb:*
by the lightning and the mirage,	*wa 'l-barqu wa 's-sarāb:*
and by the trees and the animals;	*wa 'sh-shajaru wa 'd-dawābb:*
He who is the Lord of lords;	*Rabbu 'l-arbāb:*
the Originator of all secondary causes,	*wa Musabbibu 'l-asbāb:*
the Revealer of the Book;	*wa Munazzilu 'l-Kitāb:*
the Creator of His creation	*Khāliqu khalqi-hi :*
from the dust;	*mina 't-turāb*
the Forgiver of sin;	*Ghāfiru 'dh-dhanb:*
the Accepter of repentance;	*wa Qābilu 't-tawb:*
the Stern in punishment.	*Shadīdu 'l-ʿiqāb:*
There is no god but He.	*lā ilāha illā Hū:*
In Him I have put my trust,	*ʿalai-hi tawakkaltu*
and unto Him I turn. (13:30)	*wa ilai-hi matāb.*
Allāh has told the truth, He who is	*ṣadaqa 'llāhu 'lladhī*
always Majestic,	*lam yazal Jalīlan*
always a Source of Guidance.	*Dalīlā:*
The truth He has told,	*ṣadaqa*

[521] These four lines constitute a partial and slightly paraphrased quotation of Q. 6:99.

He who is all I need	*man ḥasbī*
in the way of a Guarantor.[522]	*bi-hi Kafīlā:*
The truth He has told,	*ṣadaqa mani*
He whom I have	*'ttakhadhtu-hu*
singled out as a Trustee.[523]	*Wakīlā:*
Allāh, the Guide who shows a way	*ṣadaqa 'llāhu 'l-Hādī ilai-hi*
to reach Him, has told the truth.	*sabīlā:*
Allāh has told the truth,	*ṣadaqa 'llāhu*
and who is more truthful	*wa man aṣdaqu*
than He in telling?[524]	*min-hu qīlā.*
Allāh has told the truth,	*ṣadaqa 'llāhu*
and His communications	*wa ṣadaqa*
have conveyed the truth,	*anbā'u-h:*
and His Prophets have told the truth.	*wa ṣadaqat anbiyā'u-h:*
Allāh has told the truth,	*ṣadaqa 'llāhu*
and His blessings	*wa jalat*
have been made manifest.	*ālā'u-h:*
Allāh has told the truth,	*ṣadaqa 'llāhu*
and His earth and His heaven	*wa ṣadaqat arḍu-hu*
have also told the truth.	*samā'u-h:*
Allāh has told the truth,	*ṣadaqa 'llāhu 'l-*
[Allāh] the Unique,	*Wāḥidu 'l-*
the Eternally Pre-existent,	*Qadīm:*
the Noble, the All-Generous,	*al-Mājidu 'l-Karīm:*
the Ever-Present Witness,	*ash-Shāhidu 'l-*
the All-Knowing,	*'Alīm:*
the All-Forgiving,	*al-Ghafūru 'r-*
the All-Compassionate,	*Raḥīm:*
the Ever-Appreciative,	*ash-Shakūru 'l-*
the All-Forbearing.	*Ḥalīm:*
Say: "Allāh has told the truth;	*qul ṣadaqa 'llāh:*
so follow the creed of Abraham."	*fa-'ttabi'ū millata Ibrāhīm.*
(3:95)	
Allāh has told the truth,	*ṣadaqa 'llāhu 'l-*
[Allāh] the Almighty—	*'Aẓīmu 'lladhī*
there is no god but He—	*lā ilāha illā Hū:*
the All-Merciful,	*ar-Raḥmānu 'r-*
the All-Compassionate	*Raḥīm:*
the Ever-Living, the All-Knowing,	*al-Ḥayyu 'l-Alīm:*
the Ever-Living, the All-Generous,	*al-Ḥayyu 'l-Karīm:*

[522] This is an allusion to Q. 16:91.

[523] As Allāh Himself (Almighty and Glorious is He) has assured us in a verse *[āya]* of the Qur'ān:

And Allāh is sufficient as Trustee. (4:81)	*wa kafā bi'llāhi Wakīlā.*

[524] These words echo the question posed at the end of the verse *[āya]* of the Qur'ān:

and who is more truthful	*wa man aṣdaqu*
than Allāh in telling? (4:122)	*mina 'llāhi qīlā.*

the Ever-Living, the Everlasting,	*al-Ḥayyu 'l-Bāqī:*
He who will never die.	*lā yamūtu abadā.*
The Lord of Majesty and Honor,	*Dhu'l-jalāli wa 'l-ikrām:*
and of the Splendid Names,	*wa 'l-asmāʾi 'l-ʿiẓām:*
and of the Prodigious Blessings.	*wa 'l-minan al-jisām:*
The noble Messengers	*wa bullighati 'r-rusulu 'l-*
have also been sent	*kirām:*
with the truth.	*bi'l-ḥaqq:*
May Allāh bless our Chief,	*ṣalla 'llāhu ʿalā sayyidi-nā*
Muḥammad, and give him peace,	*Muḥammadin wa sallam:*
and peace be upon them all!	*wa ʿalai-himi 's-salām.*
And we, with respect to what Allāh,	*wa naḥnu ʿalā mā qāla 'llāhu*
our Lord,	*Rabbu-nā*
and [Muḥammad] our Chief	*wa Sayyidu-nā*
and our Master,	*wa Mawlā-nā*
have said, we are among	*mina 'sh-*
the witnesses;	*shāhidīn:*
and whatever duties	*wa mā*
they have enjoined	*awjaba*
and have made incumbent	*wa alzama*
[upon us], we do not deny	*ghairu jāḥidīn:*
[our obligation to fulfill them].	
And praise be to Allāh,	*wa 'l-ḥamdu li'llāhi*
the Lord of All the Worlds,	*Rabbi 'l-ʿālamīn:*
and His blessings be upon our Chief,	*wa ṣalawātu-hu ʿalā sayyidi-nā*
Muḥammad, the Seal of the Prophets,	*Muḥammadin khātami 'n-nabiyyīn:*
and upon his venerated forefathers,	*wa ʿalā abawai-hi 'l-mukarramaini*
Adam, our Chieftain, and	*sayyidi-nā Ādama*
Abraham, the Bosom Friend	*wa 'l-Khalīli Ibrāhīm:*
[of Allāh],	
and upon all his brethren	*wa ʿalā jamīʿi ikhwāni-hi*
meaning his fellow Prophets,	*mina 'n-nabiyyīn:*
and upon the pure members	*wa ʿalā ahli*
of his household,	*baiti-hi 'ṭ-ṭāhirīn:*
and upon his chosen Companions,	*wa ʿalā aṣḥābi-hi 'l-muntakhabīn:*
and upon his pure wives,	*wa ʿalā azwāji-hi 'ṭ-ṭāhirāti*
the Mothers of the Believers,	*ummahāti 'l-muʾminīn:*
and upon those	*wa ʿala 't-*
who follow their example	*tābiʿīna la-hum*
in active goodness	*bi-iḥsānin*
until the Day of Judgment,	*ilā yawmi 'd-dīn:*
through Your Mercy,	*ʿalai-nā maʿa-hum bi-raḥmati-ka*
O Most Merciful of the merciful!	*yā Arḥama 'r-rāḥimīn.*
Allāh has told the truth, He who is	*ṣadaqa 'llāhu*
the Lord of Majesty and Honor,	*Dhu'l-jalāli wa 'l-ikrām:*

of Splendid Might	*wa 'l-ʿaẓamati*
and Sovereign Power;	*wa 's-sulṭān:*
He who is All-Compelling,	*Jabbārun*
and cannot be repulsed;	*lā yurām:*
He who is Omnipotent,	*ʿAzīzun*
and cannot be deterred;	*lā yuḍām:*
He who is Eternally Self-Sustaining,	*Qayyūmun*
and never sleeps.	*lā yanām:*
His are the noble acts,	*la-hu 'l-afʿālu 'l-kirām:*
and the splendid gifts,	*wa 'l-mawāhibu 'l-ʿiẓām:*
and the enormous benefits,	*wa 'l-ayādi 'l-jisām:*
and the gracious favors and blessings,	*wa 'l-afḍālu wa 'l-anʿām:*
and perfection and completeness.	*wa 'l-kamālu wa 't-tamām:*
The noble angels	*tusabbiḥu la-hu 'l-malāʾikatu 'l-*
proclaim His glory,	*kirām:*
as do the animals and the reptiles,	*wa 'l-bahāʾimu wa 'l-hawāmm:*
and the winds and the clouds,	*wa 'r-riyāḥu wa 'l-ghamām:*
and the light and the darkness.	*wa 'ḍ-ḍiyāʾu wa 'ẓ-ẓalām:*
He is Allāh, the King,	*wa Huwa 'llāhu 'l-Maliku 'l-*
the Holy One,	*Quddūsu 's-*
the Source of Peace.[525]	*Salām.*
And we bear witness	*wa naḥnu ʿalā*
to that which Allāh,	*mā qāla 'llāhu*
our Lord, has said.	*Rabbu-nā*
(Glorious be His praise,	*jalla thanāʾu-h:*
and sanctified be His Names.)	*wa taqaddasat asmāʾu-h:*
His blessings have become manifest,	*wa jalat ālāʾu-h:*
and His earth and His heaven	*wa shahidat arḍu-hu*
have also borne witness,	*wa samāʾu-h:*
and His Messengers	*wa naṭaqat*
have pronounced it,	*bi-hi rusulu-hu*
and His Prophets	*wa anbiyāʾu-hu*
have been witnesses.	*shāhidūn:*
Allāh bears witness that	*shahida 'llāhu anna-hu*
there is no god but He—and [so do]	*lā ilāha illā Huwa*
the angels and the men of learning—	*wa 'l-malāʾikatu wa ulu 'l-ʿilmi*
upholding justice.	*qā'iman bi'l-qisṭ:*
There is no god but He,	*lā ilāha illā Huwa 'l-*
the Omnipotent, the All-Wise.	*ʿAzīzu 'l-Ḥakīm.*
(3:18)	
The true religion	*inna' d-dīna*
in the sight of Allāh is surrender	*ʿinda 'llāhi 'l-Islām.*
[to His will and guidance]. (3:19)	
And as for us, to that which Allāh,	*wa naḥnu bi-mā shahida 'llāhu*
our Lord, has testified,	*Rabbu-nā*

[525] This is a partial quotation of Q. 59:23.

as have the angels	*wa 'l-malāʾikatu*
and the men of learning	*wa ulu 'l-ʿilmi*
among His creatures,	*min khalqi-hi*
we too are among those	*mina 'sh-*
who bear witness.	*shāhidīn:*
This is a testimony	*shahādatun*
by which one bears witness	*shahida*
to the Omnipotent,	*bi-ha 'l-ʿAzīza 'l-*
the Praiseworthy,	*Ḥamīd:*
and by which the believer	*wa dāna*
professes obedience	*bi-ha 'l-muʾminu 'l-*
to the All-Forgiving,	*Ghafūra 'l-*
the Ever-Loving,[526]	*Wadūd:*
and he dedicates the testimony	*wa akhlaṣa bi'sh-shahādati*
to the Lord of the Throne,	*li-Dhi 'l-ʿarshi 'l-*
the All-Glorious,[527]	*Majīd:*
who will honor it with acceptance,	*yarfaʿu-hā*
as He accepts righteous	*bi'l-ʿamali 'ṣ-ṣāliḥi 'r-*
and rightly guided work.[528]	*rashīd:*
To one who utters it	*yuʿṭā qā'ilu-ha 'l-*
eternal life will be granted,	*khulūd:*
in Gardens	*fī jannati*
endowed with thornless lote-trees,	*dhāti sidrin makhḍūd:*
and clustered acacias,	*wa ṭalḥin manḍūd:*
and spreading shade,	*wa ẓillin mamdūd:*
and gushing water.[529]	*wa māʾin maskūb:*
Therein he will keep company	*yurāfiqu*
with the witness-bearing Prophets,	*fī-ha 'n-nabiyyīna 'sh-shuhūd:*
and those who bow	*wa 'r-rukkaʿu 's-*
and prostrate themselves,	*sujūd:*
and those who exert the utmost effort	*wa 'l-bādhilīna fī ṭāʿati-hi*
in paying obedience to Him.	*ghāyata 'l-majhūd.*
O Allāh, grant that we may be	*Allāhumma 'jʿal-nā*
truthful in this affirmation	*bi-hādha 't-taṣdīqi*
of the truth,	*ṣādiqīn:*
and witnesses to this truthfulness,	*wa bi-hādha 'ṣ-ṣidqi shāhidīn:*
and faithful believers	*wa bi-hādhihi 'sh-shahādati*
in this testimony,	*muʾminīn:*
and professors of Unity in this faith,	*wa bi-hādha 'l-īmāni muwaḥḥidīn:*
and sincere	*wa bi-hādha 't-*
in this profession of Unity,	*tawḥīdi mukhliṣīn:*
and certain in this sincerity,	*wa bi-hādha 'l-ikhlāṣi mūqinīn:*

526 Allāh (Exalted is He) has so described Himself in Q. 85:14.

527 Allāh (Exalted is He) has so described Himself in Q. 85:15.

528 This is an allusion to Q. 35:10.

529 This sentence includes a partial quotation of Q. 56:27–33.

and consciously aware	*wa bi-hādha 'l-*
of this certitude,	*īqāni ʿārifīn:*
and ready to acknowledge	*wa bi-hādhhi 'l-*
this awareness,	*maʿrifa muʿtarifīn:*
and penitent	*wa bi-hādha 'l-*
through this acknowledgment,	*iʿtirafi munībīn:*
and successful	*wa bi-hādhihi 'l-*
because of this repentance.	*ināba fāʾizīn:*
May we be eager	*wa fī-mā*
for that which is close to You,	*ladai-ka rāghibīn:*
and seekers	*wa li-mā*
of that which is in Your presence.	*ʿinda-ka ṭālibīn:*
May You justly vaunt our worth	*wa bāhi*
to the noble	*bi-na 'l-malāʾikata 'l-*
recording angels.[530]	*kirāma 'l-kātibīn:*
Resurrect us in the company of	*wa 'ḥshir-nā*
the Prophets	*maʿa 'n-nabiyyīna*
and the champions of truth,	*wa 'ṣ-ṣiddīqīn:*
and the martyrs	*wa 'sh-shuhadāʾi 'ṣ-*
and the righteous.[531]	*ṣāliḥīn:*
Let us not be included	*wa lā tajʿal-nā*
among those	*mim-mani*
whom the devils seduce,	*'stahwat-hu 'sh-shayāṭīn:*
distracting them	*fa-shaghalat-hu*
from their religious duty,	*ʿani 'd-dīn:*
so that they come to be	*fa-aṣbaḥa*
among the remorseful,	*mina 'n-nādimīn:*
and in the Hereafter	*wa fi 'l-ākhirati*
among the losers.	*mina 'l-khāsirīn:*
Grant us eternal life	*wa awjib la-na 'l-khulūda*
in the Gardens of bliss,	*fī jannāti 'n-naʿīm:*
through Your Mercy,	*bi-raḥmati-ka*
O Most Merciful of the merciful!	*yā Arḥama 'r-rāḥimīn.*
O Allāh, to You be the praise,	*Allāhumma la-ka 'l-ḥamd:*
for Worthy of praise are You,	*wa Anta li'l-ḥamdi Ahl:*
and You are the One	*wa Anta 'l-*
who is truly Deserving	*Ḥaqīqu*
of gracious recognition	*bi'l-minnati*
and more credit yet.	*thumma 'l-faḍl:*
To You be the praise	*la-ka 'l-ḥamdu*
for the uninterrupted flow	*ʿalā tatābuʿi*
of Your beneficence.	*iḥsāni-k:*
To You be the praise	*wa la-ka 'l-ḥamdu*
for the endless recurrence	*ʿalā tawāturi*

[530] This is an allusion to Q. 82:10–12.

[531] This is an allusion to Q. 4:69.

of Your benefaction.	*in'āmi-k:*
To You be the praise	*wa la-ka 'l-ḥamdu*
for the constant stream	*'alā tarādufi*
of Your benevolence.	*'mtināni-k.*
O Allāh,	*Allāhumma*
You instilled affection for us in the	*inna-ka 'aṭṭafta 'alai-nā*
hearts of our fathers and mothers,	*qulūba 'l-ābā'i wa 'l-ummahāti*
when we were little children,	*ṣighārā:*
and You have multiplied	*wa ḍā'afta*
Your favors to us,	*'alai-nā ni'ama-ka*
since we became adults.	*kibārā:*
You have conferred	*wa wālaita*
Your kindness upon us	*ilai-nā birra-ka*
in copious abundance.	*midrārā:*
You have not been quick	*wa jahilnā*
to punish us,	*wa mā*
although we have often	*'ājalta-nā*
acted foolishly.	*mirārā:*
To You the praise is therefore due,	*fa-la-ka 'l-ḥamdu*
O Allāh,	*'llāhumma:*
so we praise You in private	*fa-innā naḥmidu-ka*
and in public too,	*sirran wa jihārā:*
and we thank You lovingly	*wa nashkuru-ka maḥabbatan*
and of our own free will.	*wa 'khtiyārā:*
Of course the praise is due to You,	*fa-la-ka 'l-ḥamdu*
since You inspired us	*idh alhamta-nā*
to request forgiveness for our sin.	*mina 'l-khaṭa'i 'stighfārā:*
To You belongs the praise,	*wa la-ka 'l-ḥamdu*
so bestow upon us a Garden	*fa-'rzuq-nā jannatan*
[of Paradise]	
and screen from us a Fire [of Hell].	*wa 'ḥjub 'an-nā nārā:*
Do not destroy us	*wa lā tuhlik-nā*
on the Day of Resurrection,	*yawma 'l-ba'thi*
thereby putting us to shame	*fa-taj'al-nā*
among the folk assembled.	*baina 'l-ma'āshiri 'ārā:*
Do not disgrace us	*wa lā tafḍaḥ-nā*
by exposing our bad deeds,	*bi-sū'i af'āli-nā*
on the Day of our meeting with You,	*yawma liqā'i-ka*
thereby leaving us nothing to wear	*fa-taksu-nā*
but degradation and dejection.	*dhillatan wa 'nkisārā:*
[Grant these requests]	
through Your Mercy,	*bi-raḥmati-ka*
O Most Merciful of the merciful!	*yā Arḥama 'r-rāḥimīn.*
O Allāh, to You be the praise,	*Allāhumma la-ka 'l-ḥamd:*
as You have guided us unto Islām,	*ka-mā hadaita-nā li'l-Islām:*
and given us wisdom	*wa a'ṭaita-na 'l-ḥikmata*
and the Qur'ān.	*wa 'l-Qur'ān:*

O Allāh, You taught us [the Qur'ān]	*Allāhumma Anta 'allamta-nā*
before we felt any interest	*qabla raghbati-nā*
in its teaching.	*fī ta'līmi-h:*
You bestowed its grace upon us,	*wa mananta bi-hi 'alai-nā*
before we learned	*qabla 'alimnā*
how to understand it,	*bi-ma'rifati-h:*
and You singled us out to receive it,	*wa khaṣaṣta-nā bi-hi*
before we had any understanding	*qabla ma'rifati-nā*
of its merit.	*bi-faḍli-h.*
O Allāh, since this has been	*Allāhumma fa-idhā kāna dhālika*
a kindness to us,	*min faḍli-ka*
from Your bountiful grace,	*luṭfan bi-nā*
and a favor conferred upon us,	*anywa 'mtinānan 'alai-nā min ghairi*
without scheming or effort	*ḥīlati-nā*
on our part,	*wa lā quwwati-nā:*
grant us now, O Allāh,	*fa-hab la-nā 'llāhumma*
the proper observance of its Truth,[532]	*ri'āyata ḥaqqi-h:*
and the preservation of its Verses,	*wa ḥifẓa āyāti-h:*
and conduct in accordance with	*wa 'amalan*
its unequivocal precepts,	*bi-muḥkami-h:*
and faith in its ambiguous passages,	*wa īmānan bi-mutashābih-h:*
and right guidance in the	*wa hudan*
contemplation of its meaning,[533]	*fī tadabburi-h:*
and reflection on its parables	*wa tafakkuran fī amthāli-hi*
and its miraculous character,	*wa mu'jizati-h:*
and insight	*wa tabṣiratan*
into its illumination	*fī nūri-hi*
and its legislation.	*wa ḥukmi-h:*
Let us not be assailed by doubts	*lā tu'āriḍ-na 'sh-shukūku*
concerning its credibility,	*fī taṣdīqi-h:*
and let no deviation	*wa lā yakhtalij-na 'z-*
cause us to waver	*zaighu*
in the pursuit of its path.	*fī qaṣdi ṭarīqi-h.*
O Allāh, enable us to benefit	*Allāhumma 'nfa'-nā*
by the Mighty Qur'ān,	*bi-'l-Qur'āni 'l-'aẓīm:*
and let us find blessings in the signs	*wa bārik la-nā fi 'l-āyāti*
and the wise remembrance	*wa 'dh-dhikri 'l-ḥakīm:*
[it contains].[534]	
Accept [our supplication] from us,	*wa taqabbal min-nā*
for You are indeed	*inna-ka*
the All-Hearing, the All-Knowing,	*Anta 's-Samī'u 'l-'Alīm:*
and relent toward us,	*wa tub 'alai-nā*

[532] This phrase alludes to an expression used by Allāh (Almighty and Glorious is He) in Q. 57:27.

[533] This is an allusion to Q. 4:82 and 23:68.

[534] This is an allusion to Q. 3:58.

for You are indeed	*inna-ka*
the Ever-Relenting,	*Anta 't-Tawwābu 'r-*
the All-Compassionate.	*Raḥīm:*
[Grant our requests]	
through Your Mercy,	*bi-raḥmati-ka*
O Most Merciful of the merciful!	*yā Arḥama 'r-rāḥimīn.*
O Allāh, let the Qur'ān be	*Allāhumma 'j'ali 'l-Qur'āna*
the springtime of our hearts,	*rabī'a qulūbi-nā:*
and the healing of our breasts,	*wa shifā'a ṣudūri-nā:*
and the removal of our sorrows,	*wa jilā'a aḥzāni-nā:*
and the departure of our worries	*wa dhahāba humūmi-nā*
and our anxieties.	*wa ghumūmi-nā:*
[Let it be] our driver and our leader,	*wa sā'iqa-nā wa qā'ida-nā*
and our guide	*wa dalīla-nā*
to You and to Your Gardens	*ilai-ka wa ilā jannāti-ka*
the Gardens of bliss,	*jannāti 'n-na'īm:*
through Your Mercy,	*bi-raḥmati-ka*
O Most Merciful of the merciful!	*yā Arḥama 'r-rāḥimīn.*
O Allāh, let the Qur'ān be	*Allāhumma 'j'ali 'l-Qur'āna*
for our hearts an illumination,	*li-qulūbi-nā ḍiyā':*
for our eyes a clarification,	*wa li-abṣāri-nā jilā':*
for our sicknesses a medication,	*wa li-asqāmi-nā dawā':*
for our sins a purification,	*wa li-dhunūbi-nā mumaḥḥiṣā:*
and from the Fire [of Hell]	*wa mina 'n-nāri*
a means of salvation.	*mukhalliṣā.*
O Allāh,	*Allāhumma 'ksu-nā*
cause it to dress us in fine clothes,	*bi-hi 'l-ḥulal:*
and to settle us on couches	*wa askin-nā*
in the shade.	*bi-hi 'ẓ-ẓulal:*
Use it in order to shower	*wa asbigh 'alai-nā*
blessings upon us,	*bi-hi 'n-ni'am:*
and to drive misfortunes	*wa 'dfa' bi-hi*
away from us.	*'an-na 'n-niqam:*
Let it enable us,	*wa 'j'al-nā*
when recompense is due,	*bi-hi 'inda 'l-jazā'i*
to be among those	*mina 'l-*
who are successful;	*fā'izīn:*
when gracious favor is bestowed,	*wa 'inda 'n-na'mā'i*
to be among those who are grateful;	*mina 'sh-shākirīn:*
and in the face of trial	*wa 'inda 'l-*
and tribulation,	*balā'i*
to be among those	*mina 'ṣ-*
who patiently endure.	*ṣābirīn:*
Let us not be included among	*wa lā taj'al-nā*
those whom the devils seduce,	*mim-mani 'stahwat-hu 'sh-shayāṭīn:*
by using this world to tempt them	*fa-shaghalat-hu bi 'd-dunyā*

away from religious duty,	*ʿani 'd-dīn:*
so that they come to be	*fa-aṣbaḥa*
among the losers.	*mina 'l-khāsirīn:*
[Grant our requests]	
through Your Mercy,	*bi-raḥmati-ka*
O Most Merciful of the merciful!	*yā Arḥama 'r-rāḥimīn.*
O Allāh, do not let	*Allāhumma lā tajʿali 'l-*
the Qurʾān be unfruitful,	*Qurʾāna māḥilā:*
and do not let the road	*wa la 'ṣ-ṣirāṭa*
lead us nowhere.	*bi-nā zāʾilā:*
Do not cause our Prophet, our Chief	*wa lā nabiyya-nā wa sayyida-nā*
and our Mainstay, Muḥammad,	*wa sanada-nā Muḥammadan*
(Allāh bless him and give him peace)	*(ṣalla 'llāhu ʿalai-hi wa sallam)*
to disown us at the Resurrection,	*fi 'l-qiyāmati ʿan-nā*
and let him not turn	*muʿriḍan*
his back upon us.	*wa lā muwalliyā:*
Let him rather be,	*ijʿal-hu*
O our Lord and our Creator,	*yā Rabba-nā Khāliqa-nā*
O our Sustainer,	*yā Rāziqa-nā*
an intercessor who has been	*la-nā shāfiʿan*
empowered to intercede on our behalf.	*mushaffaʿā:*
Bring us to his Basin, and use his cup	*wa awrid-nā ḥawḍa-hu wa 'sqi-nā*
to offer us a drink	*bi-kaʾsi-hi*
that is so thirst-quenching,	*mashraban rawiyyā:*
so palatable and salubrious,	*sāʾighan*
that we shall never	*haniyyā:*
be thirsty again after having drunk it.[535]	*lā naẓmaʾu baʿda-hu abadā:*
Let us be neither shameful	*ghaira khazāyā*
nor disloyal,	*wa lā nākithīn:*
not guilty of denial	*wa lā jāḥidīn:*
not having earned Your wrath,	*wa lā maghḍūbin ʿalai-nā*
and not having gone astray.[536]	*wa lā ḍāllīn:*
[Grant our requests]	
through Your Mercy,	*bi-raḥmati-ka*
O Most Merciful of the merciful!	*yā Arḥama 'r-rāḥimīn.*
O Allāh, enable us to benefit	*Allāhumma 'nfaʿ-nā*
by the Qurʾān,	*bi'l-Qurʾāni 'lladhī*
the status of which	*rafaʿta*
You have exalted,	*makāna-h:*
the principles of which	*wa thabbatta*
You have established,	*arkāna-h:*
the authority of which	*wa ayyadta*
You have confirmed,	*sulṭāna-h:*
the blessings of which	*wa bayyanta*
You have explained,	*barakāta-hu*

535 See Vol.1, pp. 237–38.

536 This is an allusion to the words of Allāh (Exalted is He) in the Opening Sūra *[Sūrat al-Fātiḥa]* of the Qurʾān.

the language of which	*wa ja'alta'l-lughata 'l-*
You have caused to be	*'arabiyyata 'l-*
the eloquent Arabic tongue,[537]	*faṣīḥata lisāna-h:*
and [concerning which]	*wa*
You have said,	*qulta*
O Most Excellent of sayers	*yā 'azza*
(Glory be to Him):	*min qā'ilin subḥāna-h:*
So, when We recite it,	*fa-idhā qara'nāhu*
follow its recitation.	*fa-'ttabi' qur'ānah:*
Then upon Us	*thumma inna*
rests the task of explaining it.	*'alai-nā bayāna-h.*
(75:18,19)	
It is the best	*wa huwa aḥsanu*
of Your Books in arrangement,	*Kutubi-ka niẓāmā:*
the most lucid of them in speech,	*wa awḍaḥu-hā kalāmā:*
and the clearest of them in stating	*wa abyanu-hā*
what is lawful and unlawful.	*ḥalālan wa ḥarāmā:*
It is precise in explanation,	*muḥkamu 'l-bayān:*
manifest in demonstration,	*ẓāhiru 'l-burhān:*
securely protected from excess	*maḥrūsun mina 'z-ziyādati*
and insufficiency.	*wa 'n-nuqṣān:*
In it there is a promise and a threat,[538]	*fī-hi wa'dun wa wa'īd:*
an intimidation and a menace.	*wa takhwīfun wa tahdīd:*
Falsehood cannot come at it	*lā ya'tī-hi 'l-bāṭilu min*
from before it or behind it.	*baini yadai-hi wa lā min khalfi-h:*
[It is] a revelation	*tanzīlun*
from One who is All-Wise,	*min Ḥakīmin*
All-Praiseworthy. (41:42)	*Ḥamīd.*
O Allāh, oblige us therefore	*Allāhumma fa-awjib la-nā*
to hold it in even greater honor.	*bi-hi 'sh-sharafa 'l-mazīd:*
Enroll us in	*wa alḥiq-nā*
every auspicious act of piety,	*bi-kulli birrin sa'īd:*
and keep us employed	*wa 'sta'mil-nā*
in righteous and rightly guided work.	*fī 'l-'amali 'ṣ-ṣāliḥi 'r-rashīd:*
You are indeed the Ever-Near,	*inna-ka Anta 'l-Qarību 'l-*
the Responsive.	*Mujīb:*
[Grant our requests]	
through Your Mercy,	*bi-raḥmati-ka*
O Most Merciful of the merciful!	*yā Arḥama 'r-rāḥimīn.*
O Allāh, as You have caused us to be	*Allāhumma fa-ka-mā ja'alta-nā*
believers in it [the Qur'ān],	*bi-hi muṣaddiqīn:*
and verifiers	*wa li-mā*
of that which it contains,	*fī-hi muḥaqqiqīn:*

537 Allāh (Exalted is He) has stated this emphatically in Q. 26:192-195.

538 That is to say, the promise of blissful reward in the Garden of Paradise, and the threat of terrible torment in the Fire of Hell.

let us also be beneficiaries	*fa-'j'al-nā bi-tilāwati-hi*
of its recitation,	*muntafi'īn:*
attentive to the sweet delight	*wa ilā ladhīdhi*
of its oration,	*khiṭābi-hi mustami'īn:*
ready to take instruction	*wa bi-mā*
from its contents,	*fī-hi mu'tabirīn:*
compilers of its rules and regulations,	*wa li-aḥkāmi-hi jāmi'īn:*
obedient to its commandments	*wa li-awāmiri-hi*
and its prohibitions.	*wa nawāhī-hi khāḍi'īn:*
Let us be, at its conclusion,	*wa 'inda*
among those	*khatmi-hi*
who are tirumphantly successful.	*mina 'l-fā'izīn:*
Let us be recipients	*wa li-thawābi-hi*
of its spiritual reward,	*ḥā'izīn:*
remembering You	*wa la-ka fī jamī'i*
in all that we experience,	*shuhūdi-nā dhākirīn:*
and pinning our hopes	*wa ilai-ka fī jamī'i*
on You in all our affairs.	*umūri-nā rāji'īn:*
And grant forgiveness to us	*wa 'ghfir la-nā*
on this night of ours—to all of us—	*fī lailati-nā hādhihi ajma'īn:*
through Your Mercy,	*bi-raḥmati-ka*
O Most Merciful of the merciful!	*yā Arḥama 'r-rāḥimīn.*
O Allāh, cause us to be included	*Allāhumma 'j'al-nā*
among those	*mina 'lladhīna*
who have preserved for the Qur'ān	*ḥafiẓū li'l-Qur'āni*
its sanctity,	*ḥurmata-hu*
whenever they have held it	*lammā*
in their keeping,	*ḥafiẓū-h:*
and have glorified its dignity,	*wa 'aẓẓamū manzilata-hu*
whenever they have listened to it,	*lammā sami'ū-h:*
and have behaved	*wa ta'addabū*
with due propriety,	*bi-ādābi-hi*
whenever they have been	*lammā*
in its presence,	*ḥaḍarū-h:*
and have abided by its ordinance,	*wa 'ltazamū ḥukma-hu*
whenever they have been	*lammā*
apart from it,	*fāraqū-h:*
and have beautified its surroundings,	*wa aḥsanū jiwāra-hu*
whenever they have been	*lammā*
in its vicinity,	*jāwarū-h:*
and have dedicated its recitation	*wa arādū bi-tilāwati-hi*
to Your Noble Countenance	*Wajha-ka 'l-Karīm:*
and the abode of the Hereafter,	*wa dāra 'l-ākhira:*
and have thus attained,	*fa-waṣalū*
through its agency,	*bi-hi*
to the splendidly honorable	*ila 'l-maqāmāti 'l-*
spiritual stations.	*fākhira:*

Cause each of us, through its agency,	*wa 'jʿal-nā bi-hi*
to be someone who rises high in the	*mim-man*
ascending strata of the Gardens	*fī daraji 'l-janāni yartaqī*
[of Paradise],	
and who finds that his Prophet	*wa bi-nabiyyi-hi*
(Allāh bless him and give him peace)	*(ṣalla 'llāhu ʿalai-hi wa sallam)*
is pleased with him,	*yawma ʿarḍi-hi*
when he meets him	*wa huwa rāḍin*
on the Day of his review	*ʿan-hu yaltaqī:*
[at the Resurrection].	
For he who can rely on the Qurʾān	*fa-'l-mushtafiʿu*
for intercession	*bi'l-Qurʾāni*
is not a person in trouble.	*ghairu shaqī:*
[Grant ourrequests]	
through Your Mercy,	*bi-raḥmati-ka*
O Most Merciful of the merciful!	*yā Arḥama 'r-rāḥimīn.*
O Allāh,	*Allāhumma*
let it be a complete Qurʾanic recital	*'jʿal-hā khatmatan*
that is blessed	*mubārakatan*
for those who have recited it,	*ʿalā man qaraʾa-hā*
and those who have attended	*wa ḥaḍara-hā*
and heard it,	*wa samiʿa-hā*
and have said "*Āmīn*"	*wa ammana*
to its supplication.	*ʿalā duʿāʾi-hā:*
Send down also, O Allāh,	*wa anzil Allāhumma*
some of Your bountiful blessings	*min barakāti-hā*
to the inhabitants of houses	*ʿalā ahli 'd-dūri*
in their houses,	*fī dūri-him:*
to the inhabitants of mansions	*wa ʿalā ahli 'l-quṣūri*
in their mansions,	*fī quṣūri-him:*
to the inhabitants of seaports	*wa ʿalā ahli 'th-thughūri*
in their seaports,	*fī thughūri-him:*
and to the inhabitants	*wa ʿalā ahli 'l-*
of the two Holy Places[539]	*Ḥaramaini*
in their two Holy Places,	*fī Ḥaramai-him*
so long as those concerned	*mina 'l-*
are true believers.	*muʾminīn.*
O Allāh, and then there are	*Allāhumma*
some members	*wa ahlu 'l-*
of our religious community	*qubūri*
among the inhabitants of the graves.	*min ahli millati-nā*
Send down to them,	*anzil ʿalai-him*
in their graves,	*fī qubūri-himu 'ḍ-*
illumination and comfort.	*ḍiyāʾa wa 'l-fusḥa:*

539 The two Holy Places [*al-Ḥaramān/-ain*] are the cities of Mecca and Medina. (The third Holy Place [*thālith al-Ḥaramain*] is Jerusalem.)

Recompense them with goodness	*wa jāzi-him*
for the good they have done,	*bi'l-iḥsāni iḥsānā:*
and with forgiveness	*wa bi's-sayyi'ati*
for their bad deeds,	*ghufrānā:*
and treat us with compassion,	*wa 'rḥam-nā*
when we come to be	*idhā ṣirnā*
in the state to which they have come,	*ilā mā ṣārū ilai-h:*
through Your Mercy,	*bi-raḥmati-ka*
O Most Merciful of the merciful!	*yā Arḥama 'r-rāḥimīn.*
O Allāh, O Provider of nourishment,	*Allāhumma yā Sā'iqa 'l-qūt:*
O Hearer of the sound of the voice,	*yā Sāmi'a 'ṣ-ṣawt:*
O Clother of the bones after death,	*yā Kāsi 'l-'iẓāmi ba'da 'l-mawt:*
bless Muḥammad	*ṣalli 'alā Muḥammadin*
and the family of Muḥammad.	*wa 'alā āli Muḥammad:*
Do not leave us, on this noble	*wa lā tada' la-nā fī hādhihi 'l-*
and blessed night of ours,	*lailati 'sh-sharīfati 'l-mubārakati*
with any sin	*dhanban*
that You have not forgiven,	*illā ghafarta-h:*
nor with any care	*wa lā hamman*
that You have not dispelled,	*illā farajta-h:*
nor with any worry	*wa lā karban*
that You have not relieved,	*illā naffasta-h:*
nor with any grief	*wa lā ghumman*
that You have not removed,	*illā kashafta-h:*
nor with any misfortune	*wa lā sū'an*
that You have not banished,	*illā ṣarafta-h:*
nor with any sick person	*wa lā marīḍān*
whom You have not cured,	*illā shafaita-h:*
nor with any suffering individual	*wa lā mubtalan*
whose well-being	*illā*
You have not restored,	*'āfaita-h:*
nor with anyone guilty	*wa lā dhā*
of some misconduct	*isā'atin*
whom You have not pardoned,	*illā aqalta-h:*
nor with any overdue entitlement	*wa lā ḥaqqan*
that You have not extracted,	*illa 'stakhrajta-h:*
nor with any missing person	*wa lā ghā'iban*
whom You have not brought home,	*illā radadta-h:*
nor with any rebellious sinner	*wa lā 'āṣiyan*
whom You have not guided aright,	*illā hadaita-h:*
nor with any child	*wa lā waladan*
whom You have not	*illā*
made fit and strong,	*jabarta-h:*
nor with anyone deceased	*wa lā mayyitan*
whom You have not	*illā*
treated mercifully,	*raḥimta-h:*
nor with any need,	*wa lā ḥājatan*

connected with this world	*min ḥawāʾiji 'd-dunyā*
or the Hereafter,	*wa 'l-ākhirati*
worthy of Your approval	*la-ka fī-hā riḍan*
and important to our welfare,	*wa la-nā fī-hā ṣalāḥun*
that You have not helped us to fulfill,	*illā aʿanta-nā ʿalā qaḍāʾi-hā*
with a facility supplied by You,	*bi-yusrin min-ka*
and vitality	*wa ʿāfiyatin*
accompanied by forgiveness.	*maʿa 'l-maghfira:*
[Grant our requests]	
through Your Mercy,	*bi-raḥmati-ka*
O Most Merciful of the merciful!	*yā Arḥama 'r-rāḥimīn.*
O Allāh,	*Allāhumma*
grant us well-being and pardon us,	*ʿāfi-nā wa 'ʿfu ʿan-nā*
through Your mighty pardon,	*bi-ʿafwi-ka 'l-ʿaẓīm:*
and Your beautiful protection,	*wa sitri-ka 'l-jamīl:*
and Your eternally preexisting	*wa iḥsāni-ka 'l-*
beneficence,	*qadīm:*
O Everlasting Source of kindness,	*yā Dāʾima 'l-maʿrūf:*
O Abundant Source of goodness!	*yā Kathīra 'l-khair:*
And bless our Chief and our	*wa ṣalli ʿalā sayyidi-nā wa*
Mainstay, Muḥammad, and bless	*sanadi-nā Muḥammadin wa ʿalā*
his brethren, the Prophets, and bless	*ikhwāni-hi 'l-anbiyāʾi wa ʿalā*
his family and the angels,	*āli-hi wa 'l-malāʾikati*
and salute them	*wa sallim*
with the greeting of peace.	*taslīmā.*
Our Lord,	*Rabba-nā*
grant us mercy from Your presence,	*āti-nā min ladun-ka raḥma:*
and smooth the way for us to keep	*wa hayyiʾ la-nā*
our business on a rightly guided course,	*min amri-nā rushdā:*
and help us to succeed	*wa waffiq-nā*
in the righteous work	*li-ʿamali 'ṣ-ṣāliḥi*
that will earn us Your good pleasure,	*yurḍī-ka ʿan-nā:*
through Your Mercy,	*bi-raḥmati-ka*
O Most Merciful of the merciful!	*yā Arḥama 'r-rāḥimīn.*
O Allāh, bless Muḥammad,	*Allāhumma ṣalli ʿalā Muḥammadin*
as You have used him to guide us	*ka-mā hadaita-nā*
out of error.	*bi-hi mina 'ḍ-ḍalāla:*
O Allāh, bless Muḥammad,	*Allāhumma ṣalli ʿalā Muḥammadin*
as You have used him to rescue us	*ka-ma 'stanqadhta-nā*
from ignorance.	*bi-hi mina 'l-jahāla:*
O Allāh, bless Muḥammad,	*Allāhumma ṣalli ʿalā Muḥammadin*
as he has delivered the Message.	*ka-mā ballagha 'r-risāla:*
O Allāh, bless Muḥammad, [who is]	*Allāhumma ṣalli ʿalā Muḥammadin*
the sun of the cities and towns,	*shamsi 'l-bilād:*

the moon of the place of rest,	*wa qamari 'l-mihād:*
the beauty of the roses,	*wa zaini 'l-wirād:*
and the intercessor	*wa shafīʿi 'l-*
on behalf of sinners	*mudhnibīna*
on the Day of Summoning.[540]	*yawma 't-Tanād:*
O Allāh, bless Muḥammad,	*Allāhumma ṣalli ʿalā Muḥammadin*
and his offspring	*wa dhurriyyati-hi*
and all his Companions,	*wa jamīʿi ṣaḥābati-h:*
who came to his support,	*alladhīna qāmū bi-nuṣrati-h:*
and followed his exemplary practice,	*wa jaraw bi-sunnati-h:*
through Your Mercy,	*bi-raḥmati-ka*
O Most Merciful of the merciful!	*yā Arḥama 'r-rāḥimīn.*
O Allāh, bless Muḥammad,	*Allāhumma ṣalli*
whom You sent	*ʿalā Muḥammadini 'lladhī*
with the Truth,	*bi'l-ḥaqqi baʿathta-h:*
and to whom You attributed veracity,	*wa bi'ṣ-ṣidqi naʿatta-h:*
and whom You made remarkable	*wa bi'l-ḥilmi*
for tolerance,	*wasamta-h:*
and to whom You gave	*wa bi-Aḥmada*
the name Aḥmad,	*sammaita-h:*
and whom You have empowered	*wa fi 'l-*
to intercede for his Community	*qiyāmati fī ummati-hi*
at the Resurrection.	*shaffaʿta-h.*
O Allāh, bless Muḥammad,	*Allāhumma ṣalli ʿalā Muḥammadin*
as long as the stars shine bright,	*mā azharati 'n-nujūm:*
and bless Muḥammad,	*wa ṣalli ʿalā Muḥammadin*
as long as the clouds accumulate,	*mā talāḥamati 'l-ghuyūm:*
and bless Muḥammad,	*wa ṣalli ʿalā Muḥammadin*
O Ever-Living,	*yā Ḥayyu*
O Eternally Self-Sustaining One!	*yā Qayyūm.*
O Allāh, bless Muḥammad,	*Allāhumma ṣalli ʿalā Muḥammadin*
as long as the righteous remember him,	*mā dhakara-hu 'l-abrār:*
and bless Muḥammad	*wa ṣalli ʿalā Muḥammadin*
as long the night	*ma 'khtalafa 'l-lailu*
and the day take turns,	*wa 'n-nahār:*
and bless Muḥammad	*wa ṣalli ʿalā Muḥammadin*
and the Emigrés and the Helpers,	*wa ʿala 'l-Muhājirīna wa 'l-Anṣār:*
through Your Mercy,	*bi-raḥmati-ka*
O Most Merciful of the merciful!	*yā Arḥama 'r-rāḥimīn.*

[540] The Day of Resurrection is thus referred to in Q. 40:32,33.

The exhortation *[al-waṣiyya]*

You must realize— may Allāh	*iʿlamū—*
bestow His mercy upon you all—	*raḥima-kumu 'llāh—*
that this night of yours	*anna lailata-kum hādhihi*
is the night of bidding farewell	*lailatu 'l-wadāʿi*
to your month,	*li-shahri-kumu*
which Allāh has ennobled,	*'lladhī sharrafa-hu 'llahu*
which He has glorified,	*wa ʿaẓẓama-h:*
the value of which He has exalted,	*wa rafaʿa qadra-hu*
and which He has honored	*wa karrama-h:*
with fasting [by day] and vigil [by night],	*bi-'ṣ-ṣiyāmi wa 'l-qiyām:*
and the recitation of the Qurʾān,	*wa tilāwati 'l-Qurʾān:*
and the coming down to you	*wa nuzūli 'r-raḥmati*
therein of mercy	*fī-hi ʿalai-kum*
and approval from Allāh.	*mina 'llāhi wa 'r-riḍwān:*
Allāh has made it the lamp	*jaʿala-hu 'llāhu*
of the common folk,	*miṣbāḥa 'l-ʿāmm:*
and the means of establishing good order,	*wa wāsiṭata 'n-niẓām:*
and the glory of the principles of Islām,	*wa sharafa qawāʿidi 'l-Islām:*
which are resplendent with	*al-mushriqati*
the lights of fasting and vigil.	*bi-anwāri 'ṣ-ṣiyāmi wa 'l-qiyām:*
Allāh (Exalted is He) sent down	*anzala 'llāhu—taʿālā—*
His Book therein [in the month of Ramaḍān],	*fī-hi Kitāba-h:*
and in it He has opened	*wa fataḥa fī-hi*
His gates to the penitent.	*li't-tāʾibīna abwāba-h:*
In it no prayer of supplication	*fa-lā duʿāʾa fī-hi*
is offered without being heard,	*illā masmūʿ:*
no benefit is left	*wa lā khaira*
without being gathered,	*illā majmūʿ:*
no damage threatens	*wa lā ḍurra*
without being repulsed,	*illā madfūʿ:*
and no good deed is done	*wa lā ʿamala*
without being honorably accepted.	*illā marfūʿ:*
Fortunate and successful is he	*aẓ-ẓāfiru 'l-maimūnu*

who takes advantage	*mani 'ghtanama*
of its opportunities,	*awqāta-h:*
and a loser who misses a bargain	*wa 'l-khāsiru 'l-maghbūnu*
is he who neglects it and lets it slip by.	*man ahmala-hu fa-fāta-h:*
It is a month which Allāh	*shahrun*
has caused to be	*ja'ala-hu 'llāhu*
a means of purification for your sins,	*li-dhunūbi-kum taṭhīrā:*
and a means of atonement	*wa li-sayyi'āti-kum*
for your misdeeds.	*takfīrā:*
For those of you	*wa li-man*
who are well-behaved	*aḥsana*
in its company,	*min-kum ṣuḥbata-hu*
[He has caused it to be]	
a treasure and a radiant light,	*dhakhīratan wa nūrā:*
and, for those who fulfill	*wa li-man*
its requirements	*wafā bi-sharṭi-hi*
and observe it correctly,	*wa qāma bi-ḥaqq-hi*
a joyful and happy experience.	*faraḥan wa surūrā:*
It is a month in which pious restraint	*shahrun tawarra'a fī-hi*
is practiced even by people addicted	*ahlu 'l-fisqi*
to corrupt behavior	*wa 'l-fasād:*
and immoral conduct,	*wa zāda*
while the longing for Allāh	*fī-hi mina 'r-raghbati*
is more intensely	*ila 'llāhi*
felt by earnest and dedicated people.	*ahlu 'l-jiddi wa 'l-ijtihād:*
It is the month	*shahru*
for the reconstruction of hearts	*'amārāti 'l-qulūb:*
and the expiation of sins,	*wa kaffārāti 'dh-dhunūb:*
for paying special attention	*wa 'khtiṣāṣi 'l-*
to the mosques,	*masājid:*
by keeping them crowded	*bi'l-izdiḥāmi*
and crammed,	*wa 't-taḥāshud:*
and for the reduction of slaveholdings,	*wa hubūṭi 'l-amlāk:*
through contracts of emancipation	*bi-ṣikāki 'l-'itqi*
and manumission.	*wa 'l-fikāk:*
It is a month in which the mosques	*shahrun fī-hi 'l-masājidu*
are frequented,	*tu'mar:*
and the lamps are made to shine,	*wa 'l-maṣābīḥu tuzhar:*
and the verses	*wa 'l-āyātu*
[of the Qur'ān] are recited,	*tudhkar:*
and hearts are mended,	*wa 'l-qulūbu tujbar:*
and sins are forgiven.	*wa 'dh-dhunūbu tughfar:*
It is a month in which the mosques	*shahrun fī-hi tushriqu 'l-masājidu*
are bright with radiant lights,	*bi'l-anwār:*
and the angels make many pleas	*wa tukthiru 'l-*

for forgiveness on behalf	*malā'ikatu*
of those who are keeping the fast,	*li-ṣuwwāmi-hi mina 'l-istighfār:*
and in which	*wa yu'tiqu*
the All-Compelling One delivers—	*fī-hi 'l-Jabbār:*
each night	*fī kulli lailatin*
at the time of breaking fast—	*'inda 'l-ifṭār:*
six hundred thousand	*sitta-mi'ati alfi*
souls from the Fire.	*'atīqin mina 'n-nār:*
Gracious blessings	*wa tunazzilu*
are sent down therein,	*fī-hi 'l-barakāt:*
and charitable gifts	*wa tu'azzamu*
are magnified therein,	*fī-hi 'ṣ-ṣadaqāt:*
and bad deeds are expiated therein,	*wa tukaffaru fī-hi 's-sayyi'āt:*
and lapses are pardoned therein,	*wa tuqālu fī-hi 'l-'atharāt:*
and disasters are prevented therein,	*wa tudfa'u fī-hi 'n-nakabāt:*
and promotions are awarded therein,	*wa turfa'u fī-hi 'd-darajāt:*
and tears are mercifully	*wa turḥamu fī-hi 'l-*
spared therein,	*'abarāt:*
and therein the beautiful brides	*wa tunādī fī-hi 'l-ḥūru 'l-*
call out,	*ḥisānu*
from the Gardens [of Paradise]:	*mina 'l-jannāt:*
"Congratulations to you,	*hanī'an la-kum*
all you men and women	*yā ma'shara 'ṣ-ṣā'imīna*
who are fasting [by day],	*wa 'ṣ-ṣā'imāt:*
and all you men and women	*wa 'l-qā'imīna*
who are keeping vigil [by night],	*wa 'l-qā'imāt:*
on all the good things that Allāh	*bi-mā a'adda 'llāhu la-kum*
has prepared for you!	*mina 'l-khairāt:*
Copious blessings are in store for you,	*la-qad ghamarat-kumu 'l-barakāt:*
and your good news	*wa 'stabshara*
is welcomed with joy	*bi-kumu*
by those who inhabit	*ahlu 'l-arḍi*
the earth and the heavens."	*wa 's-samāwāt:*
So may Allāh bestow His mercy	*fa-raḥima 'llāhu*
upon any man	*'mra'an*
who prepares a bed for himself therein,	*mahhada fī-hi li-nafsi-h:*
before the advent of his funeral,	*qabla ḥulūli ramsi-h:*
and who concerns himself	*wa 'shtaghala*
with the day at hand,	*bi-yawmi-hi*
rather than his tomorrow	*'an ghadā-hu*
or his yesterday,	*wa amsi-h:*
and stocks up with provision	*wa tazawwada*
from its surplus,	*min baqiyyati zādi-h:*
for to waste it would amount	*fa-fī nafādi-hi*
to wasting his life,	*nafādu 'umri-h:*
and who shows the regret he feels	*wa aẓhara*

over having to part with his month,	*li-firāqi shahri-hi jazaʿa-h:*
and who salutes his month	*wa sallama*
with the greeting of peace,	*ʿalā shahri-h:*
and bids it farewell, and says:	*wa waddaʿa-hu wa qāl:*
"Peace be upon you,	*as-salāmu ʿalaika*
O month of Ramaḍān!	*yā shahra Ramaḍān:*
Peace be upon you,	*as-salāmu ʿalaika*
O month of fasting and vigil	*yā shahra 'ṣ-ṣiyāmi wa 'l-qiyāmi*
and recitation of the Qurʾān!	*wa tilāwati 'l-Qurʾān:*
Peace be upon you,	*as-salāmu ʿalaika*
O month of tolerance	*yā shahra 't-tajāwuzi*
and forgiveness!	*wa 'l-ghufrān:*
Peace be upon you,	*as-salāmu ʿalaika*
O month of blessings	*yā shahra 'l-barakati*
and active goodness!	*wa 'l-iḥsān:*
Peace be upon you,	*as-salāmu ʿalaika*
O month of the treasures	*yā shahra 't-tuḥafi*
and the good pleasure [of the Lord]!	*wa 'r-riḍwān:*
Peace be upon you,	*as-salāmu ʿalaika*
O month of rituals	*yā shahra 'n-nusuki*
and constant devotion to worship.	*wa 't-taʿabbud:*
Peace be upon you,	*as-salāmu ʿalaika*
O month of fasting [by day]	*yā shahra 'ṣ-ṣiyāmi*
and vigil and prayer by night!	*wa 't-tahajjud:*[779]
Peace be upon you,	*as-salāmu ʿalaika*
O month of the *tarāwīḥ*![541]	*yā shahra 't-tarāwīḥ:*
Peace be upon you,	*as-salāmu ʿalaika*
O month of the lights	*yā shahra 'l-anwāri*
and the lamps!	*wa 'l-maṣābīḥ:*
Peace be upon you,	*as-salāmu ʿalaika*
O glory of the extollers!	*yā fakhra 'l-wāṣifīn:*
Peace be upon you,	*as-salāmu ʿalaika*
O light of the tender lovers!	*yā nūra 'l-wāmiqīn:*
Peace be upon you,	*as-salāmu ʿalaika*
O garden of the worshipful!"	*yā rawḍata 'l-ʿābidīn:*
So, O month of ours,	*fa-yā*
we bid you farewell,	*shahra-nā*
but not because you are forsaken,	*ghaira muwaddaʿin waddaʿnā-k:*
and we part with you,	*wa ghaira*
but not because you are hated.[542]	*maqliyyin fāraqnā-k:*
Your daytime has been devoted	*kāna nahāru-ka*
to charitable work and fasting,	*ṣadaqatan wa ṣiyāmā:*
and your nighttime	*wa lailu-ka*
to reciting the Qurʾān	*qirāʾatan*
and keeping vigil,	*wa qiyāmā:*

[541] See Vol. 3, pp 126–35.

[542] This is an allusion to Q. 93:1–5.

so to you now, from us, comes a salutation and a farewell greeting.	*fa-ʿalai-ka min-nā* *taḥiyyatun wa salāmā.*
Shall we see you return to us again, or is death destined to overtake us, so that you do not come back to us?	*a-narā-ka taʿūdu baʿda-hā ʿalai-nā:* *aw yudriku-na 'l-manūnu* *fa-lā taʾūla ilai-nā:*
Our lamps, for your duration, were a well-known sight, and our mosques, for your duration, were constantly frequented.	*maṣābīḥu-nā* *fī-ka mashhūra:* *wa masājidu-nā* *fī-ka maʿmūra:*
But now the lamps are being extinguished, and the *tarāwīḥ* prayers are being discontinued. We are returning to our ordinary practice, and leaving the month of worshipful service.	*fa-'l-āna tanṭafi 'l-* *maṣābīḥ:* *wa tanqaṭiʿu 't-* *tarāwīḥ:* *wa narjiʿu* *ila 'l-ʿāda:* *wa nufāriqu* *shahra 'l-ʿibāda:*
If only I knew which one of us has been accepted, so that we could congratulate him on his excellent performance! Or if only I knew which one of us has been rejected, so that we could console him for his poor performance!	*fa-yā* *laita shiʿrī* *mani 'l-maqbūli min-nā* *fa-nuhanniʾa-hu bi-ḥusni ʿamali-h:* *am laita shiʿrī* *mani 'l-maṭrūdu min-nā* *fa-nuʿazziya-hu bi-sūʾi ʿamali-h:*
To you, O you who have been accepted, congratulations on Allāh's reward (Almighty and Glorious is He), and His good pleasure and His mercy, and His forgiveness and His approval, and His beneficence and His pardon, and His gracious favor and His [gift of] eternal life in the abode of His safekeeping.	*fa-yā ayyuha 'l-* *maqbūlu* *hanīʾan la-ka bi-thawābi 'llāhi—* *ʿazza wa jall—* *wa riḍwāni-hi wa raḥmati-hi* *wa ghufrāni-hi wa qabūli-hi* *wa iḥsāni-hi wa ʿafwi-hi* *wa 'mtināni-hi* *wa khulūdi-hi* *fī dāri amāni-h:*
As for you, O you who have been rejected, due to persistence in sin and transgression, and hostile aggression, and heedlessness and deviation, and wantonness and rebellion, you must bear the terrible affliction of Allāh's wrath and degradation. So where is your weeping eye? Where are your streaming tears?	*fa-yā ayyuha 'l-maṭrūdu* *bi-iḍrāri-hi* *bi-iṣrāri-hi* *wa-ṭughyāni-h:* *wa ʿudwāni-h:* *wa ghaflati-hi wa khusrāni-h:* *wa tamādī-hi wa ʿiṣyāni-h:* *la-qad ʿaẓumat muṣībatu-ka* *bi-ghaḍabi 'llāhi wa hawāni-hi* *fa-aina muqlatu-ka 'l-bākiya:* *wa aina damʿatu-ka 'l-jāriya:*

And where is	*wa aina*
your sighing and sobbing?	*zafratu-ka 'r-rāʾiḥatu 'l-ghādiya:*
Until what day have you deferred	*li-ayyi yawmin akhkharta*
your repentance?	*tawbata-k:*
Until what year have you stored	*wa li-ayyi ʿāmini 'ddakharta*
your promise away?	*ʿidata-k:*
Until some future date?	*ilā ʿāmin qābil:*
Until a year has gone by?	*wa ḥawlin ḥāʾil:*
Oh no! The span of life	*kallā fa-mā ilai-ka*
is not for you to decide,	*muddatu 'l-aʿmār:*
and its full term is not for you to know.	*wa lā maʿrifatu 'l-miqdār:*
Many an optimist has hoped	*fa-kam min muʾammilin*
to reach it [the next Fast],	*amala bulūgha-hu*
yet failed to reach it.	*fa-lam yablugh-h:*
Many a one has attained to it,	*wa kam min mudrikin la-hu*
but has not lived to complete it.	*wa lam yakhtim-h:*
Many a one has had	*wa kam*
a perfume prepared	*man aʿadda ṭīban*
for his celebration of the Festival,	*li-ʿīdi-h:*
which was then applied	*juʿila*
to his place of burial,	*fī talḥīdi-h:*
and had clothing tailored	*wa thiyāban*
for his adornment,	*li-tazyīni-h:*
which came to be a shroud	*ṣārat*
for his interment,	*li-takfīni-h:*
and has fully equipped himself	*wa mutaʾahhiban*
for his breaking of the Fast,	*li-fiṭri-h:*
only to be deposited as a pledge	*ṣāra murtahanan*
in his grave.[543]	*fī qabri-h:*
Many a one will never keep a Fast	*wa kam man lā yaṣūmu*
like this again,	*baʿda-hu siwā-h:*
though he is looking forward eagerly	*wa huwa yaṭmaʿu*
to experiencing another	*fī ghairi-hi an yarā-h:*
[month of Ramaḍān].	
So praise Allāh, O servants of Allāh,	*fa-'ḥmadu 'llāha ʿibāda 'llāhi*
for the attainment of its completion,	*ʿalā bulūghi 'khtitāmi-h:*
and beg Him to accept	*wa salū-hu*
the fasting in it,	*qabūla ṣiyāmi-h:*
and the vigil observed in it,	*wa qiyāmi-h:*
and be aware of Him	*wa rāqibū-hu*
in fulfilling His dues,	*bi-adāʾi ḥuqūqi-h:*
and hold fast to Allāh's lifeline[544]	*wa 'ʿtaṣimū bi-ḥabli 'llāhi*
and His help.	*wa tawfīqi-h:*

[543] This is an allusion to Q. 52:21 and 74:38.

[544] This is an allusion to Q. 3:103.

You must also realize—may	*wa 'ʿlamū—*
Allāh bestow His mercy upon you all—	*raḥima-kumu 'llāh—*
that you have just parted	*anna-kum fāraqtum*
with a mighty month,	*shahran ʿaẓīmā*
[a month that is]	
gracious and munificent.	*mutafaḍḍilan karīmā:*
Where are those who fasted	*aina 'ṣ-ṣuwwāmu 'l-*
and kept vigil,	*quwwām:*
your counterparts	*al-muwāfiqūna la-kum*
in the years gone by?	*fī sālifi 'l-aʿwām:*
Where are those	*wa aina man*
who used to be with you	*kāna maʿa-kum*
during the nights	*layālī shahri*
of the month of Ramaḍān,	*Ramaḍāna shāhidīn:*
bearing witness and discharging	*wa fī kulli ḥaqqi 'llāhi*
every duty to Allāh—	*muʿāmilīn:*
those fathers and mothers,	*mina 'l-ābāʾi wa 'l-ummahāti:*
and brothers and sisters,	*wa 'l-ikhwati wa 'l-akhawāti:*
and neighbors and close relatives?	*wa 'l-jīrati wa 'l-qurubāt:*
By Allāh, to them has come	*atā-hum wa 'llāhi*
the wrecker of delights,	*hādimu 'l-ladhdhāt*[784]*:*
the robber of desires,	*wa qāṭiʿu 'sh-shahawāt:*
and the separator of communities.	*wa mufarriqu 'l-jamāʿāt:*
It has left the gathering places	*fa-akhlā min-humu 'l-*
empty of them,	*mashāhid:*
and left the mosques devoid of them.	*wa ʿaṭṭala min-humu 'l-masājid:*
You see them cast	*tarā-hum*
into the bellies of the tombs.	*fī buṭūni 'l-alḥādi ṣarʿā:*
They find no defense	*lā yajidūna li-mā*
against their situation,	*hum fī-hi dafʿā:*
and they possess no power	*wa lā yamlikūna li-anfusi-him*
to harm or benefit themselves.	*ḍarran wa lā nafʿā:*
They can only wait	*yantaẓirūna*
for a Day whereon	*yawmani 'l-umamu*
the nations will be	*fī-hi ilā*
summoned to their Lord,	*Rabbi-him tudʿā:*
and all creatures will be resurrected	*wa 'l-khalāʾiqu tuḥsharu*
and hastily assembled	*ila 'l-mawqifi*
at the Place of Standing.[545]	*wa tasʿā:*
All sinews will tremble and quake	*wa 'l-farāʾiṣu tartaʿidu min hawli*
from the terror of that Day,	*dhālika 'l-yawmi jamʿā:*
and all hearts will suffer devastation	*wa 'l-qulūbu tataṣaddaʿu*
from the shattering experience	*mina 'l-ḥisābi*
of the Reckoning.	*ṣadʿā:*

[545] The earthly *mawqif*, i.e., the site at ʿArafāt where the rite of 'standing' *[wuqūf]* is performed during the Pilgrimage *[Ḥajj]*, provides a foretaste of the experience that awaits us all on the Day of Resurrection, when we shall be gathered at the Place of Standing *[al-Mawqif]* on the field of Araṣāt.

And a blast will be blown	*wa nufikha*
on the Trumpet,	*fi 'ṣ-ṣūri*
and then We shall	*fa-jamaʿnā-hum*
gather them together. (18:99)	*jamʿā:*
O servants of Allāh!	*ʿibāda 'llāhi*
whoever has restrained	*man kāna manaʿa*
his lower self	*nafsa-hu*
from that which is unlawful,	*mina 'l-ḥarām:*
during the month of Ramaḍān,	*fī shahri Ramaḍān:*
let him continue to restrain it	*fa-'l-yamnaʿ-hā fī-mā baʿda-hu*
in the ensuing months and years,	*mina 'sh-shuhūri wa 'l-aʿwām:*
for the God of the two months	*fa-inna Ilāha 'sh-shahraini*
is One,	*Wāḥid:*
and over the two periods of time	*wa Huwa ʿala 'z-zamānaini*
He is a Watchful Supervisor.	*Muṭṭaliʿun Shāhid:*
May Allāh compensate us,	*jazā-na 'llāhu*
and you too,	*wa iyyā-kum*
for the departure of	*ʿalā firāqi*
the month of blessed grace.	*shahri 'l-baraka:*
May He grant us	*wa ajzala*
our allotted portions,	*aqsāma-nā*
and grant you	*wa*
your allotted portions,	*aqsāma-kum*
of His mercy that is shared by all.	*min raḥmati-hi 'l-mushtaraka:*
May He bless us,	*wa bāraka la-nā*
and bless you,	*wa la-kum*
with His perpetual favor,	*fī baqiyyati-h:*
and may He cause us, and you,	*wa salaka bi-nā wa bi-kum*
to travel the path of His guidance,	*ṭarīqa hidāyati-h:*
through His mercy,	*bi-raḥmati-hi*
His grace and His kindness.	*wa faḍli-hi wa minnati-h.*
O Allāh,	*Allāhumma*
whatever You have apportioned,	*wa mā qasamta*
on this night,	*fī hādhihi 'l-lailati*
in the way of deliverance	*min ʿitqin*
and forgiveness,	*wa ghufrān:*
and mercy and good pleasure,	*wa raḥmatin wa riḍwān:*
and pardon and benevolence,	*wa ʿafwin wa 'mtinān:*
and munificence and benefaction,	*wa karamin wa iḥsān:*
and salvation from the Fires [of Hell],	*wa najātin mina 'n-nīrān:*
and everlasting sojourn	*wa khulūdin*
in the bliss of the Gardens	*fī naʿīmi 'l-jinān:*
[of Paradise], grant us	*fa-'jʿal*
the most copious share thereof,	*la-nā min-hu*
and the most abundant portions,	*awfara 'l-ḥaẓẓi wa ajzala 'l-aqsām:*
through Your Mercy,	*bi-raḥmati-ka*
O Most Merciful of the merciful!	*yā Arḥama 'r-rāḥimīn.*

O Allāh, as You brought us	*Allāhumma fa-ka-mā ballaghta-nā*
the month of fasting,	*shahra 'ṣ-ṣiyām:*
grant that our next year may be	*fa-'j'al 'āma-nā 'alai-nā*
one of the most	*min*
blessed of all our years,	*abraki 'l-a'wām:*
and that our coming days may be	*wa ayyāma-nā*
among the happiest of all our days.	*min as'adi 'l-ayyām:*
Accept from us	*wa taqabbal min-nā*
the fasting and the vigil	*mā qaddamnā-hu*
that we have offered up this month,	*fī-hi mina 'ṣ-ṣiyāmi wa 'l-qiyām:*
and grant us forgiveness for the sins	*wa 'ghfir la-nā ma 'qtarafnā fī-hi*
we have committed in the course of it,	*mina 'l-āthām:*
and rid us of the iniquities	*wa khalliṣ-nā*
of humankind,	*min maẓālimi 'l-anām:*
on the Day when	*yawma*
there will be no appeal	*lā yurjā*
to anyone apart from You.	*fī-hi siwā-k:*
O All-Knowing One!	*yā 'Allām:*
O Most Merciful of the merciful!	*yā Arḥama 'r-rāḥimīn.*
O Allāh, we have undertaken	*Allāhumma innā qad tawallainā*
the [daytime] fasting of our month,	*ṣiyāma shahri-nā*
and its nighttime vigil,	*wa qiyāma-hu*
though quite inadequately.	*'alā taqṣīr:*
We have discharged	*wa adainā fī-hi*
in the course of it	*min ḥaqqi-ka*
no more than a little	*qalīlan*
of much that is due to You.	*min kathīr:*
We now stand begging at Your door,	*wa qad anakhnā bi-bābi-ka sā'ilīn:*
seeking Your gracious favor,	*wa li-ma'rūfi-ka ṭālibīn:*
so do not send us away disappointed,	*fa-lā tarudda-nā khā'ibīn:*
and despairing of Your mercy.	*wa lā min raḥmati-ka āyisīn:*
We are the poor folk who need You,	*fa-naḥnu 'l-fuqarā'u ilai-k:*
the captives who stand before You.	*al-asrā baina yadai-k:*
To You our application is addressed,	*ilai-ka tawajjuhu-nā:*
and for Your gracious favor	*wa li-ma'rūfi-ka*
our petition is lodged.	*ta'arruḍu-nā:*
At Your door we have knocked,	*wa li-bābi-ka qara'nā:*
and for Your mercy we have begged,	*wa min raḥmati-ka sa'alnā:*
so treat our humility with compassion,	*fa-'rḥam khuḍū'a-nā:*
and mend our hearts,	*wa 'jbur qulūba-nā:*
and overlook our faults,	*wa 'stur 'uyūba-nā:*
and forgive our sins,	*wa 'ghfir dhunūba-nā:*
and comfort us[546] at the Resurrection,	*wa aqirra fi 'l-qiyāmati 'uyūni-nā:*
and do not turn	*wa lā taṣrif*
Your Noble Countenance	*Wajha-ka 'l-Karīma*
away from us,	*'an-nā:*

[546] Literally: "and cool our eyes."

and cause our work to be accepted,	*wa 'j'al 'amala-nā maqbūlā:*
and our striving to be acknowledged,	*wa sa'ya-nā mashkūrā:*
and grant us this night	*wa ḥazza-nā*
an abundance of good fortune.	*fī hādhihi 'l-lailati mawfūrā:*
O Allāh, if it is predetermined,	*Allāhumma in kāna*
according to Your foreknowledge,	*min sābiqi 'ilmi-ka*
that You will bring us together	*an tajmā'u-nā*
in another [Ramaḍān] like this,	*fī mithli-h:*
let it be a blessed experience for us.	*fa-bārik la-nā fī-h:*
And if You have foreordained	*wa in qaḍaita*
the termination of our life spans,	*bi-qaṭ'i ājāli-nā:*
and that something will intervene	*wa mā yaḥūlu baina-nā*
to prevent us from surviving until then,	*wa baina-h:*
let our successors be good	*fa-aḥsini 'l-khilāfata*
to those we leave behind,	*'alā bāqī-nā:*
and view our past	*wa awsi'i 'r-raḥmata*
with generous compassion.	*'alā māḍī-nā:*
Embrace us all completely	*wa 'ummu-nā jamī'an*
in Your mercy and Your forgiveness,	*bi-raḥmati-ka wa ghufrāni-k:*
and let the reunion take place	*wa 'j'ali 'l-maw'ida*
in the midst of Your Garden	*buḥbūḥa jannati-ka*
[of Paradise]	
and Your good pleasure,	*wa riḍwāni-k:*
in the company of those	*ma'a 'lladhīna an'amta 'alai-him*
to whom Allāh has granted	*mina 'n-nabiyyīna*
gracious favor—the Prophets,	*wa 'ṣ-ṣiddīqīna wa 'sh-shuhadā'i*
the champions of truth, the martyrs	*wa 'ṣ-ṣāliḥīn:*
and the righteous—and the best	*wa ḥasuna ulā'ika*
of company are they![547]	*rafīqā.*
[Grant our requests]	
through Your Mercy,	*bi-raḥmati-ka*
O Most Merciful of the merciful!	*yā Arḥama 'r-rāḥimīn.*
O Allāh,	*Allāhumma*
the occupants of the graves	*wa ahlu 'l-qubūri*
are the pledges of sins,	*rahā'inu dhunūbin*
not allowed to go free,	*lā yuṭlaqūn:*
and prisoners in solitary confinement,	*wa asārā waḥshatin*
not to be released,	*lā yufakkūn:*
and absent travellers,	*wa ghurabā'u safarin*
not expected to return.	*lā yuntaẓarūn:*
The dust of the earth has erased	*maḥat dārisātu 'th-tharā*
the good looks of their faces,	*maḥāsina wujūhi-him:*
and the vermin live beside them	*wa jāwarat-humu 'l-hawāmmu*
in the vaults of their graves,	*fī malāḥidi qubūri-him:*
for they are stiff, incapable of talking,	*fa-hum jamūdun lā yatakallamūn:*

[547] These six lines, beginning with "in the company of those...," constitute a partial quotation of Q. 4:69.

near neighbors	*wa jīrānun*
who cannot visit one another,	*qurbun lā yatazāwarūn:*
and the inhabitants of a tomb,	*wa sukkānu laḥdin*
which they cannot leave	*ila 'l-ḥashri*
until the Resurrection.	*lā yaẓ'anūn:*
Among them are doers of good	*wa fī-him muḥsinūna*
and evildoers,	*wa musī'ūn:*
and negligent types	*wa muqaṣṣirūna*
as well as hard workers.	*wa mujtahidūn:*
O Allāh, if there is someone	*Allāhumma fa-man kāna*
amongst them who is already happy,	*min-hum masrūrā:*
grant him still more dignity and joy,	*fa-zid-hu karāmatan wa ḥubūrā:*
and if anyone amongst	*wa man kāna*
them is depressed,	*min-hum malhūfā:*
replace his sadness	*fa-badhdhil ḥuzna-hu*
with joy and happiness.	*faraḥan wa surūrā.*
O Allāh,	*Allāhumma*
treat with compassion all the Muslims	*wa ta'aṭṭaf 'alā kāffati*
who have died while traveling,	*amwāt al-muslimīna 'r-rāḥilīn:*
and those who have surrendered	*wa 'l-muqīmīna 'l-*
their souls at home,	*mustaslimīn:*
through Your Mercy,	*bi-raḥmati-ka*
O Most Merciful of the merciful!	*yā Arḥama 'r-rāḥimīn.*
O Allāh, grant	*Allāhumma 'j'al*
that their graves may be	*qubūra-hum*
tunnels through which	*mafāyiḍa*
Your blessings flow,	*ṣalawāti-k:*
and places where Your gifts are stored,	*wa maqārra hibāti-k:*
and paths for Your beneficence,	*wa ṭuruqa iḥsāni-k:*
and channels for Your pardon	*wa majāriya 'afwi-ka*
and forgiveness,	*wa ghufrāni-k:*
so that [their occupants]	*ḥattā yakūnū*
may rest in peace	*ilā buṭūni 'l-alḥādi*
within the confines of their tombs,	*muṭma'innīn:*
assured of Your grace	*wa bi-jūdi-ka*
and generosity,	*wa karami-ka wāthiqīn:*
and already advanced	*wa ilā a'lā*
to Your highest degrees.	*darajāti-ka sābiqīn:*
Confer this special favor	*wa 'khṣuṣ bi-dhālika 'l-ābā'a*
on the fathers and the sons,	*wa 'l-banīn:*
and the brothers and the next of kin.	*wa 'l-ikhwata wa 'l-aqrabīn:*
[Confer it]	
before the work of demolition	*qabla an yashtamila 'l-hadmu*
wrecks the edifice completely,	*'ala 'l-binā':*
and murky gloom	*wa 'l-kadaru*

obliterates pure clarity,	*ʿala 'ṣ-ṣafāʾ:*
and the cord of hope is cut	*wa yanqaṭiʿa mina 'l-ḥayāti*
adrift from life,	*ḥablu 'r-rajāʾ:*
and the dwellings lie buried	*wa taṣīra 'l-manāzilu*
beneath the layers of earth.	*taḥta aṭbāqi 'th-tharā:*
[Confer it] before the wind	*wa qabla an*
becomes a hurricane,	*yaṣīra 'r-rīḥu wailā:*
and the drop becomes a flood,	*wa 'l-qaṭru sailā:*
and the morning turns into a night,	*wa 'ṣ-ṣubḥu lailā:*
and death drags a skirt across	*wa yasḥaba 'l-mawtu ʿalā*
the inhabitants of the heavens	*ahli 's-samāwāti*
and the earth.	*wa 'l-arḍi dhailā:*
[Confer it] before	*wa qabla an*
the grand old man cries:	*yaqūla 'sh-shaikhu 'l-kabīr:*
"White hair! What a pity!" and	*wāshaibāh:*
the eminent middle-aged man cries:	*wa yaqūla 'l-kahlu 'l-khaṭīr:*
"Disgrace! What a pity!"	*wākhajlatāh:*
and the guilty sinner cries:	*wa yaqūla 'l-mudhnibu 'l-musīʾ:*
"Failure! What a pity!"	*wākhaibatāh:*
and the young boy cries:	*wa yaqūla 'l-ḥadathu 'ṣ-ṣaghīr:*
"Disappointment! What a pity!"	*wāḥasratāh:*
[Confer it before]	
they are too ashamed	*wa ukhjilū min-hu*
and filled with dread,	*wa ashfaqū:*
and remorse has overwhelmed them,	*wa ghashiyat-hum mina 'n-nadāma:*
and their mouths have been sealed	*wa khutima ʿalā afwāhi-him*
so that they cannot speak,	*fa-lā yanṭuqū:*
and all they can do is tilt their heads,	*wa waqafū ʿalā ʿamali*
so they bow their heads in silence,	*naksi 'r-ruʾūsi fa-aṭraqū:*
and they have witnessed	*wa ʿāyanū mina 'l-ahwāli*
such terrors that	*ma waddū*
they dearly wish	*maʿa-hu anna-hum*
they had never been created.	*lam yukhlaqū:*
O Allāh, O Provider of nourishment,	*Allāhumma yā Sāʾiqa 'l-qūt:*
O Hearer of the sound of the voice,	*yā Sāmiʿa 'ṣ-ṣawt:*
O Clother of the bones after death,	*yā Kāsi ya 'l-ʿiẓāmi baʿda 'l-mawt:*
bless Muḥammad	*ṣalli ʿalā Muḥammadin*
and the family of Muḥammad.	*wa ʿalā āli Muḥammad:*
Do not leave us, on this noble	*wa lā tadaʿ la-nā fī hādhihi 'l-*
and blessed night of ours,	*lailati 'sh-sharīfati 'l-mubārakati*
with any sin	*dhanban*
that You have not forgiven,	*illā ghafarta-h:*
nor with any care	*wa lā hamman*
that You have not dispelled,	*illā farajta-h:*
nor with any worry	*wa lā karban*

that You have not relieved,	*illā naffasta-h:*
nor with any grief	*wa lā ghumman*
that You have not removed,	*illā kashafta-h:*
nor with any misfortune	*wa lā sū'an*
that You have not banished,	*illā ṣarafta-h:*
nor with any sick person	*wa lā marīḍān*
whom You have not cured,	*illā shafaita-h :*
nor with any suffering individual	*wa lā mubtalan*
whose well-being	*illā*
You have not restored,	*'āfaita-h:*
nor with anyone guilty	*wa lā dhā*
of some misconduct	*isā'atin*
whom You have not pardoned,	*illā aqalta-h:*
nor with any overdue entitlement	*wa lā ḥaqqan*
that You have not extracted,	*illa 'stakhrajta-h:*
nor with any missing person	*wa lā ghā'iban*
whom You have not made	*illā*
fit and strong,	*jabarta-h:*
nor with anyone deceased	*wa lā mayyitan*
whom You have not	*illā*
treated mercifully,	*raḥimta-h:*
nor with any need,	*wa lā ḥājatan*
connected with this world	*min ḥawā'iji 'd-dunyā*
or the Hereafter,	*wa 'l-ākhirati*
worthy of Your approval	*la-ka fī-hā riḍan*
and important to our welfare,	*wa la-nā fī-hā ṣalāḥun*
that You have not helped us to fulfill,	*illā a'anta-nā 'alā qaḍā'i-hā*
with a facility supplied by You,	*bi-yusrin min-ka*
and vitality accompanied	*wa 'āfiyatin*
by forgiveness.	*ma'a 'l-maghfira:*
[Grant our requests]	
through Your Mercy,	*bi-raḥmati-ka*
O Most Merciful of the merciful!	*yā Arḥama 'r-rāḥimīn.*
Forgive us our sins,	*ighfir la-nā dhunūba-nā*
and [forgive] our fathers	*wa li-ābā'i-nā*
and our mothers,	*wa ummahāti-nā*
and our brothers and our sisters,	*wa ikhwāni-nā wa akhawāti-nā*
and our offspring	*wa dhurriyyāti-nā*
and our close relatives,	*wa qarābāti-nā*
and our friends and our teachers,	*wa aṣdiqā'i-nā wa mu'allimī-nā:*
and those to whom	*wa man*
we have recited the Qurān,	*qara'nā 'alai-h:*
and those who have recited it to us,	*wa man qara'a 'alai-nā:*
and those from whom we have learned,	*wa ta'allamnā min-h:*
and those who have learned from us,	*wa ta'allama min-nā:*
and those who have asked us	*wa man sa'ala-na 'd-*

to pray for them,	*du'ā':*
and those whom we have asked	*wa man sa'alnā-hu 'd-*
to pray for us,	*du'ā':*
and those who have loved us	*wa man aḥabba-nā*
for Your sake,	*fī-k:*
and those whom we have loved	*wa man aḥbabnā-hu*
for Your sake,	*fī-k:*
and those who	*wa man*
have looked after us for Your sake,	*tawallā-nā fī-k:*
and those we have looked after	*wa man tawallainā-hu*
for Your sake.	*fī-k:*
[Forgive] those of them	*wa man kāna*
who are still alive,	*min-hum ḥayyā:*
and those who of them	*wa man kāna*
who are now dead.	*min-kum mayyitā:*
[Grant our requests]	
through Your Mercy,	*bi-raḥmati-ka*
O Most Merciful of the merciful!	*yā Arḥama 'r-rāḥimīn.*
O Allāh,	*Allāhumma*
O Knower of all secret things!	*yā 'Ālima 'l-khafiyyāt:*
O Dispeller of trials and tribulations!	*wa yā Dāfi'a 'l-baliyyāt:*
O You who are Responsive	*wa yā Mujība 'd-*
to supplications!	*da'awāt:*
O Remover of anxieties	*wa yā Kāshifa 'l-*
and apprehensions!	*kurubāt:*
Bless Muḥammad,	*ṣalli 'alā Muḥammadin*
the most excellent of creatures.	*afḍali 'l-bariyyāt:*
Enable us to benefit by the signs	*wa 'nfa'-nā bi-mā ṣarafta*
which You have set forth	*fī Kitābi-ka*
in Your Book,	*mina 'l-āyāt:*
and allow us to atone for our misdeeds	*wa kaffir 'an-nā*
through the practice of its recitation.	*bi-tilāwati-hi 's-sayyi'āt:*
Promote us,	*wa 'rfa'*
through the fasting and vigil	*la-nā bi-ṣiyāmi*
of the month of Ramaḍān,	*shahri Ramaḍāna wa qiyāmi-hi*
to ascending degrees in Your presence.	*'inda-ka 'd-darajāt:*
[Grant our requests]	
through Your Mercy,	*bi-raḥmati-ka*
O Knower of all secret things.	*yā 'Ālima 'l-khafiyyāt:*
Bless Muḥammad,	*ṣalli 'alā Muḥammadin*
and the family of Muḥammād.	*wa 'alā āli Muḥammad:*
Forgive, through the Qur'ān,	*wa 'ghfir bi'l-Qur'āni*
our sinful ways,	*khaṭāyā-nā:*
and through it	*wa ajzil*
bestow on us abundant gifts,	*bi-hi 'aṭāyā-nā:*

and through it heal our sick,	*wa 'shfi bi-hi marḍā-nā:*
and through it	*wa 'rḥam*
have mercy on our dead,	*bi-hi mawtā-nā:*
and through it	*wa aṣliḥ*
improve the state of our affairs,	*bi-hi umūra*
in both our religious	*dīni-nā*
and our worldly life,	*wa dunyā-nā:*
and through it	*wa 'ḥṭuṭ bi-hi*
relieve us of the burden of sins.	*ʿan-nā thaqla 'l-awzār:*
Confer on us	*wa hab la-nā*
the good qualities of the righteous.	*ḥusna shamā'ili 'l-abrār:*
Forgive us our slips and our stumbles.	*wa 'ghfir la-na 'l-zilal wa 'l-ʿithār:*
Purify our hearts	*wa ṭahhir la-na 'l-qulūba*
and our innermost beings.	*wa 'l-asrār:*
Improve through it the way we talk,	*wa ṭayyib la-nā bi-hi 'l-adhkār:*
and through it clean the way we think.	*wa ṣaffi la-nā bi-hi 'l-afkār:*
Reduce the market prices	*wa arkhiṣ*
for our benefit.	*la-na 'l-asʿār:*
Avert from us the wickedness	*wa 'ṣrif ʿan-nā*
of the bad	*sharra 'l-ashrār:*
and the cunning tricks	*wa kaida 'l-*
of the profligate.	*fujjār:*
Let us thrive on the love	*wa aḥyi-nā*
of the best of companions,	*ʿalā ḥubbi 'ṣ-ṣaḥābati 'l-akhyār:*
and unite us with them	*wa 'jmaʿ baina-nā wa baina-hum*
in the abode of permanent stability,[548]	*fī dāri 'l-qarār:*
and include us among those	*wa 'jʿal-nā min ʿutaqā'i-ka*
whom You deliver from the Fire.	*mina 'n-nār:*
And give us in this world	*wa āti-nā fi 'd-dunyā*
that which is good,	*ḥasanatan*
and in the Hereafter	*wa fī 'l-ākhirati*
that which is good,	*ḥasanatan*
and guard us against	*wa qi-nā*
the torment of the Fire [of Hell].[549]	*ʿadhāba 'n-nār:*
[Grant our requests]	
through Your mercy,	*bi-raḥmati-ka*
O Most Merciful of the merciful!	*yā Arḥama 'r-rāḥimīn.*
Praise be to Allāh	*al-ḥamdu li'llāhi*
for the bountiful gifts	*ʿalā sawābighi*
of His gracious favor,	*naʿmā'i-h:*
and His blessings be upon Muḥammad,	*wa ṣalawātu-hu ʿalā Muḥammadin*
the Seal of His Prophets,	*Khātami Anbiyā'i-h:*
and upon his family, his companions	*wa ʿalā āli-hi wa aṣḥābi-hi*
and his wives,	*wa azwāji-h:*
and may He salute them all	*wa sallama*
with many greetings of peace.	*taslīmān kathīrā.*

[548] This is an allusion to Q. 40:38,39.

[549] Q. 2:201.

This brings us to the end of the Chapter concerning
the prayers of supplication *[adʿiya]* offered
after the obligatory ritual prayers *[aṣ-ṣalawāt al-farḍ]*,
and the supplication following the recital
of the entire Qurʾān *[duʿāʾ al-khatma]*.

Praise be to Allāh, the Lord of All the Worlds!
[al-ḥamdu li'llāhi Rabbi 'l-ʿālamīn].

Concerning the Author, Shaikh ʿAbd al-Qādir al-Jīlānī

A Brief Introduction by the Translator[1]

The Author's Names and Titles

A rich store of information about the author of *Sufficient Provision for Seekers of the Path of Truth* is conveniently available, to those familiar with the religious and spiritual tradition of Islām, in his names, his surnames, and the many titles conferred upon him by his devoted followers. It is not unusual for these to take up several lines in an Arabic manuscript, but let us start with the short form of the author's name as it appears on the cover and title page of this book: *Shaikh ʿAbd al-Qādir al-Jīlānī.*

Shaikh: A term applied throughout the Islamic world to respected persons of recognized seniority in learning, experience and wisdom. Its basic meaning in Arabic is "an elder; a man over fifty years of age." (The spellings *Sheikh* and *Shaykh* may also be encountered in English-language publications.)

ʿAbd al-Qādir: This is the author's personal name, meaning "Servant [or Slave] of the All-Powerful." (The form *ʿAbdul Qādir,* which the reader may come across elsewhere, is simply an alternative transliteration of the Arabic spelling.) It has always been a common practice, in the Muslim community, to give a male child a name in which *ʿAbd* is prefixed to one of the Names of Allāh.

[1] Reproduced for the convenience of the reader, with slight modifications from the version printed on pp. xiii-xix of: Shaikh ʿAbd al-Qādir. *Revelations of the Unseen (Futūḥ al-Ghaib)*. Translated from the Arabic by Muhtar Holland. Houston, Texas: Al-Baz Publishing, Inc., 1992.

al-Jīlānī: A surname ending in *-ī* will often indicate the bearer's place of birth. Shaikh ʿAbd al-Qādir was born in the Iranian district of Gīlān, south of the Caspian Sea, in A.H. 470/1077-8 C.E. (In some texts, the Persian spelling *Gīlānī* is used instead of the arabicized form al-Jīlānī. The abbreviated form *al-Jīlī*, which may also be encountered, should not be confused with the surname of the venerable ʿAbd al-Karīm al-Jīlī, author of the celebrated work al-Insān al-Kāmil, who came from Jīl in the district of Baghdād.)

Let us now consider a slightly longer version of the Shaikh's name, as it occurs near the beginning of *Al-Fatḥ ar-Rabbānī [The Sublime Revelation]: Sayyidunā 'sh-Shaikh Muḥyi'd-Dīn Abū Muḥammad ʿAbd al-Qādir (Raḍiya'llāhu ʿanh).*

Sayyidunā 'sh-Shaikh: "Our Master, the Shaikh." A writer who regards himself as a Qādirī, a devoted follower of Shaikh ʿAbd al-Qādir, will generally refer to the latter as *Sayyidunā* [our Master], or *Sayyidī* [my Master].

Muḥyi'd-Dīn: "Reviver of the Religion." It is widely acknowledged by historians, non-Muslim as well as Muslim, that Shaikh ʿAbd al-Qādir displayed great courage in reaffirming the traditional teachings of Islām, in an era when sectarianism was rife, and when materialistic and rationalistic tendencies were predominant in all sections of society. In matters of Islamic jurisprudence *[fiqh]* and theology *[kalām]*, he adhered quite strictly to the highly "orthodox" school of Imām Aḥmad ibn Ḥanbal.

Abū Muḥammad: "Father of Muḥammad." In the Arabic system of nomenclature, a man's surnames usually include the name of his first-born son, with the prefix *Abū* [Father of—].

Raḍiya'llāhu ʿanh: "May Allāh be well pleased with him!" This benediction is the one customarily pronounced—and spelled out in writing—after mentioning the name of a Companion of the Prophet (Allāh bless him and give him peace). The preference for this particular invocation is yet another mark of the extraordinary status held by Shaikh ʿAbd al-Qādir in the eyes of his devoted followers.

Finally, we must note some important elements contained within this even longer version: *al-Ghawth al-Aʿẓam Sulṭān al-Awliyāʾ Sayyidunā 'sh-Shaikh Muḥyi'd-Dīn ʿAbd al-Qādir al-Jīlānī al-Ḥasanī al-Ḥusainī (Raḍiya'llāhu ʿanh).*

al-Ghawth al-Aʿẓam: "The Supreme Helper" (or, "The Mightiest Succor"). *Ghawth* is an Arabic word meaning: (1) A cry for aid or succor. (2) Aid, help, succor; deliverance from adversity. (3) The chief of the Saints, who is empowered by Allāh to bring succor to suffering humanity, in response to His creatures' cry for help in times of extreme adversity.

Sulṭān al-Awliyāʾ: "The Sultan of the Saints." This reinforces the preceding title, emphasizing the supremacy of the *Ghawth* above all other orders of sanctity.

al-Ḥasanī al-Ḥusainī: "The descendant of both al-Ḥasan and al-Ḥusain, the grandsons of the Prophet (Allāh bless him and give him peace)." To quote the Turkish author, Shaikh Muzaffer Ozak Efendi (may Allāh bestow His mercy upon him): "The lineage of Shaikh ʿAbd al-Qādir is known as the Chain of Gold, since both his parents were descendants of the Messenger (Allāh bless him and give him peace). His noble father, ʿAbdullāh, traced his descent by way of Imām Ḥasan, while his revered mother, Umm al-Khair, traced hers through Imām Ḥusain."

As for the many other surnames, titles and honorific appellations that have been conferred upon Shaikh ʿAbd al-Qādir al-Jīlānī, it may suffice at this point to mention *al-Bāz al-Ashhab* [The Gray Falcon].

The Author's Life in Baghdād

Through the mists of legend surrounding the life of Shaikh ʿAbd al-Qādir al-Jīlānī, it is possible to discern the outlines of the following biographical sketch:

In A.H. 488, at the age of eighteen, he left his native province to become a student in the great capital city of Baghdād, the hub of political, commercial and cultural activity, and the center of religious learning in the world of Islām. After studying traditional sciences under such teachers as the prominent Ḥanbalī jurist *[faqīh]*, Abū Sa'd 'Alī al-Mukharrimī, he encountered a more spiritually oriented instructor in the saintly person of Abu'l-Khair Ḥammād ad-Dabbās. Then, instead of embarking on his own professorial career, he abandoned the city and spent twenty-five years as a wanderer in the desert regions of 'Irāq.

He was over fifty years old by the time he returned to Baghdād, in A.H. 521/1127 C.E., and began to preach in public. His hearers were profoundly affected by the style and content of his lectures, and his reputation grew and spread through all sections of society. He moved into the school *[madrasa]* belonging to his old teacher al-Mukharrimī, but the premises eventually proved inadequate. In A.H. 528, pious donations were applied to the construction of a residence and guesthouse *[ribāṭ]*, capable of housing the Shaikh and his large family, as well as providing accommodation for his pupils and space for those who came from far and wide to attend his regular sessions *[majālis]*.

He lived to a ripe old age, and continued his work until his very last breath, as we know from the accounts of his final moments recorded in the Addendum to Revelations of the Unseen.

In the words of Shaikh Muzaffer Ozak Efendi: "The venerable 'Abd al-Qādir al-Jīlānī passed on to the Realm of Divine Beauty in A.H. 561/1166 C.E., and his blessed mausoleum in Baghdād is still a place of pious visitation. He is noted for his extraordinary spiritual experiences and exploits, as well as his memorable sayings and wise teachings. It is rightly said of him that 'he was born in love, grew in perfection, and met his Lord in the perfection of love.' May the All-Glorious Lord bring us in contact with his lofty spiritual influence!"

The Author's Literary Works

***Al-Fatḥ ar-Rabbānī* [The Sublime Revelation].** A collection of sixty-two discourses delivered by Shaikh 'Abd al-Qādir in the years A.H. 545-546/1150-1152 C.E. Arabic text published by Dār al-Albāb, Damascus, n.d. Arabic text with Urdu translation: Madīna Publishing Co., Karachi, 1989. Translated from the Arabic by Muhtar Holland. Houston, Texas: Al-Baz Publishing, Inc., 1992.

Even a non-Muslim scholar like D.S. Margoliouth was so favorably impressed by the content and style of *Al-Fatḥ ar-Rabbānī* that he wrote:[2] "The sermons included in [this work] are some of the very best in Muslim literature: the spirit which they breathe is one of charity and philanthropy: the preacher would like to 'close the gates of Hell and open those of Paradise to all mankind.' He employs Ṣūfī technicalities very rarely, and none that would occasion the ordinary reader much difficulty...."

Malfūẓāt **[Utterances].** A loosely organized compilation of talks and sayings by Shaikh ʿAbd al-Qādir, almost equal in total length to Revelations of the Unseen. Frequently treated as a kind of appendix or supplement to manuscript and printed versions of *Al-Fatḥ ar-Rabbānī*. Translated from the Arabic by Muhtar Holland. Houston, Texas: Al-Baz Publishing, Inc., 1992.

Futūḥ al-Ghaib **[Revelations of the Unseen].** A collection of seventy-eight discourses. The Arabic text, edited by Muḥammad Sālim al-Bawwāb, has been published by Dār al-Albāb, Damascus, 1986. German translation: W. Braune. *Die Futūḥ al-Gaib des ʿAbd al-Qādir*. Berlin and Leipzig: Walter de Gruyter & Co., 1933. English translations: (1) M. Aftab-ud-Din Ahmad. *Futuh Al-Ghaib [The Revelations of the Unseen]*. Lahore, Pakistan: Sh. Muhammad Ashraf. Repr. 1986. (2) Shaikh ʿAbd al-Qādir al-Jīlānī. *Revelations of the Unseen (Futūḥ al-Ghaib)*. Translated from the Arabic by Muhtar Holland. Houston, Texas: Al-Baz Publishing, Inc., 1992.

Jalāʾ al-Khawāṭir **[The Removal of Cares].** A collection of forty-five discourses by Shaikh ʿAbd al-Qādir. Arabic text with Urdu translation published by Maktaba Nabawiyya, Lahore, n.d. Translated from the Arabic by Muhtar Holland. Ft. Lauderdale, Florida: Al-Baz Publishing, Inc., 1997.

[2] In his article "ʿAbd al-Ḳādir" in *Encyclopaedia of Islam* (also printed in *Shorter Encyclopaedia of Islam*. Leiden, Netherlands: E.J. Brill, 1961).

***Sirr al-Asrār* [The Secret of Secrets].** A short work, divided into twenty-four chapters, in which "the realities within our faith and our path are divulged." English translation: *The Secret of Secrets by Ḥaḍrat ʿAbd al-Qādir al-Jīlānī*, interpreted by Shaykh Tosun Bayrak al-Jerrahi al-Halveti. Cambridge, England: The Islamic Texts Society, 1992.

***Al-Ghunya li-ṭālibī ṭarīq al-ḥaqq* [Sufficient Provision for Seekers of the Path of Truth].** Arabic text published in two parts by Dār al-Albāb, Damascus, n.d., 192 pp. + 200 pp. Translated from the Arabic (in 5 vols.) by Muhtar Holland. Hollywood, Florida: Al-Baz Publishing, Inc., 1997.

Other works attributed to Shaikh ʿAbd al-Qādir include short treatises on some of the Divine Names; litanies *[awrād/aḥzāb]*; prayers and supplications *[daʿawāt/munājāt]*; mystical poems *[qaṣāʾid]*.

May Allāh forgive our mistakes and failings, and may He bestow His blessings upon all connected with our project—especially our gracious readers! Āmīn.

Muhtar Holland

About the Translator

Muhtar Holland was born in 1935, in the ancient city of Durham in the North East of England. This statement may be considered anachronistic, however, since he did not bear the name Muhtar until 1969, when he was moved—by powerful experiences in the *latihan kejiwaan* of Subud—to embrace the religion of Islām.*

At the age of four, according to an entry in his father's diary, he said to a man who asked his name: "I'm a stranger to myself." During his years at school, he was drawn most strongly to the study of languages, which seemed to offer signposts to guide the stranger on his "Journey Home," apart from their practical usefulness to one who loved to spend his vacations traveling—at first on a bicycle—through foreign lands. Serious courses in Latin, Greek, French, Spanish and Danish, with additional smatterings of Anglo-Saxon, Italian, German and Dutch. Travels in France, Germany, Belgium, Holland and Denmark. Then a State Scholarship and up to Balliol College, Oxford, for a degree course centered on the study of Arabic and Turkish. Travels in Turkey and Syria. Then National Service in the Royal Navy, with most of the two years spent on an intensive course in the Russian language.

In the years since graduation from Oxford and Her Majesty's Senior Service, Mr. Holland has held academic posts at the University of Toronto, Canada; at the School of Oriental and African Studies in the University of London, England (with a five-month leave to study Islamic Law in Cairo, Egypt); and at the Universiti Kebangsaan in Kuala Lumpur, Malaysia (followed by a six-month sojourn in Indonesia). He also worked as Senior Research Fellow at the Islamic Foundation in Leicester, England, and as Director of the Nūr al-Islām Translation Center in Valley Cottage, New York.

* The name Muhtar was received at that time from Bapak Muhammad Subuh Sumohadiwidjojo, of Wisma Subud, Jakarta, in response to a request for a suitable Muslim name. In strict academic transliteration from the Arabic, the spelling would be *Mukhtār*. The form *Muchtar* is probably more common in Indonesia than *Muhtar*, which happens to coincide with the modern Turkish spelling of the name.

His freelance activities have mostly been devoted to writing and translating in various parts of the world, including Scotland and California. He made his Pilgrimage *[Ḥajj]* to Mecca in 1980.

Published works include the following:

Al-Ghazālī. *On the Duties of Brotherhood*. Translated from the Classical Arabic by Muhtar Holland. London: Latimer New Dimensions, 1975. New York: Overlook Press, 1977. Repr. 1980 and 1993.

Sheikh Muzaffer Ozak al-Jerrahi. *The Unveiling of Love*. Translated from the Turkish by Muhtar Holland. New York: Inner Traditions, 1981. Westport, Ct.: Pir Publications, 1990.

Ibn Taymīya. *Public Duties in Islām*. Translated from the Arabic by Muhtar Holland. Leicester, England: Islamic Foundation, 1982.

Hasan Shushud. *Masters of Wisdom of Central Asia*. Translated from the Turkish by Muhtar Holland. Ellingstring, England: Coombe Springs Press, 1983.

Al-Ghazālī. *Inner Dimensions of Islamic Worship*. Translated from the Arabic by Muhtar Holland. Leicester, England: Islamic Foundation, 1983.

Sheikh Muzaffer Ozak al-Jerrahi. *Irshād*. Translated [from the Turkish] with an Introduction by Muhtar Holland. Warwick, New York: Amity House, 1988. Westport, Ct.: Pir Publications, 1990.

Sheikh Muzaffer Ozak al-Jerrahi. *Blessed Virgin Mary*. Translation from the Original Turkish by Muhtar Holland. Westport, Ct.: Pir Publications, 1991.

Sheikh Muzaffer Ozak al-Jerrahi. *The Garden of Dervishes*. Translation from the Original Turkish by Muhtar Holland. Westport, Ct.: Pir Publications, 1991.

Sheikh Muzaffer Ozak al-Jerrahi. *Adornment of Hearts*. Translation from the Original Turkish by Muhtar Holland and Sixtina Friedrich. Westport, Ct.: Pir Publications, 1991.

Sheikh Muzaffer Ozak al-Jerrahi. *Ashki's Divan*. Translation from the Original Turkish by Muhtar Holland and Sixtina Friedrich. Westport, Ct.: Pir Publications, 1991.

Shaikh ʿAbd al-Qādir al-Jīlānī. *Revelations of the Unseen (Futūḥ al-Ghaib)*. Translated from the Arabic by Muhtar Holland. Houston, Texas: Al-Baz Publishing, Inc., 1992

Shaikh ʿAbd al-Qādir al-Jīlānī. *The Sublime Revelation (al-Fatḥ ar-Rabbānī)*. Translated from the Arabic by Muhtar Holland. Houston, Texas: Al-Baz Publishing, Inc., 1992

Shaikh ʿAbd al-Qādir al-Jīlānī. *Utterances (Malfūẓāt)*. Translated from the Arabic by Muhtar Holland. Houston, Texas: Al-Baz Publishing, Inc., 1992

Shaikh ʿAbd al-Qādir al-Jīlānī. *The Removal of Cares (Jalāʾ al-Khawāṭir)*. Translated from the Arabic by Muhtar Holland. Ft. Lauderdale, Florida: Al-Baz Publishing, Inc., 1997

Subject Index, Volume Four

BOOKS PUBLISHED BY AL-BAZ PUBLISHING INCLUDE:

1. **Revelations of the Unseen** (*Futūḥ al-Ghaib*) ($19.00)
   78 Discourses by Shaikh ʿAbd al-Qādir al-Jīlānī

2. **The Sublime Revelation** (*Al-Fatḥ ar-Rabbānī*) ($29.00)
   62 Discourses by Shaikh ʿAbd al-Qādir al-Jīlānī

3. **Utterances of Shaikh ʿAbd al-Qādir** (*Malfūẓāt*) ($16.00)

4. **The Removal of Cares** (*Jalāʾ al-Khawāṭir*) ($25.00)
   45 Discourses by Shaikh ʿAbd al-Qādir al-Jīlānī

5. **Sufficient Provision for Seekers of the Path of Truth**
   (*Al-Ghunya li-Ṭālibī Ṭarīq al-Ḥaqq*) ($110.00)
   by Shaikh ʿAbd al-Qādir al-Jīlānī (may Allāh be well pleased with him)
   This encyclopedic work is a complete resource on the inner and outer aspects of Islām. The translation has been published in 5 volumes. 1738 pages. Translated by Muhtar Holland.

Books scheduled for publication in 1997 include:

1. **Concerning the Affirmation of Divine Oneness**
   (*Risālat at-Tawḥīd)*
   by Shaikh Walī Raslān ad-Dimashqī (d. A.H. 695)
   This is a Risāla on *shirk khafī* (hidden *shirk*). *Shirk* is associating partners with Allāh. Also in the book is a commentary by Shaikh Zakariyyāʾ al-Anṣārī called "*Kitāb Fatḥ ar-Raḥmān*." Also in the book is a commentary on the commentary by Shaikh ʿAlī ibn ʿAṭiyya ʿAlawān al-Ḥamawī (d. A.H. 936) called "*Sharḥ Fatḥ ar-Raḥmān*." This is a very important book. Translated by Muhtar Holland.

2. **The Proper Conduct of Marriage in Islām** (*Ādāb an-Nikāḥ*)
   by Imām al-Ghazālī
   This is Book 12 of *Iḥyā ʿUlūm ad-Dīn*. Translated by Muhtar Holland.

3. **Fifteen Letters**
(*Khamsata ʿAshara Maktūban* otherwise known as *Maktūbāt*)
Fifteen letters by Shaikh ʿAbd al-Qādir al-Jīlānī to one of his disciples. Originally written in Persian, they were translated into Arabic by ʿAlī Ḥusāmu'd-dīn al-Muttaqī (the Devout). Translated by Muhtar Holland.

4. **Necklaces of Gems** (*Qalāʾid al-Jawāhir*)
by Shaikh Muḥammad ibn Yaḥyā at-Tādifī
A Biography of Shaikh ʿAbd al-Qādir al-Jīlānī (may Allāh be well pleased with him), on the Marvelous Exploits of the Crown of the Saints, the Treasure-trove of the Pure, the Sulṭān of the *Awliyāʾ*, the Sublime *Quṭb*, Shaikh Muḥyi'd-dīn ʿAbd al-Qādir al-Jīlānī. Translated by Muhtar Holland.

To order contact: Al-Baz Publishing, Inc.
8807 148th Ave. NE, Building E
Redmond, WA 98052

Phone: (425) 869-3923
E-mail: albaz@bellsouth.net

LaVergne, TN USA
22 January 2010
170813LV00001B/3/P

9 781882 216109